Digital Image Processing and Analysis

Bhabatosh Chanda
Dwijesh Dutta Majumder

Electronics and Communication Sciences Unit
Indian Statistical Institute
Calcutta

Prentice-Hall of India Private Limited
NEW DELHI-110 001
2008

Rs. 250.00

DIGITAL IMAGE PROCESSING AND ANALYSIS
by Bhabatosh Chanda and Dwijesh Dutta Majumder

ISBN-978-81-203-1618-8

The export rights of this book are vested solely with the publisher.

Eleventh Printing   ...   ...   **June, 2008**

Published by Asoke K. Ghosh, Prentice-Hall of India Private Limited, M-97, Connaught Circus, New Delhi-110001 and Printed by Meenakshi Art Printers, Delhi-110006.

Contents

Part II   IMAGE PROCESSING

Part III   IMAGE ANALYSIS

Foreword

Digital image processing used to be a single unified field in the early sixties and seventies. Today, it has expanded and diversified into several branches based on mathematical tools as well as applications. For instance, there are separate books dealing with fuzzy IP, morphological IP, knowledge-based IP, etc. Similarly, several books deal with diverse application specific tools for remote sensing, industrial vision, and so forth.

However, there is a need for beginners as well as practising engineers to have a reference or handbook which would give an overall exposure to the subject. The book by Bhabatosh Chanda and Dwijesh Dutta Majumder fulfils this need.

A good coverage of introductory concepts, mathematical and image preliminaries has been provided in the early chapters. These chapters will be very useful for students and other beginners who want to pursue this field for its specific applications. All the elements of image processing beginning from formation and digitization to enhancement, restoration and registration and compression techniques have been discussed in great detail.

Topics specific to remote sensing, digital photogrammetry such as stereo image processing, multi-spectral image processing, medical image processing, etc., have been covered in good length.

Image analysis issues such as segmentation, edge/line detection, feature extraction, image description and pattern recognition have been covered in great detail and all the state-of-the-art concepts have been discussed, which will be useful for students and researchers.

The book is aimed at the end-users as well as beginners, so much so that the emphasis is on providing tools rather than on mathematical proofs of their performance.

Dr. Dutta Majumder with his decades of experience has been able to sift and sort the topics and has come up with a comprehensive list of topics to make this book a valuable asset for students and researchers alike and to provide the necessary impetus for engaging in effective applications of this wide field of digital image processing. He has been ably assisted in this by Dr. Chanda. I take this opportunity to convey my appreciation to Dr. Dutta Majumder and Dr. Chanda in bringing out this well-written book.

Prof. B.L. Deekshatulu
Director
Centre for Space Science and Technology
Dehradun

Preface

With the advent of the third-generation digital computer around the middle of 1960s, the area of digital image processing and analysis has emerged as a subject of interdisciplinary study and research in physics, chemistry, biology, engineering, meteorology, space science, statistics, agriculture, and of course computer science. Two-dimensional and three-dimensional image processing and analysis today form a major area of research and development in the broad fields of pattern recognition, computer vision, machine learning and also of artificial intelligence. One of the motivation behind this spurt of activity in this field is the need felt by people to communicate with computers in a natural mode of communication in respect of diverse applications.

This motivation became much more important in early 1980s, when the fifth-generation computer systems/knowledge-based computing systems (FGCS/KBCS) were launched in different countries like Japan, USA, Europe and also in India, with the objective of designing and making automation that can carry out certain tasks as we human being perform. As a result, a new generation of applications are in the market or, are being planned not only in respect of robotics but also in respect of areas like office automation, biomedical engineering, industrial automation, meteorological prediction, high energy physics, environment and urban planning, oil and natural gas exploration, fingerprint processing, forensic investigations, restoration of images suffering from photometric and geometric distortions, multimedia and computerized video editing and video conferencing, apart from several very sophisticated military applications. The result of these efforts established image processing and computer vision as one of the fastest growing technology worldwide.

The book is an attempt to present the advances in the digital image processing analysis and recognition technology—both theory and practice—in the form of a text as well as a reference book for the benefit of computer science and electrical engineering students, teachers, professional engineers and researchers. As has already been stated, the advancements in this expanding field are largely due to the multi-disciplinary efforts of diverse subjects with that of computer science, and this book, being a comprehensive introduction to the field, will be helpful in improving the understanding among the different disciplines. An attempt has been made to provide a list of original literatures at the end of each chapter.

In Chapter 1, the perspective and engineering motivation for digital image processing and scene analysis and the requirement for different stages are presented. After an extensive list of applications, a brief description of the component of an image processing system is also discussed.

Though the mathematical level of the book is meant for senior college students in a technical discipline, such as engineering and computer science, we have provided in Chapter 2, the mathematical preliminaries of vector algebra, linear operations, orthogonal transforms such as Fourier transform, discrete sine and cosine transforms, Hartely, Walsh–Hadamard, Haar, slunt and K–L transforms, singular value decomposition, probability and statistics, fuzzy sets and their properties and the basics of mathematical morphology.

In Chapter 3, the elements of human visual system with some perceptual characteristics and pattern discrimination ability of human visual system, that are very useful in understanding image processing functions, are presented.

In chapter 4, the physical process of image formation that is continuous in space and in value is described with the help of two models—geometric model and photometric model. Recorded image is described in terms of linear position invariant transformation. Formation of digital image that is converting the analog pictures to a form suitable for processing by digital computers is described in Chapter 5. We also present some elementary definitions and concept of digital geometry that help in understanding the image processing operations.

In Chapter 6, we present image enhancement techniques that improve the quality of the image through some adhoc approaches such as contrast intensification, noise cleaning and edge sharpening, depending on quality of the image and purpose of processing. A mathematically well-formulated method for improving the image quality is the restoration technique. This is presented in Chapter 7. Here we describe some of the algebraic techniques of image restoration such as the least square estimation, singular value decomposition, and probabilistic technique that includes maximum *a posteriori* technique. We also present a homomorphic filtering method that can restore images contaminated by both additive and multiplication noise.

Chapter 8 discusses the compression of the image for a storage and its transmission. In this chapter, both lossy and loss-less compression techniques are described. Some criteria of image quality are also presented so that error introduced in the reconstructed image may be measured.

Registration methods of image-to-image, image-to-map and image-to-model, depending upon the applications, are presented in Chapter 9. Various type of geometric transformation that are used for registration are also presented. Correspondence problem relevant to stereo imaging is also discussed in this chapter.

So far we have presented methods for processing of grayscale images, where pixel value at any image point can be represented by a single valued function. But the intensity distribution of an image depends on the properties of the sensors and measuring devices, also different physical properties of objects contribute differently while generating the intensity map of the object. Such images are represented by multi-valued function, which is discussed in Chapter 10. Two major areas of this class are multispectral as in satellite images and multi-model as in medical images. Both are dealt with in details in this chapter. Processing of colour images, a special class of multispectral images are also discussed with real-life applications.

Next, we present image segmentation techniques that partition the image into meaningful regions. This partitioning is done either by region extraction or by edge detection. In Chapter 11, image segmentation by region extraction and in Chapter 12, image segmentation using edge detection are discussed. Major steps of good edge and line detection alogorithms including noise cleaning, computation of edge strength, edge linking and edge extraction are presented in Chapter 12 in some detail. For edge linking, common methods that are used are Hough transform, relaxation labelling and graph searching are also presented here.

Chapter 13 contains different methods of extracting important features, such as topological, geometrical, structural and surface features. Each of these is useful for specific class of applications. Chapter 14 describes various boundary-based and region-based schemes for object and scene descriptions. Scheme for describing objects or scene using region adjacency graph is also discussed.

An introductory treatment of basic concepts and tools for visual pattern recognition using different mathematical and heuristic approaches such as deterministic, probabilistic, fuzzy set theoretic methods, with supervised or unsupervised learning mechanism is provided in Chapter 15. Recognition of visual pattern using syntactic features is also presented here.

Some of the materials presented in the book are based on the result of research, teaching and training activities carried out by us in image processing, pattern recognition, computer vision and artificial intelligence over a long period of time at the Indian Statistical Institute. An attempt has been made to arrange the chapters in a manner so as to be helpful to the readers in tracing the growth of this newly emerging technology.

We have provided about 300 references, more than 225 line drawings and about 200 photographs along with a sufficient number of tables and algorithms, organized in 15 chapters, with problems at the end of every chapter. Solutions to some standard problems are provided as algorithms in the body of the relevant chapters.

Bhabatosh Chanda
Dwijesh Dutta Majumder

Acknowledgements

We express our gratitude to late Prof. P.C. Mahalanabis, FRS, founder director and Prof. C.R. Rao, FRS, former director of Indian Statistical Institute, who helped in laying the foundation of theoretical and experimental research in computer science, pattern recognition and image processing related areas at ISI Calcutta. We also express our thanks to Prof. J.K. Ghosh, FNA, former director and Prof. S.B. Rao, the present director of ISI for their encouragement.

A large number of M.Tech. and Ph.D. students who did their dissertation work in the area of pattern recognition and image processing under our supervision have influenced us and have contributed in the preparation of the material directly or indirectly. We take this opportunity to thank all of them without mentioning their names.

It is a pleasure to thank all our past and present colleagues at the Electronics and Communication Sciences Unit and National Centre for Knowledge-based Computing System at ISI, who worked with us in making ISI truly a centre of excellence in the areas of pattern recognition, image processing; and particularly to A.K. Dutta, J. Das, S.K. Pal, B.B. Chowdhury, N.R. Ganguly, M.K. Kundu, K.S. Roy, N.R. Pal, S.K. Parui, A. Bagchi, P. Sengupta, A. Gupta, S.R. Das, B. Umashankar, S.N. Biswas, S.E. Sarma, C.A. Murty, D.P. Mukherjee, J.K. Basak, A. Pal, P.K. Saha and P.P. Pal. We also thank all the administrative and technical staff of ECSU, namely S.K. Seal, D. Mitra and T. Bhattacharya, and particularly to Prof. J. Das, Head ECSU, for creating cooperative and resourceful environment suitable for writing this book. Our special thanks go to D.P. Mukherjee and S. Mukherjee who rendered their active participation in preparing the manuscript.

In addition, we express our appreciation to the Department of Electronics (DOE), Department of Science and Technology (DST), Council of Scientific and Industrial Research (CSIR) and Defence Research and Development Organization (DRDO) of the Government of India, and United Nations Development Programme (UNDP) for their sponsorship of R&D projects to us in the area of pattern recognition, image processing, computer vision and artificial intelligence.

Special thanks go to the publishers, Prentice-Hall of India for their help and advice during the editorial and production stages in the preparation of the book.

Finally, we wish to thank all the individuals and organizations who permitted us to use their material in the book.

Bhabatosh Chanda
Dwijesh Dutta Majumder

Part–I

Digital Image

Chapter 1

Introduction

1.1 Motivation and Perspective

The birth of digital computer has introduced to the society a machine that is much more powerful than human beings in numerical computation. The pertinent question then was whether the human capability of processing non-numerical information received from the environment as well as society, of reasoning and decision making based on non-numerical data could be incorporated in the machine with equal or more efficiency. This led to evolution of a new subject called *artificial intelligence*, which has a large area of common interest and motivation with another subject known as *pattern recognition*. A major portion of information received by a human from the environment is visual. Hence, processing visual information by computer has been drawing a very significant attention of the researchers over the last few decades. The process of receiving and analyzing visual information by the human species is referred to as *sight*, *perception* or *understanding*. Similarly, the process of receiving and analyzing visual information by digital computer is called *digital image processing and scene analysis*. The term 'image' rather than 'picture' is used here, because the computer stores and processes numerical image of a scene.

Although 'pattern recognition' and 'image processing' have a lot in common, yet they were developed as separate disciplines. Two broad classes of techniques, viz., *processing* and *analysis* have evolved in the field of digital image processing and analysis. Processing of an image includes improvement in its appearance and efficient representation. So the field consists of not only feature extraction, analysis and recognition of images, but also coding, filtering, enhancement and restoration. The entire process of image processing and analysis starting from the receiving of visual information to the giving out of description of the scene, may be divided into three major stages which are also considered as major sub-areas, and are given below:

(i) *Discretization and representation:* converting visual information into a discrete form; suitable for computer processing; approximating visual information to save storage space as well as time requirement in subsequent processing.

(ii) *Processing:* improving image quality by filtering etc.; compressing data to save storage and channel capacity during transmission.

(iii) *Analysis:* extracting image features; quantifying shapes, registration and recognition.

In the initial stage, the input is a scene (visual information), and the output is corresponding digital image. In the secondary stage, both the input and the output are images where the output is an improved version of the input. And, in the final stage, the input is still an image but the output is a description of the contents of that image. A schematic diagram of different stages is shown in Fig. 1.1.

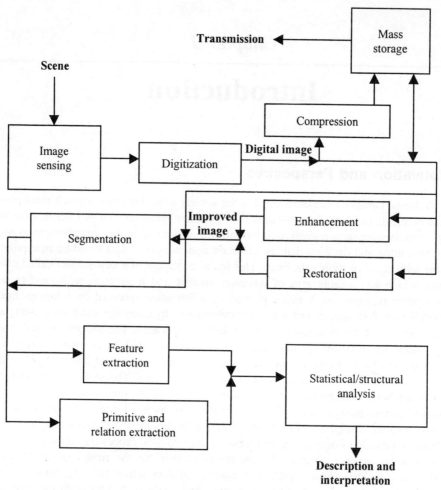

Fig. 1.1   Different stages of image processing and analysis scheme. Information flow along the outgoing link from each block.

The history of digital image processing and analysis is quite short. It cannot be older than the first electronic computer which was built way back in 1946. However, the concept of digital image could be found in literature as early as in 1920 with transmission of images through the Bartlane cable picture transmission system [McFarlane (1972)]. Images were coded for submarine cable transmission and then reconstructed at the receiving end by a specialized printing device. Attention was then concentrated on improving visual quality of transmitted (or reconstructed) images. In fact, potentials of image processing techniques came into focus with the advancement of large-scale digital computer and with the journey to the moon. Improving image quality using computer, started at Jet Propulsion Laboratory, California, USA in 1964, and the images of the moon transmitted by Ranger 7 were processed. This event can be marked as the first application of true image processing techniques [Andrews et al. (1972)]. Since 1964, the field has experienced vigorous growth [Fu and Rosenfeld (1976), Rosenfeld (1981), Rosenfeld (1984), and also see the surveys by A. Rosenfeld as appeared in *Computer Vision, Graphics and Image Processing* almost every year since 1972]. Certain efficient computer processing techniques (e.g. fast Fourier transform) have also contributed to this development.

1.2 Scenes and Images

The term *scene* stands for a landscape or a view as seen by a spectator. The scene, indoor or outdoor, we see around us is, in general, three-dimensional, i.e. each point in the scene may have different depth from the observer. However, there are scenes which can be considered as two-dimensional, i.e. points comprising the scene have equal depth. Some examples of two-dimensional scenes are:

- flat terrain seen from satellite situated at a very high altitude,
- the shadow of objects created by X-rays,
- flat polished surface of objects or thin slices seen through microscope, and
- documents printed on paper.

The Oxford dictionary defines the word *image* as the optical appearance of something produced in a mirror or through a lens. Image may be formed by other types of radiant energy and devices. However, optical images are most common and are most important. Amount of light (radiant) energy received at a point of a scene by an observer or by an image sensor varies with direction and distance of that point. Radiant energy is recorded at corresponding points on a plane to form an image. Hence, the brightness and colour recorded in an image may be represented as a function of several variables. The simplest kind of intensity (optical) image we can think of is a black-and-white (B/W) image. These images are most common and are represented by a function of two variables $g(x, y)$, where $g(x, y)$ is the grayness or brightness or intensity of the image at the spatial coordinate (x, y). A multispectral image is a vector-valued function having number of components equal to that of spectral bands and is represented by $[g_1(x, y), g_2(x, y), ..., g_n(x, y)]$ at each (x, y). The colour image is a special case of multispectral image; and if we consider intensity measured in three wavelengths corresponding to *red*, *green* and *blue*, then $g(x, y) = [g_R(x, y), g_G(x, y), g_B(x, y)]$. A temporal argument is added to represent time-varying image $g(x, y, t)$ (also called image sequences).

1.3 Applications

Digital image processing and analysis techniques are used today in a variety of problems. Many application oriented image analyzers are available and are working satisfactorily in real environment. The following are a few major application areas:

1. *Office automation:* optical character recognition; document processing; cursive script recognition; logo and icon recognition; identification of address area on envelop; etc.

2. *Industrial automation:* automatic inspection system; non-destructive testing; automatic assembling; process related to VLSI manufacturing; PCB checking; robotics; oil and natural gas exploration; seismography; process control applications; etc.

3. *Bio-medical:* ECG, EEG, EMG analysis; cytological, histological and stereological applications; automated radiology and pathology; X-ray image analysis; mass screening

of medical images such as chromosome slides for detection of various diseases, mammograms, cancer smears; CAT, MRI, PET, SPECT, USG and other tomographic images; routine screening of plant samples; 3-d reconstruction and analysis; etc.

4. *Remote sensing:* natural resources survey and management; estimation related to agriculture, hydrology, forestry, mineralogy; urban planning; environment and pollution control; cartography, registration of satellite images with terrain maps; monitoring traffic along roads, docks and airfields; etc.

5. *Scientific applications:* high energy physics; bubble chamber and other forms of track analysis; etc.

6. *Criminology:* finger print identification; human face registration and matching; forensic investigation; etc.

7. *Astronomy and space applications:* restoration of images suffering from geometric and photometric distortions; computing close-up picture of planetary surfaces; etc.

8. *Meteorology:* short-term weather forecasting, long-term climatic change detection from satellite and other remote sensing data; cloud pattern analysis; etc.

9. *Information technology:* facsimile image transmission, videotex; video-conferencing and videophones; etc.

10. *Entertainment and consumer electronics:* HDTV; multimedia and video-editing; etc.

11. *Printing and graphic arts:* colour fidelity in desktop publishing; art conservation and dissemination; etc.

12. *Military applications:* missile guidance and detection; target identification; navigation of pilotless vehicle; reconnaissance; and range finding; etc.

In addition to the above mentioned areas, another important application of image processing techniques is improvement of quality or appearance of a given image.

1.4 Components of Image Processing System

Basic components of a general-purpose image processing system are shown in Fig. 1.2. *Image sensing, digitizing, processing* and *displaying* are four principal operations performed by such a system. In the following section we describe briefly the components responsible for these tasks.

1.4.1 Image Sensor

An image sensor intercepts the radiant energy propagating from the scene, and transforms it to produce an intensity image. Two different technologies, viz., *photochemical* and *photoelectronic* are most common. Photochemical methods have the advantage of combining image formation and recording on a single entity called 'photographic film'. Photoelectronic methods, on the other hand, separate the recording process from image formation and detection. However, in the second method, recorded image can be converted more easily to a form which is suitable to computer processing.

The devices used as image sensors range from still camera to multispectral scanner on board in satellites. Television cameras are widely used and are easy to operate. There are as many as

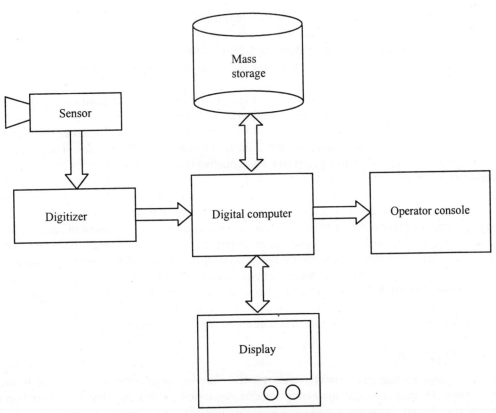

Fig. 1.2 A general-purpose image processing system.

five different systems used in television imaging: image orthicon tube, vidicon tube, iconoscope tube, image dissector tube and charge transfer devices. Most popular amongst the charge transfer devices is charge-coupled devices (commercially called CCD camera). They behave similar to an array of metal-oxide semiconductor field-effect transistors (MOSFET) in a sense that both have a source, a drain and a depletion-region. When an image is formed on a CCD array, the photons incident on the semiconductor accumulate charges in the depletion region. So during image scanning, the CCD image plane can be considered as a monolithic array of charged capacitors. Now these charges are transferred to output by applying a series of clock pulses between the source and the drain. This transfer can be made either one line at a time or a complete frame at a time; in the second case, a frame buffer would be needed to avoid data loss.

Multispectral scanners also use the same technology except some filters corresponding to different wavelength bands are added, and a full size image is recorded for each spectral band. Apart from these optical image sensors, image can also be captured in devices like X-ray scanner, radar, ultrasonic ranger, magnetic resonance imaging (MRI) system, and so on.

1.4.2 Digitizer

A *digitizer* is required input images to a digital computer, produces digital image composed of discrete intensity values at discrete positions. Most of the image sensors (photoelectronic devices) mentioned above either have suitable built-in digitizers or provide signal that can be digitized straightway by an A/D converter. However, some sensors (e.g. still camera) are purely analogue devices and their responses must be digitized before being fed to a computer. *Microdensitometer and flying spot scanner* are widely used for digitizing transparency or photograph or printed matter.

In microdensitometer, the transparency or opaque matter (photograph and printed document) is wrapped around a drum of transparent material or mounted on a flat bed. A light beam is focused on a point of the medium. In case of transparency, light is transmitted to the other side of the medium. In case of opaque matter, light is reflected from the surface. The light beam, transmitted or reflected, is made incident on a photodetector which measures and records the graylevel (intensity) at that point. The image is scanned by translating the bed or rotating the drum in relation to the light beam. Although this is a slow device, a high positional accuracy can be achieved. Flying spot scanner operates in almost similar way. The difference is, here the medium (transparency or photograph or paper) is stationary and source beam is moved to scan the image. Light source is generated by an electron beam impinging on the fluorescent surface of a cathode ray tube (CRT). The device is naturally much faster than the microdensitometer. In addition to the capability of capturing natural images, image sensors like television cameras can also digitize photographs and printed documents. Similarly, microdensitometer and flying spot scanner can also be considered as image sensors. Generally, in selection of a sensor/digitizer, system features like signal-to-noise ratio, resolution, speed and cost are to be considered.

1.4.3 Processor

Systems ranging from microcomputers to general purpose large computers are used in image processing. Dedicated image processing systems connected to host computers are very popular nowadays. Special coprocessor card (with hardware implemented image processing operators) and parallel processors are also being included in many small systems to gain speed. Interactive graphic devices are also added to provide image editing facilities. Digitized image arrays are in most cases very large. So, sufficiently large core memory should be provided with the system. In addition to this, a working system should have adequate and efficient secondary large storage facility. Magnetic tapes (spool and cartridge) and disks (starting from floppies to winchesters to removable disk packs) are the most popularly used storage media. Although image processing programs are often coded in assembly language for fast execution, the flexibility of the system can be improved by having high-level languages for use in the development phase.

Depending on the requirement various image processing architectures are designed and are available in the market. For example, machines for scientific research are different from commercial ones, as to solve a particular problem may need a special architecture. On the other hand, in industrial application, a machine needs to do a particular job in real time without the concern for its general use. Accordingly, four major distinctions are made: scientific research and commercial machines; real-time and off-line machines; machines for imaging and machine vision jobs; and machines for process control and inspection [Wilson (1993)]. Most of the image processing hardwares are based on one of the following architectural concepts:

1. *Serial* or *von Neumann architecture:* It is a low-cost traditional serial processor based on a microprocessor chip with a complex instruction set (CISC) or reduced instruction set (RISC).

2. *MIMD* (*multiple-instruction multiple-device*) *multiprocessors:* It is a small array of RISC or CISC elements and is characterized by interconnections among processors as well as

interconnections between processors and memory element. Some commonly used interconnection configurations are shown in Fig. 1.3(a).

3. *Pipelines:* It is also an MIMD architecture where identical processors are connected in a sequence as shown in Fig.1.3(b). Algorithm is decomposed and mapped to this sequence such that each processor executes only a sub-task in order. So image data go in at one end at frame rate, passes from one programmable module (processor) to the next, and finally resultant image comes out of another end at the same rate.

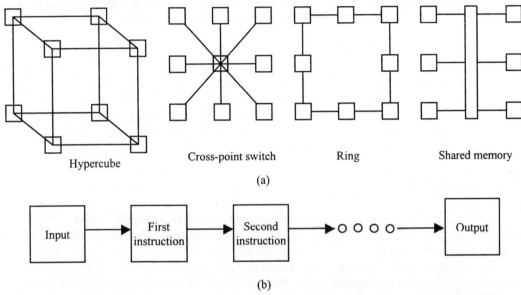

Hypercube   Cross-point switch   Ring   Shared memory

(a)

(b)

Fig. 1.3 Multiprocessor interconnections: (a) MIMD architecture, (b) pipeline architecture.

4. *Single instruction multiple device (SIMD) parallel processors*: It usually operates on image bit-planes in parallel. In that case, it is called *single-bit SIMD*. However, it may be designed to operate on the whole byte or a complete word also. In that case, it is called *word-wide SIMD*. So SIMD systems are grouped into two classes: single-bit and word-wide data flow architecture. It is characterized by interconnection scheme. Most common interconnection schemes are hypercube, mesh and linear linkage.

1.4.4 Display Unit

A display device produces and shows a visual form of numerical values stored in a computer as image array. Principal display devices are printer, TV monitor and CRTs. The printer will be described in Section 1.4.5. Any erasable raster graphics display device can be used as display unit with an image processing system. However, TV monitors (B/W or colour) are most common display devices in use. These raster devices convert image data into a video frame. One major problem is, it must refresh the screen at a rate of about 25 frames per second to avoid flicker. Since many general purpose computers are unable to transfer data at such a high speed, the entire image is kept in a memory commonly called *frame buffer*. This memory is scanned and displayed at the video rate by a *direct memory access* unit which is a special hardware independent of central processor.

1.4.5 Hard Copier

Hard copier are also non-erasable display devices. They leave permanent impression of the output image on the media, and hence the name. These devices basically are *printers* ranging from line printers to thermal and laser printers, and the medium ranges from ordinary to specialized papers. Most of the printers are *bi-level*, and specialized techniques are used to generate different *intensity or shades*. In *line printer,* graytone or shade is produced by choosing appropriate characters and overprinting many different characters at the same place. *Dot-matrix printer* and also *laser printer* can produce shades by this method. However, they can generate better quality images by printing an appropriate pattern of black dots within a white square depending on the intensity at a position. These patterns must maintain a growth sequence in which a point (position within the square) that is made black for some intensity, say *I*, will remain black for all intensity less than *I* and vice versa. Here, intensity resolution of display devices is increased at the cost of spatial resolution. The loss of spatial resolution can be avoided by another technique called *ordered dithering*. *Thermal copier* produces image by burning the surface of a special type of paper. Different shades or blackness in this device are achieved by burning to different degrees. *Colour ink-jet copier* generates desired colour at a given position by spraying four different colours: *red, green, blue* and *black* in different amount over a small area on the surface of the paper.

1.5 About This Book

This book is divided in three parts each of which consists of five chapters. These parts present (i) introduction to and basics of *digital image*, (ii) *processing* and, subsequently, (iii) *analysis* of image content, respectively.

In Chapter 1, we have presented the perspective and motivation for digital image processing and scene analysis and the requirement for different stages. After an extensive but not exhaustive list of applications we present brief description of the components of an image processing system.

Though the mathematical level of the book is within the group of senior college students in a technical discipline, such as engineering and computer science, we have provided in Chapter 2, the mathematical preliminaries of vector algebra, linear operations, orthogonal transforms such as Fourier transform, discrete cosine and sine transforms, Hartely, Walsh-Hadamard, Haar, slunt and K-L transforms, singular-value decomposition, probability and statistics, fuzzy sets and basics of mathematical morphology.

In Chapter 3, we present the elements of human visual system with some of its perceptual characteristics and pattern discrimination ability that are very useful in understanding image processing functions.

In Chapter 4, the physical process of image formation that are continuous in space and in value is described with the help of two models: geometric model and photometric model. Recorded image is described in terms of linear position-invariant transformation. Formation of digital image that is converting the analog pictures to a form suitable for processing by digital computers is described in Chapter 5. We also present some elementary definitions and concept of digital geometry that helps understanding the image processing operations.

In Chapter 6, we present image enhancement techniques that improve the quality of the image through some adhoc approaches such as contrast intensification, noise cleaning and edge sharpening, depending on quality of the image and purpose of processing. A mathematically well-formulated method for improving the image quality is restoration technique. This is presented in

Chapter 7. Here we describe some of the algebraic techniques of image restoration such as least-square estimation, singular-value decomposition and probabilistic technique such as maximum a posterior technique. We also present a homomorphic filtering method that can restore images contaminated by both additive and multiplicative noise.

After improvement of quality the image may be compressed for storage and/or transmission which we present in Chapter 8. In this chapter both lossy and lossless compression techniques are described. Some criteria of image quality are also presented so that error introduced in the reconstructed image may be measured.

In Chapter 9, we present registration methods of image-to-image, image-to-map and image-to-model depending upon the applications. Various types of geometric transformation that are used for registration are presented. Correspondence problem relevant to stereo-imaging is also discussed.

So far we have presented methods for processing of gray-scale images, where pixel value at any image point can be represented by a single-valued function. But the intensity distribution of an image depends on the properties of the sensors and measuring devices. Second, different physical properties of objects contribute differently while generating the intensity map of the object. Such images are represented by multi-valued function and we deal with such images in Chapter 10. Two major areas of this class are multi-spectral as in satellite images and multi-model as in medical images. Both are dealt with in some details in this chapter. Processing of colour images, a special class of multi-spectral images are also discussed with real life applications.

Next we present image segmentation techniques that partition the image into meaningful regions. This partitioning is done either by region extraction or by edge detection. In Chapter 11, we present image segmentation by region extraction, and in Chapter 12, we present image segmentation using edge detection. Major steps of good edge and line detection algorithms including noise cleaning, computation of edge strength and edge extraction are presented in Chapter 12, in some detail. Common methods for edge linking, such as Hough transform, relaxation labelling and graph searching, are also presented in this chapter.

In Chapter 13 we present different methods of extracting important features, like topological, geometrical, structural and surface features. Each of these is useful for specific classes of applications. Chapter 14 describes various boundary-based and region based schemes for object and scene description. Scheme for describing objects or scene using region adjacency graph is also discussed.

In Chapter 15, we provide basic concepts and tools for visual pattern recognition using different mathematical and heuristic approaches such as deterministic, probabilistic, fuzzy set theoretic methods, with supervised or unsupervised learning mechanism. Recognition of visual pattern using syntactic features is also presented.

Sufficient number of figures are provided for the sake of better presentation of various concepts as well as to show outcome of the image processing algorithms. Worked out examples and algorithmic steps are given whenever felt required. Relevant references and problems are given at end of of each chapter.

1.6 Bibliographic Note

Since its inception, digital image processing and analysis has experienced a steady growth at the hands of a large group of competent researchers. The technique is also successfully applied to solve many practical problems. Development and advancement of the subject is extensively recorded.

Today, there are a good number of journals that are explicitly dedicated to this field and a large number of conferences on this subject take place every year. A concise list of books and a few technical papers are given in the bibliography without any claim of exhaustiveness.

Bibliography

Aggarwal, J.K. Duda, R.O. and Rosenfeld A. (Eds.), *Computer Methods in Image Analysis,* IEEE Press, New York, 1977.

Ahmed, N. and Rao, K.R., *Orthogonal Transforms for Digital Signal Processing*, Springer-Verlag, New York, 1975.

Andrews, H.C. (Ed.), *Digital Image Processing,* IEEE Press, New York, 1978.

Andrews, H.C. and Hunt, B.R. *Digital Image Restoration*, Prentice-Hall, Englewood Cliffs, New Jersey, 1977.

Andrews, H.C., Tescher, A.G. and Kruger, R.P., 'Image processing by digital computers', *IEEE Spectrum*, **9**:20–32, 1972.

Ballard, D.H. and Brown, C.M., *Computer Vision,* Prentice-Hall, Englewood Cliffs, New Jersey, 1982.

Bernstein, R. (Ed.), *Digital Image Processing for Remote Sensing,* IEEE Press, New York, 1978.

Castleman, K.R., *Digital Image Processing*, Prentice-Hall, Englewood Cliffs, New Jersey, 1979.

Chaudhuri, B.B. and Dutta Majumder, D., *Two-tone Image Processing and Recognition*, Wiley Eastern Ltd., New Delhi, 1993.

Chellappa, R. and Sawchuk, A.A., *Digital Image Processing*, Vols. 1 and 2, IEEE Press, New York, 1985.

Dougherty, E.R. and Giardina, C.R., *Morphological Methods in Image and Signal Processing*, Prentice-Hall, Englewood Cliffs, New Jersey, 1988.

Duda, R.O. and Hart, P.E., *Pattern Classification and Scene Analysis*, Wiley-Interscience, New York, 1973.

Ekstrom, M.P. (Ed.), *Digital Image Processing Techniques*, Academic Press, New York, 1984.

Fu, K.S. and Rosenfeld, A., 'Pattern recognition and image processing', *IEEE Trans. on Computer*, **C-25**:1336–1346, 1976.

Fu, K.S., Gonzalez, R.C. and Lee, C.S.G., *Robotics*, McGraw-Hill, New York, 1987.

Gonzalez, R.C. and Wintz, P., *Digital Image Processing*, 2nd ed., Addison-Wesley, Reading, Massachusetts, 1987.

Hall, E.L., *Computer Image Processing and Recognition*, Academic Press, New York, 1979.

Haralick, R.M. and Shapiro, L.G., *Computer and Robot Vision*, Vols.1 and 2. Addison-Wesley, Reading, Massachusetts, 1992.

Horn, B.K.P., *Robot Vision*, MIT Press, Cambridge, Massachusetts, 1986.

Huang, T.S., *Image Sequence Processing and Dynamic Scene Analysis*, Springer-Verlag, New York, 1983.

Huang, T.S. (Ed.), *Picture Processing and Digital Filtering*, Springer-Verlag, Berlin, 1975.

Jain, A.K., *Fundamentals of Digital Image Processing*, Prentice-Hall, Englewood Cliffs, New Jersey, 1989.

Lipkin, B.S. and Rosenfeld, A., (Eds.), *Picture Processing and Psychopictorics*, Academic Press, New York, 1970.

Marr, D., *Vision*, Freeman, W.H., New York, 1982.

McFarlane, M.D., 'Digital pictures fifty years ago', *Proc. IEEE,* **60**:768–770, 1972.

Nevatia, R., *Perception*, Prentice-Hall, Englewood Cliffs, New Jersey, 1982.

Pavlidis, T., *Algorithms for Graphics and Image Processing*, Computer Science Press, Rockville, Maryland, 1982.

Pratt, W.K., *Digital Image Processing*, 2nd ed., Wiley-Interscience, New York, 1991.

Rosenfeld, A. and Kak, A.C., *Digital Picture Processing*, 2nd ed., Vols. 1 and 2. Academic Press, New York, 1982.

Rosenfeld, A. (Ed.), *Digital Picture Analysis*, Springer-Verlag, New York, 1976.

Rosenfeld, A., 'Image analysis: problems, progress and prospects', *Pattern Recognition*, **17**:3–12, 1984.

Rosenfeld, A., 'Image pattern recognition', *Proc. IEEE*, **69**:596–605, 1981.

Serra, J., *Image Analysis and Mathematical Morphology*, Academic Press, London, 1982.

Wilson, S.S., 'Image-processing architectures', in Daugherty, E.R. (Ed.), *Digital Image Processing Methods*, Marcel Dekker Inc., New York, 1993.

Young, T.Y. and Fu, K.S. (Eds.), *Handbook of Pattern Recognition and Image Processing*, Academic Press, San Diego, California, 1986.

Chapter 2

Mathematical Preliminaries

2.1 Introduction

The processing and analysing of images by computer require some basic concepts of mathematical tools available for the task. We briefly present a subset of tools that are most frequently used in image processing and analysis. It is often necessary and convenient to characterize images mathematically for understanding and designing image processing algorithms. Mathematical characterization is of utmost importance for better presentation of the problem, and subsequently, for determining an acceptable solution. Our main concern here is digital images. Naturally, mathematical tools relevant to the digital image processing get more emphasis in the following discussion. However, knowledge of mathematical tools for processing continuous signals is also important, because the digital images usually are computer presentation of the visual scenes which are continuous in time, space and intensity. The techniques are also equally useful for non-visual multidimensional signals.

We also describe some mathematical tools for uncertainty management. The concept is very useful for developing algorithms for both low- and high-level processing. A set theory based on image processing tool that has inherent capability to deal straightway with shape information is also presented.

2.2 Vector Algebra

In this section we present a brief account of vector and matrix algebraic manipulation procedures that are frequently used in image processing. A *vector* may be viewed as a convenient representation of geometrical concept of directed line segment. In general, a vector in an N-dimensional space is represented by

$$\mathbf{h} = [h(0) \quad h(1) \quad h(2) \ \dots \ h(N-1)]$$

It may be written horizontally, called *row vector*, or vertically, called *column vector*. Accordingly, the above example is a row vector. A column vector is a vertical arrangement:

$$\mathbf{v} = \begin{bmatrix} v(0) \\ v(1) \\ \vdots \\ v(N-1) \end{bmatrix} = [v(0) \ v(1) \ v(2) \ \cdots \ v(N-1)]^{\mathrm{T}} \tag{2.1}$$

The superscript T stands for transposition. The $h(i)$ (or $v(i)$) is called the i-th *element* or i-th *component* of the vector. In the following text, unless otherwise specified, we consider vectors as column vectors. A *null vector* is a vector whose all elements are zero, i.e.

$$v(r) = 0$$

for all r. Suppose $\mathbf{f}$ and $\mathbf{g}$ are two N-dimensional vectors. Then

(i) the *magnitude* or Euclidean *norm* of $\mathbf{f}$ is denoted by $\| \mathbf{f} \|$ and

$$\| \mathbf{f} \| = \{f^2(0) + f^2(1) + f^2(2) + \cdots + f^2(N-1)\}^{1/2} \qquad (2.2)$$

Norm can be defined in other ways too. A vector whose norm is one, is called a *unit vector*.

(ii) A vector can be *multiplied* by a scalar. Suppose k is a scalar, then

$$k\mathbf{f} = [kf(0) \ kf(1) \ kf(2) \ \cdots \ kf(N-1)] \qquad (2.3)$$

(iii) *Addition/subtraction* of two vectors of same dimension is defined by

$$\mathbf{f} \pm \mathbf{g} = [f(0) \pm g(0) \ f(1) \pm g(1) \ f(2) \pm g(2) \ \cdots \ f(N-1) \pm g(N-1)] \qquad (2.4)$$

(iv) $\mathbf{f}$ and $\mathbf{g}$ are equal, i.e. $\mathbf{f} = \mathbf{g}$ if $f(r) = g(r)$ for $r = 0, 1, \ldots, N-1$.

(v) The *inner* (or *dot*) *product* of two vectors of same dimension is defined by

$$\mathbf{f} \cdot \mathbf{g} = \| \mathbf{f} \| \ \| \mathbf{g} \| \cos \alpha = f(0) \ g(0) + f(1) \ g(1) + f(2) \ g(2) + \cdots + f(N-1) \ g(N-1) \qquad (2.5)$$

Here α is the angle between $\mathbf{f}$ and $\mathbf{g}$. So

$$\mathbf{f} \cdot \mathbf{f} = \| \mathbf{f} \|^2 \qquad (2.6)$$

and also

$$k(\mathbf{f} \cdot \mathbf{g}) = (k\mathbf{f}) \cdot \mathbf{g} = \mathbf{f} \cdot (k\mathbf{g}) \qquad (2.7)$$

The *projection* of $\mathbf{f}$ onto $\mathbf{g}$ is

$$\| \mathbf{f} \| \cos \alpha = \frac{\mathbf{f} \cdot \mathbf{g}}{\| \mathbf{g} \|} \qquad (2.8)$$

(vi) *Commutative property:*

$$\mathbf{f} + \mathbf{g} = \mathbf{g} + \mathbf{f} \quad \text{and} \quad \mathbf{f} \cdot \mathbf{g} = \mathbf{g} \cdot \mathbf{f} \qquad (2.9)$$

(vii) *Associative property:*

$$\mathbf{f} + (\mathbf{g} + \mathbf{h}) = (\mathbf{f} + \mathbf{g}) + \mathbf{h} \qquad (2.10)$$

(viii) *Distributive property:*

$$\mathbf{f} \cdot (\mathbf{g} + \mathbf{h}) = \mathbf{f} \cdot \mathbf{g} + \mathbf{f} \cdot \mathbf{h} \qquad (2.11)$$

A *matrix* may be considered as a set of row (or column) vectors written in a particular order. While a vector is a linear array, a matrix is, in general, a rectangular array of elements. A matrix $\mathbf{A}$ of size $M \times N$ is represented by

$$\mathbf{A} = \begin{bmatrix} a(0,0) & a(0,1) & \cdots & a(0,N-1) \\ a(1,0) & a(1,1) & \cdots & a(1,N-1) \\ \vdots & \vdots & & \vdots \\ a(M-1,0) & a(M-1,1) & \cdots & a(M-1,N-1) \end{bmatrix} \qquad (2.12)$$

where $a(r, c)$ is an arbitrary element of the matrix. The element may also be denoted by a_{rc}. We also denote a matrix containing the elements $a(r, c)$ by $[a(r, c)]$. A row vector having N elements may be considered as a matrix of size $1 \times N$, and similarly, a column vector as a matrix of size $N \times 1$. The matrix **A** is a *null matrix* if

$$a(r, c) = 0$$

for all r and c, and is denoted by **0**. If $M = N$, then the matrix is called a *square matrix*. The elements $a(r, c)$s of a square matrix are called diagonal elements if $r - c = 0$. The elements for which $r - c = k$ are called $|\,k\,|$-th upper-subdiagonal elements if k is negative, and are called $|\,k\,|$-th lower-subdiagonal elements if k is positive. Collection of all subdiagonal elements are called off-diagonal elements. A square matrix is a diagonal matrix if its off-diagonal elements are zero, i.e.

$$a(r, c) = 0$$

if $r \neq c$. A diagonal matrix is called an *identity matrix* if its diagonal elements are all one, and is denoted by **I**. Properties of a matrix **A** are discussed below:

(i) A matrix can also be multiplied by a scalar. Multiplication of a matrix **A** by a scalar k produces another matrix **X** whose elements are

$$x(r, c) = ka(r, c) \tag{2.13}$$

for all r and c.

(ii) **A** and **B** are two matrices each of size $M \times N$, then their *sum* produces another matrix **X** of size $M \times N$ whose elements are

$$x(r, c) = a(r, c) + b(r, c) \tag{2.14}$$

for all r and c. We write **X = A + B**. Also note that

$$\mathbf{A + B = B + A}$$

and

$$\mathbf{A + (B + C) = (A + B) + C}$$

where **C** is also of size $M \times N$.

(iii) **A** and **B** are two matrices of sizes $M \times L$ and $L \times N$ respectively, then their *product* gives another matrix **X** of size $M \times N$ whose elements are

$$x(r, c) = \sum_{i=0}^{L-1} a(r, i)\, b(i, c) \tag{2.15}$$

for all r and c. We write **X = AB**. Note that, in general,

$$\mathbf{AB \neq BA}$$

However,

$$\mathbf{A(BC) = (AB)C, \quad and \quad A(B + C) = (AB) + AC}$$

(iv) The *transpose* of a matrix **A** of size $M \times N$ is a matrix, say **X** of size $N \times M$ whose elements are

$$x(r, c) = a(c, r) \tag{2.16}$$

for all r and c. We write $\mathbf{X = A}^{\mathrm{T}}$. A matrix **A** is *symmetric* if

$$\mathbf{A} = \mathbf{A}^T \tag{2.17}$$

For any two matrices $\mathbf{A}$ and $\mathbf{B}$ whose product is defined following relationship holds:

$$[\mathbf{AB}]^T = \mathbf{B}^T \mathbf{A}^T \tag{2.18}$$

(v) The *trace* of a matrix $\mathbf{A}$ of size $M \times M$ is a scalar and is defined by

$$\text{tr} \, [\mathbf{A}] = \sum_{i=0}^{M-1} a(i,i) \tag{2.19}$$

If $\mathbf{A}$ and $\mathbf{B}$ are square matrices of same size then

$$\text{tr} \, [\mathbf{AB}] = \text{tr} \, [\mathbf{BA}] \tag{2.20}$$

(vi) The Euclidean *norm of a matrix* $\mathbf{A}$ is defined by

$$\| \, \mathbf{A} \, \| = \text{tr} \, [\mathbf{A}^T\mathbf{A}] \tag{2.21}$$

At this point, we recall the vector norm [Equation (2.2)] which can be rewritten as

$$\| \, \mathbf{f} \, \| = \mathbf{f}^T\mathbf{f}$$

and is a scalar. Similarly, the *inner product* or *dot product* [Equation (2.5)] can be redefined as

$$\mathbf{f} \cdot \mathbf{g} = \mathbf{f}^T\mathbf{g}$$

which is also a scalar. On the other hand, the *outer product* of two vectors $\mathbf{f}$ and $\mathbf{g}$ of M- and N-dimensions, respectively is a matrix $\mathbf{X}$ of size $M \times N$ whose elements are

$$x(r, c) = f(r) \, g(c) \quad \text{for all } r \text{ and } c \tag{2.22}$$

We write $\mathbf{X} = \mathbf{fg}^T$.

(vii) The *rank* of a matrix is defined as the number of independent rows, or equivalently, the number of the independent columns it contains. A square matrix $\mathbf{A}$ of size $M \times M$ is said to be *non-singular* if its rank is M, and *singular* if its rank is less than M. Suppose $\mathbf{A}$ is a non-singular square matrix, then there exists a unique matrix $\mathbf{A}^{-1}$, called *inverse* of $\mathbf{A}$, such that

$$\mathbf{AA}^{-1} = \mathbf{A}^{-1}\mathbf{A} = \mathbf{I} \tag{2.23}$$

If $\mathbf{A}$ and $\mathbf{B}$ are non-singular matrices of same size then

$$[\mathbf{AB}]^{-1} = \mathbf{B}^{-1} \mathbf{A}^{-1} \tag{2.24}$$

If $\mathbf{A}$ is non-singular, so is $\mathbf{A}^T$, then

$$[\mathbf{A}^T]^{-1} = [\mathbf{A}^{-1}]^T \tag{2.25}$$

Two special matrices which are of interest in designing digital filters, are *Toeplitz matrix* and *circulant matrix*. A matrix $\mathbf{A}$ is called a Toeplitz matrix if its elements are

$$a(r, c) = f(r - c) \quad \text{for all } r \text{ and } c \tag{2.26}$$

where $f(r - c)$ is a function of $(r - c)$. That means the diagonal and each of the subdiagonals of the matrix contain the same elements. Similarly a matrix $\mathbf{A}$ of size $M \times N$ is called a circulant matrix if its elements are

$$a(r, c) = f\{(r - c) \bmod N\} \text{ for all } r \text{ and } c \tag{2.27}$$

That means, like Toeplitz matrix, the diagonal and each of the subdiagonals of the circulant matrix also contain the same elements and, moreover, any row of the circulant matrix can be generated by giving the previous row a circular shift towards right.

(viii) The *quadratic form* of a vector **f** is a scalar and is defined as

$$k = \mathbf{f}^{\mathrm{T}}\mathbf{A}\mathbf{f} \tag{2.28}$$

where **A** is a square matrix. On the other hand, for a symmetric matrix **A**, the derivative of the quadratic form $\mathbf{f}^{\mathrm{T}}\mathbf{A}\mathbf{f}$ with respect to the vector **f** is a vector defined as

$$\frac{\partial[\mathbf{f}^{\mathrm{T}}\mathbf{A}\mathbf{f}]}{\partial \mathbf{f}} = 2\mathbf{A}\mathbf{f} \tag{2.29}$$

(ix) The *determinant* of a square matrix **A** of size $M \times M$ is a real valued function of elements $a(r,c)$ defined by

$$| \mathbf{A} | = \sum \pm a(0, i)\, a(1, j) \dots a(M - 1, n) \tag{2.30}$$

where summation is taken over all permutations $(i, j, \dots, n)$ of $(0, 1, \dots, M - 1)$ with a plus sign if $(i, j, \dots, n)$ is an even permutation, and with a minus sign if it is an odd permutation. Determinant of a matrix of size $M \times M$ is zero if its rank is less than M. A matrix whose determinant is zero is called a *singular matrix*, otherwise a *non-singular*.

(x) An *eigenvector* of a matrix **A** of size $M \times M$ is a vector **e** such that for some scalar λ,

$$\mathbf{A}\mathbf{e} = \lambda\mathbf{e}$$

here λ is called the *eigenvalue* of the matrix. For a $M \times M$ matrix we have M eigenvalues, may be distinct or not, and for each eigenvalue we can have one eigenvector. These eigenvalues are roots of the so-called *characteristic polynomial:*

$$| \mathbf{A} - \lambda\mathbf{I} | = 0 \tag{2.31}$$

[Interested readers may see Anton (1973), Hohn (1958), Nearing (1963) and other books on matrix theory and linear algebra for more detail.]

2.3 Linear Operations

As mentioned earlier, we present only those mathematical tools and operations which are useful for image processing. A large subset of these operations are linear in nature. Most widely used linear operations are *convolution, unitary transforms* and *discrete linear filtering*. Let Γ be an operation that maps f to g, i.e. $g = \Gamma(f)$, then Γ is said to be linear if

$$k_1 g_1 + k_2 g_2 = k_1 \Gamma(f_1) + k_2 \Gamma(f_2) = \Gamma(k_1 f_1 + k_2 f_2) \tag{2.32}$$

where k_1 and k_2 are scalars. Let us consider the convolution operation, which is a most common linear operation, in one dimensional discrete domain. Suppose f and h are two periodic sequences of elements of periods M_1 and M_2 respectively. Their convolution produces another sequence g_e of period M defined as

$$g_e(r) = \sum_{i=0}^{M-1} f_e(i)\, h_e(r-i) \tag{2.33}$$

for $r = 0, 1, 2, \ldots, M-1$, where $M \geq M_1 + M_2 - 1$. The sequences f_e and h_e are extended f and h obtained by appending zeros, i.e.

$$f_e(r) = \begin{cases} f(r) & \text{for } 0 \leq r < M_1 \\ 0 & \text{for } M_1 \leq r \leq M-1 \end{cases} \tag{2.34}$$

and

$$h_e(r) = \begin{cases} h(r) & \text{for } 0 \leq r < M_2 \\ 0 & \text{for } M_2 \leq r \leq M-1 \end{cases} \tag{2.35}$$

The extended sequences f_e and h_e are also periodic of period M. The sequences f and h are extended to avoid overlapping between the periods. We also represent convolution as

$$g(r) = f(r) * h(r)$$

Now the Equation (2.33) can be expanded to a set of M linear equations:

$$g_e(0) = h_e(0)\, f_e(0) + h_e(-1)\, f_e(1) + h_e(-2)\, f_e(2) + \cdots + h_e(-M+1)\, f_e(M-1)$$

$$g_e(1) = h_e(1)\, f_e(0) + h_e(0)\, f_e(1) + h_e(-1)\, f_e(2) + \cdots + h_e(-M+2)\, f_e(M-1)$$

$$g_e(2) = h_e(2)\, f_e(0) + h_e(1)\, f_e(1) + h_e(0)\, f_e(2) + \cdots + h_e(-M+3)\, f_e(M-1)$$

$$\vdots$$

$$g_e(M-1) = h_e(M-1)\, f_e(0) + h_e(M-2)\, f_e(1) + h_e(M-3)\, f_e(2) + \cdots + h_e(0)\, f_e(M-1) \tag{2.36}$$

Since $h_e(r)$ is periodic with period M, we can write $h_e(r) = h_e(r+M)$. Hence, the above set of equations can be represented as

$$\mathbf{g} = \mathbf{H}\mathbf{f} \tag{2.37}$$

where $\mathbf{g}$ and $\mathbf{f}$ are M-dimensional vectors:

$$\mathbf{g} = \begin{bmatrix} g_e(0) \\ g_e(1) \\ g_e(2) \\ \vdots \\ g_e(M-1) \end{bmatrix}, \quad \mathbf{f} = \begin{bmatrix} f_e(0) \\ f_e(1) \\ f_e(2) \\ \vdots \\ f_e(M-1) \end{bmatrix}$$

and $\mathbf{H}$ is a circulant matrix of size $M \times M$:

$$\mathbf{H} = \begin{bmatrix} h_e(0) & h_e(M-1) & h_e(M-2) & \cdots & h_e(1) \\ h_e(1) & h_e(0) & h_e(M-1) & \cdots & h_e(2) \\ h_e(2) & h_e(1) & h_e(0) & \cdots & h_e(3) \\ \vdots & \vdots & \vdots & \vdots & \vdots \\ h_e(M-1) & h_e(M-2) & h_e(M-3) & \cdots & h_e(0) \end{bmatrix}$$

The above formulation can trivially be extended to multi-dimensions. Discrete convolution of two- dimensional arrays is discussed in Chapter 5, where **H** is found to be block-circulant. Given a transformation

$$\mathbf{g} = \mathbf{H}\mathbf{f}$$

a common task in linear processing is to determine $\hat{\mathbf{f}}$, an estimate of **f**. If **H** is a square matrix and is invertible, then

$$\hat{\mathbf{f}} = \mathbf{H}^{-1}\mathbf{g} \tag{2.38}$$

If **H** is not square, there may exist a matrix $\mathbf{H}^{+}$, called *pseudoinverse matrix*, [Pratt (1991), Rao (1973)] such that

$$\hat{\mathbf{f}} = \mathbf{H}^{+}\mathbf{g} \tag{2.39}$$

The generalized inverse $\mathbf{H}^{-}$ may be considered as a pseudoinverse operator which satisfies the relations:

$$\mathbf{H}\mathbf{H}^{-}\mathbf{H} = \mathbf{H}, \ \mathbf{H}^{-}\mathbf{H}\mathbf{H}^{-} = \mathbf{H}$$

$$(\mathbf{H}\mathbf{H}^{-})^{\mathrm{T}} = \mathbf{H}\mathbf{H}^{-}, \ (\mathbf{H}^{-}\mathbf{H})^{\mathrm{T}} = \mathbf{H}^{-}\mathbf{H}$$

Least square inverse $\mathbf{H}^{s}$ of **H** is another example of pseudoinverse operator which satisfies the relations:

$$\mathbf{H}\mathbf{H}^{s}\mathbf{H} = \mathbf{H}, \ (\mathbf{H}\mathbf{H}^{s})^{\mathrm{T}} = \mathbf{H}\mathbf{H}^{s}$$

[Extensive treatment on the pseudoinverse and generalized inverse are available in Rao and Mitra (1971), Albert (1972), Graybill (1969).]

2.4 Orthogonal Transforms

Orthogonal transforms are useful tools for signal processing [Oppenheim and Schafer (1975), Ahmed and Rao (1975)]. Many filters have been designed so far to be applied in the transform domain. To start with, we describe how a continuous function (or signal) can be represented using a set of orthogonal functions. Suppose there is a set of continuous functions $\{\phi_0(x), \phi_1(x), \phi_2(x), \ldots\}$ of x. These functions, real or complex, are said to be *orthogonal functions* in the interval $[x_0, x_0 + X]$ if

$$\int_{x_0}^{x_0+X} \phi_i(x)\phi_j(x)\, dx = \begin{cases} k & \text{if } i = j \\ 0 & \text{otherwise} \end{cases} \tag{2.40}$$

When $k = 1$, the set is called *orthonormal*. Suppose $f(x)$ is a real valued function defined on the same interval. Then $f(x)$ can be represented by the expansion:

$$f(x) = \sum_{i=0}^{\infty} F_i\phi_i(x) \tag{2.41}$$

where F_i is the i-th *coefficient* of the expansion. Hence, F_i can be expressed as

$$F_i = \frac{1}{k}\int_{x_0}^{x_0+X} f(x)\phi_i(x)\, dx \tag{2.42}$$

for $i = 0, 1, 2, \ldots$ The orthogonal set $\{\phi_i(x)\}$ with

$$\int_{x_0}^{x_0+X} \phi_i^2(x)\, dx < \infty \qquad (2.43)$$

is said to be *closed* or *complete* if either of the following statements is true:

1. There exists no function $f(x)$ with

$$0 < \int_{x_0}^{x_0+X} f^2(x)\, dx < \infty$$

such that

$$\int_{x_0}^{x_0+X} f(x)\phi_i(x)\, dx = 0$$

for all i.

2. For any piecewise continuous function $f(x)$ with

$$0 < \int_{x_0}^{x_0+X} f^2(x)\, dx < \infty$$

and an infinitesimal $\varepsilon > 0$, there exists an M and a finite expansion:

$$\hat{f}(x) = \sum_{i=0}^{M-1} F_i \phi_i(x)$$

such that

$$\int_{x_0}^{x_0+X} \left| f(x) - \hat{f}(x) \right|^2 dx < \varepsilon \qquad (2.44)$$

The second condition states that if $\{\phi_i(x)\}$ is complete then $f(x)$ can be represented by a finite set of coefficients $\{F_0, F_1, F_2, \ldots, F_{M-1}\}$.

2.4.1 Fourier Transform

Most widely used orthogonal transform in the field of image processing is *Fourier transform* (FT). Here we present a systematic transition from the Fourier representation of function (or signal) to the Fourier transform and then to the discrete Fourier transform step-by-step [Ahmed and Rao (1975), Bracewell (1968), Lighthill (1960)].

In this case the set of orthogonal functions is $\{1, \cos i\omega_0 x, \sin i\omega_0 x\}$ defined over the period X, i.e.

$$\int_{x_0}^{x_0+X} \cos(i\omega_0 x)\cos(j\omega_0 x)\, dx = \begin{cases} X/2 & \text{if } i = j \\ 0 & \text{otherwise} \end{cases}$$

$$\int_{x_0}^{x_0+X} \cos(i\omega_0 x)\sin(j\omega_0 x)\, dx = 0$$

$$\int_{x_0}^{x_0+X} \sin(i\omega_0 x)\sin(j\omega_0 x)\, dx = \begin{cases} X/2 & \text{if } i = j \\ 0 & \text{otherwise} \end{cases}$$

where, ω_0 is the *fundamental angular frequency* and is equal to $2\pi/X$. The term $i\omega_0$ is the *harmonics*.

For simplicity let us assume $x_0 = X/2$, then $\int_{x_0}^{x_0+X}$ can be written as $\int_{-X/2}^{X/2}$. Suppose $f(x)$ is a periodic function of period X and satisfies the following conditions:

1. $\int_{-X/2}^{X/2} f^2(x)\,dx < \infty$

2. $f(x)$ has at most a finite number of discontinuities in one period.

3. $f(x)$ has at most a finite number of extrema in one period.

Then $f(x)$ can be represented by

$$f(x) = a_0 + \sum_{i=1}^{\infty} a_i \cos(i\omega_0 x) + \sum_{i=1}^{\infty} b_i \sin(i\omega_0 x) \tag{2.45}$$

Hence,

$$a_0 = \frac{1}{X}\int_{-X/2}^{X/2} f(x)\,dx \tag{2.46}$$

$$a_i = \frac{2}{X}\int_{-X/2}^{X/2} f(x)\cos(i\omega_0 x)\,dx \tag{2.47}$$

$$b_i = \frac{2}{X}\int_{-X/2}^{X/2} f(x)\sin(i\omega_0 x)\,dx \tag{2.48}$$

for $i = 1, 2, \ldots$ Now it is known that

$$\cos(i\omega_0 x) = \frac{1}{2}\exp\left(\sqrt{-1}\,i\omega_0 x\right) + \exp\left(-\sqrt{-1}\,i\omega_0 x\right)$$

$$\sin(i\omega_0 x) = \frac{1}{2\sqrt{-1}}\exp\left(\sqrt{-1}\,i\omega_0 x\right) - \exp\left(-\sqrt{-1}\,i\omega_0 x\right)$$

This allows $f(x)$ to be represented as

$$f(x) = a_0 + \frac{1}{2}\sum_{i=1}^{\infty}\left\{a_i \exp\left(\sqrt{-1}i\omega_0 x\right) + \exp\left(-\sqrt{-1}i\omega_0 x\right)\right.$$

$$\left. - \sqrt{-1}b_i\left\{\exp\left(\sqrt{-1}i\omega_0 x\right) - \exp\left(-\sqrt{-1}i\omega_0 x\right)\right\}\right]$$

or

$$f(x) = a_0 + \frac{1}{2}\sum_{i=1}^{\infty}\left[\left(a_i - \sqrt{-1}\,b_i\right)\exp\left(\sqrt{-1}i\omega_0 x\right) + \left(a_i + \sqrt{-1}\,b_i\right)\exp\left(-\sqrt{-1}i\omega_0 x\right)\right] \tag{2.49}$$

Let us define

$$F_i = \frac{1}{2}(a_i - \sqrt{-1}\,b_i)$$

From Equations (2.46), (2.47) and (2.48) first we get firstly

$$F_i = \frac{1}{X} \int_{-X/2}^{X/2} f(x) \left[\cos(i\omega_0 x) - \sqrt{-1} \sin(i\omega_0 x) \right] dx$$

or

$$F_i = \frac{1}{X} \int_{-X/2}^{X/2} f(x) \exp\left(-\sqrt{-1} i\omega_0 x\right) dx \qquad (2.50)$$

secondly, proceeding in reverse way, we get

$$F_{-i} = \frac{1}{2}\left(a_i + \sqrt{-1}\, b_i\right)$$

and finally, substituting $i = 0$ in Equation (2.50)

$$F_0 = \frac{1}{X} \int_{-X/2}^{X/2} f(x)\, dx = a_0$$

Therefore, Equation (2.49) can be rewritten as

$$f(x) = F_0 + \sum_{i=1}^{\infty} \left[F_i \exp\left(\sqrt{-1}\, i\omega_0 x\right) + F_{-i} \exp\left(-\sqrt{-1}\, i\omega_0 x\right) \right]$$

or

$$f(x) = \sum_{i=-\infty}^{\infty} F_i \exp\left(\sqrt{-1}\, i\omega_0 x\right) \qquad (2.51)$$

Substituting $X = 2\pi/\omega_0$, in Equation (2.50), we get

$$F_i = \frac{\omega_0}{2\pi} \int_{-X/2}^{X/2} f(x) \exp\left(-\sqrt{-1} i\omega_0 x\right) dx \qquad (2.52)$$

Equations (2.51) and (2.52) are called *Fourier series pair*.

Now as the period X tends to infinity (i.e. the function or signal becomes aperiodic), the harmonics $i\omega_0$ approaches continuous angular frequency ω, the fundamental angular frequency ω_0 becomes a differential angular frequency $d\omega$ and F_is' crowd in to form a continuous function $F(\omega)$. This leads to the *Fourier transform pair* in continuous domain:

$$F(\omega) = \frac{1}{2\pi} \int_{-\infty}^{\infty} f(x) \exp\left(-\sqrt{-1}\omega x\right) dx$$

$$f(x) = \int_{-\infty}^{\infty} F(\omega) \exp\left(\sqrt{-1}\omega x\right) d\omega$$

The constant $1/2\pi$ can be put in either of the above two equations. Following form is more frequently found in the image processing literature.

$$F(\omega) = \int_{-\infty}^{\infty} f(x) \exp\left(-\sqrt{-1}\omega x\right) dx \qquad (2.53)$$

$$f(x) = \frac{1}{2\pi} \int_{-\infty}^{\infty} F(\omega) \exp \sqrt{-1}\omega x \, d\omega \qquad (2.54)$$

The *discrete Fourier transform* (FT) of a sequence $\{f(r) \mid r = 0, 1, 2, \ldots, M-1\}$ of M finite valued numbers is defined as

$$F(u) = \sum_{r=0}^{M-1} f(r) \, W^{ur/M} \qquad (2.55)$$

for $u = 0, 1, 2, \ldots, M-1$. Here $W = \exp(-\sqrt{-1}\,2\pi)$ and $W^{ur/M}$ is orthogonal, i.e.

$$\sum_{r=0}^{M-1} W^{ir/M} W^{-jr/M} = \begin{cases} M & \text{if } (i-j) \text{ is zero or integer multiple of } M \\ 0 & \text{otherwise} \end{cases}$$

Similarly, *inverse discrete Fourier transform* is defined as

$$f(r) = \frac{1}{M} \sum_{u=0}^{M-1} F(u) W^{-ur/M} \qquad (2.56)$$

for $r = 0, 1, 2, \ldots, M-1$. Equations (2.55) and (2.56) are called *discrete Fourier transform pair* and conventionally represented as

$$f(r) \Leftrightarrow F(u)$$

Since the Fourier transform and its inverse are linear transforms, Equations (2.55) and (2.56) can be represented by matrix vector notation as

$$\mathbf{F} = \mathbf{W}_M \mathbf{f}$$

and

$$\mathbf{f} = \mathbf{W}_M^{-1} \mathbf{F}$$

$\mathbf{f}$ and $\mathbf{F}$ are M dimensional vectors, and $\mathbf{W}_M$ is a $M \times M$ matrix. For example, for $M = 8$, the matrix $\mathbf{W}_8$ looks like

$$\mathbf{W}_8 = \{W^{ur/8}\} = \begin{bmatrix} W^{0/8} & W^{0/8} & W^{0/8} & W^{0/8} & W^{0/8} & W^{0/8} & W^{0/8} & W^{0/8} \\ W^{0/8} & W^{1/8} & W^{2/8} & W^{3/8} & W^{4/8} & W^{5/8} & W^{6/8} & W^{7/8} \\ W^{0/8} & W^{2/8} & W^{4/8} & W^{6/8} & W^{0/8} & W^{2/8} & W^{4/8} & W^{6/8} \\ W^{0/8} & W^{3/8} & W^{6/8} & W^{1/8} & W^{4/8} & W^{7/8} & W^{2/8} & W^{5/8} \\ W^{0/8} & W^{4/8} & W^{0/8} & W^{4/8} & W^{0/8} & W^{4/8} & W^{0/8} & W^{4/8} \\ W^{0/8} & W^{5/8} & W^{2/8} & W^{7/8} & W^{4/8} & W^{1/8} & W^{6/8} & W^{3/8} \\ W^{0/8} & W^{6/8} & W^{4/8} & W^{2/8} & W^{0/8} & W^{6/8} & W^{4/8} & W^{2/8} \\ W^{0/8} & W^{7/8} & W^{6/8} & W^{5/8} & W^{4/8} & W^{3/8} & W^{2/8} & W^{1/8} \end{bmatrix}$$

Since $\mathbf{W}_M$ is *unitary* and *symmetric*, $\mathbf{W}_M^{-1} = \mathbf{W}_M^*$, where the elements of the matrix $\mathbf{W}_M^*$ are the *complex conjugate* of that of $\mathbf{W}_M$.

The discrete Fourier transform of a two dimensional array of numbers $\{f(r,c) \mid r = 0, 1, 2, ..., M - 1; c = 0, 1, 2, ..., N - 1\}$ is defined by the transform pair

$$F(u, v) = \sum_{c=0}^{N-1}\sum_{r=0}^{M-1} f(r, c)\, W^{\{(ur/M)+(vc/N)\}} \tag{2.57}$$

for $u = 0, 1, 2, ..., M - 1$ and $v = 0, 1, 2, ..., N - 1$; and

$$f(r, c) = \sum_{v=0}^{N-1}\sum_{u=0}^{M-1} F(u, v)\, W^{-\{(ur/M)+(vc/N)\}} \tag{2.58}$$

for $r = 0, 1, 2, ..., M - 1$ and $c = 0, 1, 2, ..., N - 1$. Whether continuous or discrete (or in 1-, 2-, or any dimensions) the Fourier transform coefficients are complex numbers, i.e.

$$F(u, v) = R(u, v) + \sqrt{-1}\, I(u, v)$$

where $R(u,v)$ and $I(u,v)$ are real and imaginary components respectively. It is often useful to examine the *power spectrum* $|F(u,v)|^2$ and the *phase spectrum* $\Phi(u,v)$ for designing the processing filters, where

$$|F(u, v)|^2 = R^2(u, v) + I^2(u, v)$$

$$F(u, v) = \tan^{-1} \frac{I(u, v)}{R(u, v)}$$

Figure 2.1 shows some examples of power spectra.

Since $|F(u, v)|^2 \geq 0$, to increase the visibility of the distribution of energy over the domain we have displayed $\log [|F(u, v)|^2 + 1]$ instead of just $|F(u, v)|^2$.

Below we list some properties of the Fourier transform:

1. *Linearity:*

$$af(r, c) + bh(r, c) \Leftrightarrow aF(u, v) + bH(u, v)$$

where a and b are scalars, and $F(u, v)$ and $H(u, v)$ are the Fourier transforms of $f(r, c)$ and $h(r, c)$, respectively.

2. *Shift invariance:*

$$f(r - r_0, c - c_0) \Leftrightarrow F(u, v)\, W^{\{(ur_0/M)+(vc_0/N)\}}$$

3. *Modulation:*

$$W^{\{(u_0r/M + (v_0c/N)\}} f(r, c) \Leftrightarrow F(u + u_0, v + v_0)$$

4. *Convolution:*

$$f(r, c) * h(r, c) \Leftrightarrow F(u, v)\, H(u, v)$$

Suppose the convolution on the left hand side can be represented by vector matrix notation, i.e. $\mathbf{g} = \mathbf{H}\mathbf{f}$, where $\mathbf{g}$ and $\mathbf{f}$ are MN-dimensional vectors, and $\mathbf{H}$ is a block-circulant matrix of size $MN \times MN$. Then $G(u, v) = H(u, v) F(u, v)$ indicates that the block-circulant matrix H can be diagonalized by two dimensional Fourier transform and $H(u, v)$s are its eigenvalues [Hunt (1973)]. In other words, columns of the two-dimensional Fourier transform matrix are eigenvectors of any block-circulant matrix.

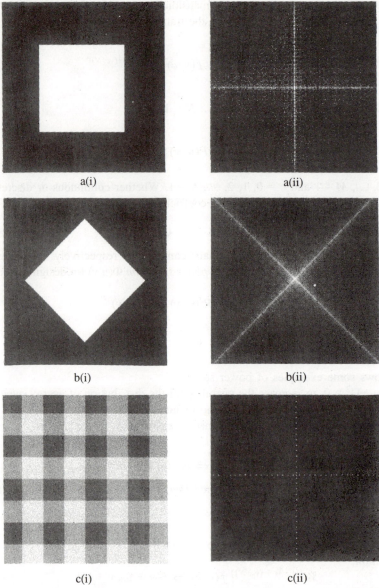

Fig. 2.1   Original images (two-dimensional array of numbers represented by variation in intensity) are shown in a(i), b(i) and c(i), the power spectra are shown in a(ii), b(ii) and c(ii).

5. *Multiplication:*

$$f(r, c)\ h(r, c) \Leftrightarrow F(u, v) * H(u, v)$$

6. *Correlation:*

$$f(r, c) * h(-r, -c) \Leftrightarrow F(u, v)\ H^*(u, v)$$

7. *Separability:*

$$\sum_{c=0}^{N-1} \sum_{r=0}^{M-1} f(r, c) W^{\{(ur/M)+(vc/N)\}} = \sum_{c=0}^{N-1} \left\{ \left(\sum_{r=0}^{M-1} f(r, c) W^{(ur/M)} \right) \right\} W^{(vc/N)}$$

$$s_{ru} = \sin\left[\frac{\pi(r+1)(u+1)}{M+1}\right] \tag{2.73}$$

The DST coefficients can also be computed using FFT algorithm. In fact, Jain (1974) first introduced DST as a fast algorithmic substitute for Karhunen-Loeve transform of a Markov process. The two-dimensional DST can be defined in exactly similar manner [Pratt (1991)].

2.4.3 Hartley Transform

We have already seen that Fourier transform coefficients are complex, so the transform may be computationally inefficient in some computing environment. To surmount this problem, a structurally similar but real valued unitary transform, called *Hartley transform*, has been proposed [Hartley (1942), Bracewell (1983), Bracewell (1986), Pratt (1991)]. The two-dimensional Hartley transform is defined by

$$F(u, v) = \frac{1}{\sqrt{MN}} \sum_{c=0}^{N-1} \sum_{r=0}^{M-1} f(r, c) \, \text{cas}\left[2\pi\left(\frac{ur}{M} + \frac{vc}{N}\right)\right] \tag{2.74}$$

and

$$f(r, c) = \frac{1}{\sqrt{MN}} \sum_{v=0}^{N-1} \sum_{u=0}^{M-1} F(u, v) \, \text{cas}\left[2\pi\left(\frac{ur}{M} + \frac{vc}{N}\right)\right] \tag{2.75}$$

where cas θ = cos θ + sin θ. It should be noted that cas θ is an orthogonal function.

2.4.4 Walsh–Hadamard Transform

So far we have discussed orthogonal transforms for which basis functions are derived from the family of sinusoids. Now we present some non-sinusoidal orthogonal transforms. In 1922, Rademacher presented a set, though not complete, of orthogonal square wave functions. Walsh (1923), however, introduced a complete set of such functions which can be used to represent any arbitrary function. The Walsh functions are defined iteratively on the interval [0,1] as follows [Hall (1979)]:

$$\phi_0(x) = 1$$

$$\phi_1(x) = \begin{cases} 1 & x < \frac{1}{2} \\ -1 & x \geq \frac{1}{2} \end{cases} \tag{2.76}$$

$$\phi_n(x) = \begin{cases} \phi_{\lfloor n/2 \rfloor}(2x), & x < \frac{1}{2} \\ \phi_{\lfloor n/2 \rfloor}(2x-1), & x \geq \frac{1}{2} \quad \text{for } n \text{ odd} \\ -\phi_{\lfloor n/2 \rfloor}(2x-1), & x \geq \frac{1}{2} \quad \text{for } n \text{ even} \end{cases}$$

where $\lfloor z \rfloor$ is the integer part of z. It should be noted that Walsh functions are ordered by *sequency*, i.e. the number of zero crossings. This is analogous to the Fourier representation where the basis functions are ordered by frequency. The coefficients of representation may be called *sequency components*. First two Walsh functions $\phi_0(x)$ and $\phi_1(x)$ are even and odd functions respectively about the point $x = \frac{1}{2}$, and every subsequent pair of functions maintains the order of even and odd functions. The rows of discrete Walsh transform matrix W_M of size $M \times M$ is generated by sampling the Walsh functions having the sequency less than or equal to $M - 1$ at equispaced M points, where M should be an integer power of 2. For $M = 8$, the matrix W_M becomes

$$W_8 = \begin{bmatrix} 1 & 1 & 1 & 1 & 1 & 1 & 1 & 1 \\ 1 & 1 & 1 & 1 & -1 & -1 & -1 & -1 \\ 1 & 1 & -1 & -1 & -1 & -1 & 1 & 1 \\ 1 & 1 & -1 & -1 & 1 & 1 & -1 & -1 \\ 1 & -1 & -1 & 1 & 1 & -1 & -1 & 1 \\ 1 & -1 & -1 & 1 & -1 & 1 & 1 & -1 \\ 1 & -1 & 1 & -1 & -1 & 1 & -1 & 1 \\ 1 & -1 & 1 & -1 & 1 & -1 & 1 & -1 \end{bmatrix}$$

Thus the elements of Walsh transform matrix are not only real, they take on the values +1 and −1 only. This results in extensive simplification in computation of sequency components by the Walsh transform. The two-dimensional Walsh transform pair is given by

$$[F(u, v)] = \frac{1}{\sqrt{MN}} \; W_M \, [f(r, c)] W_N \tag{2.77}$$

and

$$[f(r, c)] = \frac{1}{\sqrt{MN}} \; W_M \, [F(u, v)] W_N \tag{2.78}$$

A similar orthogonal transform matrix containing ±1 but with different order of sequency is due to Hadamard (1893), Pratt et al. (1969). The lowest order of Hadamard matrix is 2, and the corresponding matrix is given by

$$H_2 = \begin{bmatrix} 1 & 1 \\ 1 & -1 \end{bmatrix}.$$

The higher order matrix can easily be constructed when the order is even. In fact, if H_M be a Hadamard matrix of order M then

$$H_{2M} = \begin{bmatrix} H_M & H_M \\ H_M & -H_M \end{bmatrix}$$

is also Hadamard matrix of order $2M$. Harmuth (1969) has shown that Hadamard matrix of size $2^m \times 2^m$ (m is an integer) is equivalent to discrete Walsh matrix of same size except the order of rows. So, the transformation of discrete signal by Hadamard matrix is also called *Walsh–Hadamard transformation*. The two-dimensional Walsh Hadamard–transform pair is given by Equations (2.77) and (2.78) except that **W** be replaced by **H**. Andrews and Casparie (1970) have developed a fast algorithm for implementing the transform.

2.4.5 Haar Transform

Another orthogonal transform, called *Haar transform*, is derived from the Haar matrix [Haar (1955), Harmuth (1969), Andrews (1970)] whose elements are either -1, 0 or 1 multiplied by integer powers of $\sqrt{2}$. The main advantage of this transform is that it samples the input data sequence in coarse to fine resolution and takes the difference between the adjacent pairs. The resolution increases by a power of 2, and as a result, in the transform domain, differential energy is more and more localized. This may be revealed by the following example of a 8×8 Haar matrix.

$$\mathbf{H}_8 = \begin{bmatrix} 1 & 1 & 1 & 1 & 1 & 1 & 1 & 1 \\ 1 & 1 & 1 & 1 & -1 & -1 & -1 & -1 \\ \sqrt{2} & \sqrt{2} & -\sqrt{2} & -\sqrt{2} & 0 & 0 & 0 & 0 \\ 0 & 0 & 0 & 0 & \sqrt{2} & \sqrt{2} & -\sqrt{2} & -\sqrt{2} \\ 2 & -2 & 0 & 0 & 0 & 0 & 0 & 0 \\ 0 & 0 & 2 & -2 & 0 & 0 & 0 & 0 \\ 0 & 0 & 0 & 0 & 2 & -2 & 0 & 0 \\ 0 & 0 & 0 & 0 & 0 & 0 & 2 & -2 \end{bmatrix}$$

That means when this matrix is pre-multiplied with a vector of 8 elements the first row finds the average of the elements; the second row takes the difference between the average of first- and second- halves; the third and fourth rows take the difference between first- and second- quarters, and that of third- and fourth- quarters, and so on. A fast algorithm for M-point Haar transform requires M multiplications and $2(M-1)$ additions [Andrews and Casparie (1970)]. Two-dimensional Haar transform pair is given by

$$[F(u, v)] = \frac{1}{\sqrt{MN}} \mathbf{H}_M [f(r, c)] \mathbf{H}_N \tag{2.79}$$

and

$$[f(r, c)] = \frac{1}{\sqrt{MN}} \mathbf{H}_M [F(u, v)] \mathbf{H}_N \tag{2.80}$$

2.4.6 Slant Transform

The orthogonal sequency transforms described above are generated by sampling the square wave forms having different sequencies. On the other hand, the *slant transform* is derived from the sawtooth wave forms [Enomoto and Shibata (1971), Pratt et al. (1972)]. A slant transform matrix has a constant basis vector corresponding to zero sequency, and the slant (or sawtooth) basis vectors monotonically decrease with sequency in constant steps from a maximum to a minimum. The matrix has a sequency property and high energy compaction property. The lowest order of slant matrix is 2, and 2×2 slant matrix is identical to Hadamard matrix. The higher order slant matrix can be generated from a recursive relation [Pratt et al. (1974)]. The two-dimensional slant transform pair is given by

$$[F(u, v)] = \mathbf{S}_M [f(r, c)] \mathbf{S}_N^{\mathrm{T}} \tag{2.81}$$

and

$$[f(r, c)] = \mathbf{S}_M^{\mathrm{T}} [F(u, v)] \mathbf{S}_N \tag{2.82}$$

Where S_M represents the slant transform matrix of order M.

The transformations described so far are derived by sampling some known orthogonal functions. In the next section, we describe an orthogonal function that is derived from the statistical properties of discrete data.

2.4.7 Karhunen–Loeve Transform

Here we describe a transformation that converts discrete signals into a sequence of uncorrelated coefficients. The transformation is developed based on the statistical properties of the signal [Hotelling (1933)]. The transformation of continuous signal by similar way was suggested by Karhunen (1947) and Loeve (1948), and thus has the name *Karhunen–Loeve transform,* in short, *K-L transform.* It is also known as *Hotelling transform* and is widely used in data compression [Wintz (1972)]. This transform is different from the previous ones in the sense that in this case orthogonal transform kernel is not generated by sampling any known orthogonal function.

Consider a set of n one- or multi-dimensional discrete signals represented as column vectors $\mathbf{f}_0$, $\mathbf{f}_1$, $\mathbf{f}_2$, ..., $\mathbf{f}_{n-1}$ each having M elements. Let us denote the mean vector and covariance matrix of $\mathbf{f}_i$ ($i = 0, 1, 2, ..., n - 1$) by $\bar{\mathbf{f}}$ and Σ_f respectively. Then the r-th element of the mean vector is given by

$$\bar{f}(r) = \frac{1}{n}\sum_{i=0}^{n-1} f_i(r) \tag{2.83}$$

and the (r,c)-th element of the covariance matrix is given by

$$\Sigma_f(r,c) = \frac{1}{n}\sum_{i=0}^{n-1} \left\{ f_i(r) - \bar{f}(r) \right\}\left\{ f_i(c) - \bar{f}(c) \right\} \tag{2.84}$$

Therefore,

$$\bar{\mathbf{f}} = \frac{1}{n}\sum_{i=0}^{n-1} \mathbf{f}_i \tag{2.85}$$

and

$$\Sigma_f = \frac{1}{n}\sum_{i=0}^{n-1} \left(\mathbf{f}_i - \bar{\mathbf{f}} \right)\left(\mathbf{f}_i - \bar{\mathbf{f}} \right)^{\mathrm{T}} \tag{2.86}$$

The mean, variance, covariance, etc., are described in more detail in Section 2.6. So, $\bar{\mathbf{f}}$ is a M-dimensional vector and Σ_f is a $M \times M$ matrix. Since, Σ_f is a real symmetric matrix, we can find M *eigenvectors* $\mathbf{e}_j$ ($j = 0, 1, 2, ..., M - 1$) of Σ_f corresponding to its *eigenvalues* λ_j. Suppose we form a matrix $\mathbf{T}$ with these eigenvectors as its rows, i.e.

$$\mathbf{T} = \begin{bmatrix} \mathbf{e}_0 \\ \mathbf{e}_1 \\ \mathbf{e}_2 \\ \vdots \\ \mathbf{e}_{M-1} \end{bmatrix}$$

then we can write $\mathbf{T}^{-1} = \mathbf{T}^{T}$, and

$$\mathbf{T}\Sigma_f\mathbf{T}^{T} = \begin{bmatrix} \lambda_0 & & & & \\ & \lambda_1 & & 0 & \\ & & \lambda_2 & & \\ & 0 & & \ddots & \\ & & & & \lambda_{M-1} \end{bmatrix} \tag{2.87}$$

The K-L transform pair is then defined as

$$\mathbf{g}_i = \mathbf{T}(\mathbf{f}_i - \bar{\mathbf{f}}) \tag{2.88}$$

$$\mathbf{f}_i = \mathbf{T}^{T}\mathbf{g}_i + \bar{\mathbf{f}} \tag{2.89}$$

Now it is of interest to analyze statistical properties of $\mathbf{g}$. For example,

$$\bar{\mathbf{g}} = \frac{1}{n}\sum_{i=0}^{n-1}\mathbf{g}_i = \frac{1}{n}\sum_{i=0}^{n-1}\mathbf{T}(\mathbf{f}_i - \bar{\mathbf{f}}) = \mathbf{T}\left(\frac{1}{n}\sum_{i=0}^{n-1}\mathbf{f}_i - \frac{1}{n}\sum_{i=0}^{n-1}\bar{\mathbf{f}}\right) = \mathbf{0}$$

$$\Sigma_g = \frac{1}{n}\sum_{i=0}^{n-1}(\mathbf{g}_i - \bar{\mathbf{g}})(\mathbf{g}_i - \bar{\mathbf{g}})^{T}$$

$$= \frac{1}{n}\sum_{i=0}^{n-1}[\mathbf{T}(\mathbf{f}_i - \bar{\mathbf{f}})][\mathbf{T}(\mathbf{f}_i - \bar{\mathbf{f}})]^{T}$$

$$= \frac{1}{n}\sum_{i=0}^{n-1}[\mathbf{T}(\mathbf{f}_i - \bar{\mathbf{f}})(\mathbf{f}_i - \bar{\mathbf{f}})^{T}\mathbf{T}^{T}]$$

$$= \mathbf{T}\left[\frac{1}{n}\sum_{i=0}^{n-1}(\mathbf{f}_i - \bar{\mathbf{f}})(\mathbf{f}_i - \bar{\mathbf{f}})^{T}\right]\mathbf{T}^{T} = \mathbf{T}\Sigma_f\mathbf{T}^{T}$$

Hence,

$$\Sigma_g = \begin{bmatrix} \lambda_0 & & & & \\ & \lambda_1 & & 0 & \\ & & \lambda_2 & & \\ & 0 & & \ddots & \\ & & & & \lambda_{M-1} \end{bmatrix}$$

Since the covariance matrix of transformed vectors is a diagonal matrix, it is evident that the elements of the transformed vector $\mathbf{g}_i$ are uncorrelated. Secondly, $\Sigma_g(r, r) = \lambda_r$ implies that r-th eigenvalue is equal to the variance of $g_i(r)$ along the vector $\mathbf{e}_r$.

In case of multi-dimensional signal it may be found, sometimes, that the covariance matrix is separable. Then the transform matrix is also separable. This leads to faster computation of K-L transform.

We have seen earlier that the rows or columns of some of the orthogonal transform matrices are the eigenvectors of special square matrices. For example, Fourier transform can diagonalize circulant matrix, and discrete cosine transform can diagonalize Toeplitz matrix, etc. Now we consider diagonalization of non-square matrices.

2.5 Singular Value Decomposition

Let us consider a $M \times N$ matrix $\mathbf{A}$ having rank R, where $R \leq M$ and $R \leq N$ and $M \neq N$. Certainly the matrix is singular, i.e. its determinant is zero. The singular nature of the matrix can be studied by using a method known as *singular value decomposition* (SVD) method [Golub and Reinsch (1970), Huang and Narendra (1975), Andrews and Patterson (1976a), Andrews and Patterson (1976b)]. Now $\mathbf{AA^T}$ and $\mathbf{A^T A}$ are square matrices of size $M \times M$ and $N \times N$ respectively. Suppose $\mathbf{U}_M$ and $\mathbf{V}_N$ are two matrices composed of eigenvectors of $\mathbf{AA^T}$ and $\mathbf{A^T A}$ respectively, i.e. $\mathbf{U}_M = [u_0 \, u_1 \, u_2 \, \dots \, u_{M-1}]$ and $\mathbf{V}_N = [v_0 \, v_1 \, v_2 \, \dots \, v_{N-1}]$. Then

$$\mathbf{U}_M^T \, (\mathbf{AA^T})\mathbf{U}_M = \mathbf{D}_M \tag{2.90}$$

$$\mathbf{V}_N^T \, (\mathbf{A^T A}) \, \mathbf{V}_N = \mathbf{D}_N \tag{2.91}$$

where $\mathbf{D}_M$ ($\mathbf{D}_N$) is a $M \times M$ ($N \times N$) diagonal matrix whose first R diagonal elements are non-zero eigenvalues λ_i of $\mathbf{AA^T}(\mathbf{A^T A})$. According to SVD we can write

$$\mathbf{U}_M^T \mathbf{AV}_N = \mathbf{D} \tag{2.92}$$

where

$$
\mathbf{D} =
\begin{bmatrix}
\lambda_0 & & & & & \vdots & & \\
& \lambda_1 & & & & \vdots & 0 & \\
& & \lambda_2 & & & \vdots & & \\
& & & \ddots & & \vdots & & \\
& & & & \lambda_{R-1} & \vdots & & \\
\cdots & \cdots & \cdots & \cdots & \cdots & \cdots & \cdots & \cdots \\
& & & & & \vdots & & \\
& & 0 & & & \vdots & 0 & \\
& & & & & \vdots & &
\end{bmatrix}
$$

The top-left and bottom-right submatrices are of size $R \times R$ and $(M - R) \times (N - R)$. Now, since the outer product of $\mathbf{u}_i$ and $\mathbf{v}_i$ is a $M \times N$, the Equation (2.92) suggests that $\mathbf{A}$ can be expressed as the sum of $\mathbf{u}_i \, \mathbf{v}_i^T$ weighted by $\lambda^{1/2}$, i.e.

$$\mathbf{A} = \sum_{i=0}^{R-1} \lambda^{\frac{1}{2}} \mathbf{u}_i \mathbf{v}_i^T \tag{2.93}$$

2.6 Probability and Statistics

Generally, a *knowledge* about something is acquired through some experiments (trials) or observations. A set of conditions comprises the premises of a *trial*. A theoretically possible outcome of a trial is called an *event*. A *random event* is the result of a trial which cannot be predicted. A variable is called *random variable* if it attains its values depending on the outcome of some trial, and it has a unique value for each elementary outcome. A random variable is said to be *discrete* if the set of all its possible values is finite.

Let z be a discrete random variable whose possible and the only possible values are $z_1, z_2, ..., z_l$. So, a subset of these values may form an event. Suppose the experiment is performed n times, and the number of times z attains the value z_i is n_i. Then $n_1 + n_2 + \cdots + n_l = n$. The plot of n_i vs z_i ($i = 1, 2, ..., l$) is called a *histogram*. The ratio of the number of occurrences m ($= n_i + n_j + n_k + \cdots$) of an event A ($= \{z_i, z_j, z_k, ...\}$) to the total number of trials n is called the *relative frequency* of the event A. The *probability* of the event A, denoted by $P(A)$, is the limit of its relative frequency as n increases without bound. The event A is called *certain* if $P(A) = 1$, and *impossible* if $P(A) = 0$. The probability of its complement event is $P(\overline{A}) = 1 - P(A)$.

The probability of event A, on condition that event B has occurred, is called the *conditional probability* of event A and is denoted by $P(A \mid B)$. Two events A and B are called *independent* if the occurrence of one does not depend on the occurrence or non-occurrence of the other, i.e.

$$P(A) = P(A \mid B) = P(A \mid \overline{B}) \text{ and } P(B) = P(B \mid A) = P(B \mid \overline{A})$$

Otherwise, the events are *dependent*. The probability of *coincidence* of two events A and B is given by

$$P(A \cap B) = P(A) P(B \mid A) = P(B) P(A \mid B)$$

If A and B are independent, $P(A \cap B) = P(A) P(B)$. If A and B are *incompatible* event, then $P(A \cap B) = 0$ and $P(A \cup B) = P(A) + P(B)$. In general,

$$P(A \cup B) = P(A) + P(B) - P(A \cap B)$$

A system of events $H_1, H_2, H_3, ..., H_L$ is called a *complete group* of events if (i) $P(H_1 \cup H_2 \cup ... \cup H_L) = 1$ and (ii) $P(H_i \cap H_j) = 0$ for $i \neq j$. So, these events are incompatible and usually called *hypotheses*. Suppose an event A can take place as a result of the occurrence of one and only event H_i ($i = 1, 2, 3, ..., L$), then

$$P(A) = \sum_{i=1}^{L} P(H_i) P(A \mid H_i)$$

Now from the identity due to coincidence of two events it can be written that

$$P(A) P(H_i \mid A) = P(H_i) P(A \mid H_i)$$

Hence, the probability $P(H_i \mid A)$ of hypotheses H_i, as the event A occurs, is given by

$$P(H_i \mid A) = \frac{P(H_i) P(A \mid H_i)}{\sum_{i=1}^{L} P(H_i) P(A \mid H_i)} \qquad (2.94)$$

This is known as *Bayes formula*. The probabilities $P(H_i)$ are known before and are called *a priori probabilities*. $P(A \mid H_i)$ are the probabilities assigned to the event A. In contrary $P(H_i \mid A)$ are called *a posteriori probabilities*.

Suppose we denote the probability of discrete random variable by $p_i = P(z = z_i)$. Then the law of probability distribution can simply be represented by the following table:

z_1	z_2	z_3	$\cdots$	z_l
p_1	p_2	p_3	$\cdots$	p_l

where $\sum_{i=1}^{l} p_i = 1$. The *mathematical expectation* $\mathcal{E}(z)$ or *mean* $\overline{z}$ and *variance* σ_z^2 are defined as

$$\overline{z} = \sum_{i=1}^{l} z_i p_i \quad \text{and} \quad \sigma_z^2 = \sum_{i=1}^{l} (z_i - \overline{z})^2 p_i = z^2 - \overline{z}^2$$

In case the random variable is *continuous,* the mean and the variance are given by

$$\overline{z} = \int_{-\infty}^{\infty} z p_z(z)\, dz \quad \text{and} \quad \sigma_z = \int_{-\infty}^{\infty} (z - \overline{z})^2 p_z(z)\, dz$$

where $p_z(z)$ is the *probability density function* (p.d.f.). A continuous random variable z, all possible value of which fill a finite interval $[a,b]$, is said to be *uniformly distributed* if

$$p_z(z) = \frac{1}{b - a} \quad \text{for } a \le z \le b$$

The distribution of probability is called *normal* or *Gaussian* if

$$p_z(z) = \frac{1}{\sigma_z \sqrt{2\pi}} \exp\left\{ -\frac{(z - \overline{z})^2}{2\sigma_z^2} \right\}$$

Figure 2.2 exhibits the shape of uniform p.d.f and Gaussian p.d.f. Suppose a transformation T maps z to w, i.e. $w = T(z)$, then

$$p_w(w) = \left[p_z(z) \frac{dz}{dw} \right]_{z = T^{-1}(w)}$$

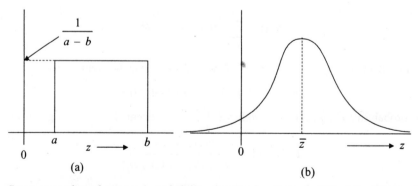

(a)　　　　　　　　　　　　　　(b)

Fig. 2.2　Some examples of common probability density functions (p.d.f.). (a) uniform distribution, (b) gaussian distribution.

Let $\mathbf{f}$ represents an M-dimensional random vector whose elements are random variables. If $\mathbf{f}$ follows a multivariate Gaussian distribution the joint p.d.f. is given by

$$p(\mathbf{f}) = \frac{1}{\sqrt{2\pi \,|\, \Sigma_{\mathbf{f}} \,|}} \exp\left\{-\frac{1}{2}(\mathbf{f} - \bar{\mathbf{f}})^{\mathrm{T}} \Sigma_{\mathbf{f}}^{-1}(\mathbf{f} - \bar{\mathbf{f}})\right\} \tag{2.95}$$

Thus $\mathbf{f}$ is characterized by its average properties:
the *mean vector*

$$\bar{\mathbf{f}} = \mathcal{E}\{\mathbf{f}\}$$

and the *covariance matrix*

$$\Sigma_{\mathbf{f}} = \mathcal{E}\{(\mathbf{f} - \bar{\mathbf{f}})\,(\mathbf{f} - \bar{\mathbf{f}})^{\mathrm{T}}\}$$

$$= \begin{bmatrix} s_{0,0} & s_{0,1} & s_{0,2} & \cdots & s_{0,M-1} \\ s_{1,0} & s_{1,1} & s_{1,2} & \cdots & s_{1,M-1} \\ s_{2,0} & s_{2,1} & s_{2,2} & \cdots & s_{2,M-1} \\ \vdots & \vdots & \vdots & \vdots & \vdots \\ s_{M-1,0} & s_{M-1,1} & s_{M-1,2} & \cdots & s_{M-1,M-1} \end{bmatrix}$$

where $s_{i,i} = \sigma_i^2$ and $s_{i,j} = \mathcal{E}(f_i - \bar{f}_i)\,(f_j - \bar{f}_j)\}$. Now the *correlation matrix* may be defined as

$$\mathbf{R} = \mathcal{E}\{\mathbf{f}\,\mathbf{f}^{\mathrm{T}}\}$$

Thus

$$\Sigma_{\mathbf{f}} = \mathbf{R} - \bar{\mathbf{f}}\,\bar{\mathbf{f}}^{\mathrm{T}}$$

If $\bar{\mathbf{f}} = \mathbf{0}$ then $\Sigma_{\mathbf{f}} = \mathbf{R}$. Secondly, if we define

$$\rho_{i,j} = \frac{s_{i,j}}{\sqrt{s_{i,i}}\,\sqrt{s_{j,j}}}$$

then covariance matrix is said to be fully normalized with the elements $\rho_{i,j} \in [-1,1]$, and is also denoted by $\mathbf{R}$. The elements of random vectors are pairwise uncorrelated if $\rho_{i,j} = 0$ for $i \neq j$. A *random sequence* of vectors can completely be characterized by the joint p.d.f. of the random variables. The sequence is called *strict sense stationary* if the joint p.d.f. is shift-invariant, and the process is called *wide sense stationary* if the correlation matrix is shift-invariant. For example, first-order stationary Markov process may be characterized by its correlation matrix $\mathbf{R}$, where

$$\mathbf{R} = \{\rho_{i,j}\} = \rho^{|i-j|}$$

and $0 < \rho < 1$. For detail discussion on elementary statistics and probability theory reader may see Goon et al. (1980), (1991) and other related books on the subject.

2.7 Fuzzy Sets and Properties

In many situations, certainty of an event can more conveniently be represented by linguistic or qualitative values than the 'probability' as discussed earlier. Imprecise value of membership of an event belonging to a set can be handled by using the *fuzzy set theoretic* approach [Pal and Dutta Majumder (1986)]. A fuzzy set A is defined as a collection of ordered pairs

$$A = \{(\mu_A(a_i),\, a_i) \mid i = 1, 2, 3, \ldots, n\}$$

The set $\{a_i \mid i = 1, 2, 3, ..., n$ and $\mu_A(a_i) > 0\}$ comprises the support of A. The grade of membership $\mu_A(a_i)$ or simply μ_i denotes the degree to which an event a_i belongs to A, and μ_i takes any real value from the interval $[0, 1]$. Thus μ_i simply reflects the ambiguity or uncertainty for an event belonging to a set. So $\mu_i = 1$ indicates a_i strictly belongs to A, $\mu_i = 0$ indicates the reverse. If $\mu_i = 0.5$, a_i is said to be the *cross-over point* in A. If the support of a fuzzy set contains only a single point then the fuzzy set is called a *fuzzy singleton*. Thus, any fuzzy set may be viewed as a union of fuzzy singletons.

Suppose A and B are two fuzzy sets defined over $X = \{x\}$ as $\{(\mu_A(x), x)\}$ and $\{(\mu_B(x), x)\}$, respectively. Basic operations and properties are then defined as follows:

1. $A \subseteq B \Rightarrow \mu_A(x) \le \mu_B(x)$, for all x

2. $A = B \Rightarrow \mu_A(x) = \mu_B(x)$, for all x

3. $C = A \cup B \Rightarrow \mu_C(x) = \max \{\mu_A(x), \mu_B(x)\}$, for all x

4. $C = A \cap B \Rightarrow \mu_C(x) = \min \{\mu_A(x), \mu_B(x)\}$, for all x

5. $A = \overline{B} \Rightarrow \mu_A(x) = 1 - \mu_B(x)$, for all x

This definition of complement fuzzy set [Zadeh (1965)] is most restrictive. There are other definitions of the set [Bellman and Giertz (1973)] which are more general. Now the given definition of complement leads to the following inequalities:

$$0 \le \min \{\mu_A(x), \mu_{\overline{A}}(x)\} \le 0.5$$

and

$$0.5 \le \max \{\mu_A(x), \mu_{\overline{A}}(x)\} \le 1$$

These inequalities, in turn, suggest

$$A \cup \overline{A} \ne X \text{ and } A \cap \overline{A} \ne \phi$$

which are different from the equivalent relations in ordinary set theory. However, other elementary properties of ordinary set operations, such as union, intersection and inversion, are satisfied by the fuzzy sets too:

$A \cup B = B \cup A$	$A \cap B = B \cap A$
$A \cup (B \cup C) = (A \cup B) \cup C$	$A \cap (B \cap C) = (A \cap B) \cap C$
$A \cup A = A$	$A \cap A = A$
$A \cup X = X$	$A \cap X = A$
$A \cup \phi = A$	$A \cap \phi = \phi$
$A \cup (B \cap C) = (A \cup B) \cap (A \cup C)$	$A \cap (B \cup C) = (A \cap B) \cup (A \cap C)$
$A \cup (A \cap B) = A$	$A \cap (A \cup B) = A$
$\overline{A \cup B} = \overline{A} \cap \overline{B}$	$\overline{A \cap B} = \overline{A} \cup \overline{B}$

$$\overline{\overline{A}} = A$$

$$(\overline{A} \cap B) \cup (A \cap \overline{B}) = (\overline{A} \cup \overline{B}) \cap (A \cup B)$$

$$(\overline{A} \cup B) \cap (A \cup \overline{B}) = (\overline{A} \cap \overline{B}) \cup (A \cap B)$$

6. $C = AB \Rightarrow \mu_C(x) = \mu_A(x)\mu_B(x)$, for all x

7. $A = B^\alpha \Rightarrow \mu_A(x) = [\mu_B(x)]^\alpha$, for all x. So, $0 < \alpha < \beta \Rightarrow A^\alpha \subseteq A^\beta$

8.   Suppose C is a bounded sum of A and B [Giles (1976)], i.e. $C = A \hat{+} B$, then

$$\mu_C(x) = \min \{1, \ \mu_A(x) + \mu_B(x)\} \text{ for all } x$$

9.   Suppose C is a bounded product of A and B [Giles (1976)], i.e. $C = A \hat{\cdot} B$, then

$$\mu_C(x) = \max \{0, \ \mu_A(x) + \mu_B(x) - 1\} \text{ for all } x$$

10. Suppose C is a bounded difference of A and B [Giles (1976)], i.e. $C = A \hat{-} B$, then

$$\mu_C(x) = \max \{0, \ \mu_A(x) - \mu_B(x)\} \text{ for all } x$$

11. Suppose C is a probabilistic sum of A and B [Giles (1976)], i.e. $C = A \tilde{+} B$, then

$$\mu_C(x) = \mu_A(x) + \mu_B(x) - \mu_A(x) \ \mu_B(x) \text{ for all } x$$

Additional definitions and properties of fuzzy sets, systems and relations are discussed in Pal and Dutta Majumder (1986), Kaufmann (1980), Dubois and Prade (1980), Kandel (1982), Mizumoto and Tanaka (1981), Mizumoto (1981).

2.8 Mathematical Morphology

Mathematical morphology increasingly has become more and more a popular tool for image processing and analysis [Serra (1982), Sternberg (1986), Giardina and Dougherty (1988), Haralick and Shapiro (1992)]. Unlike the traditional image processing techniques, the morphological techniques treat an image as an ensemble of sets. The operations are defined as an interaction between two sets: an object and a structuring element, and the language is that of set theory. Dilation and erosion are the primary operations in morphology. Other operations are formed by combining these two operations. However, dilation and erosion are constructed from even lower level operations like translation, set union and set intersection.

Suppose a rectangular domain D, a subset of a continuous domain $\mathbb{R}^2$ or of a discrete domain $\mathbb{Z}^2$, where $\mathbb{R}$ is a set of all real numbers and $\mathbb{Z}$ denotes a set of integer numbers. The morphological operators may be classified as (i) binary morphological operators and (ii) grayscale morphological operators. First, we present binary morphological operations which deal with set of points of the domain D. Let A and B are subsets of D, and t be a point in the same domain.

The *translation* of A by t, denoted by A_t, is defined as

$$A_t = \{p \in D \mid p = a + t \text{ for some } a \in A\} \tag{2.96}$$

A dilated by B, denoted by $A \oplus B$, is defined as

$$A \oplus B = \{p \in D \mid p = a + b \text{ for some } a \in A, b \in B\} \tag{2.97}$$

The set B is called the *structuring element*. Dilation can also be defined as union of translates, i.e.

$$A \oplus B = \bigcup_{b \in B} A_b \tag{2.98}$$

This definition of dilation can be rewritten as

$$A \oplus B = \{p \in D \mid \breve{B}_p \cap A \neq \phi\}$$

where $\breve{B}$ is called the *reflection* of B and is defined by

$$\breve{B} = \{p \mid p = -b \text{ for some } b \in B\}$$

A *eroded* by B, denoted by $A \ominus B$, is defined as

$$A \ominus B = \{p \in D \mid p + b \in A \text{ and for every } b \in B\} \qquad (2.99)$$

Erosion can also be defined as intersection of negative translates, i.e.

$$A \ominus B = \bigcap_{b \in B} A_{-b} \qquad (2.100)$$

This definition of erosion can be rewritten as

$$A \ominus B = \{p \in D \mid B_p \subseteq A\}$$

Dilation and erosion satisfy the duality property:

$$A \ominus B = (A^c \oplus \breve{B})^c$$

where A^c is *complement set* of the set A. A *opened* by B, denoted by $A \circ B$, is defined as

$$A \circ B = (A \ominus B) \oplus B \qquad (2.101)$$

Opening can also be expressed as

$$A \circ B = \bigcup_{B_p \subseteq A} B_p$$

A *closed* by B, denoted by $A \bullet B$, is defined as

$$A \bullet B = (A \oplus B) \ominus B \qquad (2.102)$$

Opening and closing also satisfy the duality property:

$$A \bullet B = (A^c \circ \breve{B})^c$$

Figure 2.3 shows the results of various binary morphological operations on a set A [Fig. 2.3(a)] by a structuring element B [Fig. 2.3(b)]. Results of dilation, erosion, opening and closing are shown in Figs. 2.3(c)–2.3(f) respectively. The figure shows that dilation expands a set (object) and erosion shrinks it. It also illustrates that opening suppresses sharp capes, and closing fills up thin gulfs. Opening also removes objects smaller than the structuring elements and cuts the narrow isthmuses whereas closing fills up small holes. So, the openings and closings can smooth object boundaries. It should be noted that morphological transformations are non-linear and are in general non-invertible.

Another important morphological operation is *hit-and-miss* transformation. Suppose there are two structuring elements B and C such that $B \cap C = \phi$, then hit-and-miss transformation of a set A by B and C, denoted by $A \otimes (B,C)$, is defined as

$$A \otimes (B, C) = (A \ominus B) \cap (A^c \ominus C) \qquad (2.103)$$

It can be easily shown that closing is *extensive* operation, whereas opening is *anti-extensive*, i.e.

$$A \bullet B \supseteq A, \qquad A \circ B \subseteq A$$

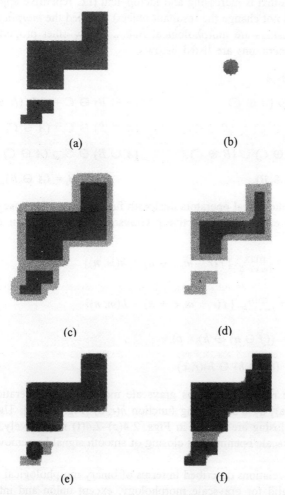

(a)   (b)

(c)   (d)

(e)   (f)

Fig. 2.3 Results of binary morphological operations: (a) object A, (b) structuring element B, (c) $A \oplus B$ (union of gray and dark regions) superposed on A (dark region), (d) $A \ominus B$ (dark region) superposed on A (union of gray and dark regions), (e) $A \circ B$ (dark region) superposed on A (union of gray and dark regions) and (f) $A \bullet B$ (union of gray and dark regions) superposed on A (dark region).

When structuring element contains the origin, dilation and erosion are also extensive and anti-extensive, respectively. However, all of these operations are *increasing*, i.e.

$$A \subseteq B \Rightarrow A \odot C \subseteq B \odot C$$

The operator $\odot$ can be replaced by any of $\oplus$, $\ominus$, $\circ$ or $\bullet$. Opening and closing operations are *idempotent* too, i.e.

$$(A \circ B) \circ B = A \circ B$$

$$(A \bullet B) \bullet B = A \bullet B$$

$$(((A \circ B) \bullet C) \circ B) \bullet C = (A \circ B) \bullet C$$

$$(((A \bullet B) \circ C) \bullet B) \circ C = (A \bullet B) \circ C$$

Now any transformation that is increasing and idempotent (i.e. repetitive application of the same transformation that does not change the resultant object) is called the *morphological filter*. In that sense, openings and closings are morphological filters. A few other properties and relations of binary morphological operations are listed below.

$$A \oplus B = B \oplus A$$

$$(A \oplus B) \oplus C = A \oplus (B \oplus C) \qquad\qquad (A \ominus B) \ominus C = A \ominus (B \oplus C)$$

$$(A \cap B) \oplus C \subseteq (A \oplus C) \cap (B \oplus C) \qquad (A \cap B) \ominus C = (A \ominus C) \cap (B \ominus C)$$

$$(A \cup B) \oplus C = (A \oplus C) \cup (B \oplus C) \qquad (A \cup B) \ominus C \supseteq (A \ominus C) \cup (B \ominus C)$$

$$A \oplus B_t = (A \oplus B)_t \qquad\qquad\qquad A \ominus B_t = (A \ominus B)_{-t}$$

The grayscale morphological operators deal with functions too. Suppose $f(r,c)$ and $h(r,c)$ are two functions defined over D and E respectively. Grayscale dilation, erosion, etc., are then defined as follows.

Dilation: $(f \oplus h)(r, c) = \max_{(m,n) \in E} \{f(r - m, c - n) + h(m, n)\}$ (2.104)

Erosion: $(f \ominus h)(r, c) = \min_{(m,n) \in E} \{f(r + m, c + n) - h(m, n)\}$ (2.105)

Opening: $(f \circ h)(r, c) = ((f \ominus h) \oplus h)(r, c)$ (2.106)

Closing: $(f \bullet h)(r, c) = ((f \oplus h) \ominus h)(r, c)$ (2.107)

Figure 2.4 presents the results of various grayscale morphological operation on a function or signal $f(r, c)$ [Fig. 2.4(a)] by a structuring function $h(r, c)$ [Fig. 2.4(b)]. The results of dilation, erosion, opening and closing are shown in Figs. 2.4(c)–2.4(f) respectively. Figures. 2.4(e) and 2.4(f) illustrate the grayscale opening and closing of smooth signal by removing sharp peaks and pits respectively.

The properties and relations described in terms of binary morphological operators, union and intersection are also valid for grayscale morphology, except union and intersection operations which need to be replaced by max (or sup) and min (or inf) respectively.

Summary

In this chapter we have presented preliminary concept of some mathematical treatments that are frequently used in digital image processing and analysis. It includes linear algebra (more specifically, vector and matrix algebra), orthogonal transforms (e.g. Fourier, Walsh, Hadamard, DST and DCT, Karhunen–Loeve, etc.), probability and fuzzy set theories for uncertainty management, and last but not the least, mathematical morphology for treating shape information. However, the treatment here is only at elementary level and interested readers may consult relevant books on the topics for more detail. The concepts recapitulated here will be used in next chapters for various types of processing and analysis.

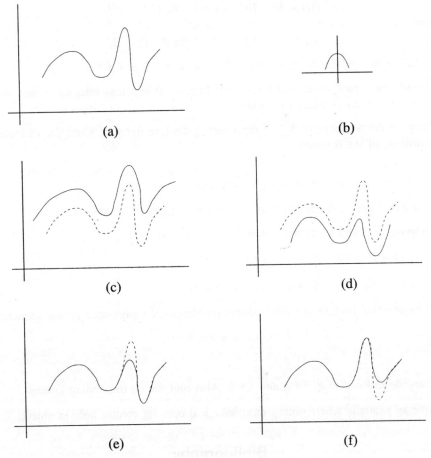

Fig. 2.4 Results of grayscale morphological operations: (a) function or signal $f(r)$, (b) structuring function $h(r)$, (c) $(f \oplus h)(r)$ (dark line) superposed on $f(r)$ (gray line), (d) $(f \ominus h)(r)$ (dark line) superposed on $f(r)$ (gray line), (e) $(f \circ h)(r)$ (dark line) superposed on $f(r)$ (gray line) and (f) $(f \bullet h)(r)$ (dark line) superposed on $f(r)$ (gray line).

Problems

1. Consider two vectors $(2\ 3\ 4)^T$ and $(3\ 1\ 2)^T$ in three-dimensional space. Find the magnitude of the vectors and the angle between them.

2. Given a matrix of size 3×3 as

$$A = \begin{bmatrix} 1 & 2 & 1 \\ 2 & 3 & 4 \\ 3 & 4 & 2 \end{bmatrix}$$

   Compute $|A|$, A^{-1}, trace of A, Euclidean norm of A, eigenvalues and eigenvectors of A.

3. Suppose two functions in one dimensional discrete domain are defined as

$$f(i) = 4i - 10 \qquad \text{for } i = 0, 1, 2, ..., 5$$

and

$$g(i) = 2 - |1 - i| \qquad \text{for } i = 0, 1, 2$$

Generate the sequences representing f and g, and compute $f * g$.

4. Define one-dimensional Fourier transform pair. Prove that imaginary part of Fourier transform of even function is zero.

5. Suppose the sequence [2 3 2 1] represents a discrete function. Compute discrete Fourier transform of the function.

6. Prove the following properties of one-dimensional Fourier transform: (i) shift-invariance and (ii) convolution. Also prove Parseval's theorem.

7. Compute Hadamard transform of the sequence given in Problem 4.

8. Suppose A, B and C are three point sets. Prove that

    (i) $(((A \bullet B) \circ C) \bullet B) \circ C = (A \bullet B) \circ C$

    (ii) $(((A \circ B) \bullet C) \circ B) \bullet C = (A \circ B) \bullet C$

9. Suppose two discrete one-dimensional functions are represented by the sequences:

    $$f = [5\ 7\ 11\ 8\ 2\ 6\ 8\ 9\ 7\ 4\ 3]$$

    $$h = [1\ 2\ 1]$$

    Compute $f \oplus h$, $f \ominus h$, $f \circ h$ and $f \bullet h$. Also plot the corresponding graphs.

10. Give an example where binary morphological opening creates hole in object.

Bibliography

Ahmed, N. Natarajan, T. and Rao, K.R., 'On image processing and a discrete cosine transform', *IEEE Trans. on Computers*, C-**23**:90–93, 1974.

Ahmed, N. and Rao, K.R., *Orthogonal Transforms for Digital Signal Processing*, Springer-Verlag, New York, 1975.

Albert, A., *Regression and the Moon-Penrose Pseudoinverse*, Academic Press, New York, 1972.

Andrews, H.C., *Computer Techniques in Image Processing*, Academic Press, New York, 1970.

Andrews, H.C. and Casparie, K., 'Orthogonal transformations', in Andrews, H.C. (Ed.), *Computer Techniques in Image Processing*, Academic Press, New York, 1970.

Andrews, H.C. and Patterson, C.L., 'Outer product expansions and their uses in digital image processing', *IEEE Trans. on Computers*, C-**25**:140–148, 1976(a).

Andrews, H.C. and Patterson, C.L., 'Singular value decomposition and digital image processing', *IEEE Trans. on Acoust., Speech, Sig. Proc.* ASSP-**24**:26–53, 1976(b).

Anton, H., *Elementary Linear Algebra*, John Wiley and Sons, New York, 1973.

Bellman, R.E. and Giertz, M., 'On the analytic formalism of the theory of fuzzy sets', *Inf. Sci.*, **5**:149–157, 1973.

Bracewell, R.M., 'The discrete Hartley transform', *J. Opt. Soc. Am.*, **73**:1832–1835, 1983.

Bracewell, R.M., *The Fourier Transform and Its Applications*, McGraw-Hill, New York, 1968.

Bracewell, R.M., *The Hartley Transform,* Oxford University Press, Oxford, 1986.

Chen, M. and Yan, P., 'A multiscaling approach based morphological filtering', *IEEE Trans. on Pattern Analysis and Machine Intelligence,* PAMI-**11**:694–700, 1989.

Cooley, J.W., and Tukey, J.W., 'An algorithm for the machine computation of complex Fourier series', *Math. Comput.*, **19**:297–301, 1965.

Dubois, D. and Prade, H., *Fuzzy Sets and Systems–Theory and Applications,* Academic Press, New York, 1980.

Enomoto, H. and Shibata, K., 'Orthogonal transform coding system for television signals', *IEEE Trans. on Electromagnetic Compatibility*, EMC-**13**:11–17, 1971.

Giardina, C.R. and Dougherty, E.R., *Morphological Methods in Image and Signal Processing*, Prentice-Hall, New Jersey, 1988.

Giles, R., 'Lukasiewicz logic and fuzzy theory', *Int. J. Man-Mach. Studies*, **8**:313–327, 1976.

Golub, G.H. and Reinsch, C., 'Singular value decomposition and least squares solutions', *Numer. Math.*, **14**:403–420, 1970.

Goon, A.M., Gupta, M.K. and Dasgupta, B., *Fundamentals of Statistics*, World Press, Calcutta, 1991.

Goon, A.M., Gupta, M.K. and Dasgupta, B., *Outline of Statistical Theory*, Vols. 1 and 2, World Press, Calcutta, 1980.

Graybill, F.A., *Introduction to Matrices with Applications in Statistics*, Wadsworth, Belmont, California, 1969.

Haar, A., 'Zur theorie der orthogonalen funktionen-system', *Math. Annalen'*, **5**:17–31, 1955.

Hadamard, J., 'Resolution d'une question relative aux determinants', *Bell Sc. Math., Ser.* 2, 17, Part I:240–246, 1893.

Hall, E.L., *Computer Image Processing and Recognition*, Academic Press, New York, 1979.

Haralick, R.M. and Shapiro, L.G., *Computer and Robot Vision*, Vols. 1 and 2, Addison-Wesley, Reading, Massachusetts, 1992.

Harmuth, H.F., *Transmission of Information by Orthogonal Functions*, Springer-Verlag, New York, 1969.

Hartley, R.V.L., 'A more symmetrical Fourier analysis applied to transmission problems', *Proc. IRE*, **30**:144–150, 1942.

Hohn, F.E., *Elementary Matrix Algebra*, Macmillan, New York, 1958.

Hotelling, H., 'Analysis of a complex statistical variable into principal components', *J. Educ. Psych.* **24**:417–441, 498–520, 1933.

Huang, T.S. (Ed.), *Picture Processing and Digital Filtering*, Springer-Verlag, Berlin, 1975.

Huang, T.S. and Narendra, P.M., 'Image restoration by singular value decomposition', *Applied Optics*, **14**:2213–2216, 1975.

Hunt, B.R., 'The application of constrained least squares estimation to image restoration by digital computer', *IEEE Trans. on Computer*, C-**22**:805–812, 1973.

Jain, A.K., 'A fast Karhunen-Loeve transform for finite discrete images', In *Proc. National Electronics Conference*, pp. 323–328, Chicago, Illinois, Oct. 1974.

Jain, A.K., 'A sinusoidal family of unitary transforms', *IEEE Trans. Pattern Analysis and Machine Intelligence*, PAMI-**1**:356–365, 1979.

Jain, A.K. and Angel, E., 'Image restoration, modelling and reduction of dimensionality', *IEEE Trans. on Computers*, C-**23**:470–476, 1974.

Kandel, A., *Fuzzy Techniques in Pattern Recognition*, John Wiley and Sons, New York, 1982.

Karhunen, H., 'On linear methods in probability theory (English tr., Selin, I. August 1960), *Technical Report Doc.*, T-**131**, The Rand Corporation, 1947.

Kaufmann, A., *Introduction to the Theory of Fuzzy Subsets—Fundamental Theoretical Elements*, Vol. I, Academic Press, New York, 1980.

Kudryavtsev, V.A. and Demidovich, B.P., *A Brief Course of Higher Mathematics*, Mir Publishers, Moscow, 1981.

Lighthill, M.J., *Introduction to Fourier Analysis and Generalized Functions*, Cambridge University Press, New York, 1960.

Loeve, M., *Fonctions Aleatoires de Seconde Ordre*. Hermann, Paris, 1948.

Maragos, P., 'Pattern spectrum and multiscale shape representation', *IEEE Trans. on Pattern Analysis and Machine Intelligence*, PAMI-**11**:701–716, 1989.

Means, R.W., Whitehouse, H.J. and Speiser, J. M., 'Television encoding using a hybrid discrete cosine transform and a differential pulse code modulator in real time', in *Proc. National Telecommunication Conference*, pp. 61–66, San Diego, California, December, 1974.

Mizumoto, M., 'Fuzzy sets and their operations', II. *Inf. Control*, **50**:160–174, 1981.

Mizumoto, M. and Tanaka, K., 'Fuzzy sets and their operations', *Inf. Control*, **48**:30–48, 1981.

Nearing, E., *Linear Algebra and Matrix Theory*, John Wiley and Sons, New York, 1963.

Oppenheim, A.V. and Schafer, R.W., *Digital Signal Processing*, Prentice-Hall, New Jersey, 1975.

Pal, S.K. and Dutta Majumder, D., *Fuzzy Mathematical Approach to Pattern Recognition*, Wiley-Eastern, Calcutta, 1986.

Papoulis, A., *Probability, Random Variables, and Stochastic Processes*, McGraw-Hill, New York, 1965.

Papoulis, A., *The Fourier Integral and Its Applications*, McGraw-Hill, New York, 1962.

Pratt, W.K., *Digital Image Processing*, 2nd ed. Wiley-Interscience, New York, 1991.

Pratt, W.K., Andrews, H.C. and Kane, J., 'Hadamard transform image coding', *Proc. IEEE,* **57**:58–68, 1969.

Pratt, W.K., Chen, W.H. and Welch, L.R., 'Slant transform image coding', *IEEE Trans. on Communication*, Com-**22**:1075–1093, 1974.

Pratt, W.K., Welch, L.R. and Chen, W.H., 'Slant transform for image coding', in *Proc. Symposium on Application of Walsh Functions*, pp. 229–234, 1972.

Rademacher, H., 'Einige sätze von allegemeinen orthogonal-funkeionen', *Math. Ann.* **87**:122–138, 1922.

Rao, C.R., *Linear Statistical Inference and Its Applications*, Wiley-Eastern, New Delhi, 1973.

Rao, C.R. and Mitra, S.K., *Generalised Inverse of Matrices and its Applications*, Wiley, New York, 1971.

Serra, J., *Image Analysis and Mathematical Morphology*, Academic Press, London, 1982.

Sternberg, S.R., 'Grayscale morphology', *Comp. Vision, Graphics, and Image Proc.* **35**:333–355, 1986.

Walsh, J.L., 'A closed set of orthogonal functions', *Am. J. Math.,* **55**:5–24, 1923.

Wintz, P.A., 'Transform picture coding', *Proc. IEEE,* **60**:809–820, 1972

Zadeh, L.A., 'Fuzzy sets', *Infor. and Control*, **8**:338–353, 1965.

Chapter 3

Visual Preliminaries

3.1 Introduction

It is important for designers and users of image processing techniques to understand the characteristics of human vision system and the underlying perceptual processes. Since the aim of the image processing and analysis techniques are to build a system that has similar capabilities as the human vision system, one must know about the formation of image in the eye, brightness adaptation and discrimination, image quality and perceptual mechanism, and should incorporate such knowledge in the processing algorithms. Many interesting studies have been carried out and the subject of visual perception has grown over centuries. Systematically organized literatures on the subject are available. However, we give here only a brief account of the discipline because of the following two reasons: (i) detail function of the different parts of human vision system and psychology of perception are still not well understood, and (ii) for convenience in computer processing, mathematical characterization of image gets more emphasis.

Human vision system consists of four major elements: (i) the eyes, (ii) the lateral geniculate body, (iii) the visual cortex in the optical lobe of the brain and (iv) the neural communication pathway from eyes to visual cortex (Fig. 3.1). A simplified diagram of the horizontal cross-section

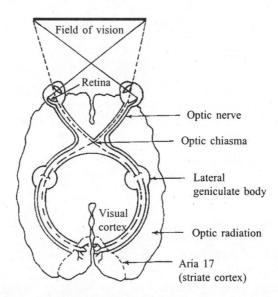

Fig. 3.1 Simplified diagram of human vision system.

of the human eye is shown in Fig. 3.2. The shape of the eye is nearly spherical with a radius of 11 mm. (approx). The outermost layer, called *sclera*, is 1 mm thick opaque membrane and merges into the transparent *cornea*. At the rear, the *optic nerve* penetrates the sclera on the nasal side. The *choroid*, the membrane that lies directly below the sclera contains a network of blood vessels which provide nutrition to the eye. The choroid being heavily pigmented reduces backscatter of light within the *optical globe*. It is divided into the *ciliary body* and the *iris diaphragm*. The iris is a nearly circular aperture which constitutes the *pupil*. It contracts and expands to control the amount of light entering the eye. The innermost membrane is the *retina*. The retinal surface contains a mosaic of *photoreceptor* cells called *rods* and *cones*.

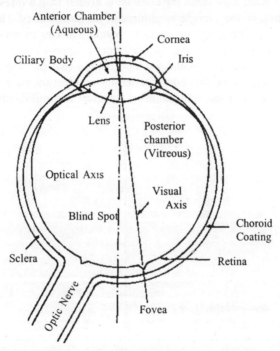

Fig. 3.2 Simplified diagram of the horizontal cross-section of human eye.

The number of cones in each eye is between 6 and 7 million and that of rods ranges from 75 to 150 million. Cones are primarily located at the centre of the retina, called *fovea* and are sensitive to colour. The cones are also responsible for acute vision and the cone vision is known as *photopic* or bright-light vision. On the other hand, the rods give an overall appearance of the scene, but are not involved in colour vision. They are sensitive to low levels of illumination. So, the rod vision is known as *scotopic* or *dim-light vision*.

A double convex *lens* made of fibrous cells is suspended directly behind the pupil. The shape of the lens can be changed to vary the effective focal length, and thus, variable viewing distance can be achieved by a single lens. The shape of the lens is controlled by the fibres of the *ciliary body*. To focus on the distant objects the lens is made relatively flat. When an eye is looking at an object the shape of the lens is controlled appropriately such that a sharp and reverse image is formed on the retinal surface. The photoreceptors convert light energy into electrical pulses through some photochemical reaction. These pulses are transmitted to the visual cortex through the optical nerve. The information reaching the visual cortex are finally decoded by the *brain*.

3.2 Brightness Adaptation and Contrast

What human eye senses are, in general, intensity images. *Intensity* and *brightness* are two different phenomena. Intensity of a light source depends on the total amount of light emitted and the solid angle from which it is emitted. Thus, intensity is a physical property and can be measured. This will be discussed in detail in Section 4.3. On the other hand, brightness is a psycho-visual concept and may be described as the sensation to the light intensity. The *contrast* may be defined as the difference in perceived brightness. Detection of a bright spot depends not only on the brightness, size (in space) and duration (in time), but also on the contrast between the spot and the background. The spot can be detected only when the contrast is greater than a threshold, called *just noticeable difference*, depending on the average brightness of the surrounding. This dependence is known as brightness adaptation. The range of intensity levels that can be adapted by the human visual system is enormous; the highest level (glare limit) is approximately 10^{10} times the lowest one (scotopic threshold). The experimental evidence shows that the brightness perceived by human visual system is a logarithmic function of intensity incident on the eye. Figure 3.3 shows a plot of subjective brightness versus light intensity (measured in millilambert). However, human eye

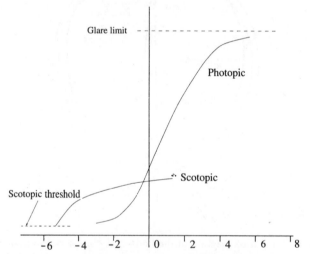

Fig. 3.3   Plot of brightness perceived by human visual system versus light intensity. Note that the response curve is linear over a significant range in the semi-log scale.

cannot operate over such an impressive dynamic range simultaneously. Rather, it roams around the complex intensity pattern (a scene) and at a particular position it adapts to an average level depending on the intensity pattern over a small neighbourhood. The total range of intensity level that eye can discriminate simultaneously is rather small compared to the entire range, and is presented by a small intersecting curve around the said level of brightness adaptation. [Interested reader may see Green and Swet (1965) for more detail.]

   In psychology, contrast sensitivity of the eye refers to the ratio of the difference in brightness B_1 (of an object) and brightness B (of its immediate surrounding) to B. It is measured by showing to an observer a pattern consisting of an extended field of uniform brightness B with a sharp-edged circular target of brightness B_1 at the centre as shown in Fig. 3.4(a). The difference $\delta B = (B_1 - B)$ in brightness is increased from zero to a level that is just noticeable. The ratio $\delta B/B$, known as *Weber ratio*, has approximately a constant value 0.02 over a wide range of brightness B. A more realistic measurement can be taken by using the pattern shown in Fig. 3.4(b). Here too, $(B_1 - B)/B$ is measured; but now the eyes adapt to the surrounding brightness B_0 which influences the contrast discriminating ability. Again as B becomes more and more different from B_0, the appearance of central target changes. If B remains constant and B_0 varies, the target appears to change from black to white. Some instances of this phenomenon are shown in Fig. 3.5.

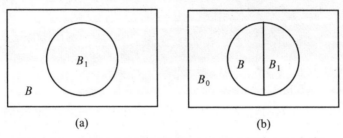

(a)   (b)

Fig. 3.4   Pattern used to measure contrast sensitivity: (a) a constant background, (b) a varying background.

Fig. 3.5   The perceived brightness of the central target is affected by the background brightness.

3.3   Acuity and Contour

The ability of human visual system to detect fine spectral details is known as *acuity*. If human visual system were linear and its response to simple stimuli such as points, lines, edges or sinusoids were known, then the detectability of complex visual stimuli could be predicted. The response to sinusoids is particularly important because it is associated with the *resolution*, one of the most important parameters relevant to acuity of the human visual system. In psychology, resolution may be defined in terms of modulation transfer function which exhibits the characteristics of a bandpass filter for a wide range of background luminances. The response is highest in the vicinity of 5 to 10 cycles per degree of angle subtended by the sinusoidal stimulus at the eye and falls off at both lower and higher spatial frequencies. Secondly, the response and, in turn, the acuity also depend on the position of the stimulus, and are greatest within about a degree of the *visual axis*.

The response of the human visual system at the *edges* or *contours* where luminance changes abruptly perceives 'overshoots'. These overshoots are present as bright bands in dark region and dark bands in bright regions (Fig. 3.6), and are known as *Mach bands*. The overshoot effects can be predicted if the spatial frequency spectrum of a step-like function is multiplied by modulation transfer function of the human visual system. Another characteristic of the human visual system is it seems to fill in the interior of a region with apparent brightness at the edge. Possibly this phenomenon guides the human visual system to fill in the gaps in the contour as shown in Fig. 3.7. [More discussion on visual illusions may be found in Luckiesh (1965)].

Fig. 3.6   Mach bands (the overshoot response of the human visual system).

Fig. 3.7   The human visual system seems to fill in the gaps in the edges.

3.4 Texture and Pattern Discrimination

Usually *texture* refers to coarseness of a surface [Brodatz (1966)]. Some examples of texture are shown in Fig. 3.8. It can describe arrangement of grains or constituent particles in the material. Visual texture, in most cases, is defined as a repetitive arrangement of some basic pattern. This repetition may not be random. However, a texture pattern normally has some degree of randomness due to randomness in basic pattern as well as due to randomness in the repetitions of basic patterns. To quantify texture, this randomness is measured by some means over a small rectangular region called *window*. Thus, texture in an image turns out to be a local property and depends on the shape and size of the window. Identifying a patch in an image as having uniform texture or discriminating different visual textures obeys the *law of similarity*. In this case, the texture property is used to produce similarity groupings.

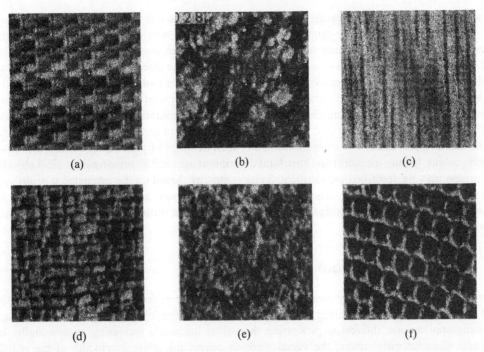

Fig. 3.8 Some examples of texture: (a) mat, (b) pebbles, (c) bark, (d) raffia, (e) grass and (f) snake-skin.

In fact, visual field is seen as consisting of a few regions rather than an array of a large number of independent points. Every region has a set of attributes which is consistent or similar over the region and is different from that of the neighbouring regions. As a result, every region should have a contour (at least partially) where the attribute changes abruptly. Not all possible combination of these regions (or contours) form figures or objects or patterns. Only some specific combinations of these regions form meaningful patterns in the visual field. Formation of the groups or patterns follows a set of rules, known as the *Gestalt laws of organization* [Zusne (1970)].

3.5 Shape Detection and Recognition

The Gestalt laws include the *law of proximity*, the *law of good continuation*, the *law of common fate* and some other laws. These laws emphasize simplicity in the shape of pattern when being formed mentally by grouping different regions in the visual field [Hochberg (1964), Nevatia (1982)]. The preferred figure usually contains least possible information. Many different arrangements of objects in a three-dimensional scene produce same two-dimensional images in the eye. It is the human visual system which uses a variety of cues to eliminate or at least to reduce the ambiguity in interpreting the objects from the image. And, in every case, it leads to simplest possible figures. For example, change in object sizes may be regarded as change in distance from the viewer, change in shape may be regarded as change in perspective, converging lines may be interpreted as receding parallel lines, and so on. Thus, distance has proved itself to be an important cue for detecting and interpreting objects. Distance cue can be obtained from *binocular parallax*, i.e. by comparing two images formed in the left and the right eyes. Distance between different objects in three-dimensional scene can also be obtained from an image sequence formed in a single eye by creating relative motion between the objects and the eye. It may be noted that if the relative position of a set of objects in the image does not change due to motion, then the visual system tends to perceive them as a single object or pattern. Among the cues which-ever leads to the simplest figure gets higher preference. The rest of the cues, if any, which are inconsistent with the interpretation chosen, already are either ignored or viewed some other way.

The detection, classification and recognition process require not only the visual system but also the memory processes. The stored information such as shape of pattern, set of attributes (like intensity, colour, texture measure) and structural description are used as *prototypes* or ideal objects. This process may be described as statistical decision making, based on the estimated *a priori* and *a posterior* probabilities, that a visual stimulus is actually present and a likelihood criterion. In recognizing visual pattern the perceptual information has a great influence, specially in estimating the prior probabilities.

3.6   Perception of Colour

So far we have considered only monochrome images. Colour provides a significant portion of visual information to human beings and enhances their abilities of object detection. In image processing applications, interest in processing the colour images is increasing exponentially. In black and white intensity image, the visual stimulus covers the entire bandwidth of the *visible spectrum* ranging from 0.4 micrometre to 0.7 micrometre. If we narrow down the bandwidth and vary the central wavelength different colours are seen.

Colour is a complex perceptual phenomenon and the sensation of colour arises due to response of three neurochemical sensors or receptors in the retina to the visible light. Suppose $h_R(v)$, $h_G(v)$ and $h_B(v)$ are the spectral sensitivities of red, green and blue receptors, respectively then due to spectral energy distribution $C(v)$ of the light source, the neural signals produced by the sensors are

$$R = \int C(v)h_R(v)\, dv$$

$$G = \int C(v)h_G(v)\, dv \qquad (3.1)$$

$$B = \int C(v)h_B(v)\, dv$$

where v represents wavelength. It is experimentally estimated that the human eye can distinguish about 350,000 different colours. A systematic way of representing and describing colours is a colour model. Although the colours can be defined using any three primary colours, the colour models discussed here are based on the normalized red, green and blue (RGB) primaries.

The first model we consider is the *RGB model* [Fig. 3.9]. It uses a Cartesian coordinate system and the subspace of interest is a unit cube. The model is used in colour TV monitor and camera. Any colour, in this model, can be defined using the weighted (weights are non-negative) sum of R, G and B components. Hence, the primaries are called the *additive primaries*. The main diagonal of the cube represents graylevel from black [at (0, 0, 0)] to white [at (1, 1, 1)]. Complement of the *RGB* model is *CMY model*. In this model three primaries, viz., cyan, magenta and yellow are obtained from red, green and blue, respectively using the relation

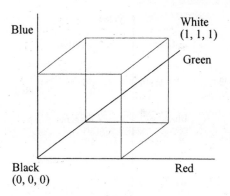

Fig. 3.9   RGB colour model.

$$\begin{bmatrix} C \\ M \\ Y \end{bmatrix} = \begin{bmatrix} 1 \\ 1 \\ 1 \end{bmatrix} - \begin{bmatrix} R \\ G \\ B \end{bmatrix} \qquad (3.2)$$

These primaries are called *subtractive primaries* because their effects are to subtract some colour from white light. The model is suitable for colour printing devices. Another important model is the *YIQ model* because of its wide use in commercial TV broadcasting. *YIQ* is a linear combination of *RGB* components for transmission efficiency and for downward compatibility with B/W TV. The components of this colour model are obtained by using the transformation

$$\begin{bmatrix} Y \\ I \\ Q \end{bmatrix} = \begin{bmatrix} 0.30 & 0.59 & 0.11 \\ 0.60 & -0.28 & -0.32 \\ 0.21 & -0.52 & 0.31 \end{bmatrix} \begin{bmatrix} R \\ G \\ B \end{bmatrix} \qquad (3.3)$$

RGB, *CMY* and *YIQ* colour models are mainly hardware oriented and none of these colour models is directly related to the intuitive colour notion of human being. One of the most popular user oriented colour models is the *HSV* (*hue, saturation and value*) *model* [Smith (1978)]. The subspace within which the model is defined is an inverted hex-cone [Fig. 3.10] of unit height with the apex at origin. Value and saturation are ranging from 0 to 1, while hue ranges from 0° to 360°. The values of *H*, *S* and *V* can be derived from normalized *R*, *G* and *B* as follows [Foley et al. (1992)].

$$mx = \max \{R, G, B\}$$

$$mn = \min \{R, G, B\}$$

$$h = \begin{cases} (g - b)/(r - mn) & \text{if } r = mx \\ 2 + (b - r)/(g - mn) & \text{if } g = mx \\ 4 + (r - g)/(b - mn) & \text{if } b = mx \end{cases}$$

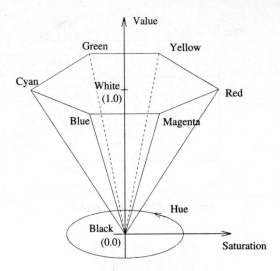

Fig. 3.10 HSV colour model..

$$H = \begin{cases} h \times 60 & \text{if } h \geq 0 \\ h \times 60 + 360 & \text{if } h < 0 \end{cases}$$

$$S = \begin{cases} 0 & \text{if } mx = mn \\ (mx - mn)/mx & \text{otherwise} \end{cases}$$

$$V = mx$$

Note that if $mx = mn$, then hue is undefined.

Another important model of this category is the *HLS* (*hue, light and saturation*) *model*. It is a double hex-cone model (Fig. 3.11) where the primaries are obtained from the normalized R, G, B in a similar way as above. In fact, mx, mn and H are exactly same as *HSV* model. L and S are determined [Foley et al. (1992)] as:

$$L = (mx + mn)/2$$

$$S = \begin{cases} (mx - mn)/(mx + mn) & \text{if } L \leq 0.5 \\ (mx - mn)/(2 - mx - mn) & \text{if } L < 0.5 \end{cases}$$

Ranges of H, L and S are same as that of H, V and S respectively in previous case. If we look at the *RGB* model along its diagonal and at *HLS* model along L-axis, both the models appear to be the same. A completely different formulation for hue and saturation are described as below:

$$\text{Hue, } H = \cos^{-1} \left[\frac{(R - G) + (R - B)}{2\sqrt{(R - G)^2 + (R - B)(G - B)}} \right] \tag{3.4}$$

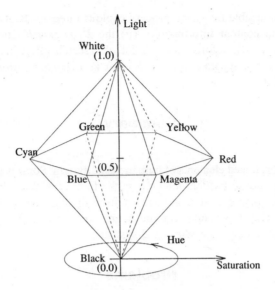

Fig. 3.11   HLS colour model.

$$\text{Intensity, } I = \frac{R + G + B}{3} \tag{3.5}$$

$$\text{Saturation, } S = 1 - \frac{3 \min\{R, G, B\}}{R + G + B} \tag{3.6}$$

So the hue ranges from 0 to 2π, while intensity and saturation vary between 0 and 1 inclusive. This is known as *HIS* (Hue, Intensity and Saturation) model of colour.

3.7   Model of Perceptual Processing

In the preceding sections, we have discussed, in brief, visual perception of simple stimuli and patterns. Understanding of how the human being abstracts certain features and attributes from a huge collection of redundant information and finally, recognizes a complex visual pattern require a complete knowledge about the visual system. Building up a successful general purpose image processing system also requires this knowledge. Unfortunately, the development of knowledge about the visual perception mechanism is still in its infancy. This development requires explicit description of functions of each and every stages between the eye and the brain. Cornsweet (1970) commented that the entire system may be composed of a very large number of repetitions of a few simple mechanisms with slight variations. Following the idea, a large number of models starting from as simple as a linear one to a highly complicated and non-linear ones have been proposed. A model close to the realistic one could have cascades of several stages consisting of filter banks, non-linear transformations, thresholding, matching and so on. However, this is still a topic of active research. Marr (1982) has suggested a hierarchical framework for the visual process. The model maps the intensity profile at the lowest level to the three-dimensional interpretation of the object space (scene) at the highest level through several stages. According to him, the framework responsible for vision process exploits three levels of representations: (i) the *primal sketch* (edge and contour information), (ii) the $2^1/_2 D$ *sketch* (surface information) and (iii) the *3D model* (volumetric information). A lot of research effort has been devoted in this direction and has become a separate subject, known as *computer vision* [Marr (1982), Horn (1986), Faugeras (1993)].

Summary

In this chapter we have presented elements of human visual system. Some perceptual characteristics, such as logarithmic response to incident intensity in the form of Weber's law, are also discussed. Brightness perception, contour detection and pattern discrimination ability of human visual system are briefly presented. These concepts can be found very useful in developing as well as understanding image processing algorithms and systems.

Problems

1. Choose 32 intensity levels from a scale calibrated as 0, 1, 2, ..., 255 such that Weber ratio between any two levels is maximum.

2. Generate a 256 × 256 image as follows.

$$h(r, c) = 255 - f(r, c)g(r, c)$$

for $r = 0, 1, 2, ..., 255$ and $c = 0, 1, 2, ...,255$, where

$$f(r,c) = \begin{cases} 255 & \text{if } (r - 128) \cos \dfrac{5n}{\pi} + (c - 128) \sin \dfrac{5n}{\pi} = 0 \text{ and } n = 0, 1, 2, ..., 71 \\ 0 & \text{otherwise} \end{cases}$$

and

$$g(r,c) = \begin{cases} 0 & 64 \le r \le 192 \text{ and } 64 \le c \le 192 \\ 1 & \text{otherwise} \end{cases}$$

Take two-dimensional Fourier transform of the image. Consider low frequency components equal to zero. Take inverse Fourier transform. Observe the effect.

3. Suppose *RGB* colour triplet for a particular colour is given by (0.3, 0.5, 0.2). Compute corresponding *YIQ* and *HSV* triplets.

Bibliography

Brodatz, P., *Textures: A Photographic Album for Artists and Designers*, Dover, New York, 1966.

Cornsweet, T.N., *Visual Perception*, Academic Press, New York, 1970.

Faugeras, O., *Three-dimensional Computer Vision: A Geometric Viewpoint*, MIT Press, Cambridge, 1993.

Foley, J., Van Daam, A., Feiner, S. and Hughes, J., *Computer Graphics: Principles and Practice*, Addison-Wesley, Reading, Massachusetts, 1992.

Green, D.M. and Swets, J.A., *Signal Detection Theory and Psychophysics*, Wiley, New York, 1965.

Hochberg, J., *Perception*, Prentice-Hall, Englewood Cliffs, New Jersy, 1964.

Horn, B.K.P., *Robot Vision*, MIT Press, Cambridge, Massachusetts, 1986.

Luckiesh, M. *Visual Illusions*, Dover, New York, 1965.

Marr, D., *Vision*, W.H. Freeman, New York, 1982.

Nevatia, R., *Perception*, Prentice-Hall, Englewood Cliffs, New Jersey, 1982.

Smith, A.R., 'Color gamut transform pairs,' *SIGGRAPH '78 Proceedings, Computer Graphics*, **12**: 12–19, 1978.

Zusne, L., *Visual Perception of Form*, Academic Press, New York, 1970.

Chapter 4

Image Formation

4.1 Introduction

The knowledge about the mechanism of image formation by the optical sensors is very important for understanding as well as developing the image processing algorithms and systems. Objects that are imaged either emit or reflect or transmit radiant energy that propagates through the space. Now this radiant energy is intercepted by the image formation system to produce a brightness pattern on a two-dimensional plane, called *intensity image*. The entire process can be looked as having two parts: (i) transforming a three-dimensional scene to a two-dimensional plane and (ii) assigning an intensity to an image point that corresponds to a particular point of the scene. In the following sections, we try to provide simple mathematical models, namely *geometric model* and *photometric model*, to describe these two sub-processes.

4.2 Geometric Model

The mapping of a three-dimensional scene to a two-dimensional image from the standpoint of coordinate transformation is presented here. To a first-order approximation of the sensing devices like the eyes, the cameras and many others, we consider an ideal *pinhole camera* [Ballard and Brown (1982)] as shown in Fig. 4.1. Assume that the light coming only through the pinhole reaches the image plane. So, the pinhole acts as the *point of projection*. The *optical axis* is defined as the perpendicular from the pinhole to the image plane. In this figure, the point of projection is at the origin of the coordinate system and is in front of the image plane, and the optical axis coincides with the Z-axis. Without losing generality, for the convenience in the subsequent analysis, we rearrange the geometry of the system so that the point of projection corresponds to a *view point* behind the image plane as shown in Fig. 4.2. As a result, the image occurs right side up unlike that in Fig. 4.1. The distance λ of the image plane from the view point may be regarded as the *focal length* in this case. Now the coordinate of a point $p(\xi, \zeta, \varsigma)$ in the image plane corresponding to a scene point $P(X, Y, Z)$ is given by

$$(\xi, \zeta, \varsigma) = \left(\frac{\lambda X}{Z}, \frac{\lambda Y}{Z}, \frac{\lambda Z}{Z} \right) \tag{4.1}$$

This mapping is known as *perspective projection*. As a special case, when the view point is at *infinity*, we have well-known *orthographic projection*.

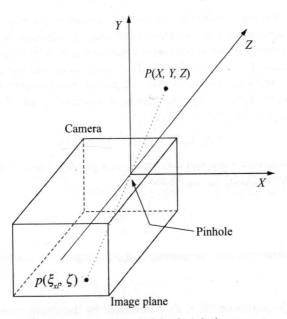

Fig. 4.1   A simple model of pinhole camera.

4.2.1   Basic Transformations

The practical cases may not be as simple as shown in Figs. 4.1 and 4.2. That means the image coordinate system may not coincide with the scene coordinate system, or the optical axis may not coincide or, even, may not be parallel with the Z-axis, or the like. So, before determining the

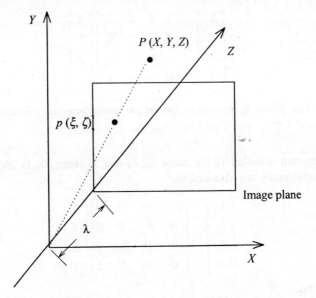

Fig. 4.2   A modified version of the model shown in Fig. 4.1.

projection from three dimensions to the two dimensions, it is better to transform the scene coordinate system to bring it in agreement with the camera (or image) coordinate system.

We start with the concept of *homogeneous coordinate system* which allows easy representation of geometric transformations [Foley et al. (1992)]. A point in an N-dimensional Euclidean space can be represented by an N-component vector. Again, an N-component vector representing N-dimensional Cartesian coordinate of a point P can be represented by an $(N+1)$-component vector called *homogeneous coordinate P_h*, i.e. for $N = 3$,

$$P(X, Y, Z) \equiv P_h(hX, hY, hZ, h)$$

Similarly, a three-dimensional Cartesian coordinate of a point Q can be obtained from the given homogeneous coordinates $Q_h(\xi_h, \zeta_h, \varsigma_h, h)$ as

$$Q = Q\left(\frac{\xi_h}{h}, \frac{\zeta_h}{h}, \frac{\varsigma_h}{h}\right) \tag{4.2}$$

For simplicity, we assume the last component of the homogeneous coordinate is 1.

Translation

Suppose a point P with coordinate (X, Y, Z) is translated by the displacement X_0, Y_0 and Z_0 along the three axes, respectively. Then the coordinate of the translated point is

$$X_T = X + X_0$$

$$Y_T = Y + Y_0$$

$$Z_T = Z + Z_0$$

Using homogeneous coordinate system, we get

$$\begin{bmatrix} X_T \\ Y_T \\ Z_T \\ 1 \end{bmatrix} = \begin{bmatrix} 1 & 0 & 0 & X_0 \\ 0 & 1 & 0 & Y_0 \\ 0 & 0 & 1 & Z_0 \\ 0 & 0 & 0 & 1 \end{bmatrix} \begin{bmatrix} X \\ Y \\ Z \\ 1 \end{bmatrix} \tag{4.3}$$

or, in short, $\mathbf{p_t} = \mathbf{Tp}$, where $\mathbf{p}$ represents the vector containing the coordinates of the point P.

Scaling

If the coordinate system is scaled by the factor S_X, S_Y and S_Z along X-, Y- and Z-axes respectively, then the scaled coordinates are obtained as

$$\begin{bmatrix} X_S \\ Y_S \\ Z_S \\ 1 \end{bmatrix} = \begin{bmatrix} S_X & 0 & 0 & 0 \\ 0 & S_Y & 0 & 0 \\ 0 & 0 & S_Z & 0 \\ 0 & 0 & 0 & 1 \end{bmatrix} \begin{bmatrix} X \\ Y \\ Z \\ 1 \end{bmatrix} \tag{4.4}$$

or, in short, $\mathbf{p_s} = \mathbf{Sp}$.

Rotation

The three-dimensional rotation is a complicated transformation and the simplest form involves rotation of a point about three coordinate axes. Rotation is measured clockwise about the said axis while looking along the axis towards the origin.

Rotation of a point (X, Y, Z) about the X-axis by an angle α is computed as

$$\begin{bmatrix} X_X \\ Y_X \\ Z_X \\ 1 \end{bmatrix} = \begin{bmatrix} 1 & 0 & 0 & 0 \\ 0 & \cos \alpha & \sin \alpha & 0 \\ 0 & -\sin \alpha & \cos \alpha & 0 \\ 0 & 0 & 0 & 1 \end{bmatrix} \begin{bmatrix} X \\ Y \\ Z \\ 1 \end{bmatrix} \tag{4.5}$$

or, in short, $\mathbf{p}_X = \mathbf{R}_X \mathbf{p}$. Similarly, rotation about Y-axis by an angle β is computed as

$$\begin{bmatrix} X_Y \\ Y_Y \\ Z_Y \\ 1 \end{bmatrix} = \begin{bmatrix} \cos \beta & 0 & -\sin \beta & 0 \\ 0 & 1 & 0 & 0 \\ \sin \beta & 0 & \cos \beta & 0 \\ 0 & 0 & 0 & 1 \end{bmatrix} \begin{bmatrix} X \\ Y \\ Z \\ 1 \end{bmatrix} \tag{4.6}$$

or, in short, $\mathbf{p}_Y = \mathbf{R}_Y \mathbf{p}$, and rotation about Z-axis by an angle γ is computed as

$$\begin{bmatrix} X_Z \\ Y_Z \\ Z_Z \\ 1 \end{bmatrix} = \begin{bmatrix} \cos \gamma & \sin \gamma & 0 & 0 \\ -\sin \gamma & \cos \gamma & 0 & 0 \\ 0 & 0 & 1 & 0 \\ 0 & 0 & 0 & 1 \end{bmatrix} \begin{bmatrix} X \\ Y \\ Z \\ 1 \end{bmatrix} \tag{4.7}$$

or, in short, $\mathbf{p}_Z = \mathbf{R}_Z \mathbf{p}$. Finally, any geometric transformation of a point can be obtained by cascading the transformations defined by $\mathbf{T}$, $\mathbf{S}$, $\mathbf{R}_X$, $\mathbf{R}_Y$ and $\mathbf{R}_Z$, and premultiplying the vector representing the homogeneous coordinate of the point.

4.2.2 Perspective Projection

Suppose by appropriate transformation (translation and rotation) the scene coordinate system is made to conform with the camera coordinate system. That means the camera lens or the view point is at the origin of the transformed coordinate system, the optical axis coincides with the transformed Z-axis, and other two axes also coincide accordingly. Thus the homogeneous coordinate of the two-dimensional image points $(h\xi, h\zeta, h)$ can be described by using the following transformation [Haralick and Shapiro (1992), Foley et al. (1992)]:

$$\begin{bmatrix} h\xi \\ h\zeta \\ h \end{bmatrix} = \begin{bmatrix} 1 & 0 & 0 & 0 \\ 0 & 1 & 0 & 0 \\ 0 & 0 & 1/\lambda & 1 \end{bmatrix} \begin{bmatrix} 1 & 0 & 0 & 0 \\ 0 & 1 & 0 & 0 \\ 0 & 0 & 1 & -\lambda \\ 0 & 0 & 0 & 1 \end{bmatrix} \begin{bmatrix} X \\ Y \\ Z \\ 1 \end{bmatrix} \tag{4.8}$$

The first transformation defined by the 4×4 matrix translates the scene coordinates by an amount of λ down the Z-axis and the second transformation performs the perspective projection on the plane. In short, the complete perspective projection can be described by $\mathbf{p}_P = \mathbf{Pp}$. Finally, the Cartesian coordinate of the transformed point is given by

$$(\xi, \zeta) = \left(\lambda \frac{X}{Z}, \lambda \frac{Y}{Z} \right) \tag{4.9}$$

Properties of perspective projection

(a) Straight lines map into straight lines

Any point of straight line in three-dimensional space having two end-points (X_1, Y_1, Z_1) and (X_2, Y_2, Z_2) can be represented by

$$\mu \begin{bmatrix} X_1 \\ Y_1 \\ Z_1 \end{bmatrix} + (1 - \mu) \begin{bmatrix} X_2 \\ Y_2 \\ Z_2 \end{bmatrix}$$

where $0 \le \mu \le 1$. The end-points map into two image points:

$$\begin{bmatrix} \lambda \dfrac{X_1}{Z_1} \\ \lambda \dfrac{Y_1}{Z_1} \end{bmatrix} \quad \text{and} \quad \begin{bmatrix} \lambda \dfrac{X_2}{Z_2} \\ \lambda \dfrac{Y_2}{Z_2} \end{bmatrix}$$

respectively.

Now any point of the three-dimensional line map into one image point is given by

$$\begin{bmatrix} \lambda \dfrac{\mu X_1 + (1 - \mu) X_2}{\mu Z_1 + (1 - \mu) Z_2} \\ \lambda \dfrac{\mu Y_1 + (1 - \mu) Y_2}{\mu Z_1 + (1 - \mu) Z_2} \end{bmatrix}$$

or

$$\begin{bmatrix} \lambda \dfrac{\mu X_1}{\mu Z_1 + (1 - \mu) Z_2} \\ \lambda \dfrac{\mu Y_1}{\mu Z_1 + (1 - \mu) Z_2} \end{bmatrix} + \begin{bmatrix} \lambda \dfrac{(1 - \mu) X_2}{\mu Z_1 + (1 - \mu) Z_2} \\ \lambda \dfrac{(1 - \mu) Y_2}{\mu Z_1 + (1 - \mu) Z_2} \end{bmatrix}$$

or

$$\frac{\mu Z_1}{\mu Z_1 + (1 - \mu) Z_2} \begin{bmatrix} \lambda \dfrac{X_1}{Z_1} \\ \lambda \dfrac{Y_1}{Z_1} \end{bmatrix} + \left(1 - \frac{\mu Z_1}{\mu Z_1 + (1 - \mu) Z_2} \right) \begin{bmatrix} \lambda \dfrac{X_2}{Z_2} \\ \lambda \dfrac{Y_2}{Z_2} \end{bmatrix}$$

Now, since

$$0 \le \frac{\mu Z_1}{\mu Z_1 + (1 - \mu)Z_2} \le 1 \quad \text{as} \quad 0 \le \mu \le 1$$

the point lies on a two-dimensional straight line having

$$\left(\lambda \frac{X_1}{Z_1}, \lambda \frac{Y_1}{Z_1} \right) \quad \text{and} \quad \left(\lambda \frac{X_2}{Z_2}, \lambda \frac{Y_2}{Z_2} \right)$$

as end-points.

(b) Further objects appear smaller

An object may be considered as a collection of points. Reduction in size then is revealed by the reduction in distance between any two points. Consider a straight line whose mid-point, length and the direction cosine vector are (X, Y, Z), $2l$ and $(a, b, c)^T$, respectively. Then the two end-points are

$$\begin{bmatrix} X \\ Y \\ Z \end{bmatrix} - l \begin{bmatrix} a \\ b \\ c \end{bmatrix} \quad \text{and} \quad \begin{bmatrix} X \\ Y \\ Z \end{bmatrix} + l \begin{bmatrix} a \\ b \\ c \end{bmatrix}$$

The end-points map into image points given by

$$\begin{bmatrix} \lambda \dfrac{X - al}{Z - cl} \\ \lambda \dfrac{Y - bl}{Z - cl} \end{bmatrix} \quad \text{and} \quad \begin{bmatrix} \lambda \dfrac{X + al}{Z + cl} \\ \lambda \dfrac{Y + bl}{Z + cl} \end{bmatrix}$$

respectively.

Now, the distance between these two image points (or length of the line connecting these points as end-points) is

$$d = \lambda \sqrt{\left(\frac{X + al}{Z + cl} - \frac{X - al}{Z - cl} \right)^2 + \left(\frac{Y + bl}{Z + cl} - \frac{Y - bl}{Z - cl} \right)^2}$$

$$= \frac{2\lambda l}{Z^2 - c^2 l^2} \sqrt{(Za - Xc)^2 + (Zb - Yc)^2}$$

Hence, d decreases as Z (the distance of the line from the view point) increases.

(c) A family of parallel straight lines which are not perpendicular to Z-axis maps into a family of concurrent straight lines

A family of parallel lines can be represented by

$$\left\{ \begin{bmatrix} X_i \\ Y_i \\ Z_i \end{bmatrix} + l \begin{bmatrix} a \\ b \\ c \end{bmatrix} \right\}$$

where (X_i, Y_i, Z_i) is a point through which the i-th line passes, l is a real number and $(a\ b\ c)^T$ is direction cosine vector of the lines. If lines are not perpendicular to Z-axis, then $c \neq 0$. The image points (ξ, ζ) corresponding to the i-th line is given by

$$\xi = \lambda \frac{X_i + al}{Z_i + cl}, \qquad \zeta = \lambda \frac{Y_i + bl}{Z_i + cl}$$

The points which are on the i-th line and are infinitely away from the view point map to the point

$$\xi = \lim_{l \to \infty} \lambda \frac{X_i + al}{Z_i + cl} = \lambda \frac{a}{c}$$

$$\zeta = \lim_{l \to \infty} \lambda \frac{Y_i + bl}{Z_i + cl} = \lambda \frac{b}{c}$$

Thus, the point is independent of (X_i, Y_i, Z_i), i.e. all lines which are perspective projections of the lines from the said family pass through the same image point

$$\left(\lambda \frac{a}{c}, \lambda \frac{b}{c} \right)$$

This common point (or the point of intersection) is called the *vanishing point*.

4.2.3 Camera Calibration

The problem of calibrating a camera is extremely important in many applications, specially in image analysis. The basic aim is to estimate the parameters of the camera in use [Fu et al. (1987)]. The parameters can be classified into two groups: *intrinsic parameters* and *extrinsic parameters* [Horn (1986)]. The intrinsic parameters of the camera are functions of the aspect ratio of the *pixels*[1], the position of image centre (or the point where the optical axis intersects the image plane), angle between the axes of the image coordinate system and focal length. The extrinsic parameters refer to the position of the camera with respect to the world coordinate system. These parameters can be measured directly. However, estimating these parameters using the camera itself as a measuring device is more convenient in many cases.

Here we describe a method for estimating the extrinsic parameters only. The intrinsic parameters are assumed to be known from the manual provided by the manufacturer of the camera. Estimating extrinsic parameters usually requires a set of image points whose world coordinates are known. The computational procedure to estimate the parameters using a set of known points is called *camera calibration*.

Projection of points in a three-dimensional world coordinate system onto a two-dimensional image plane including axis transformation can, in general, be given by using a series of linear transformations in the homogeneous coordinate system representation:

$$\begin{bmatrix} h\xi \\ h\zeta \\ h \end{bmatrix} = \mathbf{PRT} \begin{bmatrix} X \\ Y \\ Z \\ 1 \end{bmatrix} \qquad (4.10)$$

---

[1]Definition of pixel is given in Section 5.5.

$$= \mathbf{Q} \begin{bmatrix} X \\ Y \\ Z \\ 1 \end{bmatrix} \quad \text{where,} \quad \mathbf{Q} = \mathbf{PRT}$$

$$= \begin{bmatrix} q_{00} & q_{01} & q_{02} & q_{03} \\ q_{10} & q_{11} & q_{12} & q_{13} \\ q_{20} & q_{21} & q_{22} & q_{23} \end{bmatrix} \begin{bmatrix} X \\ Y \\ Z \\ 1 \end{bmatrix} \qquad (4.11)$$

So, the camera calibration problem reduces to estimating 12 unknowns $q_{00}, \ldots, q_{23}$. Now, expanding the matrix product yields

$$\text{(a)} \quad h\xi = q_{00}X + q_{01}Y + q_{02}Z + q_{03}$$
$$\text{(b)} \quad h\zeta = q_{10}X + q_{11}Y + q_{12}Z + q_{13} \qquad (4.12)$$
$$\text{(c)} \quad h = q_{20}X + q_{21}Y + q_{22}Z + q_{23}$$

Substituting Equation (c) in Equations (a) and (b) yields

$$\text{(d)} \quad q_{00}X + q_{01}Y + q_{02}Z + q_{03} = q_{20}\xi X + q_{21}\xi Y + q_{22}\xi Z + \xi q_{23} \qquad (4.13)$$
$$\text{(e)} \quad q_{10}X + q_{11}Y + q_{12}Z + q_{13} = q_{20}\zeta X + q_{21}\zeta Y + q_{22}\zeta Z + \zeta q_{23}$$

Hence, at least six points with known image and world coordinates are required to estimate the parameters. Usually, more than six points are taken and the parameters are estimated in a least-square sense.

4.3 Photometric Model

Another basic aspect of the image formation is what factors determine the intensity of light at an image point. The process depends on the characteristics (reflectance, curvature, etc.) of the object surface and the imaging situation. The imaging situation includes viewing position and distribution of light sources [Horn (1977)]. By introducing geometric and photometric model, and by treating them independently, we have basically partitioned the image formation process into a two-stage process. The partitioning may be visualized by assuming the existence of an imaginary plane between the lens and the image plane of the camera. The geometric model maps the three-dimensional scene points on this imaginary plane. The reflectance properties at different points of the scene as well as irradiance falling on them are transferred to the imaginary plane accordingly. This imaginary plane may be regarded as the *two-dimensional scene*. This is also known as the *object plane* or *ideal image*. We will use all these terms interchangeably as suited in the context. The photometric model determines the irradiance or intensity at image points depending on the object plane radiance and the transfer function of the model.

4.3.1 Intensity

Consider a spherical surface with radius ρ. Then the *angle* subtended by a small area dA_e on the surface at the centre of the sphere is

$$d\omega = \frac{dA_e}{\rho^2} \text{ steradian}$$

The total solid angle of a sphere is 4π. If a source of light radiates energy *flux* $d\Phi$ through a solid angle $d\omega$, then the *radiant intensity* $\Im$ of the source is

$$\Im = \frac{d\Phi}{d\omega} \text{ watts/steradian}$$

That means the radiant intensity $\Im$ can be defined as the amount of energy flux emitted per unit solid angle. Similarly, the power radiated from a source into a unit solid angle by a unit area is called *radiance* and is given by

$$\wp = \frac{d\Im}{dA_e} \text{ watts/steradian/sq. meter}$$

where dA_e is the projected area. On the other hand, the *irradiance* is the amount of energy flux incident on a unit area and is given by

$$I = \frac{d\Phi}{dA_i} \text{ watts/sq. meter}$$

where the energy flux $d\Phi$ is incident on the surface area dA_i.

In the image formation process, the term *intensity* refers to two different physical concepts with respect to the scene and the image. The scene intensity usually refers to the radiance, while the image intensity refers to the irradiance. We refer the distribution of light incident over the entire scene informally by the term *illumination* [Hall (1979)]. Though it is mentioned in Chapter 2 that brightness is a psychological concept, because of its strong correlation with the intensity, the term brightness is also used to mean intensity in common use. The objects in a scene either emit or transmit or reflect the light energy, where the third one is most common. Thus, as mentioned earlier, the image plane receives the light energy flux from the imaginary plane. The object plane or the (two-dimensional) scene radiance is proportional to the product of the irradiance falling on and the reflectance of the surface, i.e.

$$f(\xi, \zeta) = \Re(\xi, \zeta) \, I(\xi, \zeta) \tag{4.14}$$

where $f(\xi, \zeta)$ is the *scene radiance* (or ideal image irradiance) at the point (ξ, ζ), while $\Re(\xi, \zeta)$ and $I(\xi, \zeta)$ are the *reflectance* and irradiance respectively at that point.

4.3.2 Transformation of Energy

The energy flux radiated from the *object plane* $(\xi - \zeta$ plane) propagates through the space. An energy transformation system, which is embedded in the image formation system, intercepts the propagating energy flux and transforms it in such a manner that a distribution of intensity $g(x, y)$, called an *image*, is formed in the *image plane* (x-y plane) (Fig. 4.3). The transformation is based on three basic principles: *non-negativity*, *neighbourhood process* and *superposition* [Andrews and Hunt (1977)].

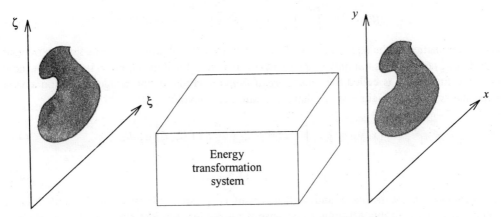

Fig. 4.3 Schematic diagram of energy transformation.

Non-negativity

The image is formed by the transport of energy flux. Since the smallest possible amount of energy either being emitted or being received is zero, the intensity distributions in both the planes are non-negative, i.e.

$$f(\xi, \zeta) \geq 0 \qquad (4.15)$$

$$g(x, y) \geq 0 \qquad (4.16)$$

Neighbourhood process

Consider a point (ξ, ζ) in an object plane and its image (x, y) in an image plane. The intensity at (x, y) depends not only on the radiant energy from the point (ξ, ζ) but also on the energy radiated from other points (possibly infinite) of the object plane. It is reasonable to assume that as the distance of a point from (ξ, ζ) increases, the contribution of energy radiated from the point to the intensity at (x, y) decreases. That means the intensity at (x, y) depends on the radiant energy propagating from a finite neighbourhood of (ξ, ζ); hence, it is called a *neighbourhood process*.

Superposition

Suppose h denotes the transfer function of an energy transformation system. The function h must be referenced to both the coordinate systems (ξ, ζ) and (x, y) to account for the change in the distribution of intensity in both the planes. Then the transformation of intensity into the image plane can be described in terms of h and the object plane radiance $f(\xi, \zeta)$ as

$$h(x, y, \xi, \zeta, f(\xi, \zeta))$$

Now, if we assume like many other energy transport processes that the irradiance is additive, the neighbourhood process principle suggests that the intensity $g(x, y)$ at (x, y) in the image plane is a sum of infinitesimal contributions from all points in the object plane, i.e.

$$g(x, y) = \int_{-\infty}^{\infty} \int_{-\infty}^{\infty} h(x, y, \xi, \zeta, f(\xi, \zeta)) \, d\xi \, d\zeta \qquad (4.17)$$

If we assume linearity for the transfer function then this equation can be rewritten as

$$g(x, y) = \int_{-\infty}^{\infty} \int_{-\infty}^{\infty} h(x, y, \xi, \zeta) f(\xi, \zeta) \, d\xi \, d\zeta \tag{4.18}$$

A close examination of the equation as well as the neighbourhood process reveals that the intensity $f(\xi, \zeta)$ at (ξ, ζ) contributes not only to the point (x, y) but also to all the points in its neighbourhood. Hence, the function h is called the *point-spread function* (PSF) of the image formation system. For the linear shift-invariant PSF we have the familiar convolution [Sondhi (1972)]:

$$g(x, y) = \int_{-\infty}^{\infty} \int_{-\infty}^{\infty} h(x - \xi, y - \zeta) f(\xi, \zeta) \, d\xi \, d\zeta \tag{4.19}$$

or

$$g(x, y) = f(x, y) * h(x, y) \tag{4.20}$$

The assumption that h is linear and shift-invariant is questionable in itself. Nevertheless, we contend ourselves with this assumption because it results in sufficient simplification in analysis. Besides these factors, the recorded image has to undergo another transformation due to the nature of response of the image sensor to the irradiance. That means

$$g(x, y) = \mathcal{C}[f(x, y) * h(x, y)] \tag{4.21}$$

$\mathcal{C}$ represents a non-linear transformation and, usually, is either logarithmic or exponential depending on the technology used in detecting and recording the image. In most of the cases, inverse transformation is provided within the system to cancel out the effect. So, we ignore $\mathcal{C}$ in the subsequent discussion.

4.3.3 Noise Process

The noise may be introduced in the image during formation and recording [Taub and Schilling (1991), Andrews and Hunt (1977)]. The noise that is introduced in a photographic film is a function of formation recording mechanism, i.e. the grains of silver that compose the developed image. The image is formed by the masses of silver deposited after development, but there is a fundamental randomness inherent in the grain deposition. First, the silver grains are randomly distributed with respect to their shapes and sizes. Second, they are located randomly in distance from one another in the film emulsion. Third, they behave randomly under similar conditions of exposure and development. In the photoelectronic technology, the noise problem is more complex. Two separate processes that likely to contribute to noise in the images are (i) random fluctuations in the number of photons and the photoelectrons on the photoactive surface of the detector and (ii) random thermal noise generated in the circuit that sense, acquire and process the signal from the detector's photoactive surface. Noise may also be introduced during the transmission of radiant energy. So, it is evident that the noise introduced in the acquired image is partly signal-dependent and partly signal-independent additive noise. Here, we assume only signal-independent additive noise that leads to

$$g(x, y) = \int_{-\infty}^{\infty} \int_{-\infty}^{\infty} h(x - \xi, y - \zeta) f(\xi, \zeta) \, d\xi \, d\zeta + \eta(x, y) \tag{4.22}$$

It is also assumed that the noise $\eta(x, y)$ follows a zero-mean Gaussian distribution. The assumption made here is again subject to criticism. However, since it makes the problem mathematically more tractable, it is common to most works on image processing. Equation (4.22) represents image intensity function in two-dimensional continuous domain. For processing image information by computer this function must be transformed to discrete form both in space and in value. The method of doing this is described in the next chapter.

Summary

In this chapter, physical process of image formation is described. The formation of image is presented with the help of two independent models: geometric model and photometric model. Noise introduced during image formation and recording is also considered. Such explicit modelling of image formation is essential for developing mathematical framework for image processing algorithms as is evident in the subsequent chapters. Finally, through some pragmatic approximation recorded, image is described in terms of a linear position-invariant transformation (i.e. convolution) and signal-independent additive noise process. However, the mathematical equation we finally derive represents an image that is continuous both in space and in value. Formation of digital image will be discussed in the next chapter.

Problems

1. Suppose an imaging system can be modelled as a pin-hole camera with 50 mm focal length. A square metal sheet of 100 sq. cm area is placed at a distance of 0.5 m in front of the camera such that optical axis of the camera passes through the centre of the metal sheet and is perpendicular to it. What will be the size of the image of the metal sheet?

2. Assume similar arrangement as described in Problem 1 except that the metal sheet is tilted by 45° about the vertical axis of the image plane. What will be the size of the image of the metal sheet?

3. If the reflectance of a surface is given by $\Re(x, y) = A + A \sin(\pi x)$ and the irradiance falling on it is given by $I(x, y) = Be^{-y^2}$. Ignoring all other factors, find out the relation between A and B such that maximum image intensity is 1.

4. Considering the basic principles of photometric model derive the equation:

$$g(x, y) = \int_{-\infty}^{\infty} \int_{-\infty}^{\infty} h(x - \xi, y - \zeta) f(\xi, \zeta) \, d\xi \, d\zeta$$

where the terms have their usual meaning.

5. Describe the sources of noise introduced in an image recorded by using (i) photochemical technology (ii) photoelectronic technology.

Bibliography

Andrews, H.C. and Hunt, B.R., *Digital Image Restoration*, Prentice-Hall, Englewood Cliffs, New Jersey, 1977.

Ballard, D.H. and Brown, C.M., *Computer Vision*, Prentice-Hall, Englewood Cliffs, New Jersey, 1982.

Foley, J., Van Daam, A., Feiner, S. and Hughes, J., *Computer Graphics: Principles and Practice*, Addison-Wesléy, Reading, Massachusetts, 1992.

Fu, K.S., Gonzalez, R.C. and Lee, C.S.G., *Robotics*, McGraw-Hill, New York, 1987.

Hall, E.L., *Computer Image Processing and Recognition*, Academic Press, New York, 1979.

Haralick, R.M. and Shapiro, L.G., *Computer and Robot Vision*, Vols. 1 and 2, Addison-Wesley, Reading, Massachusetts, 1992.

Horn, B.K.P., 'Understanding image intensities', *Artificial Intelligence*, **8**:201–233, 1977.

Horn, B.K.P., *Robot Vision*, MIT Press, Cambridge, Massachusetts, 1986.

Sondhi, M.M., 'Image restoration: the removal of spatially invariant degradation', *Proc. IEEE*, **60**:842–853, 1972.

Taub, H. and Schilling, D.L., *Principles of Communication Systems*, Tata-McGraw Hill, New Delhi, 1991.

Chapter 5

Digitization

5.1 Introduction

An image $g(x, y)$ that is detected and recorded by a sensor is primarily a continuous tone intensity pattern formed on a two-dimensional plane. This image must be converted into a form which is suitable for computer processing. The method of converting an image (or a function), which is continuous in space as well as in its value, into a discrete numerical form is called *image digitization*. This conversion may be considered as a two-step process:

1. taking measurements at regularly spaced intervals, called *sampling*, and

2. mapping the measured intensity (or value) to one of finite number of discrete levels, called *quantization*.

5.2 Sampling

Sampling is a process by which image formed over a patch in continuous domain is mapped into a discrete point with integer coordinates. The process involves two important choices: (i) the *sampling interval* and (ii) the *tessellation*. The sampling theorem provides a mathematical basis for the first one. The second choice is influenced by the connectivity and the metric to be used in the discrete domain. Therefore, image sampling may be described as the selection of a set of discrete locations in the continuous two-dimensional space; and intensity at those locations only will be considered for processing by computer. First, we describe the sampling process in one dimension, and the mathematical tool we use is the *delta function*. The delta function may be defined as

$$\delta(x - x_0) = \begin{cases} 0 & \text{when } x \neq x_0 \\ \infty & \text{otherwise} \end{cases} \tag{5.1}$$

However,

$$\int_{-\infty}^{\infty} \delta(x - x_0)\, dx = \int_{x_0-}^{x_0+} \delta(x - x_0)\, dx = 1$$

So, the function may be viewed as having an area of unity in an infinitesimal domain about x_0. Then we define a *comb function* of spacing Δx as

$$\text{comb}(x) = \sum_{r=-\infty}^{\infty} \delta(x - r\Delta x) \tag{5.2}$$

So, the comb function consists of a train of impulses as shown in Fig. 5.1(a). Suppose a one-dimensional function $g(x)$ is represented by the samples $g(r\Delta x)$, where r takes on integer values from $-\infty$ to $+\infty$ and Δx is the sampling interval. The sampled signal can then be modelled as

$$g_s(x) = g(x) \, \text{comb}(x) = g(x) \sum_{r=-\infty}^{\infty} \delta(x - r\Delta x) \qquad (5.3)$$

or equivalently,

$$g_s(x) = \sum_{r=-\infty}^{\infty} g(r\Delta x) \, \delta(x - r\Delta x) \qquad (5.4)$$

Alternatively, we can simply say that the continuous function $g(x)$ defined over a domain of length $M\Delta x$ can be sampled into a sequence $\{g(0), g(\Delta x), g(2\Delta x), ..., g((M-1)\Delta x)\}$ by taking M samples of Δx unit apart, and any sample of $g(r\Delta x)$ is given as

$$g(r\Delta x) = \int_{-\infty}^{\infty} g(x) \, \delta(x - r\Delta x) \, dx \qquad (5.5)$$

or, for brevity $g(r\Delta x)$ may be represented by $g(r)$. Then the sequence can be rewritten as $\{g(0), g(1), g(2), ..., g(M-1)\}$. The parameter to be selected here is the sampling interval, and this interval should take such a value that the original continuous function can be reconstructed exactly from its sampled sequence. For example, consider a function $g(x)$ and its Fourier transform $G(w_x)$ as shown in Figs. 5.1(c) and 5.1(d) respectively. Suppose $G(w_x) = 0$ for $w_x > W_x$. Fourier transform of the comb function, denoted by $\text{COMB}(w_x)$ is shown in Fig. 5.1(b). Now, as we know from the convolution theorem, multiplication in spatial domain [as given in Equation 5.3)] is equivalent to the convolution in the frequency domain, which means

$$G_s(w_x) = \frac{1}{\Delta x} \sum_{k=-\infty}^{\infty} G\left(w_x - \frac{k}{\Delta x}\right) \qquad (5.6)$$

The plots of $g_s(x)$ and $G_s(w_x)$ corresponding to the given $g(x)$ are shown in Figs. 5.1(e) and 5.1(f), respectively. Equation (5.6) reveals that the Fourier transform $G_s(w_x)$ of the sampled function is nothing but the summation of the shifts of the Fourier transform $G(w_x)$ of the continuous function multiplied by the constant factor $1/\Delta x$, secondly that the shift is a constant multiple of $1/\Delta x$. So, in $G_s(w_x)$, the individual repetitions of $G(w_x)$ may overlap as shown in Fig. 5.1(f), and the overlapped regions are centred at odd multiple of $1/(2\Delta x)$. We now find that exact reconstruction of function is not possible if $1/2\Delta x$ is less than W_x [Nyquist (1928)]. This is formally stated in the sampling theorem [Shannon (1949)] that establishes a relation between sampling and reconstruction of signal:

Shannon's sampling theorem

Suppose $g(x)$ is a band-limited function and its Fourier transform components $G(w_x)$ is zero for all $w_x > W_x$. Then the function $g(x)$ can be reconstructed from the samples taken at a regular interval of Δx, where

$$\Delta x \le \frac{1}{2W_x} \qquad (5.7)$$

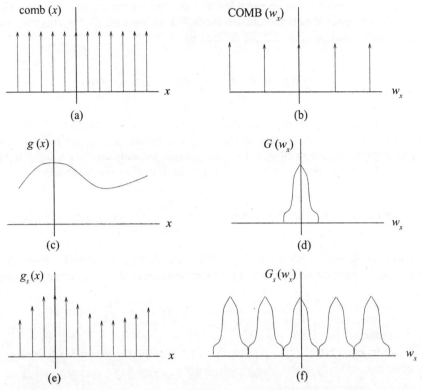

Fig. 5.1 Example showing sampling of one-dimensional function and corresponding Fourier transforms. (a) Comb function comb(x) (b) Fourier transform COMB(w_x), (c) a continuous domain function $g(x)$ (d) its Fourier transform $G(w_x)$, (e) sample $g_s(x)$ of the function $g(x)$ and (f) corresponding discrete Fourier transform $G_s(w_x)$.

Jerri (1977) has published an excellent tutorial on this topic. The objective of selecting the sampling interval satisfying the Equation (5.7) is to repeat the Fourier transform $G(w_x)$ forming $G_s(w_x)$ so that there is no overlap in the repetition. In that case $G(w_x)$ can be isolated from $G_s(w_x)$ by multiplying it with a function $H(w_x)$ in the frequency domain defined as

$$H(w_x) = \begin{cases} 1 & -W_x \leq w_x \leq W_x \\ 0 & \text{otherwise} \end{cases} \tag{5.8}$$

and thus, $g(x)$ can be recovered exactly. On the other hand, if the sampling interval Δx does not satisfy Equation (5.7) then the Fourier transform spectrum isolated from $G_s(w_x)$ by $H(w_x)$ as described above is a distorted version of $G(w)$. In the distorted version, information at high spatial frequencies interfere with that at low frequencies producing a phenomenon called *aliasing*.

The Shannon's theorem can be extended trivially to two dimensions. The sampling process for the two-dimensional functions can be modelled mathematically by making use of two-dimensional comb function [Fig. 5.2(a)] defined as

$$\text{comb}(x, y) = \sum_{c=-\infty}^{\infty} \sum_{r=-\infty}^{\infty} \delta(x - r\Delta x, y - c\Delta y) \qquad (5.9)$$

Two-dimensional sampling function comb(x, y) and its Fourier transform COMB(w_x, w_y) are shown respectively in Fig. 5.2(a) and in Fig. 5.2(b). Suppose $g(x, y)$ is a band-limited function such that its Fourier transform $G(w_x, w_y)$ is zero outside the domain $-W_x \le w_x \le W_x$ and $-W_y \le w_y \le W_y$. Now from the sampled version $g_s(x, y)$ which can be modelled as

$$g_s(x, y) = g(x, y)\text{comb}(x, y) = g(x, y) \sum_{c=-\infty}^{\infty} \sum_{r=-\infty}^{\infty} \delta(x - r\Delta x, y - c\Delta y) \qquad (5.10)$$

$G(w_x, w_y)$ and $G_s(w_x, w_y)$ are shown in Figs. 5.2(c) and 5.2(d), respectively. From these figures, we can say that the continuous function $g(x, y)$ can be recovered exactly if the sampling intervals

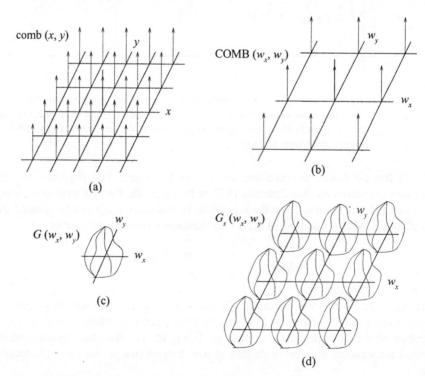

Fig. 5.2   (a) A two-dimensional sampling function comb (x, y) and (b) its Fourier transform COMB (w_x, w_y); (c) Fourier transform $G(w_x, w_y)$ of a two-dimensional continuous function and (d) its fourier transform $G_s(w_x, w_y)$.

Δx and Δy in x and y directions, respectively satisfy the following conditions:

$$\Delta x \leq \frac{1}{2W_x} \tag{5.11}$$

$$\Delta y \leq \frac{1}{2W_y} \tag{5.12}$$

It should be noted that Equation (5.10) is a two-dimensional extension of the Equation (5.3). Similarly, the extension of Equation (5.5), i.e.

$$g(r\Delta x, c\Delta y) = \int_{-\infty}^{\infty} \int_{-\infty}^{\infty} g(x, y)\, \delta(x - r\Delta x, y - c\Delta y)\, dx\, dy \tag{5.13}$$

suggests that a sampled two-dimensional function defined over a domain of size $M\Delta x \times N\Delta y$ can be considered as a two-dimensional array $\{g(0, 0), g(0, 1),\ldots, g(0, N - 1), g(1, 0), g(1, 1),\ldots, g(1, N - 1),\ldots, g(M - 1, 0), g(M - 1, 1),\ldots, g(M - 1, N - 1)\}$. That means the function is represented by $M \times N$ uniformly spaced samples over the said domain.

Apart from the sampling interval in x and y directions, another important choice relevant to the image sampling is the spatial arrangement of the sample points, called 'tessellation'. So far we have implicitly assumed the rectangular tessellation or grid. However, other types of tessellation of the image plane or simply grid, namely triangular and hexagonal, may also be used. Examples of different tessellations are shown in Fig. 5.3.

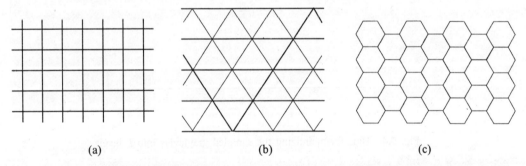

(a)   (b)   (c)

Fig. 5.3 Commonly used sampling grids: (a) rectangular, (b) triangular and (c) hexagonal.

It should be remembered that the entire treatment presented in this book considers only rectangular, more specifically, square tessellation. However, many algorithms can trivially be translated for other types of grids also. The translating process may be aided by the knowledge of the transformation of the coordinates from one type of grid to another. For example, transformations of coordinates between square grid and hexagonal grid can be defined as follows. Suppose (x_4, y_4) and (x_6, y_6) represent coordinates in square and hexagonal grids respectively. Then the transformation from square to hexagonal tessellation is given by [Wuthrich and Stucki (1991)]

$$(x_6, y_6) = \left(x_4 \frac{\sqrt{3}}{2}, y_4 + \frac{x_4}{2} \right)$$

The transformation is bijective and continuous, and hence, is invertible. Therefore,

$$(x_4, y_4) = \left(x_6 \frac{2}{\sqrt{3}}, y_6 - x_6 \frac{1}{\sqrt{3}} \right)$$

Similar transformations can be defined between other types of grids as well.

5.3   Quantization

Quantization is a process common to all kinds of signal processing by computer. The problem has been studied extensively and theoretical solutions under certain assumptions have been developed by many researchers [Panter and Dite (1951), Max (1960), Panter (1965)]. The values obtained by sampling a continuous function usually comprise an infinite set of real numbers ranging from a minimum to a maximum depending on the sensor's calibration. These values must be represented by a finite number of bits usually used by a computer to store or process any data. In practice, the sampled values are represented by a finite set of integer numbers. The mapping from the real numbers to a finite range of integers, or in other words, the process of amplitude digitization is called 'quantization'. The transformation is increasing but non-reversible.

Suppose z be a sampled value at some location of the image plane, and $z_{min} \le z \le z_{max}$. Also suppose that we want to quantize the value into one of the discrete levels $l_1, l_2,..., l_L$. Then the quantization process may be realized by dividing the entire input range into L bins each of width Δl and the i-th bin is centred at l_i (Fig. 5.4). Let the sampled value z is made to be represented by l_i by the quantization process, then the quantization error should be

$$e_q = l_i - z \tag{5.14}$$

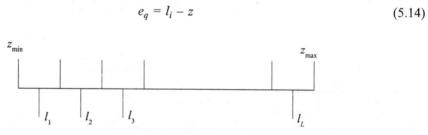

Fig. 5.4   Bins for quantizing the sampled graylevels into L levels.

It should be noted that the minimum quantization error is zero and the maximum is $\Delta l/2$. In order to incorporate this idea of quantization error we take root-mean-square of the individual errors which is

$$e_{qrms} = \sqrt{\sum_{i=1}^{L} \int_{(l_i - \Delta l)/2}^{(l_i + \Delta l)/2} (l_i - z)^2 p(z) \, dz} \tag{5.15}$$

where $p(z)$ is the p.d.f. of the sampled values, and $z_{min} = (l_1 - \Delta l)/2$ and $z_{max} = (l_L + \Delta l)/2$, then Equation (5.15) becomes

$$e_{qrms} = \sqrt{\sum_{i=1}^{L} \int_{(l_i - \Delta l)/2}^{(l_i + \Delta l)/2} (l_i - z)^2 \, dz} \tag{5.16}$$

Hence, it is apparent that the quantization process introduces noise (in terms of measurement error) in the digital image. The signal-to-noise ratio of the quantized values is

$$\frac{\sqrt{\int_{z_{\min}}^{z_{\max}} z^2 p(z)\,dz}}{\sqrt{\sum_{i=1}^{L} \int_{(l_i-\Delta l)/2}^{(l_i+\Delta l)/2} (l_i - z)^2 p(z)\,dz}} \tag{5.17}$$

One of the main criteria of image digitization is to maximize this signal-to-noise ratio.

5.4   Visual Detail in the Digital Image

The people working with digital images come across the parameter called *resolution*. The resolution is of two kinds: (i) *spatial resolution*, related to the sampling interval, and (ii) *graylevel (intensity) resolution*, related to the quantization levels. Higher the spatial resolution, greater is the sampling rate, i.e. lower is the image area $\Delta x \Delta y$ represented by each sampled point. Similarly, higher the graylevel resolution, more is the number of quantization levels, i.e. lower the quantization error. Secondly, for most of the image digitizers and digital image sensors $g(r\Delta x, c\Delta y)$ represents average intensity over an area of $\Delta x \Delta y$ at $(r\Delta x, c\Delta y)$. In Sections 5.2 and 5.3, we have presented image digitization based on sampling and quantization principles. However, in practice, the above mentioned sampling intervals and quantization levels are seldom strictly followed because of the following facts. The reconstruction of digitized image is not an essential task in most of the image processing and analysis applications. Though, the digital images with higher resolutions may be processed by comparatively simpler algorithms, they usually require more processing time and storage space. Finally, it should be kept in mind that in most of the real life applications, the resolution is limited by the capacity of the hardware in use. The finest spatial resolution is restricted by the sensors' limitation, and the quantization levels are usually represented by natural integers with a maximum that can be accommodated within a fixed number of bits (usually a byte, i.e. the number of graylevels is 256). However, in many applications, a tradeoff between the spatial and the graylevel resolutions is done to retain as much visual details in the digital image as possible with minimum amount of storage.

Suppose an image is digitized to an $M \times N$ sampled array and L intensity levels or graylevels. Then the total number of bits required to store the digital image is MNb, where $L = 2^b$. It is assumed that $l_1 = 0, l_2 = 1,..., l_L = L - 1$. For example, Fig. 5.5 shows a digital image of a

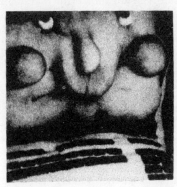

Fig. 5.5   A digital image of size 256 × 256 where number of graylevels is 256 only.

caricature of a computer terminal, where $M = N = 256$ and $L = 256$. Let us divide the image into two parts—the upper part showing the face, and the lower part showing the keys. Figs. 5.6(a)–5.6(d) show the same image but having lower spatial resolutions, i.e. 128×128, 64×64, 32×32 and 16×16, respectively. However, graylevel resolution is the same. It is clear that the effect is immediate at the keyboard region (lower part of the image), where intensity changes rapidly. While in the face region (upper part) where change in intensity is smooth, the lower spatial resolution degrades the image at much slower rate. Again, Figs. 5.7(a)–5.7(d) show the same image as in Fig. 5.5 but with graylevels quantized into 16, 8, 4 and 2 levels, respectively. Comparing the upper and the lower parts of these images with different graylevel resolutions it becomes evident that the effect of lower graylevel resolution is much more objectionable in the smooth regions (e.g. the face) than that in the busy regions (e.g. the keyboard). The images shown in Figs. 5.6 and 5.7 give a qualitative idea of visual clarity of digital image versus graylevel resolution. Hence we may argue that in a smooth scene in which spatial variation of intensity is relatively low, it is preferable to have fine quantization though the sampling rate can be low. On the other hand, in a busy scene where there is a large amount of detail, i.e. many abrupt changes in intensity, the sampling should be finer but quantization may be coarse.

It should be noted that a single image (Fig. 5.5), can be sampled and quantized at different

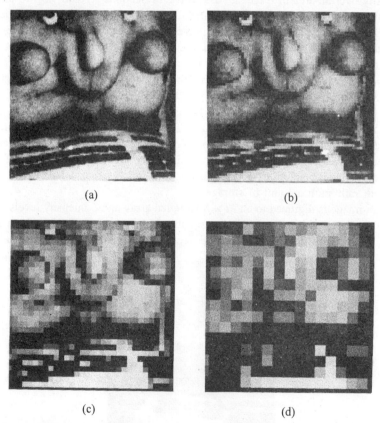

(a)   (b)

(c)   (d)

Fig. 5.6   Various sampling rates of the image shown in Fig. 5.5: (a) 128×128, (b) 64×64, (c) 32×32, (d) 16×16.

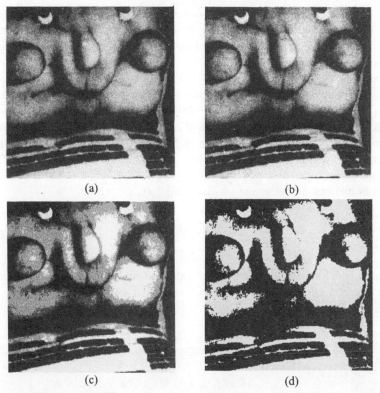

Fig. 5.7 Various number of quantization levels the image shown in Fig. 5.5: (a) 16 levels, (b) 8 levels, (c) 4 levels, (d) 2 levels.

rates at different parts of the image. This is known as *non-uniform sampling* and *non-uniform quantization*. Though not very common, non-uniform sampling and non-uniform quantization of a single image guided by the above mentioned observations can retain maximum visual detail in the digital image with minimum number of bits [Gonzalez and Wintz (1977)].

5.5 Digital Image

The discussion in the preceding section permits us to define a digital image by a finite valued function over a discrete domain $\mathscr{Z}^2$. Let us assume that the digital image domain $\mathscr{D} \subset \mathscr{Z}^2$ is a rectangular array of size $M \times N$, i.e.

$$\mathscr{D} = \{(r, c) \mid r = 0, 1, 2, ..., M - 1; c = 0, 1, 2, ..., N - 1\}$$

obtained by sampling with step size Δx and Δy along x and y directions, respectively. So a digital image $\{g(r, c)\}$ can be represented by an $M \times N$ matrix whose elements are integer numbers ranging from 0 to $L - 1$:

$$\{g(r, c)\} = \begin{bmatrix} g(0,0) & g(0,1) & \cdots & g(0, N - 1) \\ g(1,0) & g(1,1) & \cdots & g(1, N - 1) \\ \vdots & \vdots & & \vdots \\ g(M - 1,0) & g(M - 1,1) & \cdots & g(M - 1, N - 1) \end{bmatrix} \quad (5.18)$$

Each element of the matrix is called *image element, picture element, pixel, pel*, or sometimes simply, *point*. We prefer the term 'pixel'. Thus, the pixel may indicate only a location in $\mathscr{Z}^2$ (i.e. the coordinate), or it may represent the graylevel alongwith position; however, the meaning of the term will always be evident from the context.

At this point let us recall Equation (4.19) (see Section 4.3.2), which describes the image formation in continuous domain as a convolution operation between the two-dimensional scene or ideal image $f(x, y)$ and the transfer function $h(x, y)$ of the image formation system. Discrete model of image formation can be developed straightway by defining discrete convolution between two sampled periodic functions $f(r, c)$ and $h(r, c)$. Suppose the matrices representing the digital image/function $f(r, c)$ and $h(r, c)$ are of size $M_1 \times N_1$ and $M_2 \times N_2$, respectively. Based on the discussion on one-dimensional discrete convolution [see Section 2.3], it can be said that convolving f_e by h_e produces another digital image (or function) $g_e(r, c)$, where

$$g_e(r, c) = \sum_{j=0}^{N-1} \sum_{i=0}^{M-1} f(i, j) \, h(r - i, c - j) \tag{5.19}$$

for $r = 0, 1, 2, ..., M - 1$, and $c = 0, 1, 2, ..., N - 1$. Here, $M \geq M_1 + M_2 - 1$ and $N \geq N_1 + N_2 - 1$, and $f_e(r, c)$ and $h_e(r, c)$ are the elements of the extended matrices obtained by appending zeros at appropriate places, i.e.

$$f_e(r, c) = \begin{cases} f(r, c) & \text{for } 0 \leq r < M_1 \text{ and } 0 \leq c < N_1 \\ 0 & \text{for } M_1 \leq r \leq M - 1 \text{ or } N_1 \leq c \leq N - 1 \end{cases} \tag{5.20}$$

$$h_e(r, c) = \begin{cases} h(r, c) & \text{for } 0 \leq r < M_2 \text{ and } 0 \leq c < N_2 \\ 0 & \text{for } M_2 \leq r \leq M - 1 \text{ or } N_2 \leq c \leq N - 1 \end{cases} \tag{5.21}$$

Thus $f_e(r, c)$, $h_e(r, c)$ and $g_e(r, c)$ are also periodic in two dimension with periods M and N in row (or x or r) and column (or y or c) directions, respectively. For simplicity, let us write g, f and h instead of g_e, f_e and h_e, respectively. Hence, the digital image formation model including additive noise can be written as [similar to Equation (4.22) of Chapter 4 for continuous domain]:

$$g(r, c) = \sum_{j=0}^{N-1} \sum_{i=0}^{M-1} f(i, j) \, h(r - i, c - j) + \eta(r, c) \tag{5.22}$$

for $r = 0, 1, 2, ..., M - 1$, and $c = 0, 1, 2, ..., N - 1$. Now a common way to generate a column vector **g** from a given (image) matrix $\{g(r, c)\}$ is by *lexicographic ordering* of the matrix rows, i.e.

$$\mathbf{g} = \begin{bmatrix} g(0, 0) \\ g(0, 1) \\ \vdots \\ g(0, N - 1) \\ g(1, 0) \\ g(1, 1) \\ \vdots \\ g(1, N - 1) \\ \vdots \\ g(M - 1, 0) \\ g(M - 1, 1) \\ \vdots \\ g(M - 1, N - 1) \end{bmatrix} \tag{5.23}$$

The vectors **f** and η can also be formed in a similar way. Then Equation (5.22) can be represented using matrix–vector notations:

$$\mathbf{g} = \mathbf{Hf} + \eta \qquad (5.24)$$

where **g**, **f** and η are MN-dimensional vectors, and **H** is an $(MN \times MN)$ *block-circulant* matrix. The matrix **H** consists of M^2 blocks each of size $N \times N$ which are ordered in a circulant manner:

$$\mathbf{H} = \begin{bmatrix} \mathbf{H}_0 & \mathbf{H}_{M-1} & \mathbf{H}_{M-2} & \cdots & \mathbf{H}_1 \\ \mathbf{H}_1 & \mathbf{H}_0 & \mathbf{H}_{M-1} & \cdots & \mathbf{H}_2 \\ \mathbf{H}_2 & \mathbf{H}_1 & \mathbf{H}_0 & \cdots & \mathbf{H}_3 \\ \vdots & \vdots & \vdots & & \vdots \\ \mathbf{H}_{M-1} & \mathbf{H}_{M-2} & \mathbf{H}_{M-3} & \cdots & \mathbf{H}_0 \end{bmatrix} \qquad (5.25)$$

Each partition $\mathbf{H}_i$ is again a circulant matrix constructed from the elements of the i-th row of the matrix $\{h(r, c)\}$, i.e.

$$\mathbf{H}_i = \begin{bmatrix} h(i, 0) & h(i, N-1) & h(i, N-2) & \cdots & h(i, 1) \\ h(i, 1) & h(i, 0) & h(i, N-1) & \cdots & h(i, 2) \\ h(i, 2) & h(i, 1) & h(i, 0) & \cdots & h(i, 3) \\ \vdots & \vdots & \vdots & & \vdots \\ h(i, N-1) & h(i, N-2) & h(i, N-3) & \cdots & h(i, 0) \end{bmatrix} \qquad (5.26)$$

Finally, since the matrix **H** is generated from the point-spread function of the image formation process, a major source of image degradation (if any) is embedded in this matrix. So, matrix **H** is called *degradation matrix* in the image processing literature. In the rest of the discussion, the image function, the elements of image matrix or the pixels are represented by $g(r, c)$ depending on the context. Similarly, **g** would represent image function or image vector. On the other hand, the location (r, c) of a pixel or simply a pixel may be represented by p etc. Finally, as stated earlier, the value of $g(r, c)$ can take any value between O and $L - 1$ inclusive, which is given as

$$g(r, c) \in \{0, 1, 2, ..., L - 1\}$$

The convention is that $g(r, c) = 0$ represents black or the darkest possible pixel and $g(r, c) = (L - 1)$ represents white or the brightest pixel of the image. However, when $L = 2$, we have a special type of image called *two-tone image* or *binary image*. In such cases, the pixels are either black (usually having value 1) or white (usually having value zero). Alternatively, the pixel or point (r, c) with value 1 is called *object pixel* or *foreground pixel*, and the pixel with value 0 is called *background pixel*. Many binary image processing algorithms consider only the locations (coordinates) of the foreground pixels over the entire rectangular domain of the image, rather than the value of the pixels.

5.6 Elements of Digital Geometry

In this section we present some elementary definitions and concepts of digital geometry [Rosenfeld and Kak (1982)] that helps understanding the operations performed or applied on digital images and corresponding results. A frame F of a domain $\mathscr{D}$ may be defined as a subset of $\mathscr{D}$ containing pixels of the first and last rows, and pixels of the first and last columns. Let $\mathscr{Z}_1$ and $\mathscr{Z}_2$ denote two sets of integers $\{1, 3, 5, 7\}$ and $\{1, 2, 3, ..., 8\}$, respectively. Now consider Fig. 5.8, which shows a portion of rectangular image domain.

p_4	p_3	p_2
p_5	p_0	p_1
p_6	p_7	p_8

Fig. 5.8   Neighbourhood of the pixel p_0.

5.6.1   Some Important Definitions

(1) The elements of the set $\{p_i \mid i \in \mathscr{Z}_1\}$ are called *4-neighbours* of p_0, and may be denoted by $N_4(p_0)$. Similarly, the elements of the set $\{p_i \mid i \in \mathscr{Z}_2\}$ are called *8-neighbours* of p_0 and may be denoted by $N_8(p_0)$.

The 4-neighbours are also called *direct neighbours*. The domain shown in Fig. 5.8 is also called 3×3 *neighbourhood* or 3×3 *window*.

(2) A function $d(p, q)$ of the coordinates of two pixels p and q is called a *metric* or *distance function* if the following conditions are true:

1. $d(p, q) \geq 0$, and $d(p, q) = 0$ if and only if $p = q$

2. $d(p, q) = d(q, p)$

3. $d(p, q) \leq d(p, s) + d(s, q)$, where s is another pixel

Here, we consider three different distance measures, namely Euclidean, city-block and chessboard distance, and are defined as follows:

Let p and q be two discrete points in $\mathscr{Z}^2$ with coordinates (r_p, c_p) and (r_q, c_q) respectively, then the *distance* between p and q may be defined in different distance measures as under:

$$\text{Euclidean: } d_e(p, q) = \sqrt{(r_p - r_q)^2 + (c_p - c_q)^2} \tag{5.27}$$

$$\text{City-block: } d_4(p, q) = \mid r_p - r_q \mid + \mid c_p - c_q \mid \tag{5.28}$$

$$\text{Chess-board: } d_8(p, q) = \max \{\mid r_p - r_q \mid, \mid c_p - c_q \mid\} \tag{5.29}$$

City-block distance is also called *4-distance* or *Manhattan distance*. Similarly, chess-board distance is also called *8-distance* or *checker-board distance*. Set of all pixels whose distance from the pixel p is less than or equal to, say, ρ, i.e. $\{q \mid d_x(p, q) \leq \rho\}$, forms (i) a circular disc of radius ρ if 'x' is replaced by 'e', (ii) a diamond of diagonal $2\rho + 1$ if 'x' is replaced by '4' and (iii) a square of side $(2\rho + 1)$ if 'x' is replaced by '8' as shown in Fig. 5.9.

Now in terms of the distance function the 4- and 8-neighbours can be redefined as follows. A pixel q is said to be a 4-neighbour of a pixel p if and only if $d_4(p, q) = 1$ and vice versa. Similarly, A pixel q is said to be a 4-neighbour of a pixel p if $d_8(p, q) = 1$ and vice versa. Two pixels p and q are said to be connected by a 4- (8-) connected path if there exists a sequence of pixels $p = p_1, p_2, p_3, ..., p_n = q$, such that for any i, value of p_i is same as that of p and q, and $d_4(p_i, p_{i+1}) = 1[d_8(p_i, p_{i+1}) = 1]$.

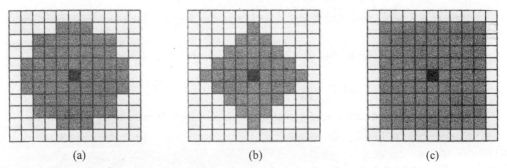

Fig. 5.9 Disks of radius 4 around pixel p (shown black in the figure) defined by various metrices. (a) Euclidean, (b) City-block, and (c) Chess-board.

(3) A set of pixels A is called *4-* (*8-*) *connected* if every pair of pixels in A is connected by a 4- (8-) connected path.

Usually, it is assumed that the objects are 8-connected and the background is 4-connected. If there exists no 4-connected path from a 0 pixel (or background pixel) to the image frame F, then the pixel is called a *hole element*. Maximal connected component of such hole elements is called a *hole*.

A *boundary pixel* of an object A is a pixel of A such that at least one of its 4-neighbours is not in A. The *boundary* of an object A is characterized by the set of its boundary pixels.

In the graylevel (multi-valued) image, there are many different types of regions rather than just two—the foreground (or the object) and the background as in binary image. Secondly, when the graylevel image is considered, the term *edge* is used to refer the boundary separating adjacent regions.

Summary

In this chapter, we have discussed formation of images that are continuous both in space and in value. Pictorial information of this form cannot be processed by digital computers. The technique of converting the said information to a form suitable for processing by digital computer is described in this chapter. The technique is called digitization which comprises two steps—sampling and quantization in sequence. As a result, we obtain digital images that are discrete, both in space and in value. All the digital image processing and analysis algorithms deal with digital images only. Here, we also present some elementary definitions and concepts of digital geometry that helps understand the image processing operators and their effects.

Problems

1. Suppose intensity distribution of an image is given by

$$f(x, y) = \{A + A \cos (3\pi x)\}\{B + B \sin (4\pi y)\}$$

for $x_{\min} \le x \le x_{\max}$ and $y_{\min} \le y \le y_{\max}$. Determine the least sampling frequency enabling exact reconstruction.

2. Suppose intensity distribution of an image is given by

$$f(x, y) = A + A \cos \pi (3x + 4y)$$

for $x_{min} \leq x \leq x_{max}$ and $y_{min} \leq y \leq y_{max}$: Determine the least sampling frequency enabling exact reconstruction.

3. Suppose the probability density function of intensity of an image is given by

$$p(z) = \frac{2}{10} - \frac{2}{100} z \quad \text{for} \ 0 \leq z \leq 10$$

Determine 8 quantization levels such that the root-mean-square error is minimum.

4. Consider the following sub-image.

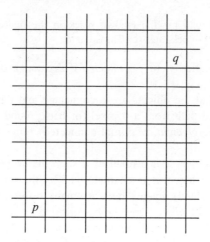

Determine (i) Euclidean, (ii) city-block and (iii) chess-board distance between p and q. Count the number of all possible paths in each case.

Bibliography

Gonzalez, R.C. and Wintz, P., *Digital Image Processing*, Addison-Wesley, Massachusetts, 1977.

Jerri, A.J., 'The Shannon sampling theorem—its various extensions and applications: a tutorial review' *Proc. IEEE*, **65:**1565–1596, 1977.

Max, J. 'Quantizing for minimum distortion', *IRE Trans. on Information Theory*, **6:**7–12, 1960.

Nyquist, H., 'Certain topics in telegraph transmission', *Trans. of AIEE*, **47:**617–644, 1928.

Panter, P.F., *Modulation Noise and Spectral Analysis Applied to Information Transmission.* McGraw-Hill, New York, 1965.

Panter, P.F. and Dite, W., 'Quantizing distortion in pulse-count modulation with non-uniform spacing of levels', *Proc. IRE*, **39:**44–48, 1951.

Rosenfeld, A. and Kak, A.C., *Digital Picture Processing*, 2nd ed., Vols. 1 and 2, Academic Press, New York, 1982.

Shannon, C.H., 'Communication in the present of noise', *Proc. IRE*, **37:**10–21, 1949.

Wuthrich, C.A. and Stucki, P., 'An algorithmic comparison between square- and hexagonal-based grids', *Computer Vision, Graphics and Image Processing*, **53:**324–339, 1991.

Part–II

Image Processing

Chapter 6

Image Enhancement

6.1 Introduction

Whenever an image is converted from one form to another, such as digitizing, transmitting, scanning, etc., some form of degradation occurs at the output. Secondly, no imaging system, however accurate it be, can produce an exact replica of the scene (or ideal image). All such degraded image may be modelled using Equation (5.24)

$$\mathbf{g} = \mathbf{Hf} + \eta$$

Since the matrix $\mathbf{H}$ is generated from the point-spread function of the image formation process, a major source of image degradation (if any) is embedded in this matrix. So, matrix $\mathbf{H}$ is called *degradation matrix* in the image processing literature. Improvement in the quality of these degraded images can be achieved by the application of restoration and/or enhancement technique. *Restoration* may be defined as an attempt to estimate the original (or ideal) image by applying effective inversion of the degrading phenomenon. This requires an a priori model of the degradation process. When no such knowledge is available the quality of an image may be improved for specific application by some ad hoc process called *image enhancement*. So essentially, any technique is a fair game for enhancement if the resulting image provides additional information which were not readily apparent in the observed image. The term 'specific' is important, because the enhancement technique which is suitable for biomedical images can be a total catastrophe for remotely sensed images. Secondly, the quality of an image depends on the purpose for which the image is acquired or displayed. The image may be intended for human viewing or for processing and analysis by the computer. Consequently, the fidelity of an image may be measured in various ways. The measurements can be grouped into two classes—subjective criteria and objective criteria. An example of objective fidelity criteria is signal-to-noise ratio. Hence, by the term *image enhancement* we mean improvement of the appearance of an image by increasing dominance of some features, or by decreasing ambiguity between different regions of the image. It should be noted that enhancement of certain features may be achieved at the cost of suppressing others. The enhancement techniques can be divided into three categories:

1. Contrast intensification
2. Noise cleaning or smoothing and
3. Edge sharpening or crispening

The algorithms are developed using one of the two basic approaches: *spatial-domain techniques* and *frequency-domain techniques*. The term 'spatial-domain' refers to the discrete image domain defined as

$$\{(r, c) \mid r = 0, 1, 2,..., M - 1; \quad c = 0, 1, 2,..., N - 1\}$$

Spatial-domain operators directly operate on the pixel values $g(r,c)$ of the image and can be expressed as

$$\tilde{g}(r, c) = T(g(r, c), Q(r, c)) \tag{6.1}$$

for all r and c, where $Q(r, c)$ is the set of graylevels of the neighbouring pixels. T is the operator, in general, defined over some neighbourhood of (r, c), and the operation is the convolution. Some of these operators are also called *filters*. The operator has its simplest form when it is defined over a single pixel, i.e. over 1×1 neighbourhood. The operation then becomes an *intensity mapping*. Secondly, the transformation function may or may not depend on the coordinate (r, c). Accordingly the operator is called *local* or *global* respectively.

On the other hand, in frequency-domain, the operators are always global and are called *filters*. Filtering the image information can be expressed as

$$\tilde{G}(u, v) = \mathfrak{I}(u, v) \, G(u, v) \tag{6.2}$$

for all u and v. Hence, frequency-domain refers to a rectangular array of discrete coordinates resulting from orthogonal transform, commonly known as Fourier transform. The term 'frequency', in this case, has cropped up from the concept of fundamental angular frequency and their harmonics defining the Fourier transform kernel. The image is first transformed to the frequency-domain, then the transformed image is passed through a suitable filter, and finally the filtered information is mapped back to the spatial-domain by an inverse transform operation.

6.2 Contrast Intensification

One of the most common defects found in the recorded image is its poor contrast. This degradation may be caused by inadequate lighting, aperture size, shutter speed and/or non-linear mapping of the image intensity. The effect of such defects is reflected on the range and shape of the graylevel histogram of the recorded image. In this case, the contrast can be improved by scaling the graylevel of each pixel, so that image graylevel occupy entire dynamic range available. The operation may be called *histogram stretching*, since the graylevel histogram reveals the overall appearance of the image. Figure 6.1 shows an example of histogram stretching, where Fig. 6.1(a) is the graylevel histogram of the input image, Fig. 6.1(b) shows the transformation function that maps the input graylevel m to the output graylevel l, and Fig. 6.1(c) is the graylevel histogram of the processed (enhanced) image. The transformation function $l = T(m)$ must satisfy the following conditions:

1. $T(m)$ must be monotonically increasing in the interval $[m_{\min}, m_{\max}]$, i.e.

$$m_1 < m_2 \Rightarrow l_1 = T(m_1) \le l_2 = T(m_2)$$

That means that transformed graylevel l must preserve the order from black to white.

2. $l_{\min} \le l \le l_{\max}$, i.e. transformed graylevel must lie within the allowed range of graylevel.

where $[l_{\min}, l_{\max}]$ and $[m_{\min}, m_{\max}]$ are the available graylevel range and the graylevel range in the given image, respectively.

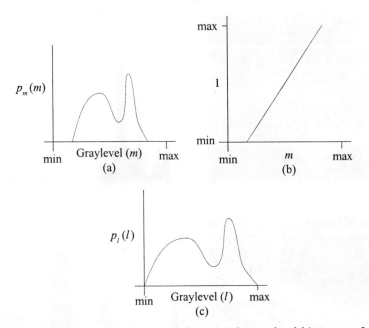

Fig. 6.1 An example of graylevel histogram stretching: (a) the graylevel histogram of the input image, (b) the transformation function, (c) the graylevel histogram of the processed (enhanced) image.

6.2.1 Linear Stretching

Here the transformation function can be represented by a straight line having slope $(l_{max} - l_{min})/(m_{max} - m_{min})$. So

$$l = T(m) = \frac{l_{max} - l_{min}}{m_{max} - m_{min}} (m - m_{min}) + l_{min} \tag{6.3}$$

This transformation function shifts and stretches the graylevel range (and consequently the graylevel histogram) of the input image to occupy the entire dynamic range $[l_{min}, l_{max}]$. The transformation may also be written as

$$\tilde{g}(r, c) = \frac{l_{max} - l_{min}}{m_{max} - m_{min}} \{g(r, c) - m_{min}\} + l_{min} \tag{6.4}$$

The slope of the transformation function is always greater than or equal to 1. If the slope is 1, there is no enhancement. In fact, image is enhanced only when the slope is much greater than 1. Figure 6.2 shows the result of linear stretching. Sometimes only a portion of the graylevel range of the input image is strongly stretched to emphasize certain features of the image. For example, the transformation defined over $[l_{min}, l_{max}]$

$$l = \begin{cases} \dfrac{[3a - b - 2l_{min}] m + [b - a]l_{min}}{2[a - l_{min}]} & \text{for } l_{min} \leq m < a \\[3mm] \dfrac{4m - a - b}{2} & \text{for } a \leq m \leq b \\[3mm] \dfrac{[2l_{max} + a - 3b]m + [b - a]l_{max}}{2[l_{max} - b]} & \text{for } b < m \leq l_{max} \end{cases} \tag{6.5}$$

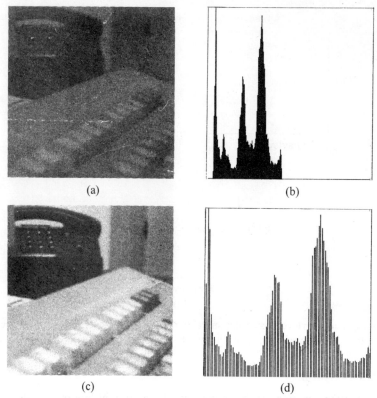

(a)   (b)

(c)   (d)

Fig. 6.2 Result of linear stretching: (a) original image, (b) graylevel histogram of (a), (c) enhanced image, (d) graylevel histogram of (c).

stretches the subrange $[a, b]$ by a factor of 2. The remaining portion of the entire graylevel range, i.e. $[l_{min}, a)$ and $(b, l_{max}]$ have been compressed to satisfy the condition 2. This is known as *piecewise stretching*. It should also be noted that the rate of stretching changes abruptly at $m = a$ and at $m = b$. Smoother changes may be achieved by employing non-linear transformation function.

Example   Suppose m be the graylevel of input image which has to be transformed to l by linear stretching. Then l is the graylevel of the output image. Let n_i and n'_i are the numbers of pixel having i-th graylevel in the input and the output images, respectively. Suppose for an 8-level image we have the following frequency table for the input graylevels.

i	0	1	2	3	4	5	6	7
n_i	0	0	a	b	c	d	e	0

Also given that a and e are greater than zero. So $m_{min} = 2$ and $m_{max} = 6$ and, since we are considering 8-level image, $l_{min} = 0$ and $l_{max} = 7$. Therefore, Equation (6.3) becomes

$$l = \frac{7}{4} (m - 2)$$

For $m = 3$. we have $l = 1.75 \approx 2$ and for $m = 4$ we have $l = 3.5 \approx 4$, and so on. Finally, we have the following frequency table for the output graylevels:

i	0	1	2	3	4	5	6	7
n'_i	a	0	b	0	c	d	0	e

∎

6.2.2 Non-linear Stretching

When the graylevel histogram shows high population of pixels in the lower graylevel zone of the gray scale, we may want to stretch this portion more at the cost of compressing the higher graylevel zone. In that case, it is customary to use logarithmic or similar type of transformation function. Secondly, when the image sensor exhibits an exponential response to the irradiance, then logarithmic transformation function is of particular importance to neutralize the effect. An example of such function is given below:

$$l = l_{max} \frac{\ln (m - m_{min} + 1)}{\ln (m_{max} - m_{min} + 1)} + l_{min} \tag{6.6}$$

or

$$\tilde{g}(r, c) = l_{max} \frac{\ln \{g(r, c) - m_{min} + 1\}}{\ln \{m_{max} - m_{min} + 1\}} + l_{min} \tag{6.7}$$

Such transformation functions are also useful when$\{g(r, c)\}$ occupies a very wide dynamic range. Fourier power (or amplitude) spectrum images are displayed using this transformation. Square root, cube root, or in general, n-th root functions are also useful in such situations.

   Example Suppose m be the graylevel of input image which has to be transformed to output image graylevel l by logarithmic stretching. Let n_i and n'_i are the numbers of pixel having i-th graylevel in the input and the output images respectively. Suppose for an 8-level image we have the following frequency table for the input graylevels.

i	0	1	2	3	4	5	6	7
n_i	a	b	c	d	e	f	g	h

Also given that a and h are greater than zero. So, $m_{min} = 0$ and $m_{max} = 7$, and since we are considering an 8-level image, $l_{min} = 0$ and $l_{max} = 7$. Therefore, Equation (6.6) becomes

$$l = 7 \frac{\ln (m + 1)}{\ln 8}$$

For $m = 1$ we have $l = 2.3 \approx 2$ and for $m = 2$ we have $l = 3.7 \approx 4$, and so on. Finally, we have the following frequency table for the output graylevels.

i	0	1	2	3	4	5	6	7
n'_i	a	0	b	0	c	$d+e$	f	$g+h$

∎

On the other hand, exponential or power law transformation functions are useful when the graylevel histogram shows high population of pixels in the high graylevel zone of the gray scale. These functions are also able to cancel the effect of logarithmic response of the image sensor to the irradiance. A transformation function of this class can be developed by incorporating the property of human visual system [Chanda et al. (1983, 1984), Foley et al. (1992)] as described below.

There is considerable experimental evidence indicating that the just-noticeable difference δB in brightness over the brightness B in its neighbourhood is approximately proportional to B (Weber's law). Thus the higher the B, δB must also be higher for visual detectability. Hence, $(\delta B + B)/B$ is constant and is equal to Weber ratio plus one. The discrete graylevels $\{l_i\}$ of the enhanced image can be chosen in such a way that ratio of l_{i+1} ($\equiv B_i + \delta B_i$) and l_i ($\equiv B_i$) be same for all i. Assuming $k = m_{max} - m_{min} + 1$ and $C = l_{i+1}/l_i$, we may write

$$\frac{l_2}{l_1} = \frac{l_3}{l_2} = \cdots = \frac{l_k}{l_{k-1}} = C$$

or

$$l_k = C \, l_{k-1} = C^2 \, l_{k-2} = \cdots = C^{k-1} l_1$$

So

$$C = \left(\frac{l_k}{l_1} \right)^{\frac{1}{m_{max} - m_{min}}}$$

Now $l_k = l_{max}$ and $l_1 = l_{min}$. Hence, graylevel m of the input image is mapped to the corresponding graylevel l in the enhanced image by the following transformation

$$l = l_{min} \left(\frac{l_{max}}{l_{min}} \right)^{\frac{m - m_{min}}{m_{max} - m_{min}}} \tag{6.8}$$

or

$$\tilde{g}(r, c) = l_{min} \left(\frac{l_{max}}{l_{min}} \right)^{\frac{g(r, c) - m_{min}}{m_{max} - m_{min}}} \tag{6.9}$$

This transformation recalibrates the grayscale in such a way that the difference in perceived brightness or contrast is same between any two consecutive graylevels. As a result, the overall perceived contrast of the image increases. It should be noted that implementation of this transformation must shift the grayscale to avoid l_{min} be equal to zero.

Example Suppose m be the graylevel of input image which has to be transformed to output image graylevel l by exponential stretching. Let n_i and n_i' are the numbers of pixel having i-th graylevel in the input and the output images, respectively. Suppose for an 8-level image we have the following frequency table for the input graylevels:

i	0	1	2	3	4	5	6	7
n_i	a	b	c	d	e	f	g	h

Also given that a and h are greater than zero. So $m_{min} = 0$ and $m_{max} = 7$, and since we are considering an 8-level image, $l_{min} = 0 + 1 = 1$ and $l_{max} = 7 + 1 = 8$. After transformation gray scale should be shifted back to its original position. Therefore, Equation (6.8) becomes

$$l = 8^{\frac{m}{7}} - 1$$

For $m = 1$ we have $l = 0.34 \approx 0$ and for $m = 2$ we have $l = 0.81 \approx 1$, and so on. Finally, we have the following frequency table for the output graylevels:

i	0	1	2	3	4	5	6	7
n_i^t	$a + b$	$c + d$	e	f	0	g	0	h

Results of logarithmic and exponential stretching are shown in Figs. 6.3 and 6.4 respectively.

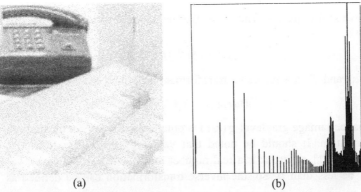

| (a) | (b) |

Fig. 6.3 Result of logarithmic stretching: (a) enhanced image, (b) graylevel histogram of (a). Original image is the same as in Fig. 6.2(a).

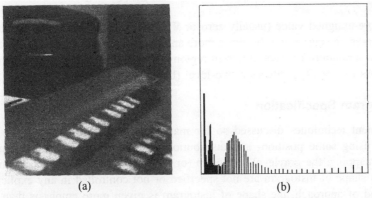

| (a) | (b) |

Fig. 6.4 Result of exponential stretching: (a) enhanced image, (b) gravlevel histogram of (a). Original image is the same as in Fig. 6.2(a).

6.2.3 Fuzzy Property Modification

The technique used here is based on the modification of pixel values in the fuzzy property domain [Pal and King (1980, 1981)]. To enter into this domain from the spatial domain values represented by $\{g(r, c)\}$ an S-type membership function, M, may be used. Where M is defined as

$$\mu(r, c) = M(g(r, c)) = \left[1 + \frac{l_{max} - g(r, c)}{F_d}\right]^{-F_e} \tag{6.10}$$

The fuzzifiers F_d and F_e are both greater than or equal to one. Exact values of F_d and F_e are selected in such a way that $M(l_t) = 0.5$ where l_t ($l_{min} \le l_t \le l_{max}$) is a threshold graylevel (also called *cross-over point*). The value of l_t is, of course, problem-dependent. The idea of enhancement operation is to decrease the membership values that are below 0.5 and to increase the same that are above 0.5. The transformation

$$T_1(\mu) = \begin{cases} 2\mu^2 & \text{for } 0 \le \mu \le 0.5 \\ 1 - 2(1 - \mu)^2 & \text{for } 0.5 \le \mu \le 1 \end{cases} \tag{6.11}$$

satisfies the above said objective. Therefore, the fuzzy property $\mu(r, c)$ of the pixels are modified by

$$\tilde{\mu}(r, c) = T_i(\mu(r, c)) \tag{6.12}$$

for $i = 1, 2, 3,\ldots$ and T_i is a recursive transformation defined as

$$T_i(\mu(r, c)) = T_1(T_{i-1}(\mu(r, c))) \tag{6.13}$$

Finally, the enhanced image graylevel $\tilde{g}(r, c)$ is obtained from $\tilde{\mu}(r, c)$ by applying an appropriate inverse transformation. It should be noted that values of $\mu(r, c)$ are restricted in the interval $[\alpha, 1]$, and not in $[0, 1]$, where α is a real number and $0 < \alpha \le 1$. However, value of $\tilde{\mu}(r, c)$ at some (r, c) can be less than α. So, the inverse transformation can be defined as

$$\tilde{g}(r, c) = \begin{cases} M^{-1}(\tilde{\mu}(r, c)) & \text{for } \alpha \le \tilde{\mu}(r, c) \le 1 \\ k & \text{for } \tilde{\mu}(r, c) < \alpha \end{cases} \tag{6.14}$$

where k is a pre-assigned value (usually zero or $M^{-1}(\alpha)$ depending on the problem in hand).

As i increases, the curve of T_i becomes more and more steeper near cross-over point resulting in less and less ambiguity between different regions. Thus, enhancement of the given image can be achieved. As $i \to \infty$, T_i produces a two-level (binary) image.

6.2.4 Histogram Specification

The enhancement techniques discussed so far map input image graylevel to the graylevel of output image using some position- and distribution-independent transformation function. As a result of this mapping, the graylevel histogram (or the p.d.f.) may change to certain extent. The changes in the shape of histogram are not specified or not controlled in any explicit manner. In a different kind of approach, the shape of histogram is given more emphasis than the previous ones [Gonzalez and Fittes (1975, 1977)]. It is evident that the shape of graylevel histogram gives an idea about the overall appearance of an image. For example, an image with a positively-skewed graylevel histogram [Fig. 6.5(a)] looks more bright than an image with negatively-skewed graylevel histogram [Fig. 6.5(b)]. This is because, in the former image the number of pixels having high gray values are greater than that in the latter image. It is believed that an image may be enhanced by mapping the input graylevels in such a way that the graylevel histogram (or the p.d.f.) of the processed image attains a desired shape. The simplest kind of these techniques is *histogram equalization*.

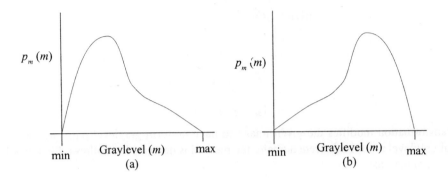

Fig. 6.5 Examples of (a) positively-skewed and (b) negatively-skewed histogram.

It is known that if there are L events with probability p_i associated with i-th event ($i = 0$, 1, 2, ..., $L - 1$) such that $\sum_{i=0}^{L-1} p_i = 1$, then the *entropy* or *information content* can be defined as

$$E = -\sum_{i=0}^{L-1} p_i \log p_i \qquad (6.15)$$

The entropy is maximum when p_i = constant for all i, i.e. every event has equal probability. In this case the constant = $1/L$. In the context of image processing, a pixel attains a particular graylevel which may be considered as an event. The entropy in an image is maximized when all graylevels have the same probability or the frequency of occurrence. That means the graylevel histogram or the p.d.f. would be uniform. In other words, every graylevel has equal importance in the appearance of the image.

For the time being, let us assume that the image graylevel is a continuous variable and lying in the interval [0, 1]. Suppose m and l represent the graylevels of input and output images, and $p_m(m)$ and $p_l(l)$ are their respective p.d.fs. It is seen experimentally (and also mentioned in the context of non-linear stretching) that if $p_m(m)$ be positively skewed then exponential stretching gives better result than that of linear stretching, whereas, if $p_m(m)$ be negatively skewed it is the logarithmic stretching that gives better result. In general, it may be argued that if the slope of the transformation be proportional to $p_m(m)$, i.e. if

$$\frac{dT(m)}{dm} = \frac{dl}{dm} = cp_m(m)$$

where c is a constant, then we should have reasonably good result. Supposing $c = 1$, we have the following transformation

$$l = T(m) = \int_0^m p_m(x)\, dx \qquad (6.16)$$

to modify the graylevels of the image, where x is a dummy variable representing input graylevel. Then the p.d.f. $p_l(l)$ of the transformed image is

$$p_l(l) = \left[p_m(m)\frac{dm}{dl} \right]_{m=T^{-1}(l)}$$

$$= \left[p_m(m)\frac{1}{p_m(m)} \right]_{m=T^{-1}(l)}$$

$$= [1]_{m=T^{-1}(l)} = 1$$

So, the transformation modifies the given image to have uniform graylevel p.d.f. irrespective of its original graylevel p.d.f. In discrete domain, the method is described as follows. First, we define the following notations:

M = Number of rows in the given digital image

N = Number of columns in the given digital image

$\{0, 1, 2, ..., l_{max} = L - 1\}$ = Allowable graylevels in the given digital image

n_i = Number of pixels having graylevel i

p_i = Probability that a pixel have graylevel $i = \dfrac{n_i}{M \times N}$

m_i = i-th Normalized graylevel in the given digital image = $\dfrac{i}{L - 1}$

l_i = i-th Graylevel in the output image

Using these notations, the transformation function is given as

$$l_i = (L - 1) \sum_{j=0}^{i} p_j \tag{6.17}$$

So, in the transformed image the number of pixels having graylevel l_i is same for all i. In other words, the height of the graylevel histogram of the transformed image is equal throughout its range, hence the name of this method. However, due to quantization error, uniformity of the graylevel histogram of the output image is achieved only approximately. The fact is revealed in Fig. 6.6 that presents the result of histogram equalization technique as in the following example.

 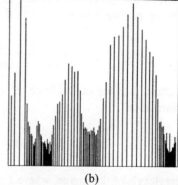

(a)   (b)

Fig. 6.6   Result of histogram equalization: (a) enhanced image, (b) gray-level histogram of (a). Original image is the same as in Fig. 6.2(a).

Example Suppose m be the graylevel of input image which has to be transformed to output image graylevel l by histogram equalization technique. Let n_i and n_i' are the numbers of pixel having i-th graylevel in the input and the output images, respectively. Suppose for an 8-level image of size 64×64 we have the following frequency table for the input graylevels.

m	0	1	2	3	4	5	6	7
n_m	123	78	281	417	639	1054	816	688

We see that $\sum_{m=0}^{7} n_m = 4096$, which is again equal to 64×64. So, probability $p_m = \dfrac{n_m}{4096}$ and cumulative probability $c_m = \sum_{i=0}^{m} p_i$. Then output graylevel is computed as $l = 7c_m$. The steps are revealed more vividly in the following table:

m	n_m	p_m	c_m	l
0	123	0.03	0.03	$0.21 \approx 0$
1	78	0.019	0.049	$0.34 \approx 0$
2	281	0.069	0.118	$0.82 \approx 1$
3	417	0.102	0.22	$1.54 \approx 2$
4	639	0.156	0.376	$2.62 \approx 3$
5	1054	0.257	0.633	$4.43 \approx 4$
6	816	0.199	0.832	$5.82 \approx 6$
7	688	0.168	1.0	7

Finally, we have the following frequency table for the output graylevels:

l	0	1	2	3	4	5	6	7
n_l	201	281	417	639	1054	0	816	688

■

It should be noted that if we modify the graylevel of an image that has uniform p.d.f. using inverse of the transformation given in Equation (6.16), then we will get an image that will have a p.d.f. similar to $p_m(m)$. Exploiting this knowledge, we can obtain any shape of the graylevel histogram by processing the given image in the following way. Suppose $p_m(m)$ and $p_l(l)$ represent the graylevel p.d.fs. of input and output images and m and l are respective graylevels. Also, suppose that k represents graylevel of some intermediate image result, i.e.

$$k = T_1(m) = \int_0^m p_m(x)\, dx$$

and

$$k = T_2(l) = \int_0^l p_l(x)\, dx$$

and in both the cases, either for $k = T_1(m)$ or for $k = T_2(l)$, $p_k(k)$ is uniform. Hence, the transformation

$$l = T_2^{-1}(T_1(m)) \tag{6.18}$$

achieves the desired result. This method is known as the *histogram specification*. Usually the shape of the graylevel histogram of the output image is specified interactively by graphics input device.

6.2.5 Modifying Graylevel Co-occurrence Matrix

Although histogram-based techniques are quite effective, sometimes a histogram cannot provide sufficient information required for processing. In those cases, it is desirable to use higher order image statistics such as *graylevel co-occurrence matrix* [Haralick (1979), Haralick et al. (1973)]. The idea (of image enhancement using graylevel co-occurrence matrix) is to choose a threshold that corresponds to the maximum of the average contrast of the image. Then using this threshold as a parameter, a transformation is devised to give a desirable shape to the co-occurrence matrix (or histogram).

Let $\{0, 1, 2, ..., L-1\}$ denotes the set of possible graylevels of a digital image with $M \times N$ pixels. Consider two pixels (r, c) and $(r + d \cos \theta, c - d \sin \theta)$. The latter pixel is at a distance d from the former one in the direction θ measured counter-clockwise with the vertical axis of the image. Then the gray level co-occurrence matrix $\mathbf{C}_\theta$ for the direction θ may be defined as $\mathbf{C}_\theta = \{\mathbb{C}_{\theta, m_1, m_2}\}$, where the (m_1, m_2)-th element of $\mathbf{C}_\theta$ is

$$\mathbb{C}_{\theta, m_1, m_2} \sum_{c=0}^{N-1} \sum_{r=0}^{M-1} \psi \ (g(r, c) = m_1 \wedge g(r + d \cos \theta, c - d \sin \theta) = m_2) \qquad (6.19)$$

If $\psi = 1$ the argument is true, otherwise, $\psi = 0$. For simplicity, d is taken to be 1 and θ is integer multiple of π. It is assumed that $g(M, c) = g(0, c)$, $g(r, N) = g(r, 0)$, $g(-1, c) = g(M-1, c)$ and $g(r, -1) = g(r, N-1)$. It is easy to see that $\mathbf{C}_\theta$ is an $L \times L$ matrix with $\mathbf{C}_0 = \mathbf{C}_\pi^T$ and $\mathbf{C}_{\pi/2} = \mathbf{C}_{3\pi/2}^T$, and also

$$\sum_{i=0}^{L-1} \mathbb{C}_{\theta, i, k} = \sum_{i=0}^{L-1} \mathbb{C}_{\theta, k, i} = n_k \qquad (6.20)$$

for all k, where n_k denotes the frequency of pixels having graylevel k. So, the co-occurrence matrix C (independent of direction) can now be computed as

$$\mathbb{C} = \{\mathbb{C}_{m_1, m_2}\} = \frac{1}{4}(\mathbf{C}_0 + \mathbf{C}_{\pi/2} + \mathbf{C}_\pi + \mathbf{C}_{3\pi/2}) \qquad (6.21)$$

For large M and N, the relative frequency of co-occurrence $P_{m_1, m_2} = \mathbb{C}_{m_1, m_2}/MN$ represents approximately the joint probability mass of the discrete variables m_1 and m_2. Henceforth, the co-occurrence matrix be assumed to have the elements P_{m_1, m_2} in place of $\mathbb{C}_{m_1, m_2}$.

For a given threshold t' let us define the average contrast in the given image as

$$\text{Con}_{m_1, m_2} (t') = \frac{\sum_{m_1=0}^{t'} \sum_{m_2=t'+1}^{L-1} (m_1 - m_2)^2 \, P_{m_1, m_2}}{\sum_{m_1=0}^{t'} \sum_{m_2=t'+1}^{L-1} P_{m_1, m_2}}$$

$$+ \frac{\sum_{m_1=t'+1}^{L-1} \sum_{m_2=0}^{t'} (m_1 - m_2)^2 \, P_{m_1, m_2}}{\sum_{m_1=t'+1}^{L-1} \sum_{m_2=0}^{t'} P_{m_1, m_2}} \qquad (6.22)$$

Detail derivation of this equation will be presented in Chapter 11. The graylevel t is called the *threshold of maximum average contrast* [Chanda et al. (1985), Chanda and Dutta Majumder (1988)], if

$$\text{Con}_{m_1, m_2}(t) = \max_{t'} \{\text{Con}_{m_1, m_2}(t')\} \tag{6.23}$$

In the discrete domain the transformation for output graylevel l is given by

$$l = \left\{ \left(\sum_{\alpha=0}^{m_1-1} \sum_{\beta=0}^{L-1} P_{\alpha,\beta} + \sum_{\beta=0}^{m_2} P_{m_1,\beta} \right) A_{t_0} - t_0^{2\lambda+1} \right\}^{\frac{1}{2\lambda+1}} + t_0 \tag{6.24}$$

where λ is a positive integer and $A_{t_0} = (L - 1 - t_0)^{2\lambda+1} + t_0^{2\lambda+1}$. Thus, for $0 \le m_1$, m_2 (or simply $m) \le L - 1$, we have $0 \le l \le L - 1$. The transformed threshold t_0 of the maximum average contrast can be obtained as

$$t_0 = (L - 1) \frac{\{a'/(1 - a')\}^{\frac{1}{2\lambda+1}}}{1 - \{a'/(1 - a')\}^{\frac{1}{2\lambda+1}}} \tag{6.25}$$

where

$$a' = \sum_{\alpha=0}^{t-1} \sum_{\beta=0}^{L-1} P_{\alpha,\beta} + \sum_{\beta=0}^{t} P_{t,\beta} \tag{6.26}$$

Experimental results are presented in Fig. 6.7.

6.2.6 Local Contrast Stretching

The linear and non-linear stretching as well as histogram and co-occurrence matrix modification methods discussed in the previous sections are *global*, in a sense that pixel intensities are modified by a position invariant transformation function. If the scene is illuminated by incident light of widely varying intensity, then it may happen that minimum and maximum graylevels in the recorded image are very close to $l_{\min}$ and $l_{\max}$ respectively, but the contrast over a small region is very poor. In such situation, there is very little scope to improve contrast by global transformation of graylevel. So, it is often necessary to stretch the contrast over a small area. The technique by which this can be achieved is called the *local contrast stretching*.

One interesting method suggested by Dorst (1982) has the following steps (assuming $l_{\min} = 0$ and $l_{\max} = L - 1$).

Step 1: Compute graylevel histogram over an $n \times n$ neighbourhood around the candidate pixel (r, c). Suppose l_l and l_h are the lowest and the highest graylevels in that region. Local graylevel range $(l_h - l_l)$ may be considered as a measure of local contrast.

Step 2: Modify graylevel at (r, c) as

$$\tilde{g}(r, c) = \begin{cases} \gamma\, g(r, c) - \dfrac{(\gamma - 1)(L - 1)l_l}{(L - 1) - (l_h - l_l)} & \text{if } (l_h - l_l) \le \dfrac{L - 1}{\gamma} \\[3mm] (L - 1) \dfrac{g(r, c) - l_l}{l_h - l_l} & \text{otherwise} \end{cases} \tag{6.27}$$

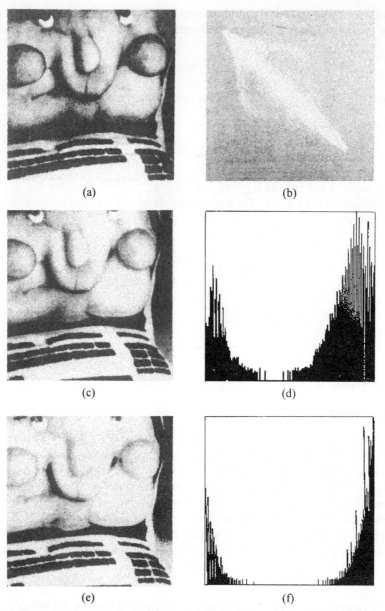

Fig. 6.7 Result of co-occurrence matrix modification: (a) original image, (b) graylevel co-occurrence matrix of the original image, (c) enhanced image for $\lambda = 1$, (d) graylevel histogram of (c), (e) enhanced image for $\lambda = 3$, (f) graylevel histogram of (e).

Here γ is the gain of the filter and is a global parameter supplied by the user. Figure 6.8 show the result of this algorithm for $n = 5$ and $\gamma = 2$. To make the filter noise insensitive, outliers are discarded by defining l_l and l_h as graylevels with percentile $L\%$ and $H\%$ respectively in the local histogram.

(a)   (b)   (c)

Fig 6.8   Result of local contrast stretching [Dorst (1982)] for $\gamma = 2$: (a) original image, (b) enhanced image
for $n = 3$, (c) enhanced image for $n = 5$.

In another approach [Narendra and Fitch (1981)], local graylevel statistics over a small neighbourhood is used to define the filter. For example, mean graylevel $\overline{g}(r, c)$ of pixels around an $n \times n$ neighbourhood of (r, c) may be a measure of local brightness. Similarly, the graylevel variance $\sigma^2(r, c)$ may be a measure of local contrast. The idea is to increase the contrast to greater degree if the initial local contrast is low. So, the gain $\gamma(r, c)$ should be inversely proportional to the local variance, i.e.

$$\gamma(r, c) = k \frac{\overline{g}}{\sigma^2(r,c)}, \qquad 0 < k \leq 1$$

where $\overline{g}$ is the global mean of image graylevel and k is a user-defined parameter. Hence, the transformation function is defined as

$$\tilde{g}(r, c) = \begin{cases} \gamma(r, c)[g(r, c) - \overline{g}(r, c)] + \overline{g}(r, c) & \text{if } \sigma^2(r, c) > t \\ g(r, c) & \text{otherwise} \end{cases} \qquad (6.28)$$

Here the transformation function amplifies the difference between the graylevel at the candidate pixel and the local brightness, and at the same time it preserves the local brightness level. Hence, the local contrast of the image is greatly increased. The threshold t prevents smooth regions from being rough.

6.3   Smoothing

Smoothing operation is used primarily to diminish the effect of spurious noise and to blur the false contours that may be present in a digital image. These unwanted effects may be due to detection and recording error or transmission channel noise or digitization error or some combination of these factors. During removal of noise, smoothing techniques may degrade the sharp important details. Smoothing algorithms have been developed in both spatial domain and frequency domain.

If we assume the absence of degradation except additive noise during the formation of image, Equation (5.22) is simplified to

$$g(r, c) = f(r, c) + \eta(r, c) \qquad (6.29)$$

for $r = 0, 1, 2, ..., M - 1$ and $c = 0, 1, 2, ..., N - 1$. In matrix-vector notation we may write this equation as

$$\mathbf{g} = \mathbf{f} + \eta \tag{6.30}$$

Equation (6.30) is same as Equation (5.24) except that the degradation matrix $\mathbf{H}$ is replaced by an identity matrix. Here we need to find some transformation T_{sm} which reduces the effect of spurious noises, i.e.

$$\overline{g}(r, c) = T_{sm} [g(r, c), Q(r, c)] \tag{6.31}$$

where $Q(r, c)$ is the set of graylevels of the neighbouring pixels.

6.3.1 Image Averaging

Suppose noise $\eta(r, c)$ is a zero mean pairwise uncorrelated. Then a set of n noisy images $\{g_i (r, c)\}$ can be given by

$$g_i (r, c) = f(r, c) + \eta_i (r, c) \tag{6.32}$$

Also suppose that $\eta_i(r, c)$ follows the same distribution for all i, $\sigma_\eta^2(r, c)$ be its variance. The assumptions are approximately valid if we consider, say, transmission channel noise only. That means if an image $f(r, c)$ is transmitted n times over some communication channel we may receive a set of noisy images $\{g_1(r, c), g_2(r, c), ..., g_n(r, c)\}$ at the receiver end. The objective is to recover $f(r, c)$ from the given set $\{g_i(r, c)\}$. By averaging n such images we get

$$\overline{g}(r, c) = \frac{1}{n}\sum_{i=0}^{n} g_i(r, c) = f(r, c) + \frac{1}{n}\sum_{i=0}^{n} \eta_i(r, c) = f(r, c) + \overline{\eta}(r, c)$$

for all r and c. Since noise has zero mean, for large n, $\overline{g}(r, c)$ approaches $f(r, c)$ and

$$\sigma_{\overline{\eta}(r, c)}^2 = \sigma_{\overline{g}(r, c)}^2 = \frac{1}{n}\sigma_{\eta(r, c)}^2$$

tends to zero as n increases. Though the method is very simple, registration[1] of different images might be a problem (Fig. 6.9).

6.3.2 Mean Filter

For a given image, noise cleaning methods are based on the concept of graylevel homogeneity within a neighbourhood. The techniques primarily replace the graylevel of the candidate pixel by some other graylevel that is more consistent with that over the neighbourhood around it. The noise is assumed to have zero mean and is assumed to be independent for any two pixels. Usually, noise is modelled to follow either uniform or Gaussian or some other symmetric distribution. Secondly, the scene is, in most of the cases, assumed to be a part of the planar world. As a result, the regions in the image have either constant or linearly varying graylevel. In other words, the intensity profile of the ideal (noise free) image can be represented by piecewise linear patches. Suppose

---

[1]Registration may be defined as placing more than one images in appropriate position with respect to each other.

Fig. 6.9 Result of image averaging technique. First eight images, in raster order, are noisy ones. Bottom-right image is the average of the first eight images.

graylevel at any pixel (m, n) within a neighbourhood $N_{(r, c)}$ around the candidate pixel (r, c) is modelled as

$$f(m, n) = A(m - r) + B(n - c) + C \qquad (6.33)$$

where A, B and C are constants for the equation of a plane. Therefore,

$$f(r, c) = C \qquad (6.34)$$

and

$$g(m, n) = f(m, n) + \eta(m, n) \qquad (6.35)$$

$$= A(m - r) + B(n - c) + C + \eta(m, n) \qquad (6.36)$$

Now to estimate the parameters A, B and C we minimize the error

$$e^2 = \sum_{(m,n) \, \in N_{(r,c)}} [\hat{A}(m - r) + \hat{B}(n - c) + \hat{C} - g(m, n)]^2 \qquad (6.37)$$

Taking partial derivatives of e^2 with respect to $\hat{A}$, $\hat{B}$ and $\hat{C}$, and equating them to zero, we get

$$\frac{\partial e^2}{\partial \hat{A}} = \sum_{(m,n) \, \in N_{(r,c)}} [\hat{A}(m - r) + \hat{B}(n - c) + \hat{C} - g(m, n)](m - r) = 0 \qquad (6.38)$$

$$\frac{\partial e^2}{\partial \hat{B}} = \sum_{(m,n) \, \in N_{(r,c)}} [\hat{A}(m - r) + \hat{B}(n - c) + \hat{C} - g(m, n)] \, (n - c) = 0 \qquad (6.39)$$

$$\frac{\partial e^2}{\partial \hat{C}} = \sum_{(m,n)\,\in N_{(r,c)}} [\hat{A}(m - r) + \hat{B}(n - c) + \hat{C} - g(m, n)] = 0 \tag{6.40}$$

If the neighbourhood under consideration be symmetric, i.e.

$$\sum_{(m,n)\,\in N_{(r,c)}} (m - r) = 0 \quad \text{and} \quad \sum_{(m,n)\,\in N_{(r,c)}} (n - c) = 0$$

Then, solving Equations (6.38)–(6.40) yields

$$\hat{C} = \frac{\Sigma_{(m,n)\,\in N_{(r,c)}} g(m, n)}{\Omega} \tag{6.41}$$

where Ω is the number of pixels in the neighbourhood $N_{(r,c)}$. In practice, $N_{(r,c)}$ is a $(2k + 1) \times (2k + 1)$ square around (r, c). In that case, the smooth graylevel $\bar{g}(r, c)$ is given by

$$\bar{g}(r, c) = \frac{1}{(2k + 1)(2k + 1)} \sum_{n=-k}^{k} \sum_{m=-k}^{k} g(m, n) \tag{6.42}$$

The value of k can be 1, 2, ..., etc. Masks are shown in Figs. 6.10(a) and 6.10(b) for $k = 1$ and $k = 2$, respectively. The operation is also called the *simple averaging* and can be represented by convolution as

$$\bar{g} = g * w_k \tag{6.43}$$

where w_k is called the *kernel* or *mask*. For $k = 2$, the result is shown in Fig. 6.11(b).

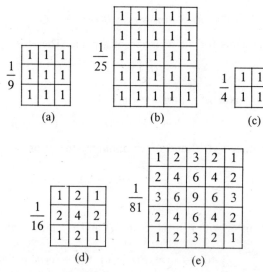

(a)   (b)   (c)

(d)   (e)

Fig. 6.10 Common masks used for noise cleaning by moving average filtering: (a) 3×3 and (b) 5×5 used in simple averaging, (c) the smallest symmetric mask (2×2) that can be used in simple averaging, (d) mask for weighted averaging that is generated by convolving the mask shown in (c) by itself, (e) a mask used for weighted averaging that is generated by convolving the mask (a) with itself.

The masks may be applied repetitively. The smallest symmetric mask of size 2×2 is shown in Fig. 6.10(c). Suppose this mask is used twice to remove the noise. Then

$$\bar{g} = (g * w) * w = g * (w * w) = g * w^{(2)}$$

The mask $w^{(2)}$ is shown in Fig. 6.10(d). We see that $w^{(2)}$ contains different weights at different positions. However, the weights are placed symmetrically with respect to the centre position. In general, any symmetric mask whose values are non-negative and decrease monotonically with distance from the centre position can be used for noise cleaning. The operation can be expressed as

$$\bar{g}(r, c) = \frac{\sum_{n=-k}^{k} \sum_{m=-k}^{k} w(m, n)g(m, n)}{\sum_{n=-k}^{k} \sum_{m=-k}^{k} w(m, n)} \tag{6.44}$$

Hence, all pixels within the neighbourhood contribute to the average value. The result of applying this method with a 5×5 mask [as shown in Fig. 6.10(e)] is shown in Fig. 6.11(c). These types of unselected averaging blur the edges and other sharp details as well. Secondly, the selection of mask size is a non-trivial task; because with the increase in size the edges and sharp details are blurred to a greater degree, even though the noise removal ability of the operator is more.

6.3.3 Ordered Statistic Filter

Problem of blurring the edges during smoothing can partly be overcome by *ordered statistic filter*. In the weighted averaging method smooth graylevel $\bar{g}(r, c)$ is obtained by a linear combination of $g(m, n)$ over a neighbourhood where weights are dependent on their relative position within the neighbourhood. On the other hand, in the ordered statistic filter [Bovik et al. (1983)], the weights are dependent on the order of the sorted graylevel over the neighbourhood. Suppose x_i ($i = 0, 1, 2,..., \Omega - 1$) represent the graylevel at the pixels in the neighbourhood region, and $x_{[i]}$ represent the same sorted in ascending order. Therefore, $x_{[0]}$ is the minimum graylevel while $x_{[\Omega-1]}$ is the maximum graylevel in the neighbourhood. The ordered statistic filter obtains the graylevel at the pixel (r, c) of the smooth image by the relation

$$\bar{g}(r, c) = \sum_{i=0}^{\Omega-1} w_i x_{[i]} \tag{6.45}$$

where w_i is the i-th weight.

Median filter

One of the most popular order statistic filter is the *median filter* [Tukey (1971)]. If Equation (6.45) is used to define the median filter, then we get

$$w_i = \begin{cases} 1 & \text{if } i = \dfrac{\Omega-1}{2} \\ 0 & \text{otherwise} \end{cases} \tag{6.46}$$

where Ω is an odd number. Median filter is very effective to remove impulsive noise. The result of median filter over a 5×5 neighbourhood is shown in Fig. 6.11(d). Though median filter is one of the most popular noise cleaning operator, its straightforward processing is remarkably slow. To speed-up the processing, fast median filter is designed [Chaudhuri (1983)]. Separable median filters have also been suggested by many researchers [Narendra (1981), Nodes and Gallagher (1983)].

Another order statistic filter is the *midrange filter* [Arce and Fontana (1988)] which may be defined by Equation (6.45) with

$$w_i = \begin{cases} \dfrac{1}{2} & \text{if } i = 0 \\[2mm] \dfrac{1}{2} & \text{if } i = \Omega - 1 \\[2mm] 0 & \text{otherwise} \end{cases} \tag{6.47}$$

In other words,

$$\bar{g}(r, c) = \frac{1}{2}(x_{[0]} + x_{[\Omega-1]}) \tag{6.48}$$

This filter is useful when the noise distribution has light and smooth tails. When the noise distribution has fat tails, one may use *trimmed-mean filter* [Bedner and Watt (1984)] defined as

$$\bar{g}(r, c) = \frac{1}{\Omega - 2k} \sum_{i=k}^{\Omega-k-1} x_{[i]} \tag{6.49}$$

So, here, simple average of only central $\Omega - 2k$ sorted values is taken.

Max-min and min-max filters

Max-filter and *min-filter* are also order statistic filters [Nakagawa and Rosenfeld (1978)]. They are defined as

$$\bar{g}(r, c) = \max_i \{x_{[i]}\} \tag{6.50}$$

$$\bar{g}(r, c) = \min_i \{x_{[i]}\} \tag{6.51}$$

respectively. In other words, the max and min operators may be defined in terms of Equation (6.45), where

$$\text{for max filter, } w_i = \begin{cases} 1 & \text{if } i = \Omega - 1 \\ 0 & \text{otherwise} \end{cases}$$

$$\text{for min filter, } w_i = \begin{cases} 1 & \text{if } i = 0 \\ 0 & \text{otherwise} \end{cases}$$

In general, these operators are defined as

$$g(r, c) = \max_{(m,n) \in N_{(r,c)}} g(m, n) \tag{6.52}$$

and

$$\bar{g}(r, c) = \min_{(m,n) \in N_{(r,c)}} g(m, n) \tag{6.53}$$

However, these operators alone cannot remove noise in the image. But when cascaded, i.e. if we apply max and min operators alternately they can remove certain kind of noise, such as salt-and-pepper noise, very efficiently. It should be noted that once max-min (or min-max) filter is applied then further application of it does not change the image. However, if min-max and max-min filters are applied alternately then result approaches towards median filtered image. Results of min-max and max-min filters over a 3×3 neighbourhood are shown in Figs. 6.11(f) and 6.11(g), respectively.

Morphological filter

A comparison of Equations (6.52) and (6.53) with Equations (2.104) and (2.105) reveals that max and min filters are special cases of graylevel dilation and erosion in two-dimensional space. Suppose h be a structuring element that is defined over the domain E, and the value of h at every pixel $(r, c) \in E$ is zero. Let us call such structuring element the *zero-height rod structuring element*. Now, if the shape of E be the same as that of $N_{(r, c)}$ with the origin at its centre, then

$$(g \oplus h)\,(r, c) = \max_{(m,n) \in N_{(r,c)}} g(m, n) \tag{6.54}$$

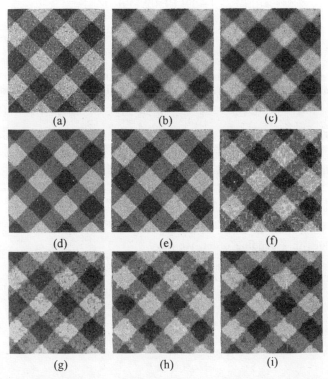

Fig. 6.11 Result of smoothing techniques. Figures (a) to (i) are arranged in left-to-right and top-to-bottom fashion. (a) original image. (b) result of mean filter over a 5×5 neighbourhood, (c) result of weighted averaging using a 5×5 mask as shown in Fig. 6.10(e), (d) result of median filter over a 5×5 neighbourhood, (e) result of edge-preserving smoothing over a 7×7 neighbourhood for $\lambda = 4$, (f) result of min-max filter over a 3×3 neighbourhood (g) result of max-min filter over a 3×3 neighbourhood, (h) result of min-max-max-min filter over a 3×3 neighbourhood. (i) result of max-min-min-max filter over a 3×3 neighbourhood.

$$(g \ominus h)(r, c) = \min_{(m,n) \in N_{(r,c)}} g(m, n) \tag{6.55}$$

Hence, it is evident that the morphological opening is equivalent to the min-max and the closing is equivalent to the max-min filters, respectively. Hence, Figs. 6.11(f) and 6.11(g) may also be described as the results of opening and closing morphological filters, respectively, using a 3×3 rod structuring element. As said earlier, max-min and min-max are increasing and idempotent. If we apply opening and closing alternately then we have the *alternating sequential filter* (ASF). In case of binary image, openings and closings are extremely useful for removing pepper noise and salt noise, respectively. Figures 6.11(h) and 6.11(i) show the results of two different ASFs, where max and min are computed using a 3×3 rod structuring element.

Example Consider the following figure where each small rectangle represents a pixel and the value inside it is graylevel at that pixel. Hence the whole array represents a digital image $g(r, c)$ of size 5×5. The centre pixel $g(2, 2)$ is marked by underline.

0	1	0	6	7
2	0	1	6	5
1	1	7	5	6
1	0	6	6	5
2	5	6	7	6

Suppose we smooth the image in a spatial domain using a 3×3 neighbourhood. Then for mean filter:

$$\overline{g}(2, 2) = \frac{1}{9}[0 + 1 + 6 + 1 + 7 + 5 + 0 + 6 + 6] = 3.55 \approx 4$$

For weighted average filter [using the mask shown in Fig. 6.10(d)]:

$$\overline{g}(2, 2) = \frac{1}{9}[1 \times 0 + 2 \times 1 + 1 \times 6 + 2 \times 1 + 4 \times 7 + 2 \times 5 + 1 \times 0 + 2 \times 6 + 1 \times 6]$$
$$= 7.33 \approx 7$$

By sorting the values in ascending order, we have
$$0, \ 0, \ 1, \ 1, \ 5, \ 6, \ 6, \ 6, \ 7$$

Hence, for median filter:
$$\overline{g}(2, 2) = 5$$

For min filter:
$$\overline{g}(2, 2) = 0$$

For max filter:
$$\overline{g}(2, 2) = 7 \qquad \blacksquare$$

6.3.4 Edge-preserving Smoothing

Conventional mean filtering, though simple and popular, cannot preserve edges in the image. For edge-preserving smoothing, we modify mean filter in the following way. The basic idea is to consider masks of various shapes and to position them at various places around the pixel which is to be smoothened. Then the average value of pixels belonging to each mask and some measure of homogeneity in the value of pixels belonging to that mask are computed. Finally, the smoothened value of the said pixel is computed by taking contributions of these average values proportional to corresponding homogeneity. Tomita and Tsuji (1977) used square masks, while Nagao and Matsuyama (1979) used square, pentagonal and hexagonal masks. In both the works, the average value corresponding to the mask that has the maximum homogeneity is taken as the smoothened value. Thus, average value of pixels that belong to the mask lying across an edge is never considered to compute the smoothened value. As a result, blurring of edge is avoided. A more general approach has been suggested by Chanda et al. (1983, 1984) as described below.

Consider the blocks B_1, B_2, B_3, B_4, B_5, B_6, B_7 and B_8 around the candidate pixel (r, c) to be smoothened as shown in Fig. 6.12(a). Suppose g_b is the average graylevels of pixels in the neighbourhood which is the union of these blocks. Let us modify $g(r, c)$, the graylevel of pixel (r, c), to $\bar{g}(r, c)$ such that it has a component of ratio of difference $g_b - g(r, c)$ to $g(r, c)$. The idea comes from Weber's ratio in human visual response. Thus, let

$$\bar{g}(r, c) = g(r, c)\left[1 + \gamma\frac{g_b - g(r, c)}{g(r, c)}\right] \tag{6.56}$$

where $0 < \gamma < 1$ is a weighting factor. This allows reasonable flexibility to a picture for adaptation. On simplification, Equation (6.56) takes the form

$$\bar{g}(r, c) = (1 - \gamma)\,g(r, c) + \gamma g_b \tag{6.57}$$

which is nothing but the weighted average of $g(r, c)$ and g_b, and can also be expressed by proper choices of weights α and β as

$$\bar{g}(r, c) = \frac{\alpha}{\alpha + \beta}g(r, c) + \frac{\beta}{\alpha + \beta}g_b \tag{6.58}$$

Let the average of graylevels of pixels within and on the boundary of B_i $(i = 1, 2, 3,..., 8)$ is g_{b_i}, then we can write

$$\bar{g}(r, c) = \frac{\alpha g(r, c)}{\alpha + \Sigma_{i=1}^{8}\beta_i} + \frac{\Sigma_{i=1}^{8}(\beta_i g_{b_i})}{\alpha + \Sigma_{i=1}^{8}\beta_i} \tag{6.59}$$

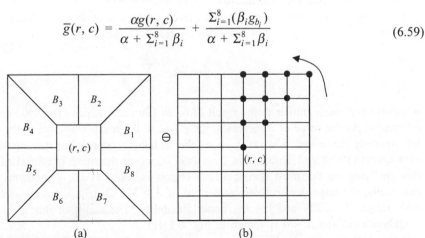

(a)   (b)

Fig. 6.12   (a) Sub-neighbourhoods B_1, B_2, etc., around candidate pixels, (b) discrete version of a triangular mask.

Now, g_{b_i} is given by

$$g_{b_i} = \frac{k\mu_i - g(r, c)}{k - 1} \tag{6.60}$$

where $(k - 1)$ is the number of pixels in block B_i and μ_i is the average graylevel including the candidate pixel (r, c). From Equations (6.59) and (6.60), we obtain

$$\bar{g}(r, c) = \frac{\alpha g(r, c)}{\alpha + \Sigma_{i=1}^{8} \beta_i} + \frac{\Sigma_{i=1}^{8} \left[\beta_i \dfrac{k\mu_i - g(r, c)}{k - 1} \right]}{\alpha + \Sigma_{i=1}^{8} \beta_i}$$

$$= \frac{1}{\alpha + \Sigma_{i=1}^{8} \beta_i} \left[\alpha - \frac{\Sigma_{i=1}^{8} \beta_i}{k - 1} \right] g(r, c) + \frac{k}{k - 1} \left[\frac{\Sigma_{i=1}^{8} \beta_i \mu_i}{\alpha + \Sigma_{i=1}^{8} \beta_i} \right] \tag{6.61}$$

If we put, $\alpha = \Sigma_{i=1}^{8} (w_i)^{\lambda}$ and $\beta_i = (k - 1)w_i^{\lambda}$ in Equation (6.61), then

$$\bar{g}(r, c) = \frac{\Sigma_{i=1}^{8} (w_i^{\lambda} \mu_i)}{\Sigma_{i=1}^{8} w_i^{\lambda}} \tag{6.62}$$

where, w_i is the new weighting factor and λ is any non-negative quantity which can be treated as a parameter of the filter. So, it is evident that μ_i is the mean graylevel of the pixels lying on i-th triangular mask as shown in Fig. 6.12(b). Suppose, σ_i denotes the correponding standard deviation in graylevel. The weighting factor may be defined as

$$w_i = \frac{\min \{\sigma_i \mid i = 1, 2, \ldots, 8\}}{\sigma_i}$$

where σ_i is taken as a measure of heterogeneity, then w_i is greater if the region under the mask is homogeneous and vice-versa. Now for different values of λ, the resulting filter [Equation (6.62)] smooths out spurious noises and preserve edges with different degrees.

For $\lambda = 0$, the graylevel of smoothened image becomes

$$\bar{g}(r, c) = \sum_{i=1}^{8} \frac{\mu_i}{8} \tag{6.63}$$

which is very much similar to the result of mean filter and which cleans the spurious noise most efficiently. As the value of λ increases, the effect of the mean graylevel of the region with lower homogeneity decreases. Also as $\lambda \to \infty$, the technique approaches towards that of Nagao and Matsuyama (1979) and Tomita and Tsuji (1977), where the mean graylevel of only those pixels that are lying on the most homogeneous region is taken as the smoothened graylevel. Thus, practically, the edge is effectively preserved, if $\lambda > 32$. Clearly, the method can operate with a wide range of quality and has the better flexibility. The result of this technique for a 7×7 neighbourhood and $\lambda = 4$ is shown in Fig. 6.11(e).

One of the major aspects in smoothing technique is the choice of the size of the neighbourhood. Because both the efficiency and the effectiveness of neighbourhood operators depend on the size of the mask used. A higher size of mask yields better noise cleaning but consequently gives rise to other difficulties such as blurring of the fine details. A compromise approach is to use a small mask and to iterate for better estimation.

6.3.5 Low-pass Filtering

Noise that causes sharp transition in graylevel contributes heavily to the high-frequency components of the Fourier transform of the image. This leads us to believe that suppression of high-frequency components removes such noise to some extent. Let us consider Equation (6.29). Taking the Fourier transform of the observed image $g(r, c)$ we can produce

$$G(u, v) = F(u, v) + N(u, v) \tag{6.64}$$

where, $G(u, v)$, $F(u, v)$ and $N(u, v)$ represent the Fourier transform of $g(r, c)$, $f(r, c)$ and $\eta\ (r, c)$, respectively. Suppose $T(u, v)$ is the impulse response of a filter in the Fourier domain. The filtered information is obtained by multiplying $T(u, v)$ with $G(u, v)$ for each (u, v) as in Equation (6.2), i.e.

$$\tilde{G}(u, v) = T\ (u, v)\ G(u, v)$$

Finally, smoothened image $\tilde{g}(r, c)$ is obtained by taking inverse Fourier transform of $\tilde{G}(u, v)$. Most popular and the simplest filter for this purpose is the ideal low-pass filter that may be defined as

$$T(u, v) = \begin{cases} 1, & \text{if } u^2 + v^2 \leq F_c \\ 0, & \text{otherwise} \end{cases} \tag{6.65}$$

where F_c is a predefined constant equivalent to *cut-off frequency* in one-dimension. The filter is radially symmetric and completely attenuates Fourier components that lie outside the circle of radius F_c and passes everything unaffected inside it. The main problem of this approach is that the filter de-emphasizes the edge information, because, like noise, edges also contribute to the high-frequency components. As a result, edges become blurred in the smoothened image. This problem may be avoided, only to some extent, if the rate of transition of response of the filter function from 1 to 0 is slowed down. With this idea, filters like *trapezoidal filter*, *exponential filters*, *Butterworth filter*, etc, are designed [Gonzalez and Wintz (1977)]. All these filters are radially symmetric too. They are more commonly called *low-emphasis filter*. Secondly, since

$$G(u, v)\ T(u, v) \Leftrightarrow g(r, c) * t(r, c)$$

where $t(r, c)$ is the impulse response of the filter in the spatial domain. Hence the low-pass filtering is equivalent to the weighted averaging technique as described earlier.

6.4 Image Sharpening

We have already explained that image degradation generally involves blurring. Being an integration operation blurring attenuates high spatial frequency components which suggests that observed/recoded image can be enhanced by differentiation in spatial domain. So, using spatial domain technique, the graylevel of sharpened image $g'(r, c)$ may be obtained as

$$g'(r, c) = \nabla^2 g(r, c) \tag{6.66}$$

where ∇^2 is Laplacian which is linear, rotation invariant, second-order derivative operator. In discrete domain, $\nabla^2 g$ is approximated in different types of connectivity as under:

Using 4-connectivity,

$$g'(r, c) = \nabla^2 g(r, c)$$

$$= \frac{1}{4}[g(r - 1, c) + g(r + 1, c) + g(r, c - 1)$$

$$+ g(r, c + 1) - 4g(r, c)] \tag{6.67}$$

$$= g_{b4} - g(r, c) \tag{6.68}$$

and using 8-connectivity,

$$g'(r, c) = \nabla^2 g(r, c)$$

$$= \frac{1}{8}[g(r - 1, c - 1) + g(r - 1, c) + g(r - 1, c + 1)$$

$$+ g(r, c - 1) + g(r, c + 1) + g(r + 1, c - 1)$$

$$+ g(r + 1, c) + g(r + 1, c + 1) - 8g(r, c)] \tag{6.69}$$

$$= g_{b8} - g(r, c) \tag{6.70}$$

where g_{bn} represents the average graylevel of n-nearest neighbours. However, problem due to simple application of the Laplacian operator is that the sharpened image $g'(r, c)$ contains only the enhanced edges, and the graylevels of different smooth regions are mapped to almost same graylevels (approximately zero). Hence, $g'(r, c)$ cannot be further used for region extraction (where more than two types of regions are present in the original image). This problem can be surmounted by adding grayvalues of the observed image with the negative of the Laplacian. The method is called *crispening*. So, the crispened image is defined as

$$g'(r, c) = g(r, c) - \nabla^2 g(r, c) \tag{6.71}$$

where the graylevels of all different smooth regions are left unaffected. In discrete domain, we may write using 4-connectivity,

$$g'(r, c) = g(r, c) - [g_{b4} - g(r, c)] = 2\,g(r, c) - g_{b4} \tag{6.72}$$

and using 8-connectivity,

$$g'(r, c) = g(r, c) - [g_{b8} - g(r, c)] = 2\,g(r, c) - g_{b8} \tag{6.73}$$

Example Consider the following figure where each small rectangle represents a pixel and the value inside it is graylevel at that pixel. Hence whole array represents a digital image $g(r, c)$ of size 5×5. The centre pixel $g(2, 2)$ is marked by underline.

0	1	0	6	7
2	0	1	6	5
1	1	_7_	5	6
1	0	6	6	5
2	5	6	7	6

Suppose we sharpen the image in spatial domain using Laplacian. Then, due to Equation (6.67):

$$g'(r, c) = \frac{1}{4}(1 + 1 + 5 + 6 - 4 \times 7) = -3.75 \approx -4$$

due to Equation (6.69):

$$g'(r, c) = \frac{1}{8}[0 + 1 + 6 + 1 + 5 + 0 + 6 + 6 - 8 \times 7] = -3.875 \approx -4$$

due to Equation (6.72):

$$g'(r, c) = 2 \times 7 - \frac{1}{4}(1 + 1 + 5 + 6) = 10.75 \approx 11$$

due to Equation (6.73):

$$g'(r, c) = 2 \times 7 - \frac{1}{8}[0 + 1 + 6 + 1 + 5 + 0 + 6 + 6) = 10.875 \approx 11 \qquad \blacksquare$$

The problem associated with implementation of Equations (6.68), (6.70), (6.72) and (6.73) is that all of them increase the effect of noise rather than reducing it. We recall Equation (5.24) where the observed image vector $\mathbf{g}$ is related to original image vector $\mathbf{f}$ and noise η as $\mathbf{g} = [H]\mathbf{f} + \eta$ or

$$g(r, c) = h(r, c) * f(r, c) + \eta(r, c) \qquad (6.74)$$

for $r = 0, 1, 2,..., M - 1$ and $c = 0, 1, 2, ..., N - 1$. $h(r, c)$ is the blurring operator. Presence of noise term $\eta(r, c)$ restricts us to use the Laplacian indiscriminately. So, we are to find out a transformation T_{sh} which sharpens or highlights the edge information and reduces the effect of spurious noises, i.e.

$$g'(r, c) = T_{sh}(g(r, c), Q(r, c)) \qquad (6.75)$$

where $Q(r, c)$ is the set of graylevels of the neighbouring pixels. We incorporate a characteristic of human visual system in deriving the sharpening transformation, since human visual system can smooth and sharpen an image simultaneously. In the section describing edge-preserving smoothing, it has already been mentioned that incorporation of human visual response to smooth an image leads us to select the transformation function of the form [see Equation (6.56)]

$$\overline{g}(r, c) = g(r, c)\left[1 + \gamma\frac{g_{bn} - g(r, c)}{g(r, c)}\right] \qquad (6.76)$$

Since, we are interested in obtaining a sharpened image from a smooth one, sharpening transformation can be given by [from Equation (6.76)]

$$g(r, c) = \frac{1}{1 - \gamma}\overline{g}(r, c) - \left(\frac{1}{1 - \gamma} - 1\right)g_{bn} \qquad (6.77)$$

Using prior notations for sharpening technique, this equation can be rewritten as

$$g'(r, c) = \gamma' g(r, c) - (\gamma' - 1)g_{bn} \qquad (6.78)$$

where γ' $(1 < \gamma' < \infty)$ is a new weighting factor. It can be shown that for different values of γ' and n, Equation (6.78) works in various ways. For example, for $\gamma' = 2$ and $n = 4$, Equation (6.78) becomes similar to Equation (6.72); for $\gamma' = 2$ and $n = 8$, Equation (6.78) becomes similar to Equation (6.73). Again when $\gamma' \gg 1$, Equation (6.78) becomes similar to either of Equations (6.68) and (6.70) multiplied by the constant γ'/n. Equation (6.78) can also be represented as

$$g'(r, c) = \frac{\alpha + \beta}{\alpha} g(r, c) - \frac{\beta}{\alpha} g_{bn} \tag{6.79}$$

for $\alpha > 0$ and $\beta > 0$. During identification or recognition of a scene, human visual system does not sharpen the image in all possible directions. In fact, it tries to enhance the edges only in the direction of maximum variance of graylevels, so in developing an equivalent transformation we should break up the entire neighbourhood of the candidate pixel (r, c) into the blocks B_1, B_2, B_3, B_4, B_5, B_6, B_7 and B_8 as shown in Fig. 6.12(a). Let the average graylevels of pixels lying within and on the boundary of block B_i ($i = 1, 2, 3,..., 8$) be g_{bi}. So, Equation (6.79) can be written as

$$g'(r,c) = \frac{\alpha + \Sigma_{i=1}^{8} \beta_i}{\alpha} g(r, c) - \frac{\Sigma_{i=1}^{8} (\beta_i g_{b_i})}{\alpha} \tag{6.80}$$

where g_{b_i} can be obtained from the relation given in Equation (6.60). Substituting Equation (6.60) in Equation (6.80) and simplifying, we obtain

$$g'(r, c) = g(r, c) - \frac{\Sigma_{i=1}^{8} [\beta_i \{\mu_i - g(r, c)\}]}{\alpha(k - 1)/k} \tag{6.81}$$

Putting $\beta_i = (w_i')^\lambda$ and $\alpha = k\Sigma_{i=1}^{8}(w_i')^\lambda/(k - 1)$, we get

$$g'(r, c) = g(r, c) - \frac{\Sigma_{i=1}^{8} [(w_i')^\lambda \{\mu_i - g(r, c)\}]}{\Sigma_{i=1}^{8} (w_i')^\lambda} \tag{6.82}$$

where w_i' is the weighting factor and λ is a non-negative quantity which can be treated as the parameter of the transformation function. μ_i and σ_i are the same as described in the edge-preserving smoothing technique. Here, we use the same triangular mask as shown in Fig. 6.12(b). Then, w_i' is given by

$$w_i' = \frac{\sigma_i}{\max\{\sigma_i\}}$$

Human visual system has another property that it can detect and ignore any isolated noisy pixel in a smooth region. This property may be incorporated here by defining new graylevel as

$$g'(r, c) = \begin{cases} \Sigma_{i=1}^{8} \dfrac{\mu_i}{8} & \text{if } \max\{\sigma_i\} - \min\{\sigma_i\} < t_\sigma \\[4mm] g(r, c) - \dfrac{\Sigma_{i=1}^{8}[(w_i')^\lambda \{\mu_i - g(r, c)\}]}{\Sigma_{i=1}^{8} (w_i')^\lambda} & \text{otherwise} \end{cases} \tag{6.83}$$

where t_σ is a threshold and is chosen *a priori* based on smoothness. Value of t_σ is usually very low because the presence of peak noise in a smooth region is revealed by the fact that the variances in graylevel in all directions are almost same. Equation (6.83) forms a band-pass filter in spatial domain. This can characterize human visual system approximately [Hall (1979)]. It is observed that, for different values of λ, the sharpening transformation [Equation (6.82)] sharpens the image to different degree. As the value of λ increases contributions due to masks having higher non-homogeneity (or variance) increases. If $\lambda \to \infty$, $g'(r, c)$ is obtained by taking the contribution of the masks having the highest variance only.

Results of this algorithm are shown in Figs. 6.13 and 6.14. Figure 6.13(a) is obtained by adding random noise to an ideal synthetic image and then blurring it, and Fig. 6.14(a) is obtained by adding random noise to Fig. 6.13(a). One of the major problems of this algorithm is the selection of the values for λ and k. Because both the efficiency and the effectiveness of the neighbour weighting algorithms depend on the size of the neighbourhood (or mask) as well as the weightages. A bigger size of mask makes the algorithm more insensitive to noise, but consequently it thickens the enhanced edges and some fine details may be lost. It is already explained that λ = 0 or $\lambda > 32$ leads to two extreme cases.

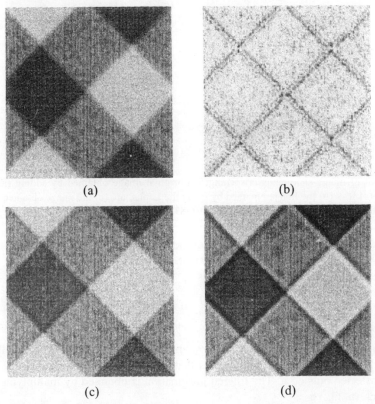

(a)   (b)

(c)   (d)

Fig. 6.13 Results of image sharpening and crispening: (a) original image, (b) the image obtained by using the Laplacian, (c) the image obtained by subtracting (b) from (a), (d) the result of Equation (6.83) for $\lambda = 4$ and $t_\sigma = 15$.

6.4.1 High-pass Filtering

As argued in Section 6.3.5, edges between two different regions contribute heavily to the high-

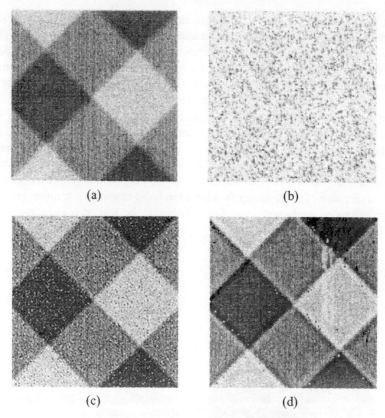

Fig. 6.14 Result of image sharpening/crispening: (a) original image obtained by adding random noise to Fig. 6.13(a), (b) the image obtained by using the Laplacian, (c) the image obtained by subtracting (b) from (a), (d) the result of Equation (6.83) for $\lambda = 4$ and $t_\sigma = 15$.

frequency components of the Fourier transform of the image. Therefore, highlighting high-frequency components we can sharpen edges to some extent. Most popular and the simplest filter for this purpose is the ideal high-pass filter defined as

$$T(u, v) = \begin{cases} 1, & \text{if } u^2 + v^2 > F_c \\ 0, & \text{otherwise} \end{cases} \tag{6.84}$$

where F_c is a predefined constant equivalent to *cut-off frequency*. The filter is radially symmetric and completely attenuates Fourier components that lie inside the circle of radius F_c and passes everything unaffected outside it. The filtered information is obtained by multiplying $T(u, v)$ with $G(u, v)$ for each (u, v), i.e.

$$G'(u, v) = G(u, v) \, T(u, v) \tag{6.85}$$

Finally, sharpened image $g'(r, c)$ is obtained by taking the inverse Fourier transform of $G'(u, v)$. The main problem of this approach is that noise is also enhanced because it contributes to the high-frequency components. This problem may be avoided to some extent by using suitable high-emphasis filters like *trapezoidal filter*, *exponential filter*, *Butterworth filter*, etc., where the rate of transition of response of the filter from 0 to 1 is slowed down [Gonzalez and Wintz (1977)].

6.4.2 Homomorphic Filtering

Let us assume a point-spread function of the image formation process in a unity transformation and noise-free situation. Then the matrix H in Equation (5.24) is an identity matrix and η is a zero vector. Equation (4.14) suggests that observed image $g(r, c)$ is the product of the irradiance falling on the reflectance of the surface [as in Equation (4.14)], i.e.

$$g(r, c) = R(r, c)I(r, c) \qquad (6.86)$$

where $R(r, c)$ and $I(r, c)$ are the reflectance and irradiance respectively at the point (r, c). In ideal case, I is assumed to be constant. But if illumination over the scene varies, i.e. $I(r, c)$ be different at different location, then some degradation is introduced in the image. This degradation may be considered as an example of *multiplicative noise*. In practice, variation in $I(r, c)$ is much less than that of $R(r, c)$. So, such degradation may be corrected as under:

1. Take logarithm of graylevel of the observed image at each pixel. That gives

$$\log [g(r, c)] = \log [R(r, c)] + \log [I(r, c)] \qquad (6.87)$$

   So, multiplicative noise now has become additive noise. Secondly, since 'logarithm' is an increasing mapping, variation in $\log [I(r, c)]$ is much less than that of $\log [R(r, c)]$.

2. Take the Fourier transform of $\log [g(r, c)]$ and then suppress the noise $\log [I(r, c)]$ by passing it through a *high-pass filter* (HPF). Then take inverse Fourier transform of the outcome of the HPF.

$$\tilde{g}_l(r, c) = \mathbf{F}^{-1} [\mathbf{H}(u, v)\mathbf{F}\{\log [g(r, c)]\}] \qquad (6.88)$$

3. Finally, take exponential of values $\tilde{g}_l(r, c)$ at every (r, c) and scale them to 0–255 to obtain the enhanced image $\tilde{g}(r, c)$.

The technique is called *homomorphic filtering* [Stockham, Jr. (1972)]. Note that to avoid computing logarithm of zero, 1 is first added to $g(r, c)$ and then the subsequent manipulation is done accordingly.

Summary

In this chapter, image enhancement techniques that improve the quality of image through some ad hoc approach are presented. The methods described can be classified into three groups: contrast intensification, noise cleaning, and edge sharpening. Any particular technique that may be applied on an image depends on subjective quality of the image as well as the purpose of processing of the said image.

Finally, it should be noted that more than one enhancement techniques may be applied to achieve the desired result. However, selection of suitable methods and the order in which they are applied are completely ad hoc in nature and depend on the users choice. A more systematic and mathematically well-founded method for improving the image quality is the restoration technique which will be discussed in the next chapter.

Problems

1. An 8-bit input image has to be enhanced by stretching graylevel range [96, 169] by a factor of 2. The remaining parts of the grayscale should be compressed at a uniform rate. Write down the graylevel transformation function for the purpose.

2. A 12-bit image has to be displayed on an 8-bit display device. Suggest a suitable transfer function such that displayed image shows as much intensity variation as possible.

3. (a) Graylevel histogram of an image is given below.

Graylevel	0	1	2	3	4	5	6	7
Frequency	400	700	1350	2500	3000	1500	550	0

Compute the graylevel histogram of the output image obtained by enhancing the input by the histogram equalization technique.

(b) Give an example where histogram equalization technique compresses the discrete graylevel range of the image.

4. State the underlying assumptions and derive the expression of mean filter.

5. Prove that order statistic filtering commutes with any linear monotonically increasing transformation.

6. Generate a 256-level noisy image by adding an uniformly distributed noise in the interval [−50, 50] with zero mean to a good contrasted image. Observe the performance of (i) mean filter, (ii) median filter, (iii) max-min filter and (iv) min-max filter. Note the time required in each case.

7. Generate a noisy image by adding the Gaussian noise with $\mu = 0$ and $\sigma = 16$. Observe the performance of (i) mean filter, (ii) median filter, (iii) max-min filter and (iv) min-max filter. Note the time required in each case.

8. Show that crispened image can be obtained by convolving it with the mask:

0	−1	0
−1	5	−1
0	−1	0

Bibliography

Ahuja, N. and Rosenfeld, A., 'A note on the use of second-order graylevel statistics for threshold selection', *IEEE Trans. on Syst., Man, and Cybern.* SMC-**8**:895–898, 1978.

Arce, G.R. and Fontana, S.A., 'On the midrange estimator', *IEEE Tr. on Acous. Speech and Signal Proc.* ASSP-**36**:920–922, 1988.

Bedner, J.B. and Watt, T.L., 'Alpha-trimmed mean and their relationships to median filters', *IEEE Tr. on Acous. Speech and Signal Proc.* ASSP-**32**:145–153, 1984.

Bovik, A.C., Huang, T.S. and Munson, D.C., 'A generalization of median filtering using linear combinations of order statistics'. *IEEE Trans. Acous., Speech, and Signal Processing*, ASSP-**31:**1342–1350, 1983.

Chanda, B., Chaudhuri, B.B. and Dutta Majumder, D., 'Some techniques for image enhancement, edge detection, and smoothing', *J. Inst. Electron. and telecomm. Engrs.*, **29:**189–193, 1983.

Chanda, B., Chaudhuri, B.B. and Dutta Majumder, D, 'Some algorithms for image enhancement incorporating human visual response', *Pattern Recognition*, **17:**423–428, 1984.

Chanda, B., Chaudhuri, B.B. and Dutta Majumder, D, 'On image enhancement and threshold selection using graylevel cooccurrence matrix', *Pattern Recognition Letters*, **3:**243–251, 1985.

Chanda, B. and Dutta Majumder, D, 'A note on use of graylevel cooccurrence matrix in threshold selection', *Signal Processing*, **15:**149–167, 1988.

Chaudhuri, B.B, 'Efficient algorithm for image enhancement', *Proc. IEEE*, **130:**91–97, 1983.

Deravi, F. and Pal, S.K., 'Graylevel thresholding using second-order statistics', *Pattern Recognition Letters*, **1:**417–422, 1983.

Dorst, L., 'A local contrast enhancement filter', in *Proc. of the 6th Intl. Conference on Pattern Recognition*, pp. 604–606, Munich, Germany, 1982.

Foley, J., Van Daam, A., Feiner, S. and Hughes, J., *Computer Graphics: Principles and Practice*, Addison-Wesley, Reading, Massachusetts, 1992.

Gonzalez, R.C. and Fittes, B.A., 'Graylevel transformations for interactive image enhancement', in *Proc. 2nd Conf. on Remotely Manned Systems*, pp. 17–19, 1975.

Gonzalez, R.C. and Fittes, B.A., 'Graylevel transformations for interactive image enhancement', *Mechanism and Machine Theory*, **12:**111–122, 1977.

Gonzalez, R.C. and Wintz, P., *Digital Image Processing,* Addison-Wesley, Reading, Massachusetts, 1977.

Hall, E.L., *Computer Image Processing and Recognition,* Academic Press, New York, 1979.

Haralick, R.M., 'Statistical and structural approaches to texture', *Proc. IEEE*, **67:**786–804, 1979.

Haralick, R.M., Shanmugam, K. and Dinstein, I., 'Textural features for image classification', *IEEE Trans. on Syst., Man, and Cybern.* SMC-**3:**610–621, 1973.

Kittler, J., Illingworth, J., Foglein, J. and Paler, K., 'An automatic thresholding algorithm and its performance', in *Proc. 7th Int. Conf. on PR*, pp. 287–289, Montreal, 1984.

Nagao, M. and Matsuyama, T., 'Edge preserving smoothing', *Computer Graphics and Image Processing*, **9:**394–407, 1979.

Nakagawa, Y. and Rosenfeld, A., 'A note on the use of local min and max operation in digital picture processing', *IEEE Tr. on System, Man and Cybern.*, SMC-**8:**632–635, 1978.

Narendra, P.M., 'A separable median filter for image noise smoothing', *IEEE Tr. on Patt. Anal. and Mach. Intell.* PAMI-**3:**20–29, 1981.

Narendra, P.M. and Fitch, R.C., 'Real-time adaptive contrast enhancement', *IEEE Trans. on Pattern Analysis and Machine Intelligence*, PAMI-**3:**655–661, 1981.

Nodes, T.A. and Gallagher, N.C., 'Two-dimensional root structures and convergence properties of the separable median filter', *IEEE Tr. on Acous. Speech and Signal Proc.*, ASSP-**31:**1350–1365, 1983.

Pal, S.K. and King, R.A., 'Image enhancement using fuzzy sets', *Electron. Letters*, **16:**376–378, 1980.

Pal, S.K. and King, R.A., 'Image enhancement using smoothing with fuzzy sets', *IEEE Trans. on Syst., Man, and Cybern.*, SMC-**11:**494–501, 1981.

Rosenfeld, A. and Kak, A.C., *Digital Picture Processing*, 2nd ed., Vols. 1 and 2, Academic Press, New York, 1982.

Stockham, T.G., Jr. 'Image processing in the context of a visual model', *Proc. IEEE*, **60:**828–842, 1972.

Tomita, F. and Tsuji, S., 'Extraction of multiple regions by smoothing in selective neighbourhoods', *IEEE Trans. on System, Man and Cybern,* SMC-**7:**107–109, 1977.

Tukey, J., *Exploratory Data Analysis*, Addison-Wesley, Menlo Park, California, 1971.

Weszka, J.S. and Rosenfeld, A., 'Threshold evaluation technique,' *IEEE Trans. on System, Man, and Cybern.*, SMC-**8:**622–629, 1978.

Chapter 7

Restoration

7.1 Introduction

One of the major application areas of image processing techniques is improving the quality of recorded images. No imaging system gives images of perfect quality because of degradations caused by various reasons. So, the image needs to be restored for subsequent computer processing and/or human viewing. Image restoration technique deals with those images that have been recorded in the presence of one or more sources of degradation. The *restoration* technique can be defined as the estimation of the original image or ideal image from the observed one by the effective inversion of degradation phenomena through which the scene was imaged. This technique requires the knowledge of the degradation phenomena. All deterministic models (whether linear or non-linear, space-invariant or space-variant) are based upon the concept of a point-spread function. We shall concentrate on linear, space-invariant degradation model given by Equation (5.22):

$$g(r, c) = \sum_{j=0}^{N-1} \sum_{i=0}^{M-1} f(i, j)h(r - i, c - j) + \eta(r, c)$$

for $r = 0, 1, 2, ..., M - 1$, and $c = 0, 1, 2, ..., N - 1$. In matrix–vector notation [Equation (5.24)]:

$$\mathbf{g} = \mathbf{Hf} + \eta$$

where $\mathbf{g}$, $\mathbf{f}$ and η are MN-dimensional vectors, and $\mathbf{H}$ is a $MN \times MN$ block circulant matrix. Here, h or $\mathbf{H}$ represents the degradation process embedded in the image formation process. There are various sources of such degradation which may be grouped into the following categories:

1. Point degradation
2. Spatial degradation
3. Temporal degradation
4. Chromatic degradation
5. Combination of the above

Since we have assumed the neighbourhood process for the image formation (see Chapter 4), we consider only the *spatial degradation*. Some common examples of the spatial degradation are (i) atmospheric turbulence, (ii) motion blur and (iii) defocussed system. Space-invariant point-spread function for these types of blurring may be described as follows:

1. Severely defocussed lens with circular aperture stop [Goodman (1968)]:

$$H(\omega_x, \omega_y) = \frac{J_1(a\rho)}{a\rho}, \quad \rho = \sqrt{\omega_x^2 + \omega_y^2} \tag{7.1}$$

where $J_1(.)$ stands for the first order Bessel function.

2. Long-term exposure of atmospheric turbulence [McGlamery (1967)]:

$$H(\omega_x, \omega_y) = \exp\left\{-\frac{(\omega_x^2 + \omega_y^2)}{2\sigma^2}\right\} \tag{7.2}$$

3. Uniform motion blur [Andrews and Hunt (1977)]:

$$H(\omega_x, \omega_y) = \frac{\sin a(\omega_x \cos\theta + \omega_y \sin\theta)}{\omega_x \cos\theta + \omega_y \sin\theta} \tag{7.3}$$

$H(\omega_x, \omega_y)$ is the Fourier domain representation of two-dimensional point-spread function in continuous domain. In discrete domain, $H(\omega_x, \omega_y)$ may be replaced by $H(u, v)$. Another source of degradation is, of course, additive noise η.

Thus, the digital image restoration problem can be viewed by obtaining an approximation to f, say $\hat{f}$, given the observed image g and the degradation matrix H due to the point-spread function. The knowledge about η may be limited to information about its statistical nature. We find out an inverse operator Φ, which gives the restored image.

One of the most essential issues to be considered is the fact that image restoration is an ill-conditioned problem at best and a singular problem at worst which may be explained briefly as follows. We have already stated that the image restoration problem is to find the inverse transformation such that

$$\Phi(g) \rightarrow \hat{f} \tag{7.4}$$

In Fourier domain, Φ is called the *filter function* $P(u, v)$. Mathematically, the problem of image restoration corresponds to the existence and uniqueness of the inverse operator. Both the existence and uniqueness phenomena are important. If the inverse operator does not exist then there is no mathematical basis for asserting that f can be recovered from g. The problem for which there is no inverse operator, i.e. Φ does not exist is said to be *singular*. In that case, the denominator of $P(u, v)$ is equal to zero for some (u, v). On the other hand, Φ may exist but *not unique*. In that case, there may be more than one Φ, which is dependent on f. Finally, even if Φ exists and is unique, it may be *ill-conditioned* (or *near-singular*), by which we mean that a trivial perturbation in g can produce non-trivial perturbation in $\hat{f}$. That is, there exists ε, which can be made arbitrarily small such that

$$\Phi(g + \varepsilon) = \hat{f} + \delta \tag{7.5}$$

where $\delta \gg \varepsilon$; δ is not arbitrarily small and hence cannot be ignored. This happens when denominator of $P(u, v)$ becomes nearly equal to zero at some (u, v). In fact, the solution of the digital image restoration problem is obtained by the solution of an ill-conditioned system of linear equations [Equation 7.5].

7.2   Minimum Mean-square Error Restoration

Suppose we wish to design a filter that can estimate original images from the observed ones optimally in a minimum mean-square error (MMSE) sense for a large number of images. All the images have undergone the same degradation phenomenon and noise come from the same population. So the i-th recorded image $\mathbf{g}_i$ can be expressed as

$$\mathbf{g}_i = \mathbf{H}\mathbf{f}_i + \eta_i \tag{7.6}$$

Let the estimated image be $\hat{\mathbf{f}}_i$ corresponding to $\mathbf{g}_i$. Since our image formation model is linear and space-invariant, we consider similar model for the restoration filter Φ too which may be represented by the pre-multiplying $\mathbf{g}_i$ by the matrix $\mathbf{P}$. Hence,

$$\hat{\mathbf{f}}_i = \mathbf{P}\mathbf{g}_i \tag{7.7}$$

Thus the corresponding error vector $\mathbf{e}_i$ is obtained as

$$\mathbf{e}_i = \mathbf{f}_i - \hat{\mathbf{f}}_i \tag{7.8}$$

where the elements of the error vector $\mathbf{e}_i$ may be positive or negative. To force the error to be a non-negative quantity we consider $\mathbf{e}_i^T\,\mathbf{e}_i$ an error in estimating i-th image. For brevity, let us drop the subscript i in the following analysis. The MMSE criterion requires the mean error over the entire ensemble of the images under consideration be minimum. Thus, we pose the optimization problem as

$$\text{minimize } \{\varepsilon\{(\mathbf{e}^T\mathbf{e})\} = \text{minimize } [\varepsilon\{\text{Tr}(\mathbf{e}\mathbf{e}^T)\}] \tag{7.9}$$

ε and Tr represent *expectation* and *trace* operator respectively.

Substituting Equations (7.6), (7.7) and (7.8) into the optimization criterion given in Equation (7.9), we obtain the objective function $J(\mathbf{P})$. Thus

$$\begin{aligned}
J(\mathbf{P}) &= \varepsilon[\text{Tr}\{[\mathbf{f} - \mathbf{P}(\mathbf{H}\mathbf{f} + \eta)][\mathbf{f} - \mathbf{P}(\mathbf{H}\mathbf{f} + \eta)]^T\}] \\
&= \varepsilon[\text{Tr}\{(\mathbf{f} - \mathbf{P}\mathbf{H}\mathbf{f} - \mathbf{P}\eta)(\mathbf{f} - \mathbf{P}\mathbf{H}\mathbf{f} - \mathbf{P}\eta)^T\}] \\
&= \varepsilon[\text{Tr}\{(\mathbf{f} - \mathbf{P}\mathbf{H}\mathbf{f} - \mathbf{P}\eta)(\mathbf{f}^T - \mathbf{f}^T\mathbf{H}^T\mathbf{P}^T - \eta^T\mathbf{P}^T)\}] \\
&= \varepsilon[\text{Tr}(\mathbf{f}\mathbf{f}^T - \mathbf{f}\mathbf{f}^T\mathbf{H}^T\mathbf{P}^T - \mathbf{f}\eta^T\mathbf{P}^T - \mathbf{P}\mathbf{H}\mathbf{f}\mathbf{f}^T + \mathbf{P}\mathbf{H}\mathbf{f}\mathbf{f}^T\mathbf{H}^T\mathbf{P}^T \\
&\quad + \mathbf{P}\mathbf{H}\mathbf{f}\eta^T\mathbf{P}^T - \mathbf{P}\eta\mathbf{f}^T + \mathbf{P}\eta\mathbf{f}^T\mathbf{H}^T\mathbf{P}^T + \mathbf{P}\eta\eta^T\mathbf{P}^T)] \tag{7.10}
\end{aligned}$$

Since both Tr and ε are linear operators, they can be interchanged. Secondly, we have assumed signal-independent noise, i.e. $\varepsilon\{\eta\mathbf{f}^T\} = \varepsilon\{\mathbf{f}\eta^T\} = \mathbf{0}$. Also, note that $\text{Tr}\{A\} = \text{Tr}\{A^T\}$. Hence, Equation (7.10) becomes

$$J(\mathbf{P}) = \text{Tr}[\mathbf{R}_f - 2\mathbf{P}\mathbf{H}\mathbf{R}_f + \mathbf{P}\mathbf{H}\mathbf{R}_f\mathbf{H}^T\mathbf{P}^T + \mathbf{P}\mathbf{R}_\eta\mathbf{P}^T] \tag{7.11}$$

where $\mathbf{R}_f$ and $\mathbf{R}_\eta$ are *auto-correlation* matrices defined as $\mathbf{R}_f = \varepsilon\{\mathbf{f}\mathbf{f}^T\}$ and $\mathbf{R}_\eta = \varepsilon\{\eta\eta^T\}$, respectively. So, for $J(\mathbf{P})$ be minimum, we differentiate $J(\mathbf{P})$ with respect to $\mathbf{P}$ and equate the derivative to zero. That yields

$$-2\mathbf{R}_f\mathbf{H}^T + 2\mathbf{P}\mathbf{H}\mathbf{R}_f\mathbf{H}^T + 2\mathbf{P}\mathbf{R}_\eta = \mathbf{0}$$

$\mathbf{0}$ is a null column vector. Hence, the filter matrix $\mathbf{P}$ is given by

$$\mathbf{P} = \mathbf{R_f}\mathbf{H}^{\mathrm{T}}(\mathbf{H}\mathbf{R_f}\mathbf{H}^{\mathrm{T}} + \mathbf{R}_\eta)^{-1} \tag{7.12}$$

The correlation matrices $\mathbf{R_f}$ and $\mathbf{R}_\eta$ are in block-Toeplitz form. However, for mathematical tractability, we assume them in block-circulant form, so that they can be diagonalized by a two-dimensional Fourier transform. In case of image restoration, this is a close approximation of real situation. Therefore, in Fourier domain we have

$$\hat{F}(u, v) = P(u, v)\, G(u, v) = \frac{H^*(u, v)}{|H(u, v)|^2 + \dfrac{R_\eta\,(u, v)}{R_f\,(u, v)}}\, G(u, v) \tag{7.13}$$

for $u = 0, 1, 2, ..., M - 1$, and $v = 0, 1, 2, ..., N - 1$. $P(u, v)$, $H(u, v)$, $R_f\,(u, v)$ and $R_\eta(u, v)$ are Fourier transform coefficients of $\mathbf{P}$, $\mathbf{H}$, $\mathbf{R_f}$ and $\mathbf{R}_\eta$ respectively, and $H^*(u, v)$ is complex conjugate of $H(u, v)$. This filter is also known as *Wiener filter*.

7.3   Least-square Error Restoration

Minimum mean-square error estimation provides a filter that produces optimal restoration in an average sense over an ensemble of images, but it cannot ascertain optimal restoration of a particular image. This may be obtained by the *method of least-square*. In absence of any knowledge about noise we may treat it as a measurement error. So, to restore a particular image, we minimize the difference between the observed image and the re-degraded estimated image. Thus, the objective function $J(\hat{\mathbf{f}})$ is given by

$$J(\hat{\mathbf{f}}) = \|\mathbf{g} - \mathbf{H}\hat{\mathbf{f}}\|^2 = \mathbf{g}^{\mathrm{T}}\mathbf{g} - \mathbf{g}^{\mathrm{T}}\mathbf{H}\hat{\mathbf{f}} - \hat{\mathbf{f}}^{\mathrm{T}}\mathbf{H}^{\mathrm{T}}\mathbf{g} + \hat{\mathbf{f}}^{\mathrm{T}}\mathbf{H}^{\mathrm{T}}\mathbf{H}\hat{\mathbf{f}} \tag{7.14}$$

Now to find $\hat{\mathbf{f}}$ such that $J(\hat{\mathbf{f}})$ be minimum, differentiate Equation (7.14) with respect to $\hat{\mathbf{f}}$ and then equate the result to zero. This yields

$$-2\mathbf{H}^{\mathrm{T}}\mathbf{g} + 2\mathbf{H}^{\mathrm{T}}\mathbf{H}\hat{\mathbf{f}} = 0$$

Hence, the estimated image can be obtained as

$$\hat{\mathbf{f}} = (\mathbf{H}^{\mathrm{T}}\mathbf{H})^{-1}\mathbf{H}^{\mathrm{T}}\mathbf{g} = \mathbf{H}^{-1}\mathbf{g} \tag{7.15}$$

In the Fourier domain, we have

$$\hat{F}(u, v) = \frac{G(u, v)}{H(u, v)} \tag{7.16}$$

for $u = 0, 1, 2, ..., M - 1$, and $v = 0, 1, 2, ..., N - 1$. Main problem of this method is $H(u, v)$ becomes zero for some (u, v). This may happen when the matrix $\mathbf{H}$ is singular because the number of independent equations is less than the number of unknowns in the set of linear equations given by Equation (5.22). This problem is very common especially when point-spread function is symmetric. In this case, we can have a family of solutions (restored images). To select a solution from that family we employ the *constrained least-square estimation* approach as described below.

7.4   Constrained Least-square Error Restoration

The method of 'constrained least-square' can be defined as the optimization of some criterion of goodness or quality of image subject to the constraint that residual norm between the image and the re-degraded estimated image be equal to the norm of the noise vector [Hunt (1973)]. Suppose, we define the measure of some image quality by $\| \mathbf{Q}\hat{\mathbf{f}} \|^2$. So, our objective is to minimize $\| \mathbf{Q}\hat{\mathbf{f}} \|^2$ subject to the constraint $\| \mathbf{g} - \mathbf{H}\hat{\mathbf{f}} \|^2 = \| \eta \|^2$. The addition of equality constraint in the minimization problem can be handled without difficulty by using the method of Lagrange multiplier, where the constraint is expressed in the form $\lambda (\| \mathbf{g} - \mathbf{H}\hat{\mathbf{f}} \|^2 - \| \eta \|^2)$ and then append it to the function $\| \mathbf{Q}\hat{\mathbf{f}} \|^2$. Hence, $\hat{\mathbf{f}}$ is obtained by minimizing the objective function $J(\hat{\mathbf{f}})$, where

$$J(\hat{\mathbf{f}}) = \| \mathbf{Q}\hat{\mathbf{f}} \|^2 + \lambda (\| \mathbf{g} - \mathbf{H}\hat{\mathbf{f}} \|^2 - \| \eta \|^2)$$
$$= \hat{\mathbf{f}}^T\mathbf{Q}^T\mathbf{Q}\hat{\mathbf{f}} + \lambda (\mathbf{g}^T\mathbf{g} - \mathbf{g}^T\mathbf{H}\hat{\mathbf{f}} - \hat{\mathbf{f}}^T\mathbf{H}^T\mathbf{g} + \hat{\mathbf{f}}^T\mathbf{H}^T\mathbf{H}\hat{\mathbf{f}} - \eta^T\eta) \qquad (7.17)$$

where λ is the *Lagrange multiplier* and is a constant. Differentiating Equation (7.17) with respect to $\hat{\mathbf{f}}$ and setting the result equal to zero yields

$$\frac{\partial J(\hat{\mathbf{f}})}{\partial \hat{\mathbf{f}}} = 0 = 2\mathbf{Q}^T\mathbf{Q}\hat{\mathbf{f}} + 2\lambda (-\mathbf{H}^T\mathbf{g} + \mathbf{H}^T\mathbf{H}\hat{\mathbf{f}})$$

Then the solution obtained for $\hat{\mathbf{f}}$ is given by

$$\hat{\mathbf{f}} = (\mathbf{H}^T\mathbf{H} + \gamma\mathbf{Q}^T\mathbf{Q})^{-1}\mathbf{H}^T\mathbf{g} \qquad (7.18)$$

where, $\gamma = 1/\lambda$. In Fourier domain, we have

$$\hat{F}(u, v) = \frac{H^*(u, v)}{H^*(u, v)H(u, v) + \gamma Q^*(u, v)Q(u, v)} G(u, v) \qquad (7.19)$$

for $u = 0, 1, 2, ..., M - 1$, and $v = 0, 1, 2, ..., N - 1$.

Here, various types of goodness criterion are considered. For example, one may want to maximize signal-to-noise ratio, or in other words, minimize noise-to-signal ratio. In this case $\mathbf{Q}^T\mathbf{Q} = \mathbf{R_f}^{-1}\mathbf{R}_\eta$. Thus in the Fourier domain, the estimated image is given as

$$\hat{F}(u, v) = \frac{H^*(u, v)}{H^*(u, v)H(u, v) + \gamma\dfrac{R_\eta(u, v)}{R_\mathbf{f}(u, v)}} G(u, v) \qquad (7.20)$$

for $u = 0, 1, 2, ..., M - 1$, and $v = 0, 1, 2, ..., N - 1$. On comparing Equation (7.20) with Equation (7.13), we see that Equation (7.20) is same as the Wiener filter except the parameter γ, so it is called the *parametric Wiener filter*. Another, goodness criterion may be smoothness of the restored image. In that case, $\mathbf{Q}\hat{\mathbf{f}}$ measures the variation in intensity in the restored image. That means $q(r,c)$ represents the Laplacian [Gonzalez and Wintz (1977)].

Another interesting criterion may be the independence between the restored image and the additive noise [Chanda et al. (1984a), (1984b)]. In this case we define the criterion based on a measure of cross-correlation between the estimated image and the noise process. The correlation coefficient $\rho(r, c)$ between the image and noise is given by

$$\rho(m, n) = \frac{1}{MN} \sum_{c=0}^{N-1} \sum_{r=0}^{M-1} \eta(r, c)\, \hat{f}(r + m, c + n) \qquad (7.21)$$

for $m = 0, 1, 2, ..., M - 1$, and $n = 0, 1, 2, ..., N - 1$. Equation (7.21) can be represented in matrix–vector notation as

$$\rho = A\hat{f} \tag{7.22}$$

where A is a block-circulant matrix of size $MN \times MN$ and is composed of noise graylevels. Matrix A consists of M^2 partitions, each partition being of size $N \times N$ and ordered according to

$$A = \begin{bmatrix} A_0 & A_{M-1} & A_{M-2} & \cdots & A_1 \\ A_1 & A_0 & A_{M-1} & \cdots & A_2 \\ A_2 & A_1 & A_0 & \cdots & A_3 \\ \vdots & \vdots & \vdots & & \vdots \\ A_{M-1} & A_{M-2} & A_{M-3} & \cdots & A_0 \end{bmatrix}$$

where the partition A_j is constructed from the j-th row of $\eta(j, k)$ as follows:

$$A_j = \begin{bmatrix} \eta(j, 0) & \eta(j, N-1) & \eta(j, N-2) & \cdots & \eta(j, 1) \\ \eta(j, 1) & \eta(j, 0) & \eta(j, N-1) & \cdots & \eta(j, 2) \\ \eta(j, 2) & \eta(j, 1) & \eta(j, 0) & \cdots & \eta(j, 3) \\ \vdots & \vdots & \vdots & & \vdots \\ \eta(j, N-1) & \eta(j, N-2) & \eta(j, N-3) & \cdots & \eta(j, 0) \end{bmatrix}$$

Since the correlation between two independent process should be zero, our objective is to minimize $\| A\hat{f} \|^2 = \hat{f}^T A^T A \hat{f}$ subject to the constraint $\| g - H\hat{f} \|^2 = \| \eta \|^2$.

Therefore, from Equation (7.18), we get

$$\hat{f} = (H^T H + \gamma A^T A)^{-1} H^T g \tag{7.23}$$

Let the noise term be point-wise uncorrelated, i.e.

$$\sum_{c=0}^{N-1} \sum_{r=0}^{M-1} \eta(r, c) \, \eta(r + m, c + n) = 0$$

for all m and n but not both equal to zero. Then a straight-forward analysis leads to

$$A^T A = \frac{1}{MN} E_\eta I \tag{7.24}$$

where I is the identity matrix of size $MN \times MN$ and E_η is the average energy or power of noise function, where

$$E_\eta = \frac{1}{MN} \sum_{r=0}^{M-1} \sum_{c=0}^{N-1} \eta^2(r, c) \tag{7.25}$$

Let μ_η is the mean value of the noise gray levels and σ_η is its variance, then

$$\mu_\eta = \frac{1}{MN} \sum_{r=0}^{M-1} \sum_{c=0}^{N-1} \eta(r, c)$$

and

$$\sigma_\eta = \frac{1}{MN} \sum_{r=0}^{M-1} \sum_{c=0}^{N-1} [\eta(r, c) - \mu_\eta]^2$$

$$= \frac{1}{MN} \sum_{r=0}^{M-1} \sum_{c=0}^{N-1} \eta^2(r, c) - \frac{2}{MN} \mu_\eta \sum_{r=0}^{M-1} \sum_{c=0}^{N-1} \eta(r, c) + \mu_\eta^2$$

$$= E_\eta - 2\mu_\eta\mu_\eta + \mu_\eta^2$$

$$= E_\eta - \mu_\eta^2$$

Thus

$$E_\eta = \mu_\eta^2 + \sigma_\eta \tag{7.26}$$

If we assume $\mu_\eta = 0$, then

$$E_\eta = \sigma_\eta \tag{7.27}$$

Combining Equations (7.23) and (7.24), we obtain

$$\hat{\mathbf{f}} = \left(\mathbf{H}^T\mathbf{H} + \gamma \frac{1}{MN} E_\eta \mathbf{I} \right)^{-1} \mathbf{H}^T\mathbf{g} \tag{7.28}$$

Hence, in Fourier domain we have

$$\hat{F}(u, v) = \frac{H^*(u, v)}{|H(u, v)|^2 + \gamma E_\eta} G(u, v) \tag{7.29}$$

for $u = 0, 1, 2, ..., M - 1$, and $v = 0, 1, 2, ..., N - 1$.

As already said, image restoration using inverse filtering technique occasionally encounters computational difficulties when the denominator vanishes or tends to vanish for some values of (u, v). However, it is evident that $|H(u, v)|^2$ is real and non-negative, and E_η, being average noise energy, presents a significant positive value. Now the incident, that denominator of the filter function becomes zero or very nearly equal to zero, completely depends on the value of γ. It will be shown in the next section that if the average noise energy be greater than zero but less than the average energy of the observed image, which is most common in practice, then the value of γ is greater than zero. Hence the denominator is sufficiently greater than zero and $\hat{F}(u, v)$ can be computed uniquely.

Solving Equation (7.28) [or Equation (7.29)] subject to the constraint $\| \mathbf{g} - \mathbf{H}\hat{\mathbf{f}} \|^2 = \| \eta \|^2$, we obtain the values of γ and $\hat{\mathbf{f}}$ [or $\hat{F}(u, v)$]. Equation (7.28) represents MN number of linear equations and the constraint identity represents a non-linear equation. Since it is difficult to solve simultaneously a non-linear equation and a set of linear equations, we try to find γ by iterative technique. To avoid computations required to find inverse Fourier transform of $\hat{F}(u, v)$ and then to find $\mathbf{H}\hat{\mathbf{f}}$ during the estimation of γ, we apply Parseval's theorem to the constraint identity and obtain

$$\frac{1}{MN} \sum_{u=0}^{M-1} \sum_{v=0}^{N-1} |G(u, v) - H(u, v)\hat{F}(u, v)|^2 = \frac{1}{MN} \sum_{u=0}^{M-1} \sum_{v=0}^{N-1} |N(u, v)|^2 = MNE_\eta \tag{7.30}$$

where $N(u, v)$ is the (u, v)-th Fourier transform coefficient of noise $\eta(r, c)$. It is clear that the error in estimation of $\mathbf{f}$ depends on γ only. Let us define corresponding error function as

$$e(\gamma) = \frac{1}{MN} \sum_{u=0}^{M-1} \sum_{v=0}^{N-1} | G(u, v) - H(u, v)\hat{F}(u, v) |^2$$

$$= \frac{1}{MN} \sum_{u=0}^{M-1} \sum_{v=0}^{N-1} \left| G(u, v) - \frac{|H(u, v)|^2 G(u, v)}{|H(u, v)|^2 + \gamma E_\eta} \right|^2$$

or

$$e(\gamma) = \frac{1}{MN} \sum_{u=0}^{M-1} \sum_{v=0}^{N-1} \frac{\gamma^2 E_\eta^2 \, | G(u, v) |^2}{[|H(u, v)|^2 + \gamma E_\eta]^2} \tag{7.31}$$

Therefore, value of γ is selected to satisfy

$$e(\gamma) = MNE_\eta \pm \varepsilon_a \tag{7.32}$$

where ε_a is an accuracy factor. From Equation (7.31) we see that $e(\gamma)$ is a piecewise monotonic increasing function. This implies that finding γ by iterative method is not a difficult problem.

7.4.1 Lower Bound of γ

We are yet to exploit the fact that the filter, as described by Equation (7.29), results in a minimization rather than maximization of the function $J(\hat{\mathbf{f}})$. From the calculus of several variables we have the following sufficient condition:

$$\frac{\partial J^2(\hat{\mathbf{f}})}{\partial \hat{\mathbf{f}}^2} = \begin{bmatrix} \dfrac{\partial J^2}{\partial \hat{f}_0^2} & \dfrac{\partial J^2}{\partial \hat{f}_1 \partial \hat{f}_0} & \dfrac{\partial J^2}{\partial \hat{f}_2 \partial \hat{f}_0} & \cdots & \dfrac{\partial J^2}{\partial \hat{f}_{MN-1} \partial \hat{f}_0} \\[2mm] \dfrac{\partial J^2}{\partial \hat{f}_0 \partial \hat{f}_1} & \dfrac{\partial J^2}{\partial \hat{f}_1^2} & \dfrac{\partial J^2}{\partial \hat{f}_2 \partial \hat{f}_1} & \cdots & \dfrac{\partial J^2}{\partial \hat{f}_{MN-1} \partial \hat{f}_1} \\[2mm] \dfrac{\partial J^2}{\partial \hat{f}_0 \partial \hat{f}_2} & \dfrac{\partial J^2}{\partial \hat{f}_1 \partial \hat{f}_2} & \dfrac{\partial J^2}{\partial \hat{f}_2^2} & \cdots & \dfrac{\partial J^2}{\partial \hat{f}_{MN-1} \partial \hat{f}_2} \\[2mm] \vdots & \vdots & \vdots & & \vdots \\[2mm] \dfrac{\partial J^2}{\partial \hat{f}_0 \partial \hat{f}_{MN-1}} & \dfrac{\partial J^2}{\partial \hat{f}_1 \partial \hat{f}_{MN-1}} & \dfrac{\partial J^2}{\partial \hat{f}_2 \partial \hat{f}_{MN-1}} & \cdots & \dfrac{\partial J^2}{\partial \hat{f}_{MN-1}^2} \end{bmatrix}$$

is a positive definite matrix. That means all eigenvalues of this matrix must be greater than zero. Here [from Equation (7.17)]

$$\frac{\partial J(\hat{\mathbf{f}})}{\partial \hat{\mathbf{f}}} = 2\mathbf{A}^T\mathbf{A}\hat{\mathbf{f}} + 2\lambda(-\mathbf{H}^T\mathbf{g} + \mathbf{H}^T\mathbf{H}\hat{\mathbf{f}})$$

and

$$\frac{\partial J^2(\hat{\mathbf{f}})}{\partial \hat{\mathbf{f}}^2} = 2\mathbf{A}^T\mathbf{A} + 2\lambda\mathbf{H}^T\mathbf{H} = \frac{2}{MN} E_\eta\mathbf{I} + 2\lambda\mathbf{H}^T\mathbf{H}$$

So, $\partial^2 J / \partial \hat{f}^2$ is also a block-circulant matrix of size $MN \times MN$ which can be diagonalized by a two-dimensional Fourier transform. The eigenvalues of this matrix are $2E_\eta + 2\lambda |H(u, v)|^2$, where

$$E_\eta + \lambda |H(u, v)|^2 > 0 \qquad (7.33)$$

for $u = 0, 1, 2, ..., M - 1$, and $v = 0, 1, 2, ..., N - 1$. Therefore, the Lagrange multiplier must satisfy the condition:

$$\lambda > \frac{-E_\eta}{|H(u, v)|^2}$$

for $u = 0, 1, 2, ..., M - 1$, and $v = 0, 1, 2, ..., N - 1$. Equivalently,

$$\lambda > - \min_{(u,v)} \left\{ \frac{E_\eta}{|H(u, v)|^2} \right\}$$

Hence, the parameter γ of filter function must satisfy either $\gamma \geq 0$ or

$$\gamma < - \max_{(u,v)} \left\{ \frac{|H(u, v)|^2}{E_\eta} \right\} = \gamma_1 \text{ (say)}$$

Now if the restoration problem is singular, i.e. $H(u, v) = 0$ for at least one pair of (u, v), then γ must be positive. Otherwise, γ may assume negative value. In order to determine the circumstances which may lead to a negative value of γ, the error function defined by Equation (7.31) will be explored in some greater detail.

7.4.2 Monotonicity in the Error Functions

Taking the derivative of Equation (7.31) with respect to γ, we get

$$\frac{de(\gamma)}{d\gamma} = \frac{1}{MN} \sum_{u=0}^{M-1} \sum_{v=0}^{N-1} \frac{2\gamma E_\eta^2 |H(u, v)|^2 |G_e(u, v)|^2}{[|H(u, v)|^2 + \gamma E_\eta]^3} \qquad (7.34)$$

Now for $\gamma > 0$ we have $|H(u, v)|^2 + \gamma E_\eta > 0$ [see Equation (7.33)] and for $\gamma < \gamma_1$ we have $H^2(u, v) + \gamma E_\eta < 0$, for all u and v. So,

$$\frac{de(\gamma)}{d\gamma} \begin{cases} > 0 & \text{for } \gamma > 0 \\ > 0 & \text{for } \gamma < \gamma_1 \end{cases} \qquad (7.35)$$

Therefore, the error function is a monotonically increasing function in both the range of γ, i.e. $(-\infty, \gamma_1)$ and $[0, \infty)$, respectively. In order to gain further insight into the behaviour of error as a function of γ we can evaluate $e(\gamma)$ at some particular values of γ.

$$\left. \begin{array}{l} e(\gamma) \big|_{\gamma=0} = 0 \\[2mm] e(\gamma) \big|_{\gamma \to \pm\infty} = \dfrac{1}{MN} \sum\limits_{u=0}^{M-1} \sum\limits_{v=0}^{N-1} |G(u, v)|^2 \\[4mm] e(\gamma) \big|_{\gamma \to \gamma_1} \to \infty \end{array} \right\} \qquad (7.36)$$

From Equations (7.35) and (7.36), we can sketch a typical $e(\gamma)$ versus γ curve as shown in Fig. 7.1. This figure reveals that γ will assume negative values if and only if average energy of noise is greater than that in the observed image, i.e.

$$MNE_\eta > \frac{1}{MN} \sum_{u=0}^{M-1} \sum_{v=0}^{N-1} |G(u, v)|^2 \qquad (7.37)$$

However, such situations seldom occur.

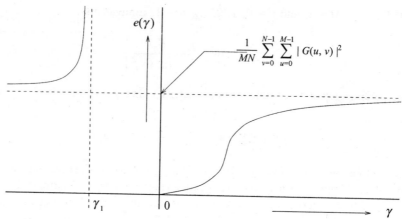

Fig. 7.1 A typical plot of error in estimation as a function of γ.

7.4.3 A Concise Algorithm for Restoration

In describing the algorithm for constrained least-square estimation method using signal-noise correlation criterion as described in previous sections, we assumed that the noise energy satisfies the following condition:

$$0 < MNE_\eta \le \frac{1}{MN} \sum_{u=0}^{M-1} \sum_{v=0}^{N-1} |G(u, v)|^2$$

The assumption is most common in real life situation too. This enables us to consider monotonically increasing part of the plot of $e(\gamma)$ versus γ, where $\gamma > 0$. The monotonicity of $e(\gamma)$ implies that there is only one unique value of γ such that $e(\gamma) = MNE_\eta$ and an iterative process is sufficient to find that unique value [Dines and Kak (1977), Dutta Majumder et al. (1989)]. The following steps summarize the proposed algorithm.

Algorithm 7.1

Step 1: Based on the knowledge of physical degradation process compute the elements of the matrix $[h(r, c)]$ of size $M \times N$.

Step 2: Compute $H(u, v)$ by two-dimensional Fourier transform of $h(r, c)$.

Step 3: Compute $G(u, v)$ by two-dimensional Fourier transform of the observed image $g(r, c)$.

Step 4: If average noise energy E_η (or power) is not known, calculate it from the mean and variance using Equation (7.26).

Step 5: Choose an initial value of γ (>0). Find the estimation error $e(\gamma)$ as given by Equation (7.31).

Step 6: Modify the value of γ as follows:

(a) Increase the value of γ, if $e(\gamma) < MNE_\eta - \varepsilon_a$.
(b) Decrease the value of γ, if $e(\gamma) > MNE_\eta - \varepsilon_a$.

Find new estimation error $e(\gamma)$ as given by Equation (7.31).

Step 7: Repeat Step 6 until following is satisfied:

$$MNE_\eta - \varepsilon_a \le e(\gamma) \le MNE_\eta + \varepsilon_a$$

Step 8: For acceptable value of γ, i.e. if $MNE_\eta - \varepsilon_a \le e(\gamma) \le MNE_\eta + \varepsilon_a$, determine $\hat{F}(u, v)$ using Equation (7.29). Then find $\hat{f}(r, c)$ by applying two-dimensional inverse Fourier transform on $\hat{F}(u, v)$.

Now if

$$MNE_\eta > \frac{1}{MN} \sum_{u=0}^{M-1} \sum_{v=0}^{N-1} |G(u, v)|^2$$

which seldom occurs in practice, the above algorithm will remain the same except that Step 5 is modified as: "Choose an initial value of $\gamma(<\gamma_1)$...". Secondly, this algorithm can easily be modified for other types of goodness criteria. Results of the least-square and constrained least-square restoration techniques using a controlled degraded image are shown in Fig. 7.2. Figure 7.2(a) shows a reasonably good quality image of a scene consisting of a keyboard, a telephone, a part of display terminal, etc. Image of the same scene is taken with a slightly out-of-focus lens arrangement and a uniformly distributed noise is added to it. Degraded image, thus obtained, is shown in Fig. 7.2(b). Restored images by the least-square and constrained least-square estimation techniques are shown in Figs. 7.2(c) and (d), respectively.

7.5 Restoration by Singular Value Decomposition

Let us recall Equation (7.15) where restored image is given by

$$\hat{\mathbf{f}} = \mathbf{H}^{-1}\mathbf{g} \tag{7.15}$$

Now if H is singular, H^{-1} does not exist. In that case, we may obtain the restored image $\hat{\mathbf{f}}$ as [see Equation (2.39)]

$$\hat{\mathbf{f}} = \mathbf{H}^+\mathbf{g} \tag{2.39}$$

where $\mathbf{H}^+$ is the pseudoinverse matrix of $\mathbf{H}$. The main advantage of the pseudoinverse matrix is that it always exists irrespective of singular nature of $\mathbf{H}$ or non-uniqueness of the solution of the set of linear Equations given in Equation (5.24). Substituting Equation (5.24) in Equation (2.39),

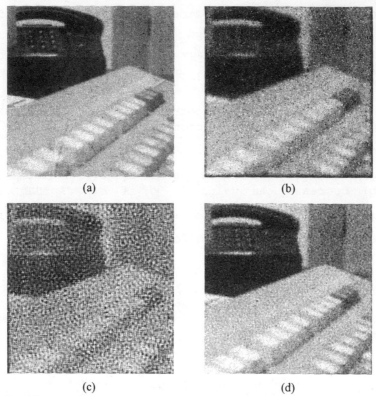

Fig. 7.2   Results of least squares restoration techniques: (a) degradation-free and reasonably good quality imgae, (b) degraded image of the same scene obtained by defocussing and by adding uniformly distributed noise; note that signal-to-noise ratio is 13.1 dB, (c) restored image using the least-square method, (d) restored image using the constrained least-square method using signal–noise correlation constraint.

we have

$$\hat{\mathbf{f}} = \mathbf{H}^{+}\mathbf{H}\mathbf{f} + \mathbf{H}^{+}\eta \tag{7.38}$$

The first term on the right-hand side of Equation (7.38) is equivalent to least-square estimation neglecting the noise term. However, in many cases the noise part contributes heavily to the recorded image **g**. One way of dealing with the noise term is to use singular value decomposition (SVD) to calculate the pseudoinverse [Huang and Narendra (1975)]. As in Section 7.5, matrix **H** can be decomposed as

$$\mathbf{H} = \sum_{i=0}^{MN-1} \lambda_i^{\frac{1}{2}} \mathbf{u}_i \mathbf{v}_i^{\mathrm{T}} \tag{7.39}$$

where $\mathbf{u}_i$ and $\mathbf{v}_i$ are i-th eigenvectors of $\mathbf{HH}^{\mathrm{T}}$ and $\mathbf{H}^{\mathrm{T}}\mathbf{H}$ respectively, and λ_i is the i-th eigenvalue of either of these matrices. Therefore, the pseudoinverse $\mathbf{H}^{+}$ of $\mathbf{H}$ may be expressed as

$$\mathbf{H}^{+} = \sum_{i=0}^{MN-1} \lambda_i^{-\frac{1}{2}} \mathbf{v}_i \mathbf{u}_i^{\mathrm{T}} \tag{7.40}$$

Hence, Equation (7.38) becomes

$$\hat{\mathbf{f}} = \left(\sum_{i=0}^{MN-1} \lambda_i^{-\frac{1}{2}} \mathbf{v}_i \mathbf{u}_i^T \right) \mathbf{H}\mathbf{f} + \left(\sum_{i=0}^{MN-1} \lambda_i^{-\frac{1}{2}} \mathbf{v}_i \mathbf{u}_i^T \right) \eta \qquad (7.41)$$

Suppose λ_is are arranged in descending order. Then the effectiveness of SVD in presence of noise can be explained as follows. Each term in the first summation on the right-hand side of Equation (7.41) has more or less the same magnitude, while the magnitudes of the terms in the second summation increases with i [Huang and Narendra (1975)]. As we consider more and more terms in the summations in Equation (7.41) the first summation approximates the original image more and more faithfully, but at the same time noise term also becomes increasingly significant. As a result, signal-to-noise ratio in the restored image decreases. Hence, we trade off between the amount of noise and the quality of signal by choosing the number of terms in the summation. Suppose, first R terms produce visually optimum restoration to the user, then

$$\hat{\mathbf{f}} = \sum_{i=0}^{R-1} \lambda_i^{-\frac{1}{2}} \mathbf{v}_i \mathbf{u}_i^T \mathbf{H}\mathbf{f} + \sum_{i=0}^{R-1} \lambda_i^{-\frac{1}{2}} \mathbf{v}_i \mathbf{u}_i^T \eta = \sum_{i=0}^{R-1} \lambda_i^{-\frac{1}{2}} \mathbf{v}_i \mathbf{u}_i^T \mathbf{g} \qquad (7.42)$$

Major drawback of this approach is its computational cost, because it involves computation of eigenvalues and eigenvectors of a very large size matrix. This problem may be surmounted partially if the degrading function $h(x, y)$ [or $h(r, c)$] be separable.

7.6 Restoration by Maximum a Posterior Estimation

The strategy, here, is to develop a probability density for the original image $\mathbf{f}$ conditioned upon the recorded image $\mathbf{g}$ and then maximize the conditional density to generate the estimate $\hat{\mathbf{f}}$ [Hunt (1975)].

Suppose the sampled noise vector η be described by the multivariate normal p.d.f.

$$p(\eta) = \{(2\pi)^{MN/2} \mid \mathbf{R}_\eta \mid^{1/2}\}^{-1} \exp\{-(\eta - \overline{\eta})^T \mathbf{R}_\eta^{-1} (\eta - \overline{\eta})\} \qquad (7.43)$$

where $\overline{\eta}$ and $\mathbf{R}_\eta$ are the mean vector and the covariance matrix of the sampled noise, respectively. The noise is assumed to be zero-mean stationary, so the matrix $\mathbf{R}_\eta$ is of block-Toeplitz form. Original image intensity vector $\mathbf{f}$ is also assumed to be a sample from an underlying random process. So, a Gaussian process fluctuating about a positive mean may be chosen as the model for image intensities. This assumption is unrealistic at least for two reasons. First, graylevel histograms of images reveal that in some cases intensities cannot be modelled by the Gaussian statistics. Second and more important is the Gaussian process generates negative values, no matter how large be the positive mean. However, if the variance is that very small compared to the mean, then a large positive mean implies only a very small portion of the values are negative. In that case, the model is a reasonable approximation of the real situation and we adopt it for mathematical tractability. Thus $\mathbf{f}$ is described by the multivariate normal p.d.f.

$$p(\mathbf{f}) = \{(2\pi)^{MN/2} \mid \mathbf{R}_\mathbf{f} \mid^{1/2}\}^{-1} \exp\{-(\mathbf{f} - \overline{\mathbf{f}})^T \mathbf{R}_\mathbf{f}^{-1} (\mathbf{f} - \overline{\mathbf{f}})\} \qquad (7.44)$$

where $\overline{\mathbf{f}}$ and $\mathbf{R}_\mathbf{f}$ are mean vector and covariance matrix of the original image vector, respectively.

Now given the recorded image **g**, the p.d.f. of **f** conditioned on **g** is determined using the Bayes' rule

$$p(\mathbf{f} \mid \mathbf{g}) = \frac{p(\mathbf{g} \mid \mathbf{f}) p(\mathbf{f})}{p(\mathbf{g})} \qquad (7.45)$$

Taking logarithm on both sides, we get

$$\ln(p(\mathbf{f} \mid \mathbf{g})) = \ln\{p(\mathbf{g} \mid \mathbf{f})\} + \ln\{p(\mathbf{f}) - \ln p(\mathbf{g})\} \qquad (7.46)$$

The maximum a posterior estimate is derived by differentiating Equation (7.46) with respect to **f** and equating the result to zero. Thus

$$\frac{\partial \ln(p(\mathbf{f} \mid \mathbf{g}))}{\partial \mathbf{f}} = \frac{\partial \ln(p(\mathbf{g} \mid \mathbf{f}))}{\partial \mathbf{f}} + \frac{\ln(p(\mathbf{f}))}{\partial \mathbf{f}} = 0 \qquad (7.47)$$

The term involving $p(\mathbf{f})$ is available from Equation (7.44) and the term involving $p(\mathbf{g} \mid \mathbf{f})$ may be obtained from Equation (7.43), because the condition of **g** on **f** is describable in terms of p.d.f. of η, i.e.

$$p(\mathbf{g} \mid \mathbf{f}) = \{(2\pi)^{MN/2} \mid \mathbf{R}_\eta \mid^{1/2}\}^{-1} \exp\{-(\mathbf{g} - \mathbf{Hf})^{\mathrm{T}} \mathbf{R}_\eta^{-1} (\mathbf{g} - \mathbf{Hf})\} \qquad (7.48)$$

since $\overline{\eta} = \mathbf{0}$. Substituting Equations (7.44) and (7.48) in Equation (7.47) and simplifying, we obtain

$$\hat{\mathbf{f}} = \overline{\mathbf{f}} + \mathbf{R}_{\mathbf{f}}\mathbf{H}^{\mathrm{T}}\mathbf{R}_\eta^{-1} (\mathbf{g} - \mathbf{H}\hat{\mathbf{f}}) \qquad (7.49)$$

Now from Equation (7.49), we see that a priori mean image is an explicit part of the estimate. If no a priori knowledge is available about the mean image, $\overline{\mathbf{f}}$ is assumed to be a constant and any non-negative value may be chosen as the constant. The solution of Equation (7.49) is found iteratively as follows.

Suppose given an initial guess $\hat{\mathbf{f}}_i$ of the restored image. Then

$$\hat{\mathbf{f}}_i = \overline{\mathbf{f}} + \mathbf{R}_{\mathbf{f}}\mathbf{H}^{\mathrm{T}}\mathbf{R}_\eta^{-1} (\mathbf{g} - \mathbf{H}\hat{\mathbf{f}}_{i-1})$$

for $i = 1, 2, 3, \ldots$ Iteration stops if some goodness criterion is satisfied. An example of such criterion may be $\| \hat{\mathbf{f}}_i - \hat{\mathbf{f}}_{i-1} \|^2 < \varepsilon$, where ε is a predefined tolerance threshold. The iteration can be speeded-up by approximating $\mathbf{R}_{\mathbf{f}}$ and $\mathbf{R}_\eta$ by block-circulant matrix and transforming Equation (7.49) to the Fourier domain.

7.7 Restoration by Homomorphic Filtering

Image restoration techniques described in the previous sections are applicable when image formation models consider additive noise only. Here we describe a method for additive as well as multiplicative noise. The situation may better be described with an example so as to restore an image of earth surface taken from a satellite in a cloudy situation as described below.

7.7.1 Distortion Model and Range of Parameters

Recovery of true ground reflectance from the recorded image is not possible when the cloud cover is too thick to allow ground reflectance information to reach the sensor. Thus, the algorithm presented here is applicable when obscuration is atmospheric haze and thin cloud cover [Chanda and Dutta Majumder (1991)]. Discrete model for image formation is described in Fig. 7.3. The

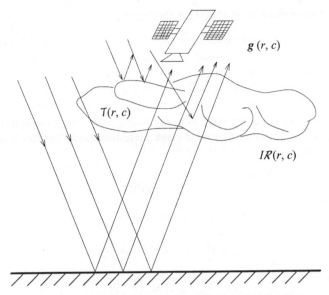

Fig. 7.3   Schematic model for satellite image formation.

figure depicts the formation of an image of earth surface when a thin cloud cover exists over the region of interest. We assume, here, that the transmittance $T(r, c)$ of cloud cover plus the reflectance of it equals one (i.e. we ignore the diffusion factor). We also assume that the sun illumination I is constant over the earth surface. These assumptions lead us to Equation (7.50) where $g(r, c)$ is the image recorded by the sensor.

$$g(r, c) = IR(r, c)\, T(r, c) + I\{1 - T\}(r, c)\} \qquad (7.50)$$

Various terms on the right-hand side of Equation (7.50) are described as under:

- $R(r, c)$ — is the ground reflectance which we want to restore from recorded information $g(r, c)$, and $0 \le R(r, c) \le 1$. $R(r, c) = 0$ corresponds to black region, and $R(r, c) = 1$ corresponds to the brightest region in the image of the earth surface.

- $T(r, c)$ — is transmittance through cloud and $0 < T(r, c) \le 1$. $T(r, c) = 0$ and 1 reflect the opaque and transparent nature of the cloud respectively. $T(r, c) = 0$ is not considered here, because in that case information about ground reflectance cannot reach the sensor and, consequently, we cannot ascertain the restoration of $R(r, c)$. It is assumed that $T(r, c)$ has relatively low spatial frequency content compared to the ground reflectance $R(r, c)$.

- I — is the sun illumination. Its value is assumed to be maximum value of the dynamic range of the sensor.

A careful examination of Equation (7.50) reveals that $g(r, c)$ attains the value I only when $R(r, c) = 1$, otherwise, the maximum possible value of $g(r, c)$ is less than I. Thus $0 \le g(r, c) \le I$. Here the 'noise' due to cloud is not strictly multiplicative [e.g. attenuation of ground reflectance information, $IR(r, c)\, T(r, c)$] or additive [e.g. reflection from cloud cover, $I\{1 - T(r, c)\}$], but is a combination of the two. For simplicity, effects of other photometric degradation and sensor noise are not considered here.

7.7.2   Filtering Procedure and Related Problems

For removing the effects of cloud cover over the earth surface, one of the methods may be that the spatial and spectral properties of cloud be modelled by a universal cloud model and the sun-angle and, finally, discarding the spatial frequency content corresponding to cloud from that of cloudy images. In this case, once the spatial frequency content of cloud is modelled, the filter to be applied is more or less fixed. However, having such a model suitable for the image in hand is non-trivial. A more pragmatic approach is to estimate a filter which can remove the cloud noise best in some sense, say minimum of squared error. Here the second approach is adopted. A high-emphasis filter and its complement is used to restore the image based on the assumption that image of cloud contains only low spatial frequencies. These filters can most conveniently be implemented in the Fourier domain. Before applying Fourier transformation we rearrange Equation (7.50) to get

$$g'(r, c) = T(r, c)R'(r, c) \qquad (7.51)$$

where

$$g'(r, c) = 1 - g(r, c)/I \qquad (7.52)$$

and

$$R'(r, c) = 1 - R(r, c) \qquad (7.53)$$

Taking the logarithm on both sides of Equation (7.51) yields

$$\ln g'(r, c) = \ln T(r, c) + \ln R'(r, c) \qquad (7.54)$$

Taking the Fourier transform of $\ln g'(r, c)$, we get

$$G'(u, y) = T(u, v) + R'(u, v) \qquad (7.55)$$

where

$$G'(u, v) = F\ (\ln g'(r, c))$$
$$T(u, v) = F\ (\ln T(r, c))$$
$$R'(u, v) = F\ (\ln R'(r, c))$$

Suppose signal is assumed to be $\ln R'(r, c)$ and noise is assumed to be $\ln T(r, c)$, then in the transform domain noise is additive only. Secondly, cloud noise or transmittance $T(r, c)$ has relatively low spatial frequency components compared to the signal $R'(r, c)$, so has $\ln T(r, c)$ compared to $\ln R'(r, c)$. So, we can separate $T(u, v)$ by using a low-pass filter and get $\ln T(r, c)$ by applying inverse Fourier transform to $T(u, v)$. Finally we get $T(r, c)$, estimated transmittance of cloud cover, by exponentiating the output of inverse Fourier transform. Similarly, $R'(r, c)$ can be obtained by first using a high-pass filter (i.e. complement of the said low-pass filter) and then exponentiating the filter output.

The main problem with this approach is in selecting the parameter values for the filters. Since $R'(r, c)$ also [along with $T(r, c)$] contributes to low spatial frequencies, the filters, either low-emphasis or high-emphasis, cannot be ideal in this case. This compels us to take tapered-shaped filters. Figure 7.4 shows the cross-sectional view of the filters with the parameters α and β. Here, the responses are piecewise linear which is the simplest shape of this type. The entire procedure is described in Fig. 7.5 by means of a block diagram. Hence, our problem is to search for values of α and β for which we obtain a visually good restored image. However, the selection of α and β may be assisted by detecting minimum error in estimation. The error $e(\alpha, \beta)$ in estimation may be defined as squared error between the recorded signal and the redegraded estimated signal, i.e.

$$e(\alpha, \beta) = \sum_{c=0}^{N-1} \sum_{r=0}^{M-1} [g'(r, c) - g(r, c)]^2 \qquad (7.56)$$

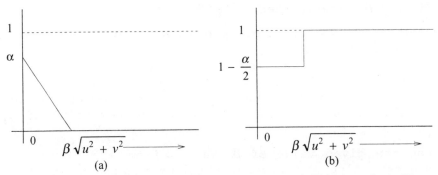

Fig. 7.4 Cross-sectional views of (a) low-emphasis and (b) high-emphasis filters.

The iteration and selection of parameters are performed by the 'INFerence' block of the diagram shown in Fig. 7.5. Detail of search algorithm may be described as follows:

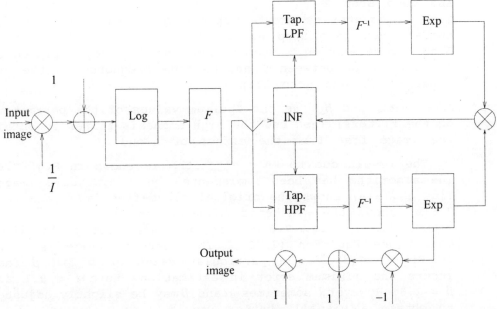

Fig. 7.5 Block diagram of the algorithm for removing the effect of cloud.

Algorithm 7.2

Step 1: Choose a random number between 0 and 1 as an initial value of α. Assign a large value to e_{min} and 0 to β. Record these values of α and β as α_{opt} and β_{opt}, respectively. Set the counter to zero.

Step 2: Use a given value of α. Vary β from its lowest to the highest value and compute $e(\alpha, \beta)$. Choose β for which $e(\alpha, \beta)$ is minimum. Increase the counter reading.

Step 3:   If $e(\alpha, \beta)$ < e_{min} then

update: $e_{min} = e(\alpha, \beta)$, $\alpha_{opt} = \alpha$ and $\beta_{opt} = \beta$. Reset the counter and goto Step 4.
Else if counter reading is greater than a given maximum iteration number then goto Step 6.
Else choose another random number (not already explored as a value of α) between 0 and 1 as the new value of α, and goto Step 2.

Step 4:   Use the given value of β. Vary α from its lowest to the highest value and compute $e(\alpha, \beta)$. Choose α for which $e(\alpha, \beta)$ is minimum. Increase the counter reading.

Step 5:   If $e(\alpha, \beta)$ < e_{min} then

update: $e_{min} = e(\alpha, \beta)$, $\alpha_{opt} = \alpha$ and $\beta_{opt} = \beta$. Reset the counter and goto Step 2.
Else if counter is greater than a given maximum iteration number then goto Step 6.
Else choose another random number (not already explored as a value of β) between 0 and maximum frequency as the new value of β, and goto Step 4.

Step 6:   Accept α_{opt} and β_{opt} as the optimum values of the parameters of the filters. Then use the high-emphasis filter to obtain the image free from the effect of cloud.

The result due to this algorithm is shown in Fig. 7.6. The algorithm has been implemented on a synthetic image. Figure 7.6(a) shows the original cloud-free image and Fig. 7.6(b) shows the synthetic image of the cloud cover. The cloudy image, Fig. 7.6(c), is generated using the given model [see Equation (7.50)]. The restored image is shown in Fig. 7.6(d) for a particular value of α and β that incurs the minimum error in estimation. Here $\alpha = 0.1$ and $\beta = 2.5$. However, sometimes α and β may be slightly adjusted to obtain a visually better result.

7.8   Other Methods

As is already said earlier that the knowledge about degradation may come in the form of parametric or non-parametric statistical models, or analytical (deterministic) models. Using Gaussian models for image and noise statistics, maximum a posterior (Bayes') estimate of restored image that is corrupted by space-variant degradation process can be derived [Hunt (1977)]. Other approaches to Bayes' analysis for image restoration have been formulated in recursive forms [Habibi (1972), Nahi (1972)]. Restoration of image by maximizing information content or *entropy* has been suggested by Burch et al. (1983). Because of great success in the one-dimensional signal processing,

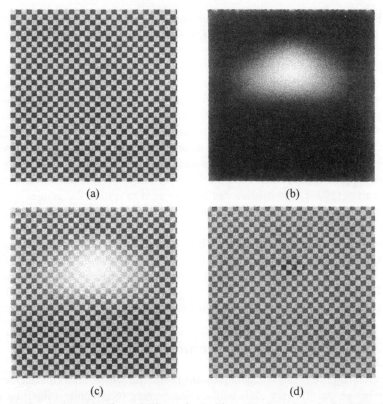

(a)   (b)

(c)   (d)

Fig. 7.6 The result of restoration by a high-emphasis filter: (a) the original cloud-free image, (b) the synthetic image of the cloud, (c) the synthetic cloudy image of (a), (d) the restored image.

there have been many attempts to extend Kalman filtering technique to two-dimensional image processing. In the two-dimensional cases, the enormity of data calls particularly for an efficient recursive processor. Another problem opposing this extension is that the specification of recursive model requires that the 'past', the 'present' and the 'future' be defined. It is, of course, trivial to do so for one-dimensional signal. For image data, however, there is no unique way to specify these. Early efforts to achieve a truly recursive two-dimensional Kalman filter were of only limited success because of both the difficulty in establishing a suitable two-dimensional recursive model and also the high dimension of the resulting state vector. Because of the aforementioned factors, computational load was found to be excessive. The problem surmounted by introducing some approximations like strip processor that updates a line segment at a time, and 'reduced update' Kalman filter (that processes elements near the present point) [Woods and Rademan (1977)]. Computational cost can also be reduced by introducing circulant matrix approximation for the banded Toeplitz structured image degradation matrices [Biemond et al. (1983)] or by using semicausal model for the recursive filtering [Jain (1977)].

Space-variant degradation and restoration models are treated in [Sahasrabudhe and Kulkarni (1979), Sawchuk (1972)]. Though non-linear methods require elaborate and costly computational procedures these cannot be overlooked, because they represent more realistic situations. Non-linear restoration methods may come directly from the image formation and recording system [Hunt (1977)]. A second situation in which non-linear image restoration may arise is from constraints. For example, inclusion of a simple constraint that all the pixels of the restored image should have non-negative value in the linear formulation leads to non-linear restoration technique [Andrews and Hunt (1977)].

Most of the linear restoration methods can be classified into two broad categories: (i) least square methods and (ii) constrained least square methods. The problem of least squares filtering of pictures with a deterministic PSF was solved by Helstrom (1967). However, one of the most important problems, namely, the ill-conditioned or singular nature of image restoration cannot be dealt with by the use of the least-squares criterion. Because of ill-condition or singularity of the image restoration problem, no unique inverse of degrading phenomenon exists. In such cases, one may use pseudoinverse technique for image restoration. Computational requirements to implement this technique is quite high. A fast computational technique for pseudoinversion is described in Pratt and Davarian (1977). The method can also be used to restore the images degraded through space-variant PSF [Sahasrabudhe and Kulkarni (1979)]. The singularity problem can also be handled by a more powerful optimization criterion, namely, minimum mean-square-error (MMSE) estimation. MMSE filter can be derived from both a priori and a posterior knowledge. The MMSE filter derived from a priori knowledge is usually referred to as a traditional Wiener filter [Andrews and Hunt (1977)]. The derivation of MMSE filter using a posterior knowledge is dealt with in Trussel and Hunt (1978). Degradation specific restoration technique has also been formulated and implemented in early days. One such example may be found in Slepian (1967) for motion blur.

Summary

In this chapter, image restoration techniques are presented which, like enhancement techniques, also improve image quality. However, unlike enhancement techniques, restoration techniques do it by removing the effects of degradation in strict mathematical sense. So, these methods are applicable only when mathematical model of image degradation is available, and the original (degradation free) image is estimated by applying inverse operation on the recorded (degraded) image.

This chapter presents mostly algebraic techniques of image restoration, such as minimum mean-square estimation, least-square estimation and constrained least-square estimation techniques. Singular value decomposition technique is also presented. The chapter includes one of the most popular statistical approach, namely, maximum a posterior estimation technique. All these methods assume additive noise only. Finally, a homomorphic filtering method is described which can restore images contaminated by both additive and multiplicative noise arisen from a practical situation.

After the improvement of quality the image may be compressed for storage/transmission or may be passed to image analysis methods for further processing. Those methods are discussed in the subsequent chapters.

Problems

1. Suppose intensity distribution of image of a point source can be approximated by a cone with radius of base equal to 3. Write down the degradation function of image formation.

2. What is meant by singularity and ill-condition in relation to image restoration? Derive expression of restored image using the least-square approach. Comment on the singularity of this filter.

3. Take a good quality image. Degrade it with the function given in Problem 1 and add the Gaussian noise with $\mu = 0$ and $\sigma = 10$. Restore the image using the constrained least-square estimation where goodness criterion is assumed that the signal and noise are independent.

4. Derive Wiener filter for image restoration using the minimum mean-square approach.

Bibliography

Andrews, H.C. and Hunt, B.R., *Digital Image Restoration*, Prentice-Hall, Englewood Cliffs, New Jersey, 1977.

Biemond, J., Rieske, J. and Garbands, J.J., 'A fast kalman filter for images degraded by both blur and noise', *IEEE Trans. on Acoustics Speech and Signal Proc.* ASSP-**31**:1248–1256, 1983.

Burch, S.F., Gull, S.F. and Skilling, J., 'Image restoration by a powerful maximum entropy method', *Computer Graphics and Image Proc.* **23**:113–128, 1983.

Chanda, B., Choudhuri, B.B. and Dutta Majumder, D., 'Application of least-square estimation technique for image restoration using image-noise correlation constraint', *IEEE Trans. on Systems, Man and Cybern.*, SMC-**14**:515–519, 1984a.

Chanda, B., Choudhuri, B.B. and Dutta Majumder, D., 'An efficient least-squares biomedical image restoration using image-noise correlation criterion', *J. IETE*, **30**:80–85, 1984b.

Chanda, B. and Dutta Majumder, D., 'An iterative algorithm for removing the effect of thin cloud cover from landsat imagery', *Mathematical Geology*, **23**:853–860, 1991.

Dines, K.A. and Kak, A.C., 'Constrained least-squares filtering', *IEEE Trans. on Acous. Speech and Signal Proc.* ASSP-**25**:346–350, 1977.

Gonzalez, R.C. and Wintz, P., *Digital Image Processing*, Addison-Wesley, Massachusetts, 1977.

Goodman, J.W., *Introduction to Fourier Optics*, John Wiely & Sons, New York, 1968.

Habibi, A. 'Two-dimensional Bayes estimate of image', *Proc. IEEE*, **60**:878–883, 1972.

Helstrom, C.W., 'Image restoration by the method of least squares', *J. Opt. Soc. America*, **57**:297–303, 1967.

Huang, T.S. and Narendra, P.M., 'Image restoration by singular value decomposition', *Applied Optics*, **14**:2213–2216, 1975.

Hunt, B.R., 'The application of constrained least squares estimation to image restoration by digital computer', *IEEE Trans. on Computer*, C-**22**:805–812, 1973.

Hunt, B.R., 'Digital image processing', *Proc. IEEE*, **63**:693–708, 1975.

Hunt, B.R., 'Bayes method in non-linear digital image restoration', *IEEE Trans. on Computer*, C-**26**:216–219, 1977.

Jain, A.K., 'A semicausal model for recursive filtering of two-dimensional images', *IEEE Trans. on Computer*, C-**26**:343–350, 1977.

Dutta Majumder, D., Chanda, B. and Mali, P.C., 'Mathematical tools for image restoration and data compression', *J. Inst. Electronics and Telecomm. Engrs.*, **35:**120–135, 1989.

McGlamery, B.L., 'Restoration of turbulence degraded images', *Jour. Opt. Soc. Amer.*, **57:**293–297, 1967.

Nahi, N.E., 'Role of recursive estimation in statistical image enhancement', *Proc. IEEE*, **60:**872–877, 1972.

Pratt, W.K. and Davarian, F., 'Fast computational techniques for pseudo-inverse and Wiener image restoration', *IEEE Trans. on Computer*, C-**26:**571–588, 1977.

Sahasrabudhe, S.C. and Kulkarni, A.D., 'Shift-variant image degradation and restoration using SVD', *Computer Graphics and Image Processing*, **9:**203–212, 1979.

Sawchuk, A.A., 'Space-variant image motion degradation and restoration', *Proc. IEEE*, **60:**854–861, 1972.

Slepian, D., 'Restoration of photographs blurred by image motion', *Bell Systems Tech. J.* **46:**2353–2362, 1967.

Trussel, H.J. and Hunt, B.R., 'Notes on nonlinear image restoration by maximizing a posteriori probability', *IEEE Trans. on Acous. Speech and Signal Proc.* ASSP-**26:**174–176, 1978.

Woods, J.W. and Rademan, C.H., 'Kalman filtering in two dimensions', *IEEE Trans. on Information Theory*, IT-**23:**473–482, 1977.

Chapter 8

Image Compression

8.1 Introduction

Users of digital image processing techniques usually have to handle a large volume of data. Storing image data for future use needs large storage space. Similarly transmitting image data in reasonable time needs wide channel capacity. To reduce these requirements the technique we use is called *data compression*. So, compression techniques represent (almost) same pictorial information in a more compact form by removing redundancies. In essence, compression techniques represent image data using fewer bits than what is required for original image. Thus this class of techniques may also include *feature extraction/selection* procedures. To understand the basic concept of compression techniques let us consider the following example in which a digital signal (or image, in case of two dimension) is represented by a vector $\mathbf{g}$ having M elements, i.e $\mathbf{g} = (g_0 \; g_1 \; g_2 \; \cdots \; g_{M-1})^\mathrm{T}$, where g_j represents j-th sampled value. Also suppose that every element of the vector is coded by b bits. So, total number of bits required to represent this digital signal is Mb. Now suppose that the vector $\mathbf{g}$ is transformed to another vector $\mathbf{G}$, say, by a transformation matrix $\mathbf{T}$, i.e.

$$\mathbf{G} = \mathbf{Tg} \tag{8.1}$$

where $\mathbf{G}$ can be represented by K bits. This may be achieved either by retaining only $M'(<M)$ elements of $\mathbf{G}$ or by encoding the elements of $\mathbf{G}$ in such a way that the average number of bits per element is $b'(<b)$. In the former case $K = M'b$, and in the latter case $K = Mb'$. Thus the amount of data reduction is given by

$$C = \frac{Mb - K}{Mb} \times 100\% \tag{8.2}$$

With reference to earlier discussion retaining M' elements of $\mathbf{G}$ is actually same as feature extraction. Therefore, the major steps of data compression procedure is (i) *transformation,* (ii) *feature selection* and (iii) *encoding* as shown in Fig. 8.1.

Now suppose we reconstruct the digital signal from $\mathbf{G}$ and obtain $\tilde{\mathbf{g}}$. Hence, any discrepancy between $\tilde{\mathbf{g}}$ and $\mathbf{g}$ is considered as error introduced by the compression technique. Usually amount of error increases with reduction in the amount of data. So, the objective of the compression technique is to achieve maximum C without introducing objectionable error. If amount of error

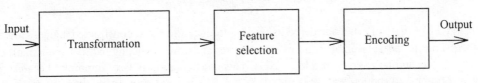

Fig. 8.1 Schematic diagram representing the major steps of data compression procedure.

145

introduced is zero we call it *error-free compression* or *loss-less compression*; otherwise it is a *lossy compression*. Loss-less compression is perfectly invertible. That means original image can be exactly recovered from its compressed representation. The encoder–decoder pairs that incur zero error are also referred to as *information processing*. In case of lossy compression, perfect recovery of original image is not possible. On the other hand, amount of data reduction is usually more in case of lossy compression than that of loss-less compression. In fact, following Shanon source entropy concept it can be shown that maximum amount of data reduction that can be achieved through loss-less compression technique is

$$\frac{b - H}{b} \times 100\%$$

where H is the entropy associated with $\mathbf{g}$ [Abramson (1963)].

8.2   Error Criterion

To judge the performance of a lossy compression technique we need to decide upon using the error criterion. The error criteria commonly used may be classified into two broad groups: (i) *objective criteria* and (ii) *subjective criteria* [Gonzalez and Wintz (1987)]. The first group of measures need mathematical formulation and restricted to statistical sense only; while it is very difficult to standardize the second group of measures as it involves human observers. Let us denote the original image and the reconstructed image by $g(r, c)$ and $\tilde{g}(r, c)$, respectively. Suppose the images are of size $M \times N$.

8.2.1   Objective Criteria

The objective error criterion most often used is the *mean-squared* one. This is defined as

$$e_{\text{ms}} = \frac{1}{MN} \sum_{c=0}^{N-1} \sum_{r=0}^{M-1} \{g(r, c) - \tilde{g}(r, c)\}^2 \tag{8.3}$$

Sometimes *root-mean-squared* (rms) error is preferred over mean-squared one. The rms error criterion is defined as

$$e_{\text{rms}} = \left[\frac{1}{MN} \sum_{c=0}^{N-1} \sum_{r=0}^{M-1} \{g(r, c) - \tilde{g}(r, c)\}^2 \right]^{1/2} \tag{8.4}$$

However, values of mean-squared as well as root-mean-squared error criteria depend on the range of values of the $g(r, c)$. So, it is better to normalize the error measure with respect to signal energy. As a result, we arrive at an error criterion commonly known as *signal-to-noise* ratio defined as

$$e_{\text{SNR}} = \frac{\sum_{c=0}^{N-1} \sum_{c=0}^{M-1} \{g(r, c) - \tilde{g}(r, c)\}^2}{\sum_{c=0}^{N-1} \sum_{r=0}^{M-1} g^2(r, c)} \tag{8.5}$$

Here, $\{g(r, c) - \tilde{g}(r, c)\}^2$ is considered as noise introduced in the reconstructed signal. However, all these criteria measure error in an average sense, and cannot distinguish between small error at many pixels and large error at a few pixels. This consideration is very important because same type of error may produce widely different visual effect depending on the context of the local neighbourhood of the noisy pixels.

8.2.2 Subjective Criteria

The subjective error measure is performed as follows. Original image and the reconstructed image are shown to a large group of examiners. Each examiner assigns grade to the reconstructed image with respect to the original image. These grades may be drawn from a subjective scale divided as, say, excellent, good, reasonable, poor, unacceptable [Frendendall and Behrend (1960)]. However, the scale can, of course, be divided into a coarser or finer bins. Finally, based on grades assigned by all the examiners, an overall grade is assigned to the reconstructed image. Complement of this grade gives an idea of the subjective error.

8.3 Lossy Compression

In this section, we present transform and sub-band compression techniques. Here input vector is approximated either by a subset of linear transform coefficients or by a set of parameters associated with a pattern or by index to another vector close to it. In such cases, the decompression method must undo the transformation either by inverse transform or by regeneration of the graylevel pattern with the stored parameters or by using a look-up table, respectively.

8.3.1 Transform Compression

Let us assume that $\mathbf{T}$ represents orthogonal transformation matrix that maps $\mathbf{g}$ onto another orthogonal space [Clarke (1985)]. It can be shown that Karhunen–Loeve (K–L) transform is the optimum transform for signal representation with respect to mean-squared error sense [Ahmed and Rao (1975)]. Secondly, if we retain only M' elements of $\mathbf{G}$, then mean-squared error incurred is minimum of sum of $(M - M')$ eigenvalues of covariance matrix of $\mathbf{g}$. This is because the discrete signal is converted into a sequence of uncorrelated coefficients [Habibi and Wintz (1971)]. As described in Chapter 2, K–L transformation matrix is developed based on the statistical properties of the signal. We present the steps of K–L transform approach for image compression with an example as under.

Given an image of size $N \times N$ where gray values of pixels are considered as random variables and within a small block they are highly correlated. Let us divide the image into n number of blocks each of size $m \times m$ (see Fig. 8.2) and denote the blocks by $g_i(r, c)$ for $i = 0, 1, 2, \ldots,$

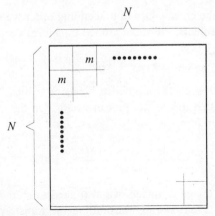

Fig. 8.2 Blocks of size $m \times m$ of an $N \times N$ image.

$n-1$. Now we form column vectors $\mathbf{g}_i$s having M elements corresponding to each block by lexicographic ordering of the pixels, where $M = m^2$. Let us denote mean vector and covariance matrix of $\mathbf{g}_i$ ($i = 0, 1, 2, ..., n-1$) by $\bar{\mathbf{g}}$ and Σ_g, respectively. It should be noted that $\Sigma_g(k, k)$ is the variance of the k-th element of the image vector $\mathbf{g}$. Let us denote it also by $\sigma_g^2(k)$. Suppose the k-th element of the column vector $\mathbf{g}$ corresponds to the (r, c) pixel of the image block (or the image), then $\sigma_g^2(k) = \sigma_g^2(r, c)$. Now we can find M eigenvectors $\mathbf{e}_j$ ($j = 0, 1, 2, ..., M-1$) of Σ_g corresponding to its eigenvalues λ_j. The orthogonal transform matrix $\mathbf{T}$ is formed by these eigenvectors as its rows. So the covariance matrix of $\mathbf{G}$ can be obtained as

$$\Sigma_G = \mathbf{T}\Sigma_g\mathbf{T}^T = \begin{bmatrix} \lambda_0 & & & & \\ & \lambda_1 & & 0 & \\ & & \lambda_2 & & \\ & 0 & & \ddots & \\ & & & & \lambda_{M-1} \end{bmatrix}$$

Let us assume that the eigenvalues are arranged in descending order. If not, we can have them arranged in desired order just by shuffling the rows of $\mathbf{T}$ (i.e. the eigenvectors of Σ_g) accordingly. Now, since Σ_G is a diagonal matrix we can say the elements of the vector $\mathbf{G}_i$, i.e. the pixel values $G_i(u, v)$ of transformed image block are uncorrelated. As before, $\Sigma_G(k, k)$ is the variance of the k-th element of the transformed image vector $\mathbf{G}$. Let us denote it by $\sigma_G^2(k)$, then $\sigma_G^2(k) = \sigma_G^2(u, v)$. In statistics, this technique is called *factor analysis* or *principal component analysis*. Finally, if we want to retain only M' elements of the vector $\mathbf{G}$, then the transformation matrix $\mathbf{T}$ as in Equation (8.1) is a $M' \times M$ matrix formed by first M' eigenvectors as its rows. Therefore, we obtain transform vector $\mathbf{G}_i$ having M' elements as $\mathbf{G}_i = \mathbf{T}(\mathbf{g}_i - \bar{\mathbf{g}})$. It can be shown that if j-th element of the transform vector is discarded, then mean-square error is increased by λ_j. Hence, by discarding last $(M - M')$ elements of transform vector the amount of error introduced in signal representation is given by

$$e(M') = \sum_{j=M'+1}^{M} \lambda_j$$

Thus by (virtually) arranging the eigenvalues in descending order we minimize the error incurred due to discarding $(M - M')$ elements. From the pruned transform vector, original image vector is reconstructed as

$$\tilde{\mathbf{g}}_i = \mathbf{T}^T\mathbf{G}_i + \bar{\mathbf{g}} \tag{8.6}$$

Now suppose elements of both $\mathbf{g}$ and $\mathbf{G}$ are coded by using b bits. Then we need $nM'b$ bits to store n transform blocks and $M'b$ bits to store mean vector. On the other hand, to store original image we need nMb bits. Therefore,

$$C = \frac{nM - (n+1)M'}{nM} \times 100\%$$

Since eigenvectors vary from image to image, we also need to store/transmit the transformation matrix $\mathbf{T}$ of size $M' \times M$. To avoid storing/transmitting the transformation matrix we may use some standard orthogonal transforms such as Fourier, Walsh, Hadamard, Haar, discrete cosine, etc. [Wintz (1972)]. Unfortunately, no other transform can diagonalize the covariance matrix in general. Diagonalizing capability of a transformation can be used for comparing its performance with that of K–L transformation for a given matrix. Suppose Σ_G^{tr} denotes transformed covariance matrix due to any transformation tr, i.e.

$$\Sigma_G^{tr} = T_{tr} \Sigma_g T_{tr}^T$$

It can be shown that diagonalization of covariance matrix is equivalent to the maximization of variance of a random variable. So, the *merit* of a transformation may be defined with respect to K–L transformation as [Dutta Majumder et al. (1989)]

$$\text{Merit (tr)} = \frac{\sum_{j=0}^{M-1} [\Sigma_G^{tr}(j,j) - \Sigma_g(j,j)]^2}{\sum_{j=0}^{M-1} [\lambda_j - \Sigma_g(j,j)]^2} \tag{8.7}$$

It can be seen that for any transformation matrix other than K–L transform, $0 \leq \text{Merit (tr)} < 1$. However, when we select M' rows of a standard orthogonal transformation matrix for image data compression, it is assumed that $\sigma_G^2(u, v)$, the variance of $G(u, v)$, is known a priori. If it is not known, we may estimate the value through modelling the class of images to be compressed. Let us assume that the images or image blocks can be described statistically by a first-order Markov process. To reduce computational cost let us also assume that the rows and the columns can be treated independently, and the variance of all the pixel values of the input image $g(r, c)$ is σ_g^2. So, we have the covariance matrices for the rows and columns, respectively, as

$$\Sigma_{g(r)} = \sigma_g^2 R_r \quad \text{and} \quad \Sigma_{g(c)} = \sigma_g^2 R_c$$

where

$$R_r = \begin{bmatrix} 1 & \rho_r & \rho_r^2 & \cdots & \rho_r^{M-1} \\ \rho_r & 1 & \rho_r & \cdots & \rho_r^{M-2} \\ \rho_r^2 & \rho_r & 1 & \cdots & \rho_r^{M-3} \\ \vdots & \vdots & \vdots & & \vdots \\ \rho_r^{M-1} & \rho_r^{M-2} & \rho_r^{M-3} & \cdots & 1 \end{bmatrix}$$

and

$$R_c = \begin{bmatrix} 1 & \rho_c & \rho_c^2 & \cdots & \rho_c^{M-1} \\ \rho_c & 1 & \rho_c & \cdots & \rho_c^{M-2} \\ \rho_c^2 & \rho_c & 1 & \cdots & \rho_c^{M-3} \\ \vdots & \vdots & \vdots & & \vdots \\ \rho_c^{M-1} & \rho_c^{M-2} & \rho_c^{M-3} & \cdots & 1 \end{bmatrix}$$

Corresponding covariance matrices in the transform domain are given by

$$\Sigma_{G(u)}^{tr} = T_{tr} \Sigma_{g(r)} T_{tr}^T \quad \text{and} \quad \Sigma_{G(v)}^{tr} = T_{tr} \Sigma_{g(c)} T_{tr}^T$$

Finally, the variance of the (u, v)-th element of the transform image block (or the transform image) can then be computed as

$$\Sigma_G^{tr}(k,\ k) = \sigma_G^2(u,\ v) = \Sigma_{G(u)}^{tr}(u)\Sigma_{G(v)}^{tr}(v)$$

Under the said assumptions performance of Discrete Cosine transform is almost same as that of K–L transform. Secondly, $\Sigma_G^{tr}(k,\ k)$ is maximum for $k = 0$ and it decreases very rapidly as k increases. For other transforms also we observe similar characteristics except rate of decrement is less and monotonicity of decrement is not consistent. However, considering computational cost and quality, Fourier transform usually is the choice next to K–L transform for image data compression. Figure 8.3 shows results of transform compression using K–L transform and Fourier transform.

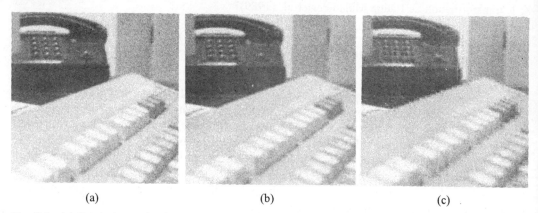

| (a) | (b) | (c) |

Fig. 8.3 (a) Original gray-level image, where number of bits per pixel is 8, (b) image reconstructed from K–L transform compressed image where number of bits per pixels is 2, (c) image reconstructed from Fourier transform compressed image where number of bits per pixels is 2.

The technique of principal component analysis or the transform compression techniques can be straightaway used for compressing multi-spectral images. Here vectors are formed by the values due to different spectral bands at the same pixel position of the same scene and is represented by $[g_1(r,\ c)\ g_2(r,\ c)\ \dots\ g_M(r,\ c)]^T$ at each $(r,\ c)$. The method is suitable for satellite image data compression and analysis where almost same information can be preserved using much less number of transformed bands [Richard (1986)].

8.3.2 Block Truncation Compression

In the previous section we have described methods of lossy compression by selecting important features in transform domain. Here we present a compression technique that processes data in the spatial domain itself. Basic idea of this method is to split the image into a number of small non-overlapping square blocks and then graylevels within each block are approximated by one of two graylevels l_1 and l_2. These graylevels l_1 and l_2 are so chosen that mean and variance of original and approximated graylevels of each block be the same. Suppose an image of size $N \times N$ is divided into n number of blocks each of size $m \times m$. Let us assume that graylevels within i-th block is approximated as

$$\tilde{g}_i(r,\ c) = \begin{cases} l_1 & \text{if } g_i(r,\ c) < \text{thres} \\ l_2 & \text{otherwise} \end{cases} \qquad (8.8)$$

for all (r, c), where *thres* represents a predefined threshold for converting a graylevel image into a binary image. Suppose the number of pixels in the i-th block that have approximated value equal to l_1, is M_1, and that equal to l_2 is M_2. So $M_1 + M_2 = m^2 = M$ (say). Now we have

$$\bar{g}_i = \frac{1}{M} \sum_{r=0}^{m-1} \sum_{c=0}^{m-1} g_i(r, c) \tag{8.9}$$

$$\overline{g_i^2} = \frac{1}{M} \sum_{r=0}^{m-1} \sum_{c=0}^{m-1} g_i^2(r, c) \tag{8.10}$$

As we have said earlier, average graylevel of $g_i(r, c)$ and that of $\tilde{g}_i(r, c)$ are the same, i.e.

$$\frac{1}{M}(M_1 l_1 + M_2 l_2) = \frac{1}{M} \sum_{r=0}^{m-1} \sum_{c=0}^{m-1} g_i(r, c)$$

and the variance of graylevel within these blocks are also the same, i.e.

$$\frac{1}{M}[M_1(l_1 - \bar{g}_i)^2 + M_2(l_2 - \bar{g}_i)^2] = \frac{1}{M} \sum_{r=0}^{m-1} \sum_{c=0}^{m-1} \{g_i(r, c) - \bar{g}_i\}^2$$

or

$$M_1 l_1^2 + M_2 l_2^2 + (M_1 + M_2)\bar{g}_i^2 - 2(M_1 l_1 + M_2 l_2)\bar{g}_i = \sum_{r=0}^{m-1} \sum_{c=0}^{m-1} [g_i^2(r, c) + \bar{g}_i^2 - 2\bar{g}_i g_i(r, c)]$$

or

$$M_1 l_1^2 + M_2 l_2^2 + M\bar{g}_i^2 - 2M\bar{g}_i \bar{g}_i = \sum_{r=0}^{m-1} \sum_{c=0}^{m-1} g_i^2(r, c) + M\bar{g}_i^2 - 2\bar{g}_i \sum_{r=0}^{m-1} \sum_{c=0}^{m-1} g_i(r, c)$$

or

$$M_1 l_1^2 + M_2 l_2^2 = \sum_{r=0}^{m-1} \sum_{c=0}^{m-1} g_i^2(r, c)$$

Therefore, l_1 and l_2 are obtained by solving the following two equations:

$$\frac{1}{M}(M_1 l_1 + M_2 l_2) = \bar{g}_i \tag{8.11}$$

$$\frac{1}{M}(M_1 l_1^2 + M_2 l_2^2) = \overline{g_i^2} \tag{8.12}$$

Solving Equations (8.11) and (8.12) subject to constraint $l_1 < l_2$, we obtain

$$l_1 = \bar{g}_i - \sigma \sqrt{\frac{M_2}{M_1}} \tag{8.13}$$

$$l_2 = \overline{g}_i + \sigma \sqrt{\frac{M_1}{M_2}} \tag{8.14}$$

where $\sigma = \sqrt{\overline{g_i^2} - \overline{g}_i^2}$.

Threshold may be set as average graylevel, i.e. thres = $\overline{g}_i$. One may also choose threshold as follows. Suppose pixels values $\{g_i(r, c) \mid r = 0, 1, \ldots m - 1 \text{ and } c = 0, 1, \ldots, m - 1\}$ are arranged in ascending order to get $\{g^{(0)}, g^{(1)}, \ldots, g^{(M - 1)}\}$. Then

$$\text{thres} = \begin{cases} g^{(k)} & \text{if } g^{(k)} - g^{(k-1)} > g^{(j)} - g^{(j-1)} \text{ for all } j, \text{ and } j \neq k \\ \overline{g}_i & \text{otherwise} \end{cases}$$

This means that the threshold is selected based on the largest difference in graylevel. Let us consider the following example for better understanding of this compression technique.

Example   Figure 8.4(a) shows a 4×4 block which is a part of a large graylevel image. Average graylevel and standard deviation of graylevels within this block is 74 (approx.), and 86.78 (approx) respectively. Compressed image blocks obtained by using average graylevel threshold and threshold corresponding to the largest graylevel difference respectively are represented by binary images as shown in Figs. 8.4(b) and 8.4(d) along with the values of l_1 and l_2. In these figures, graylevels less than threshold are represented by 0 and those greater than or equal to threshold are by 1. Thus the whole block can be represented by 16 bits and values of l_1 and l_2. Secondly, for Fig. 8.4(b) $M_1 = 8$ and $M_2 = 8$, and for Fig. 8.4(d) $M_1 = 6$ and $M_2 = 10$. Values of l_1 and l_2 are computed using Equation (8.13) and Equation (8.14), respectively. For Fig. 8.4(b), $l_1 = 29$ and $l_2 = 119$, and for Fig. 8.4(d) $l_1 = 16$ and $l_2 = 109$. So, for each compressed block two extra bytes (i.e. 16 bits) are needed to store these values. Finally, a block is reconstructed based on these values and the corresponding binary image. Hence, image block reconstructed from Fig. 8.4(b) is shown in Fig. 8.4(c), and that from Fig. 8.4(d) in Fig. 8.4(e).   ■

It is clear from the aforesaid approximation method that the i-th block of a graylevel image can be represented by two values l_1 and l_2, and binary image block whose pixels have value 0 or 1. In fact, the value 0 is assigned to the pixels that have approximated value l_1 and the value 1 to the pixels that have approximated value l_2. It can be shown that if $g(r, c)$ is represented by b bits, then b bits can reliably represent the values of l_1 and l_2 rounded to integers. Since a binary image of size $m \times m$ needs M bits to be represented, then the amount of data reduction is given by

$$C = \frac{Mb - M - 2b}{Mb} \times 100\% \tag{8.15}$$

Hence the method is useful when $m \geq 2$, where $b = 8$. However, as m increases the quality of compressed image deteriorates. It is shown that almost no distortion is visible when $m = 4$ [Delp and Mitchell (1979)] and still achieves $C = 75\%$. An example of image reconstructed from block truncation coded real image is shown in Fig. 8.5. Finally, this method can be implemented on hardware very easily [Rosenfeld and Kak (1982)].

17	22	20	140
19	26	136	95
25	126	69	98
133	73	92	94

(a)

0	0	0	1
0	0	1	1
0	1	0	1
1	0	1	1

$l_1 = 29, \quad l_2 = 119$

(b)

0	0	0	1
0	0	1	1
0	1	1	1
1	1	1	1

$l_1 = 16, \quad l_2 = 109$

(d)

29	29	29	119
29	29	119	119
29	119	29	119
119	29	119	119

(c)

16	16	16	109
16	16	109	109
16	109	109	109
109	109	109	109

(e)

Fig. 8.4 Example showing block truncation coding: (a) original graylevel image block of size 4 × 4, (b) compressed image using average graylevel as threshold, (c) reconstructed image from (b), (d) compressed image using the threshold selected based on the largest difference in graylevel, (e) reconstructed image from (d).

Fig. 8.5 Result of block truncation coding for $m = 4$. Original graylevel image is same as in Fig. 8.3(a) where number of bits per pixel is 8.

8.3.3 Vector Quantization Compression

Here we present *vector quantization compression* technique as is described by Gray et al. (1992). Other methods may be found in Abut (1990). Like transform, compression image domain is divided into, say, n non-overlapping blocks of size $m \times m$. Then by lexicographic ordering the pixel values within each block, we form an M-dimensional vector $\mathbf{g}_i$, where $M = m^2$. Usually, value of m is small. When the encoder has some predefined M-dimensional vectors $\mathbf{X}_j$ in its database, the input to the encoder (or data compressor) is g_i and the output is k (see Fig. 8.6), such that

$$d(g_i, \mathbf{X}_k) \le d(g_i, \mathbf{X}_j) \qquad \text{for all } j \tag{8.16}$$

where d is a *metric*. However, if we have more than one $\mathbf{X}_k$ that satisfy Equation (8.16), then we may select one among them arbitrarily. The decoder (or decompressor) works exactly reverse way. Here the input is a code word k and the output is the corresponding vector $\mathbf{X}_k$ obtained through simple table look-up operation.

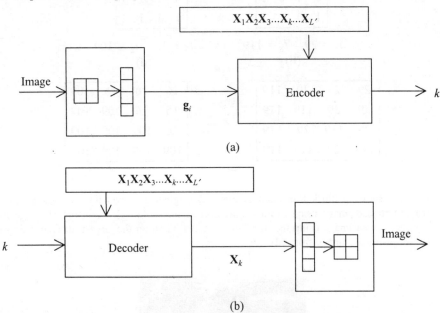

(a)

(b)

Fig. 8.6   Schematic diagram of (a) encoder and (b) decoder for vector quantization compression technique.

Thus the vector $\mathbf{g}_i$ is represented by another vector that is reasonably close to it. So, we see that unlike transform compression vector, quantization compression technique approximates data in the spatial domain itself. Suppose the number of vectors stored in the encoder is L', where $L' = 2^{n'}$. Then j can be represented by n' bits. So, the amount of data reduction is

$$C = \frac{Mb - n'}{Mb} \times 100\%$$

For example, if $m = 2$ and the original image has 256 graylevels, and if the encoder contains 1024 predefined vectors, then $C \approx 69\%$. As m increases we achieve greater data reduction, but consequently quality of compressed image falls and computational cost increases exponentially. Figure 8.7 shows the result of this compression technique for $m = 2$ and $n' = 8$. The remaining question yet to be answered is, how to decide upon the vectors $\mathbf{X}_j$s stored in the encoder as well as the decoder. There are various methods proposed in the literature [Gersho and Gray (1992), Abut(1990)]. We present a simple one, as follows.

Fig. 8.7   Result of vector quantization compression technique for $m = 2$ and $n' = 8$. Original graylevel image is same as Fig. 8.3(a) where number of bits per pixel is 8.

Each vector $\mathbf{g}_i$ can be represented by a point in an M-dimensional space. So, each image can be represented by n points in that space. Now from the desired amount of data reduction we first compute n'. The points accumulated (due to one or more images) in that space are divided into L' cluster[1]. Finally, a representative (usually the centroid) of a cluster is selected as the vector $\mathbf{X}_j$. So from L' clusters, we get L' number of vectors. In practice, not all the clusters are equally populated. Hence further data reduction is possible by assigning variable length code to the index (i.e. j) to the vectors. Naturally, an index to representative of a highly populated cluster is given a shorter code than that of less populated cluster. Huffman coding technique (described in the next section) may be used to assign codes to these indexes.

8.4   Loss-less Compression

It is explained in Section 8.1 that the data reduction (i.e. C) can also be achieved by encoding the pixel values in such a way that the average number of bits b' used to represent each pixel be much less than b, the number of bits used to represent each pixel originally. Here we are not discarding any information as is done in lossy compression, but we represent more frequently occurring values by shorter codes and the less occurring values by longer codes. Hence the data compression we achieve, if any, incur zero error. This method is suitable for those images where frequencies of different graylevels vary widely.

Suppose the image contains L different graylevels $i = 0, 1, 2, ..., L - 1$, and n_i denotes frequency of occurrence of pixels having graylevel i. Then the probability of occurrence of graylevel i in the image is

$$p_i = \frac{n_i}{\Sigma_{i=0}^{L-1} n_i}$$

Let us define entropy H associated with the graylevel as

$$H = -\sum_{i=0}^{L-1} p_i \log_2 p_i$$

---

[1]Details of clustering technique is presented in Chapter 15.

Entropy is a measure of randomness in the set of random variables. For example, if one of the random variables of a set occurs with probability 1, then outcome is always known in advance. So, there is no randomness and entropy attains its lowest value, i.e. $H = 0$. On the other hand, when all the variables are equally likely, i.e. $p_0 = p_1 = \cdots = p_{L-1} = 1/L$, then the randomness is maximized and the entropy attains its greatest value $\log_2 L$. In image graylevel encoding process, entropy represents total amount of information associated with the image through its pixel values. So, H is a measure of randomness in occurrence of graylevels in the image. Randomness in occurrence of graylevel in the image is also reflected in the number of average bits required to represent them. Thus, there must exist a relation between H and b' for an image. In fact, if pixel values, i.e. graylevels are independent of each other then H is the lower bound of b'. In other words, b' cannot be less than H in loss-less compression.

8.4.1 Huffman Coding

The most efficient technique to assign binary words of unequal length to the graylevels is due to Huffman (1952). The method is basically source encoding that reduces the number of bits required to represent an image by making use of graylevel statistics. Note that the image can be reconstructed perfectly from the compressed data. Huffman encoding scheme has two major steps: construction of probability tree and assigning code word two to each node of the constructed tree. The algorithm may be described as follows:

Algorithm

Step 1: Construct a tree based on the graylevel frequencies n_i.

1(a): Compute probability p_i associated with each graylevel. Consider these graylevels as terminal nodes or lowest level nodes of a tree.

1(b): Add two lowest probabilities to form a node at higher level. So, probability associated with the newly-formed node is equal to the sum of those two probabilities.

(Note: If more than two probabilities satisfy the condition to be added at a certain level, any two may be selected arbitrarily from them.)

1(c): Every other node forms a node at the higher level and the same probability is associated with it.

1(d): Repeat Steps 1(b) and 1(c) until we reach at a single node, namely root node.

So, we have constructed a binary tree. However, a speciality of this tree is that at each level only one node splits into two nodes.

Step 2: Assign binary code words to each graylevel depending on its probability.

2(a): Assign a null code to the root node.

2(b): Whenever a node splits into two nodes, the code

corresponding to the right child is constructed by appending a '1' to the code at the said node and for left child a '0' is appended.

2(c): Code at any node that have single child is assigned to the child node.

2(d): Repeat Steps 2(b) and 2(c) until terminal nodes are reached.

Binary code word assigned to each node should now be used to represent corresponding graylevel. It is clear that assigned code words are of unequal length.

From this algorithm we see that the higher probabilities seldom add with other during the construction of the probability tree. Consequently, very few splits occur along the path from the root node to the terminal node with high probability. So the binary code corresponding to this graylevel is constructed by appending very few '0' or '1' bits. As a result, length of the said code should be small. On the other hand, binary code word assigned to the graylevel having low probability should be long. Suppose the length of the i-th graylevel is l_i. Then

$$b' = \sum_{i=0}^{L-1} p_i l_i \tag{8.17}$$

The technique may be better clarified with an example as given below. Let us consider an image having 8 different graylevels. Normalized frequency or probabilities of each graylevel is shown in Fig. 8.8. We constructed the probability tree as described in Algorithm 9.1 and assigned Huffman code to each graylevel accordingly. Figure 8.8(a) shows the construction of the tree and Fig. 8.8(b) shows the way the codes are generated. We see from the example that shorter codes are assigned to more probable graylevels and longer codes to less probable graylevels. So average number of bits required per pixel is

$$b' = 0.05 \times 5 + 0.008 \times 6 + 0.022 \times 6 + 0.06 \times 4$$
$$+ 0.18 \times 3 + 0.13 \times 3 + 0.07 \times 3 + 0.48 \times 1$$
$$= 2.29$$

Now entropy for this image considering the graylevels is

$$H = - (0.05 \times \log_2 0.05 + 0.008 \times \log_2 0.008 + 0.022 \times \log_2 0.022 + 0.06 \times \log_2 0.06$$
$$+ 0.18 \times \log_2 0.18 + 0.13 \times \log_2 0.13 + 0.07 \times \log_2 0.07 + 0.48 \times \log_2 0.48)$$
$$= -2.24$$

Hence, in this case $b' > H$. Figure 8.9 shows another example where $b' = H$. As before, Fig. 8.9(a) shows the construction of the probability tree and Fig. 8.9(b) shows the way the codes are generated. Here $b' = H = 1.999$. If we use BCD code or gray code or any other equal length code, then we would require 3 bits per pixel for the images considered in these examples. So in both the examples we achieve significant compression without introducing any error by using Huffman coding scheme.

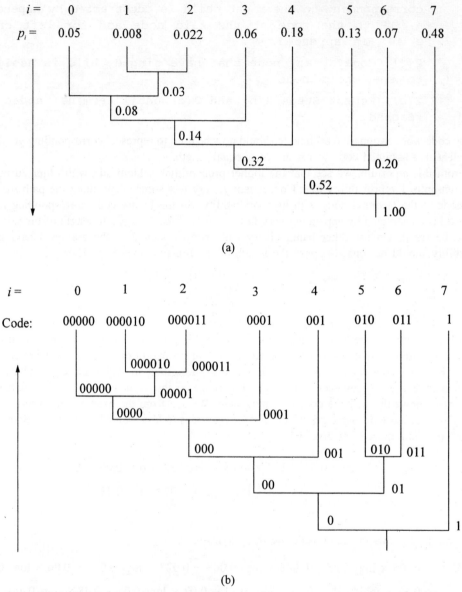

Fig. 8.8 Example showing Huffman coding scheme: (a) construction of probability tree, (b) assignment of code words.

We may define a *compact code* as one whose average word length is less than or equal to that of any uniquely decodable code for the same set of input probabilities [Gonzalez and Wintz (1987)]. It should be noted that Huffman code is a compact code, or simply a minimum-length code. However, compression may be achieved through Huffman coding scheme only when graylevels are highly unequally distributed. The images which do not satisfy this criterion may be converted in such a way that the histogram of the transformed image becomes sharply peaked.

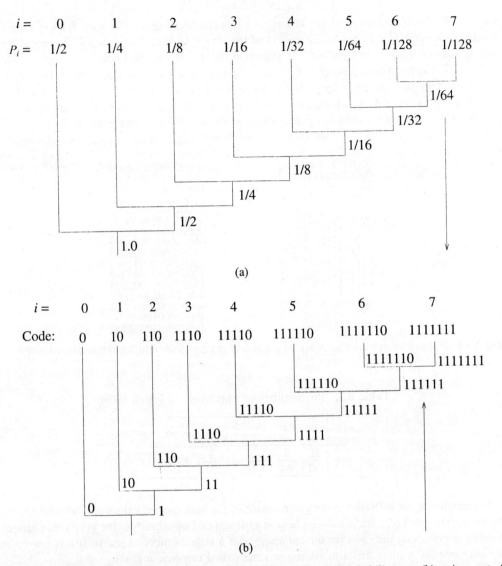

Fig. 8.9 Example showing Huffman coding scheme: (a) construction of probability tree, (b) assignment of code words.

An example of such transformation is taking the difference between graylevels of adjacent pixels, i.e.

$$g'(r, c) = \begin{cases} g(r, c) & \text{for } r = 0 \\ g(r, c) - g(r - 1, c) & \text{for } r > 0 \end{cases} \tag{8.18}$$

for all c, or

$$g'(r, c) = \begin{cases} g(r, c) & \text{for } c = 0 \\ g(r, c) - g(r, c - 1) & \text{for } c > 0 \end{cases} \tag{8.19}$$

for all r. To illustrate the use of this technique let us consider Fig. 8.10. Figure 8.10(a) shows the pixel values of a 16×16 image. Graylevel of the image lies between 0 and 7. So, equal length coding scheme needs 3 bits per pixel to represent the graylevels. Secondly, since $p_i = \frac{1}{8}$ for $i = 0, 1, \ldots, 7$, Huffman code also needs 3 bits per pixel. Now by using Equation (8.18), we get a transformed image as shown in Fig. 8.10(b). The probabilities of graylevel present in the transformed image is shown in Table 8.1. It may be noted that probability density function sharply peaked at graylevel 0. Hence, if we encode the graylevels of the transformed image using Huffman coding scheme, we achieve $b' = 1.3$. That means a significant reduction in data can be achieved.

```
0000222244446666        0000200020002000
0000222244446666        0000200020002000
0000222244446666        0000200020002000
0000222244446666        0000200020002000
0000111122223333        0000100010001000
0000111122223333        0000100010001000
0000111122223333        0000100010001000
0000111122223333        0000100010001000
1111333355557777        1000200020002000
1111333355557777        1000200020002000
1111333355557777        1000200020002000
1111333355557777        1000200020002000
4444555566667777        4000200020002000
4444555566667777        4000200020002000
4444555566667777        4000200020002000
4444555566667777        4000200020002000
```

Fig. 8.10 (a) An example of digital image whose graylevel range from 0 to 7, (b) transformed image of (a) obtained by using Equation (8.18).

Table 8.1 Probabilities of graylevels in Fig. 8.10(b)

i	0	1	2	3	4	5	6	7
p_i	$\frac{50}{64}$	$\frac{7}{64}$	$\frac{6}{64}$	0	$\frac{1}{64}$	0	0	0

Though it is not reflected in the given example, the transformed values may also be negative. However, this kind of transformations help in efficient coding whenever the graylevel changes at a uniform rate along the rows (or the columns) over a large number of pixels. If this rate be zero we may employ a more efficient coding scheme called *run-length coding*.

8.4.2 Run-length Coding

Suppose the value of pixels (i.e. graylevel) along a row of a digital image are given by a sequence of integers $g_0, g_1, g_2,$ and so on. Then the graylevel along this row may be represented by a set of ordered pairs (l_i, n_i), where n_i is the number of consecutive pixels that have same value and l_i is that value. In other words, n_i is the length of the run of constant graylevel and, hence, the name of the coding scheme [Wilkins and Wintz (1970)]. For example, consider the following string of integers as a sequence of pixel values along a row of an image:

33333355555555222222222222222233311111111144444444444444444222222

Thus run-length encoding scheme represents this row as:

$$(3, 6), (5, 8), (2, 15), (3, 3), (1, 9), (4, 17), (2, 6)$$

Similar representation is generated for all the rows of the entire image. Thus significant data reduction can be achieved if the run-lengths are large, or in other words, number of ordered pairs is small. Suppose maximum graylevel present in the image is L and the number of pixels in each row is N. Then using equal length code we need $\log_2 L$ bits to store l_i and $\log_2 N$ bits for n_i; that means each ordered pair needs $\log_2 L + \log_2 N$ bits. Usually, n_i is much less than N; that means many code words using $\log_2 N$ bits either are not used or are used seldom. Hence, further data reduction may be achieved using Huffman codes for n_i. This encoding scheme can be extended to two-dimensions. Two examples of such extension are *predictive differential quantizer (PDQ)* and *double delta coding (DDC)* [Gonzalez and Wintz (1987)].

In case of binary image, where pixel can have one of the two values, 0 and 1, further reduction of data is possible. Since, at the start of every run the pixel value toggles between 0 and 1, we need not keep l_i except the first run. Thus, a row can be represented by a sequence of integers: $(l, n_0, n_1, n_2, ...)$, where l is the value of the first pixel of the row so it is either 0 or 1. Consider the following example which represents a row of a binary image.

$$11111111111000000000000000011111100000000011111111111111111111000000$$

This row can be represented by $(1, 11, 15, 6, 9, 17, 6)$. Here, one may use Huffman code also to represent n_is. Another approach could be representing a row by the runs of 1-pixels only. In that case a row is represented by a set of ordered pairs $\{(r_i, n_i) \mid i = 0, 1, 2, ... \}$, where r_i represents the horizontal coordinate of the first pixel of a run of 1-pixels and n_i the number of 1-pixels in that run. Using this method, the above row can be represented by $\{(0, 11), (26, 6), (41, 17)\}$. Thus each ordered pair requires $2\log_2 N$ bits to store the information. During reconstruction rest of the row is filled with 0s. Two-dimensional extension of this approach is to represent a block at a time rather than a run.

8.4.3 Block Coding

A binary image consists of black blobs, i.e. connected components (or sets) of 1-pixels, against a white background consisting of 0-pixels. Hence, a binary image can be represented by a set of maximal blocks of 1-pixels only. One of the simplest shapes of such blocks is square. In that case, a binary image can be represented by a set of ordered triples: $\{(r_i, c_i, n_i) \mid i = 0, 1, 2, ...,\}$ where (r_i, c_i) represents the coordinate of, say, top-left corner of the i-th maximal square of 1-pixels only, and n_i represents the number of 1-pixels on each side of that square [Rosenfeld and Kak (1982)]. By the term *maximal square*, we mean a square that is not a subset of any other square; however, its intersection with another square may be non-empty. Let us consider a binary image as shown in Fig. 8.11(a). Assuming top-left corner of the image as origin, maximal squares of 1-pixels, i.e. the black regions of the image, are represented by this method as $\{(1, 3, 7), (2, 7, 4), (9, 6, 5), (12, 9, 3)\}$. Similarly, the black portion of the image shown in Fig. 8.11(b) is represented by $\{(2, 4, 9), (3, 4, 9), (4, 4, 9), (5, 4, 9)\}$. So, Fig. 8.11(b) may be represented more efficiently if in place of upright square we consider upright rectangle. In that case, black blobs are presented by a set of quadruples $\{(r_i, c_i, v_i, h_i) \mid i = 0, 1, 2, ...,\}$, where (r_i, c_i) is the same as before, and v_i and h_i are the number pixels on the vertical side and horizontal side, respectively. Other shapes that can be used for efficient representation of binary image can be diamond, circle, etc. These types of coding, i.e. representing black blobs using regular geometric shapes assumes that the boundary of the connected components of 1-pixels matches with boundary of the shape used for representation at most of the places subject to a scale factor. However, when the black blobs and, in turn, its complement (i.e. background in a binary image) can be decomposed into a few large non-overlapping rectangles the image may be more compactly represented by a special type of data structure called *quad tree*, and thus data compression is achieved.

```
0000000000000000     0000000000000000     0000000000000000
0001111111000000     0000000000000000     0000011110000000
0001111111100000     0000111111111000     0000011111000000
0001111111100000     0000111111111000     0000011111100000
0001111111100000     0000111111111000     0000011111110000
0001111111100000     0000111111111000     0001111001111000
0001111111000000     0000111111111000     0001110000111000
0001111111000000     0000111111111000     0011100001110000
0000000000000000     0000111111111000     0011100111100000
0000001111100000     0000111111111000     0011111110000000
0000001111100000     0000111111111000     0011111000000000
0000001111100000     0000111111111000     0011110000000000
0000001111110000     0000111111111000     0001111110000000
0000001111110000     0000111111111000     0000111111110000
0000000001110000     0000000000000000     0000011111111000
0000000000000000     0000000000000000     0000000000000000
       (a)                  (b)                  (c)
```

Fig. 8.11   Some examples of binary images.

8.4.4   Quad Tree Coding

For simplicity let us start with a string of 0s and 1s representing a row of a binary image and consider it as the *root node* of a binary tree. Now the tree is constructed as follows. If a node contains all 0s or all 1s retain it as the *leaf node*; otherwise, call it an *intermediate node* and split it into two *child nodes*. Each child node represents a string of length exactly half of their *parent node*. This splitting is carried on until no intermediate node exists. Thus the entire row can be represented by a set of leaf nodes which contains its level in the tree and value of pixels in string represented by the node. Level of a node gives the size of the string represented by that node. For example, if the root node, i.e. the node at level 0, of the tree represents a string of length 2^n, then the node at level i represents a string of length 2^{n-i}. Quad tree coding is a two-dimensional extension of the binary tree coding described above. Here the whole image is considered as the root node of the quad tree and intermediate nodes are split into four quadrants. Exactly the same procedure is followed to construct the tree. So, if the original image is of size $2^m \times 2^n$ then the i-th level node of tree represents a region of size $2^{m-i} \times 2^{n-i}$, and each leaf node contains either all 1-pixels or all 0-pixels. Hence, the image is represented by a set of leaf nodes only.

Example   Figure 8.12(a) shows a row of a binary image shown in Fig. 8.12(c). Size of the image is 8×8. Binary tree constructed based on the row is shown in Fig. 8.12(b). Quad tree corresponding to Fig. 8.12(c) is shown in Fig. 8.12(d).   ∎

Both block coding and quad tree coding assume that the contours of regions should be smooth as well as should have very regular geometric shape. For example, quad tree coding assumes most part of the contour should be either horizontal or vertical line segments. When these assumptions are not satisfied by the given image, data reduction cannot be achieved by these coding methods. In that case, the shapes may efficiently be represented by its boundary information as described in the next section.

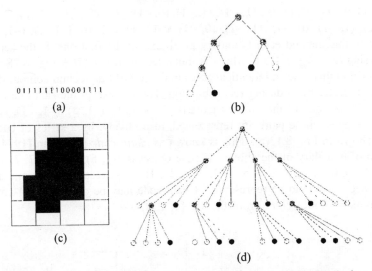

$$0 1 1 1 1 1 1 1 0 0 0 1 1 1 1$$

(a)   (b)

(c)

(d)

Fig. 8.12   An example of tree coding. Black leaf nodes represent all 1 (or black) pixels; white leaf nodes all 0 (or white) pixels, (a) a string of 0s and 1s representing a row of binary image, (b) binary tree representing (a), (c) a binary image, (d) quad tree representing (c).

8.4.5   Contour Coding

Suppose as we walk along the boundary of an object in a binary image and the direction of movement changes rapidly. An example of such an object is shown in Fig. 8.11(c). Such images may be compressed to some extent by retaining sequences of the coordinates (r_i, c_i) of boundary pixels only. Let us call the first pixel of the sequence an *indicator pixel* of the contour. For example, the object in Fig. 8.11(c) can be represented by two sequences $\{(1, 5), (1, 6), (1, 7), (1, 8), (2, 9), (3, 10), (4, 11), (5, 12), (6, 12), (7, 11), (8, 10), (8, 9), (9, 8),...\}$ and $\{(4, 7), (4, 8), (5, 9), (6, 10), (7, 9), (8, 8), (8, 7), (9, 6), (9, 5), (8, 4), (7, 4), (6, 5), (5, 6)\}$. Here $(1, 5)$ and $(4, 7)$ are indicator pixels of two given contours. The original image can be reconstructed simply by drawing the contour of the objects followed by polygon filling as used in computer graphics methodologies. Now suppose the size of the image is $M \times N$ and the number of boundary pixels is K. So we need MN bits to store the original image, whereas $K(\log_2 M + \log_2 N)$ bits are needed to store the coordinates of boundary pixels. Thus the method is useful when

$$K \ll \frac{MN}{\log_2 MN} \qquad (8.20)$$

The same boundary information may be represented using smaller number of bits if we take relative position (r_i', c_i') of a pixel with respect to the previous pixel in the sequence instead of the absolute one, where

$$(r_i', c_i') = \begin{cases} (r_i, c_i) & \text{if } i = 0 \\ (r_i - r_{i-1}, c_i - c_{i-1}) & \text{if } i > 0 \end{cases} \qquad (8.21)$$

So value of r_i' and c_i' come from the set $\{-1, 0, 1\}$. Using this approach boundary information of the example object as shown in Fig. 8.11(c) can be represented as $\{(1, 5), (0, 1), (0, 1), (0, 1),$

(1, 1), (1, 1), (1, 1), (1, 1), (1, 0), (1, –1), (1, –1), (0, –1), (1, –1), ...} and {(4, 7), (0, 1), (1, 1), (1, 1), (1, –1), (1, –1), (0, –1), (1, –1), (0, –1), (–1, –1), (–1, 0), (–1, 1), (–1, 1)}. It can be observed that in this method each boundary pixel, except the first one of the sequence, can be represented using (2 + 2 =) 4 bits which is much less than $\log_2 M + \log_2 N$. Secondly, unlike the previous one, in this case and identical cases in the rest of this section contour drawing should start from the indicator pixel during reconstruction. Thirdly, except the first one of the sequence all other (r_i', c_i')s are one of the ordered pairs (0, 1), (–1, 1), (–1, 0), (–1, –1), (0, –1), (1, –1), (1, 0), (1, 1). Suppose these pairs are represented, respectively, by a series of codes: 0, 1, 2, 3, 4, 5, 6, 7 as shown in Fig. 8.13(a). This is known as *chain code* [Freeman (1974)]. Chain code representation of boundary of the above example object is {(1, 5), 0, 0, 0, 7, 7, 7, 7, 6, 5, 5, 4, 5, ...} and {(4, 7), 0, 7, 7, 5, 5, 4, 5, 4, 3, 2, 1, 1}. Hence, except the first one all elements of the sequence needs 3 bits to be represented. Chain code may be defined for 4-connectivity too. In that case possible codes come from the set {0, 1, 2, 3}.

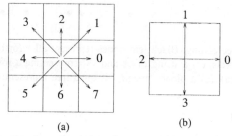

(a)   (b)

Fig. 8.13(a)   Chain codes using 8-connectivity, (b) chain codes using 4-connectivity or crack codes.

It is clear from the aforesaid description that chain code presents the direction of move as we step from centre of one pixel to the centre of its neighbouring pixel. But if we walk along the edge or crack between two neighbouring pixels, then the direction of moves is just 4 as shown in Fig. 8.13(b). We call this code as *crack code* [Rosenfeld and Kak (1982)]. This is similar to chain code too in case of 4-connectivity. Using crack code, contour of the regions in example image [Fig. 8.11(c)] can be written as {(1, 5), 0, 0, 0, 0, 3, 0, 3, 0, 3, 0, 3, 0, 3, 3, 2, 3, 2, 3, 2, 2, 3, 2, 2, 3, 2, 3, 0, 0, 0, ...} and {(4, 7), 0, 0, 3, 0, 3, 2, 3, 2, 2, 3, 2, 2, 1, 1, 0, 1, 0, 1}. In general, the number of elements in the sequence of crack code is greater than that of chain code for the same region. On the other hand, crack code can be represented using 2 bits only. Second and most important characteristic of contour coding technique using crack code is that it can straightaway be extended for graylevel images.

A graylevel image can be represented by contour coding using crack code as follows. Each region of the image that have uniform graylevel is represented by crack code of the contour enclosing the region as before except the coordinate of the indicator pixel follows the graylevel of the region. Thus, if we consider Fig. 8.11(c) as a graylevel image with two levels only then the contour coding scheme represents the image as {1, (1, 5), 0, 0, 0, 0, 3, 0, 3, 0, 3, 0, 3, 0, 3, 3, 2, 3, 2, 3, 2, 2, 3, 2, 2, 3, 2, 3, 0, 0, 0, ...}, {0, (4, 7), 0, 0, 3, 0, 3, 2, 3, 2, 2, 3, 2, 2, 1, 1, 0, 1, 0, 1}, and so on. Algorithm for contour coding using either chain code or crack code have two parts—first part detects exactly one indicator pixel for each contour, and the second one tracks the contour of the region and generates the corresponding chain/crack codes [Graham (1967), Wilkins and Wintz (1970)]. During reconstruction each contour is generated followed by filling the enclosed region with the given graylevel. The process is repeated for all the contours.

However, it should be noted that a contour may be nested (or completely enclosed) by another. When reconstructed outer contours should be considered first.

8.5 Other Methods

Among other methods, image data compression using *wavelet transform* [Antomini (1992), Lewis (1992)] and *fractal block coding* [Jacquin (1992), Fisher et al. (1992)] are becoming popular nowadays, because of large compression ratio. Both are lossy compression techniques; wavelet transform compression technique is very much similar to that of DCT. However, for a given image quality wavelet transform coding achieves higher compression ratio than that due to DCT. Compression ratio as high as 200:1 may be achieved by this method. In other words, given desired compression ratio (or amount of data reduction), the quality of image compressed by wavelet transform is significantly better than that by DCT. In fact, the blocking effect is much less in the former case because its basic functions overlap one another and decay smoothly to zero at their end points. Another advantage of wavelet transform over DCT is that the former can much easily be implemented on hardware. Here, a low-pass filter and a high-pass filter are applied on the input image along horizontal and vertical directions. Output of the filters are sub-sampled by a factor 2. Suppose output of these operations are denoted by L and H. Then these outputs are combined to get the sub-bands: HH, HL, LH and LL. Among them first three are retained. The process is repeated on the last one, i.e LL to generate next level of decomposition. So, after the first level of decomposition we have 4 sub-bands, 7 sub-bands at the second level, 10 at the third level, and so on. One of the most important parameters to decide upon is the number of coefficient should be preserved to compress the image.

In terms of the conjecture proposed by Mandelbrot (1982) a random line/surface may be assumed to be composed of geometrically self-similar objects of small size. On the other hand, if we subject an initial scale to certain iterative map, after large number of iterations we arrive at a random surface. Randomness of the surface depends on the nature of map and the number of iterations. More random the surface is, more the embedding surface it fills. To quantify the degree of randomness of the surface vis-a-vis its space filling capacity, a dimension is defined. The value of this new dimension is greater than the topological dimension of the surface, but is less than the dimension of the embedding space. It is fractional in nature and is called the *fractal dimension* of the surface. The iterative map that builds the surface is called the *iterative function system* (IFS) of the surface. In case of an image, surface may be formed by pixel values plotted over a two-dimensional plane. Therefore, an image may be described in terms of a set of mathematical rules (IFS) which can be represented using relatively much less number of bits. As a result, large amount of data reduction can be achieved. The value of compression ratio in this case may go up to 1000:1 depending on the image to be coded. However, computational cost of encoding process is usually very high, because a large number of iterations is needed by the IFS to converge. This encoding process (i.e. determining IFS) is, usually, aided by the fractal dimension of the image to be compressed. To reduce the computational cost, image is partitioned to small square blocks and then fractal block coding procedure is applied.

Sometimes various compression techniques are combined to achieve the largest possible data reduction and still a high quality compressed image can be obtained. For example, video image may be compressed by applying motion compensation for temporal compression, transform coding for spatial compression and Huffman coding for statistical compression [Jain (1996)].

Summary

Image compressing techniques, by which image information can be represented by less number of bits, are very useful for image transmission from one point to other and also for image archival purpose. Many image compression techniques incur losses such that some error (with respect to the original image) are introduced in the image reconstructed from its compressed representation. These kinds of techniques are called lossy compression. On the other hand, there are techniques that provide lossless compression. Thus, along with compression ratio, amount of error introduced should also be considered during selection/development of compression methods.

In this chapter both lossy and lossless compression techniques are described. Various criteria of image quality are also presented, so that error introduced in the reconstructed image may be measured. Some compression techniques, presented here, are derived from standard signal/data compression methodologies, while others are developed by exploiting the characteristics of digital images. However, basic idea in all the cases is to process the image to extract features, and then compression is achieved by discarding less important features and/or through compact representation of those features. In the subsequent chapters we will see other kinds of image processing techniques based on the image features.

Problems

1. Generate a set of vectors

$$(x_0 \ y_0)^T, \ (x_1 \ y_1)^T, \ (x_2 \ y_2)^T, \ ..., \ (x_n \ y_n)^T,$$

   where

$$x_i = i + \eta_{2i} \text{ and } y_i = 3i + 7 + \eta_{2i+1}$$

   and η_i is random number coming from uniformly distributed population between -10 and 10. Compute K–L transform of the data. Give physical interpretation of transformation in two-dimensional space. What would be the amount of error incurred if only one element of transformed vector is retained?

2. Graylevels of a 4×4 block (ordered lexicographically) are as follows:

   74 78 75 123 77 79 115 128 76 82 118 125 75 116 124 130

   Suggest a code to represent the graylevels in the block using block-truncation coding scheme. What is the amount of error incurred?

3. Find a set of code words and average word length using Huffman coding scheme for a set of input graylevels with probabilities as given below.

Input	S_1	S_2	S_3	S_4	S_5	S_6	S_7	S_8
Probability	0.02	0.15	0.03	0.15	0.05	0.20	0.10	0.30

   Compute the lowest possible average bits per graylevel required to represent this data.

4. Divide a 256×256 image into non-overlapping blocks each of size 16×16. Form column vectors from each block by lexicographic ordering. Compute the mean vector and covariance matrix. Using the Fourier transform compression technique compute the merit of Fourier

transform for diagonalizing this covariance matrix. Compute also the amount of error incurred and average bits per pixel when (i) 16, (ii) 24 or (iii) 32 elements of transformed vectors are retained.

5. Divide a 256×256 image into non-overlapping blocks each of size 16×16. Form column vectors from each block by lexicographic ordering. Compute the mean vector and covariance matrix. Using Hadamard transform compression technique compute the merit of Hadamard transform for diagonalizing this covariance matrix. Compute also the amount of error incurred and average bits per pixel when (i) 16, (ii) 24 or (iii) 32 elements of transformed vectors are retained.

Bibliography

Abramson, A., *Information Theory and Coding*, McGraw-Hill, New York, 1963.

Abut, Ed.H., *Vector Quantization: IEEE Reprint Collection*, IEEE Press, New Jersey, USA, 1990.

Ahmed, N. and Rao, K.R., *Orthogonal Transforms for Digital Signal Processing*, Springer-Verlag, New York, 1975.

Antomini, M., 'Image coding using wavelet transform', *IEEE Trans. on Image Proc.* **1**:205–220, 1992.

Clarke, R.J., *Transform Coding of Images*, Academic Press, Orlando, 1985.

Delp, E.J. and Mitchell, O.R., 'Image compression using block truncation coding', *IEEE Trans. on Commn.* COM-**27**:1335–1342, 1979.

Fisher, Y., Jacobs, E.W. and Boss, R.D., 'Fractal image compression using iterated transforms', in Storer, J.A. (Ed.), *Image and Text Compression,* Kluwer Academic Publishers, Boston, 1992.

Freeman, H., 'Computer processing of line drawing images', *ACM Computing Survey*, **6**:57–97, 1974.

Frendendall, G.L. and Behrend, W.L., 'Picture quality — procedures for evaluating subjective effects of interference', *Proc. IRE*, **48**:1030–1034, 1960.

Gersho, A. and Gray, R.M., *Vector Quantization and Signal Compression*, Kluwer Academic Publishers, Boston, 1992.

Gonzalez, R.C. and Wintz, P., *Digital Image Processing*, 2nd ed., Addison-Wesley, Reading, Massachusetts, 1987.

Graham, D.N., 'Image transmission by two-dimensional contour coding', *Proc. IEEE*, **55**:336–346, 1967.

Gray, R.M., Cosman, P.C. and Riskin, E.A., 'Image compression and tree structured vector quantization', in Storer, J.A. (Ed.), *Image and Text Compression*, Kluwer Academic Publishers, Boston, 1992.

Habibi, A. and Wintz, P.A., 'Image coding by linear transformations and block quantization', *IEEE Trans. on Commn.*, COM-**19**:50–62, 1971.

Huffman, D.A., 'A method for the construction of minimum redundancy codes', *Proc. IRE*, **40:**1098–1101, 1952.

Jacquin, A., 'Image coding based on a fractal theory of integrated contractive image transformation', *IEEE Trans. on Image Proc.*, **1:**18–30, 1992.

Jain, P.C., 'Advances in video signal compression and its applications', *IETE Tech. Review*, **6:**293–298, 1996.

Lewis, A.S., 'Image compression using 2d-wavelet transform', *IEEE Trans. on Image Proc.*, **1:**244–250, 1992.

Dutta Majumder, D., Chanda, B. and Mali, P.C., 'Mathematical tools for image restoration and data compression', *J. Inst. Electronics and Telecomm. Engrs.*, **35:**120–135, 1989.

Mandelbrot, B.B., *The Fractal Geometry of the Nature*, Freeman, New York, 1982.

Richards, J.A., *Remote Sensing Digital Image Analysis: An Introduction*, Springer-Verlag, New York, 1986.

Rosenfeld, A. and Kak, A.C., *Digital Picture Processing*, 2nd ed., Vols. 1 and 2, Academic Press, New York, 1982.

Wilkins, L.C. and Wintz, P.A., 'Studies on data compression, Part I: Picture coding by contours, Part II: Error analysis of run-length codes', Technical Report TR–EE 70–17, School of Electrical Engineering, Purdue University, Lafayette, Indiana, 1970.

Wintz, P.A., 'Transform picture coding', *Proc. IEEE,* **60:**809–820, 1972.

Chapter 9

Registration

9.1 Introduction

Registration establishes feature-based correspondence between related image pairs. Take an example of medical imaging system. The computer aided tomography (CT) highlights specific features in the image of a human organ. The magnetic resonance imaging (MRI) depicts another set of features in the MR image of the same human organ. Therefore, to enhance the medical information, it may be necessary to *fuse* both the CT and MR images of almost identical cross-sections of a human organ. The process of information fusion in this case requires establishing correspondence between different shape-based features of CT and MR images. This is an example of registration.

Registration is also a process of mapping between a temporal sequence of image frames. To estimate wind speed and direction, specially over sea surface, meteorologists take the help of two consecutive satellite images taken at half-hourly interval. A specific cloud cluster is identified in both the images. The shift of cloud cluster in the second image with respect to the first one in the sequence provides the wind velocity. This further requires satellite image registration.

Establishing a correspondence means matching of identical shapes in the related image pair. This requires geometric transformation of one image onto the other. This is detailed in the next section. This enables mapping between related image pairs so that the accuracy of matching could be determined. The transformation needs a set of features in both the images. These features are known as *landmarks*. In some cases, even for a change in view point, the features remain invariant. We discuss this in Section 9.2.2. Similar problem exists in the case of binocular vision. It is always required to establish a correspondence between the image formed at left eye with that at the right eye. Human solves this problem *intelligently*. How is it done in the case of machine stereo vision? For details, refer to Section 9.3. An extensive survey on image registration techniques may be found in Brown (1992).

9.2 Geometric Transformation

The mapping between the related image pairs is achieved using geometric transformations. The analysis is based on the familiar pinhole camera model [Thompson (1966)] of image formation. The transformation is restricted to planar models and are part of plane-to-plane *collineations*, that means, a line remains a line even after object-to-image projections [see Chapter 4]. Projection from planar surface model is considered because of its abundance in man-made environment. Also, many surfaces can be considered *locally* planar and their mathematical analyses are much simpler compared to any other complex class of surfaces.

Change in view point or relative motion between the camera and object planes introduces distortion in the features of an image. A circle appears to be an ellipse when observed from a *non-fronto-parallel* vantage point. The geometric transformation models are used to parameterize this object-to-image distortion. However, certain features of object shape remain intact or preserved even after such transformations. These features are commonly known as *invariants*. For example, the length of a vector remains unchanged after its rotation. In the following descriptions of the transformation groups, invariant features are mentioned. This properties could be utilized while mapping related image pairs or to find correspondence.

Before we go into the details of transformation geometry, we state the notations used in this chapter. For convenience of the reader, vectors are written in bold font (*e.g.* $\mathbf{x}$) while matrices are written in typewriter font (*e.g.* $\mathbf{X}$).

9.2.1 Plane-to-plane Transformations

The plane-to-plane transformations describe world model to image mappings and vice versa. We begin their descriptions starting from the plane projective group. These transformations can be represented by a *group* since they satisfy the group axioms of *closure*, *identity*, *inverse* and *associativity*. While there exists more general transformations [Mundy and Zisserman (1992)] than projectivities, the detail discussion of those is beyond the scope of this text.

The plane projective group.   A projective transformation or *projectivity* from one projective plane to another plane is a non-singular 3×3 matrix acting on homogeneous coordinates.

$$\begin{pmatrix} x_1 \\ x_2 \\ x_3 \end{pmatrix} = \begin{pmatrix} t_{11} & t_{12} & t_{13} \\ t_{21} & t_{22} & t_{23} \\ t_{31} & t_{32} & t_{33} \end{pmatrix} \begin{pmatrix} X_1 \\ X_2 \\ X_3 \end{pmatrix} \tag{9.1}$$

or

$$\mathbf{x} = \mathbf{T X} \tag{9.2}$$

The transformation matrix $\mathbf{T}$ has eight degrees of freedom because only the ratio of homogeneous coordinates is significant and there are eight ratios among nine elements of $\mathbf{T}$. Properties like concurrency, collinearity, order of contact (intersection, tangency, inflections), tangent discontinuities and cusps and cross-ratio are preserved under projective transformation [Mundy and Zisserman (1992)].

The plane affine group.   In the case of affine transformation, the matrix $\mathbf{T}$, as in Equation (9.2), takes the form:

$$\mathbf{T} = \begin{pmatrix} t_{11} & t_{12} & t_{13} \\ t_{21} & t_{22} & t_{23} \\ 0 & 0 & t_{33} \end{pmatrix} \tag{9.3}$$

Affine transformation has six degrees of freedom and is equivalent to the combined effects of translation, rotation, isotropic scaling and shear (non-uniform scaling in some direction). Properties like parallelism, ratio of lengths of collinear or parallel segments (e.g. mid-points), ratio of areas, linear combination of vectors are invariant under affine transformation [Mundy and Zisserman (1992)].

The plane similarity group. This is a specialization of the affine transformation without shear and is equivalent to an Euclidean transformation composed with an isotropic scaling. This has four degrees of freedom and occurs when the world plane is parallel to the image plane, i.e. under *fronto-parallel* viewing condition. Ratio of lengths, angles are preserved under plane similarity transform [Mundy and Zisserman (1992)].

The plane Euclidean group. The Euclidean transformation matrix is shown in Equation (9.4). Here, the top 2×2 sub-matrix of $\mathbf{T}$ is a rotation matrix and $\mathbf{t} = (t_1, t_2)^T$ is a translation vector. It has three degrees of freedom.

$$\mathbf{T} = \begin{pmatrix} r_{11} & r_{12} & t_1 \\ r_{21} & r_{22} & t_2 \\ 0 & 0 & 1 \end{pmatrix} \tag{9.4}$$

Lengths, angles, areas are preserved under the Euclidean transform [Mundy and Ziserman (1992)].

The motivation for using a specific transformation geometry depends on the physical imaging process. While the plane projective group is a *perspective* phenomenon, the transformation due to affine group is the effect of a special type of *weak perspective* where the parallel lines in the object remain parallel in the image. Following are the heuristic helps in selecting the appropriate plane-to-plane transformation. When the distance between the image plane at the camera and the object plane is less than the maximum dimension of the object along the viewing direction, the object-to-image transformation is of projective type. The example of parallel railway track that appears to meet at a vanishing point is a case of projective transformation. The similarity or Euclidean transformation is due to orthographic projection for *fronto-parallel* viewing.

There is a strict hierarchy of plane-to-plane transformations beginning from the plane projective group followed by affine, similarity and Euclidean. Each group inherits the invariances of the more general transformations of the preceding groups, but also have extra invariances. For example, all the invariant parameters of plane projective group remain invariant for plane affine group. Additionally, parallelism is maintained even after affine object-to-image transformation. The hierarchy and the range of transformations are shown in Fig. 9.1.

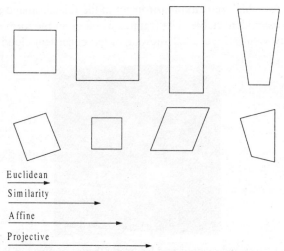

Fig. 9.1 The hierarchy of plane-to-plane transformations ranging from Euclidean to plane projective group.

9.2.2 Mapping

In this context, mapping is a process of transformation between related image pairs. We restrict our discussion within the purview of transformations described in Section 9.2.1. The process of mapping involves the two specific steps:

- Detection and matching of a set of landmarks
- Estimating transformation between corresponding landmarks.

Detection and matching of a set of landmarks

Landmarks are object specific stable features present in the image. Naturally, the process of detection of landmark depends on the specific application involved. Figure 9.2 is the edge image of a spanner while points *A*, *B*, *C* and *D* could be taken as landmarks. There are *significant* changes of curvature at these points. They are also *stable* features in the sense that these points will still be the high curvature points even after affine or projective object-to-image transformation of the spanner. In this case, calculation of convex hull [Preparata and Shamos (1985), Mukherjee (1994)] on the closed contour of the spanner should generate these landmark points.

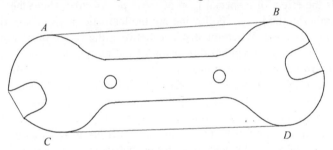

Fig. 9.2   Points *A*, *B*, *C* and *D* are landmarks of the spanner image. These are the points where the convex hull of the spanner contour parts away from the original contour.

The basic philosophy of landmark detection stems from the idea of invariance, i.e. the identification of features which remain *almost* intact in the related image pairs. At the same time the features must be *easily* identifiable. The features could be in the form of geometric primitives or in terms of intensity values. Figure 9.3 shows a bright consistent cloud mass generally known

Fig. 9.3   Example of intensity- and shape- based landmark: the *tracer* cloud of INSAT image detects cloud motion vector.

as *tracer* clouds. The displacement of this cloud mass in a sequence of geostationary satellite images gives wind speed and direction. This tracer cloud is an example of intensity and shape specific landmarks. Even though various domain specific techniques of landmark detection are in existence, still the expert assisted semi-automatic methodólogy gives better result compared to the automatic detection process. The detection of tracer cloud is such an example. There are other kinds of invariant features that could be utilized for image registration. For example, Wong and Hall (1978) used invariant moment features to register radar images with optical ones. While Goshtasby (1985) used similar kind of features for registering satellite images of visible and infra-red bands.

Two important applications of landmark detection and matching are in areas of biomedical and satellite image processing. In both the cases, the main objective is to achieve registration of images so that imaged information is enhanced. The following is a brief discussion on various registration techniques in these areas.

- *Biomedical images*: A convenient method is to detect a known set of patterns or regular grid in the image. Such techniques are also applicable to satellite imageries. In case of biomedical images, the markers are usually of two types:

1. *Object intrinsic and extrinsic markers:* Intrinsic markers are a bit generalized and preferred over extrinsic ones for better accuracy and retrospective viewing of images. These markers can be any one or a combination of signature points, centroids of segmented regions, contours and surfaces [Pelizzari et al. (1989), Collignon et al. (1994)]. Signature points are usually inflexion points where *significant* change in curvature or cornerity is demonstrated. Surface or contour based methods are better compared to point based methods when point landmarks from a small region of interest (ROI) are used to map a comparatively larger area of correspondence.

   Object extrinsic markers are either 'point-like' or specially designed fixtures which is attached onto the skin of patient for registration. The major problem for point-like markers is that they cannot achieve subslice accuracy. Note that different biomedical imaging protocols display 3D rendered images after interpolating a number of 2D slice images of a human organ. The point-like markers may miss the entire purpose if it falls within the interslice gap. To surmount the problem markers of synthetic material [Elsen et al. (1993)] that are easily applicable to the patient's skin and both MRI and CT compatible are used. The design has also been extended for SPECT images where marker is filled with radioactive fluids. The detection of such markers either in CT or MR images are mostly semi-automatic and hence fairly accurate.

2. *Patient specific markers:* These markers are generated by expert radiologist. The process relies on anatomical features particular to a patient and may include specific pathology like tumour or lesion of the patient's affected organ. As any other expert guided process, it is subjective, tedious and hence time-consuming.

- *Satellite images:* In this case two important applications are addressed utilizing the concept of mapping. First, geometric distortions introduced in the remote-sensed imageries are corrected after establishing correspondence between the map of a geographical region and its satellite image. Secondly, registration of two satellite images of the identical geographical region taken at two different dates can give a measure of change of certain observed parameters. For example, depletion of forest cover could be monitored registering sequence of satellite images taken over a span of time.

To correct geometric distortions in the satellite images, two sets of coordinate systems are defined. Let (u, v) be the coordinate system of the map while (x, y) is the coordinate system of the corresponding image. The objective is to define a set of function ϕ_1 and ϕ_2 [Richards (1986)] such that

$$u = \phi_1(x, y) \quad \text{and} \quad v = \phi_2(x, y) \qquad (9.5)$$

These functions could be linear, second order or even cubic polynomials. The higher the order, more is the number of correspondences needed to be established in order to solve the coefficients of Equation (9.5). Care must be taken for mapping functions higher than second degree as it may introduce error in evaluating coefficients of functions ϕ_1 and ϕ_2 rather than removing the geometric distortions. Once ϕ_1 and ϕ_2 are evaluated to a reasonable degree of accuracy, any point of the image could be located in the map and vice-versa.

The accuracy of the process depends on accurate localization of image features in the map. The image features generally chosen are prominent man-made structures like road intersections, runways, bridges or natural features like river bends or coastline features. These points which are used for correspondence are commonly known as *ground control points* (GCP). Typically, a second degree mapping function may take the following form [Richards (1986)]:

$$u = a_0 + a_1 x + a_2 y + a_3 x^2 + a_4 xy + a_5 y^2$$
$$v = b_0 + b_1 x + b_2 y + b_3 x^2 + b_4 xy + b_5 y^2 \qquad (9.6)$$

This requires a minimum of six GCP correspondences. However, for all practical purposes, more numbers of GCPs are used than what are required. In such case, a linear least square solution is obtained as discussed in Section 9.2.2.

Estimation of cloud motion vector that we have discussed at the onset of this chapter, is an example of image-to-image registration. In the 'picture-duplet' algorithm, two images are taken at half-hourly interval. Since both images are taken from the same imaging system, for example, a geostationary satellite like INSAT or GMS, they are already registered to the same scale and orientation. For convenience, let the first image in the sequence be the source image while the second one is the destination image. The problem here is to identify a cloud mass in both source and destination images. The drift of this cloud mass during the half hour period gives the wind speed and direction. The correspondence between the source and destination images is determined based on a measure of similarity of the local intensity map. For every small sub-image region, typically a 15 × 15 (pixel) square grid in one image, a similar sub-image region is found in the second image. The similarity is based on correlation value and a number of correlation measures are being used depending on the application domain. The scheme works as follows:

1. For every $p \times p$ sub-image of the source image, select a search window w_d in the destination image. Note that the centre of $p \times p$ sub-image of the source and the centre of w_d of the destination are the same.

2. For every $p \times p$ overlapping sub-image within w_d of destination image, a gray-value-based feature is calculated and compared with that of the candidate sub-image of the source. For the best match between sub-images of the source and destination (within the search window w_d), a correspondence is established. Figure 9.4 explains the scheme of determining correspondence.

3. Various gray value based features are being used to measure similarity. Also the use of a particular feature, to a large extent, depends on the specific domain. The similarity (or dissimilarity) measures are classified as:

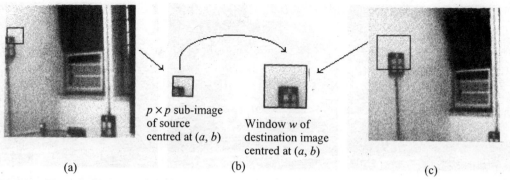

$p \times p$ sub-image of source centred at (a, b)

Window w of destination image centred at (a, b)

(a) (b) (c)

Fig. 9.4 The schematic for establishing correspondence between stereo pair images (a) and (c). The correspondence is determined based on gray value based correlation measure. Source sub-image and destination window are shown in (b).

(i) Maximum cross-correlation measure (MCC)

(ii) Sum of absolute value difference measure (SAVD)

(iii) Sum of squared difference measure (SSD)

The model for similarity-based matching could be given by:

$$g_d(x, y) = \mathbf{T}g_s(x, y) + m + \eta(x, y) \tag{9.7}$$

The grayvalue distribution of the $p \times p$ mask of the source is $g_s(x, y)$ whereas $g_d(x, y)$ is that of sub-image in the destination (within search space w_d). The transformation $\mathbf{T}$ is responsible for the mapping from the source to the destination while m is a bias term modelling the possible differences in mean intensity level. The parameter η is assumed to be zero mean Gaussian noise independent of image signal.

The correlation measure between $g_s(x, y)$ and $g_d(x, y)$ is straightforward to calculate:

$$C = \frac{\sum\sum \{g_s(x, y) - \overline{g}_s\}\{g_d(x, y) - \overline{g}_d\}}{\sqrt{\sum\sum \{g_s(x, y) - \overline{g}_s\}^2} \sqrt{\{g_d(x, y) - \overline{g}_d\}^2}} \tag{9.8}$$

and the dissimilarity measures SAVD and SSD between $g_s(x,y)$ and $g_d(x,y)$ may be given by

$$d_{\text{SAVD}} = \sum\sum |g_s(x, y) - g_d(x, y)| \tag{9.9}$$

$$d_{\text{SSD}} = \sum\sum \{g_s(x, y) - g_d(x, y)\}^2 \tag{9.10}$$

Figure 9.5 shows the result of SAVD scheme. The analysis is carried out on a pair of INSAT images taken at 5:00 and 5:30 GMT in December, 1993. Figures 9.5(a) and 9.5(b) are source and destination images respectively. A set of cloud motion vectors are drawn only on the contour (vertices of polygon approximating the contour) of the tracer cloud mass of the source image in Fig. 9.5(a).

The result reveals an important insight into this problem. Note that a number of cloud motion vectors are shown on almost all the vertices instead of a unique one. The problem with such a scheme is that the similarity between intensity maps of the source and destination is typically multimodal instead of desired unimodal type. In Fig. 9.5(a), CMVs with correlation matching (between source and destination sub-images) value higher than 0.8 are plotted.

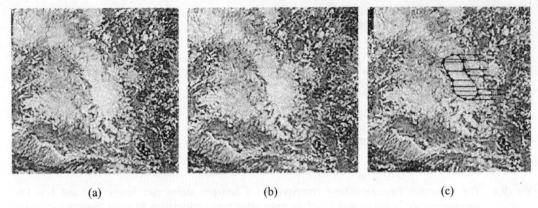

(a)   (b)   (c)

Fig. 9.5 The half-hourly image duplet: (a) source image and (b) destination image, (c) cloud motion vectors are drawn on the source image based on gray value similarity measure between the source and destination image.

Canonical frame registration

So far we have discussed registration where correspondence is established between either object-to-image or image to image. There could even be a situation where we need to bring the features of two images into a single unified space other than the two image spaces in question. This space is what we refer here as a canonical frame. From Section 9.2.1, we know that a planar affine mapping needs three point correspondence while a projective mapping requires four to solve the eight degrees of freedom. Therefore, an affine canonical frame could take a shape of a triangle while a projective space can take the form of a square. In case of affine canonical mapping, the affine transformation matrix is evaluated between three landmark points on the image or any of its feature and the three vertices of the triangular canonical frame. The transformation thus evaluated is then used to map all the image features onto the canonical frame. Similar transformations are undertaken using four landmark points of the image and four vertices of projective canonical frame.

Take the example of spanner image in Fig. 9.6(a). The two opposite (major) concavities of the spanner are identical. However, as the image is captured under affine imaging condition, the concavities appear to be unequal in size. Affine canonical frame registration could be used to prove that the concavities are equal. The algorithmic steps are as follows:

- Detect edge of the spanner image[1] and trace the edge pixels in a specific direction (either clockwise or anti-clockwise). *Significant* concavities are extracted for each closed contour after computing the convex hull and setting a threshold on concavity height and width. The concavity entrance and exit points mark significant changes in curvature. Also at these points, the convex hull of the shape parts away from the edge map. The concavity height point is the farthest point on the concavity from the line joining the concavity entrance and exit points. The length between the concavity entrance and exit points is the width of the concavity. Figure 9.7(b) shows these different parameters to select and specify significant concavities.

---

[1]Edge detection techniques are discussed in Chapter 12.

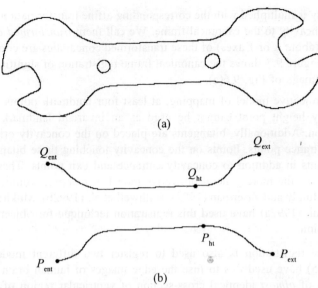

(a)

(b)

Fig. 9.6 (a) Affine image of boundary of a spanner and (b) the different parameters of a *significant* concavity, namely, concavity entrance, exit and height points.

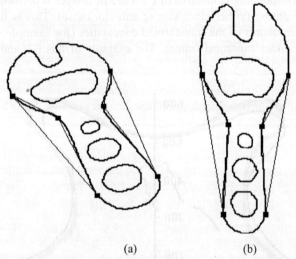

(a)   (b)

Fig. 9.7 (a) Significant concavities of the spanner image of Fig. 9.6(a) are mapped to triangular canonical frame, (b) the construction to determine landmark points for projective canonical frame registration. Notice the similarity between the transformed curves.

- The concavity entrance, exit and height points denote point 'landmarks' used for canonical frame registration. These points are invariant under affine imaging condition. The affine matrix which transforms these three points to the corresponding points of a triangle with vertices at, say, (−1, 0), (1, 0) and (0, 1) is computed. The transformation equation is explained in the next section. Two different affine matrices are obtained after mapping two sets of landmark points (from two concavities) to the canonical frame. Every edge pixel of a concavity is multiplied with the corresponding affine transformation matrix to transfer the entire concavity to the canonical frame. We call them *transformed concavities*. Areas or moments (about X or Y axes) of these transformed concavities are compared for the test of equality. Figure 9.7 shows the canonical frame registration of significant concavities of the spanner image of Fig. 9.6(a).

- In case of projective model of mapping, at least four landmark points are needed. Also, the concavity height point cannot be used as an invariant landmark under projective transformation. Additionally, bitangents are placed on the concavity originating from the concavity entrance points. Points on the concavity touching these bitangents are the two invariant points in addition to concavity entrance and exit points. These four points are sufficient to use the more general projective model of mapping. Similar applications are reported in Mundy and Ziserman (1992), Rothwell et al. (1992b), Mukherjee et al. (1993). Rothwell et al. (1992a) have used this registration technique for object recognition even under occlusion.

Canonical frame registration is also used to register two different modalities of images. Banerjee et al. (1995) have used this to fuse the edge images of human brain organ. These are CT and MR images of *almost* identical cross-section of ventricular region of the same person. They have exploited concavities of ventricle region of human brain for registration using both affine and projective model. The technique of mapping is essentially the same as what is described above. Matching of corresponding landmarks of CT and MR images is performed from the tracing order of the ventricle contour (either clockwise or anti-clockwise). This is further verified from the derived geometric measures of the transformed concavities (for example, areas and moments of transformed curves under canonical frame). The example of this CT and MR registration is shown in Fig. 9.8.

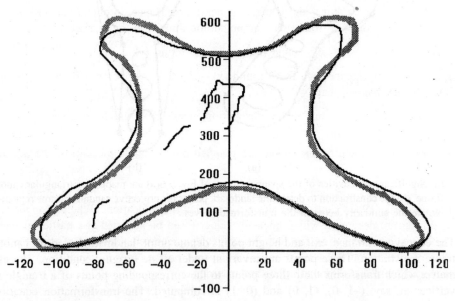

Fig. 9.8 The example of registration of edge maps of human ventricles obtained from CT and MR images [Banerjee et al. (1995)].

Estimating transformation between landmark points

The 2D affine model of registration is given by:

$$\begin{bmatrix} x' \\ y' \end{bmatrix} = \begin{bmatrix} a & b \\ d & e \end{bmatrix} \begin{bmatrix} x \\ y \end{bmatrix} + \begin{bmatrix} t_x \\ t_y \end{bmatrix} \quad . \tag{9.11}$$

The point (x', y') is the affine transformed image of the point (x, y). The 2×2 matrix stands for rotation, scaling and shearing while the vector (t_x, t_y) stands for object-to-image translation. The transformation has six degrees of freedom and three correspondences are required to evaluate the affine parameters. Note that three landmark points are used for the affine transformation of the image of spanner in the last section.

In quite a few practical problems, it may be necessary to detect more correspondence than necessary. In such cases, the transformation problem could be solved as a overdetermined case and various numerical techniques like pseudoinverse or Levenberg–Marquadart methods [Mukherjee and Dutta Majumder (1993)] could be used to find the transformation for registration.

9.2.3 Problems in Discrete Domain

Since we are interested in mapping digital images from one (source) coordinate system to another (destination), at this point we should mention some typical problems associated with such mapping between discrete coordinate systems. We may employ either Equation (9.6) or Equation (9.11) or some other transformation functions suitable for the problem in hand. Required parameters are estimated as discussed in the previous sections. In general, Equation (9.5) is used to compute destination coordinate may be computed from source coordinate (r, c) as

$$u = \phi_1(x, y) \quad \text{and} \quad v = \phi_2(x, y) \tag{9.12}$$

where r and c are integers, but u and v are, in general, not. Hence, to obtain integer coordinates for destination image one can round the computed coordinates to the nearest integer, i.e.

$$k = \text{round } (u) \quad \text{and} \quad l = \text{round } (v)$$

where round (x) is an integer such that $| \text{ round } (x) - x | \le 0.5$. Now since *round* is not strictly monotonic,[2] it may happen that

1. there exist some locations in the destination image onto which no pixel of the source image is mapped, and

2. several pixels of the source image are mapped onto a single location of the destination image.

In the first case, some intermediate pixels of the destination image are void of intensity values [Rosenfeld and Kak (1982)], and thus holes are created at those locations. Whereas, in the second case it is difficult to decide on which intensity value would be assigned at a particular location. One solution may be accepting the last intensity value received. But in that case the spatial distribution of intensity in the destination image depends on the order in which (r, c) are picked-up. However, a more legitimate solutions are in order.

---

[2]That means $x_1 < x_2$ does not imply round (x_1) < round (x_2).

Reverse mapping

Instead of computing destination coordinates from the source ones, we employ a mapping that works in the reverse direction. That means, here, we compute source coordinates from destination coordinates (k, l) as

$$x = \psi_1(k, l) \quad \text{and} \quad y = \psi_2(k, l) \tag{9.13}$$

Again k and l are integers, but x and y are, in general, not. However, integer coordinates can be obtained as before by rounding, i.e.

$$r = \text{round } (x) \quad \text{and} \quad c = \text{round } (y)$$

Thus, all the locations of the destination image receive some intensity value from the source image. However, because of the *round* operation it may happen here also that

1. there exist some locations in the source image which have no contribution to the destination image, and

2. intensity of a single pixel of source image are mapped onto several locations of the destination image.

Thus intensity values at all pixels of the source image are not transferred to the destination image with equal importance. To surmount this problem one may adopt the method called *graylevel interpolation*.

Graylevel interpolation

The objective of the *graylevel interpolation* is to generate intensity information at any location from the intensity values of the neighbouring pixels. Before we understand how to interpolate grayvalues, let us consider the situation that an image $g_d(k, l)$ is computed from a given image $g_s(r, c)$ using some transformation as given in Equation (9.13). To calculate graylevels at the destination image $g_d(k, l)$, the following steps are usually taken:

- Take each pixel location (k, l) of $g_d(k, l)$ and apply reverse transformation [Equation (9.13)].

- The resultant pixel location (x, y) due to Step 1, corresponds to a definite location in the original source image $g_s(r, c)$.

- If both the coordinates x and y are integers, the intensity value at $g_s(x, y)$ is directly substituted at the destination image point (k, l). Else, the intensity value at the non-integer coordinate (x, y) of the image $g_s(r, c)$ is calculated by interpolating the intensities at neighbouring pixels, and then it is transferred to the destination image point (k, l). The second case is a more likely situation and hence there exists a need for graylevel interpolation.

The simplest interpolation is obviously the linear interpolation technique. Consider the situation in Fig. 9.9 where the interpolated graylevel at (x, y) is to be determined. The pixel point (x, y) is enclosed by the pixels (r, c), $(r + 1, c)$, $(r + 1, c + 1)$ and $(r, c + 1)$, such that $r \le x \le r + 1$ and $c \le y \le c + 1$ where r and c represent the integer part of x and y, respectively. That means $r = \text{floor } (x)$ and $c = \text{floor } (y)$. For linear interpolation let us assume, $d_x = x - r = x - \text{floor } (x)$ and $d_y = y - c = y' - \text{floor } (y)$. Therefore, $0 \le d_x, d_y \le 1$. Then the interpolated grayvalue at (x, y) is given by:

$$g_s(x, y) = (1 - l) \left[(1 - k) g_s(r, c) + k g_s(r + 1, c) \right]$$
$$+ l \left[(1 - k) g_s(r, c + 1) + k g_s(r + 1, c + 1) \right] \tag{9.14}$$

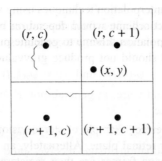

Fig. 9.9 Location (x, y) and its enclosing pixels whose grayvalues are used to compute grayvalue at (x, y) by bilinear interpolation.

This scheme is commonly referred to as *bilinear interpolation* [see Fig. 9.10(c)].

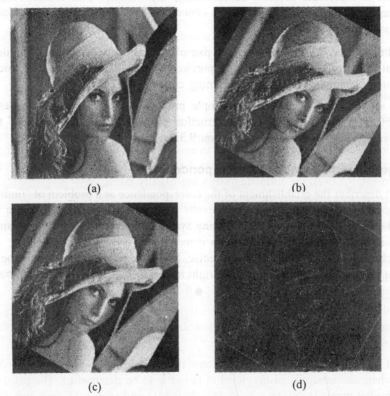

Fig. 9.10 The figure in (b) and (c) are the rotated images of (a). The pixel values of the image (b) is calculated using nearest-neighbour approach and that of (c) by bilinear interpolation, (d) shows the difference between (b) and (c).

Instead of interpolation if we take

$$g_s(x, y) = g_s(\text{round } (x), \text{round } (y)) \tag{9.15}$$

the scheme is called the *nearest-neighbour* mapping as described at the beginning of Section 9.2.3.

More sophisticated graylevel interpolation techniques using second or third order polynomials could be used. However, the exact scheme would depend on both the nature of transformation and image. For example, the interpolation scheme to generate pixel values of a rotated version of a binary image (black and white) should not produce grayvalues other than black or white.

9.3   Stereo Imaging

The human visual system is the perfect example of stereo vision. Both of our eyes generate two intensity maps of the scene in our retinal plane. Alternately, an object is being viewed from two different positions. These two image frames are then registered and subsequently fused into a single intensity image. Even though this registration and fusion mechanism is not fully understood, it is possible for us to recover the depth information of an object which, otherwise, is lost in the case of a single image. The same mechanism has also been used in the case of machine vision and a number of algorithms are at work to recover depth from a pair of stereo images.

So far as the objective of this chapter is concerned, there are clearly two issues involved in stereo imaging problem:

- Find the correspondence between the pair of stereo image. A number of algorithms to this effect has already been discussed in previous sections. We will see in Section 9.3.1 how the stereo geometry helps in determining correspondence.

- The second issue is relatively a simple problem to solve once the correspondence is established. It is basically a reconstruction problem where the depth of the object is recovered. This is described in Section 9.3.2.

9.3.1   Algorithms to Establish Correspondence

Horn (1986) describes the establishment of the correspondence as a problem of 'finding conjugate points'. In case of stereo image pair, there exists a left camera (eye) image and a right camera (eye) image captured using a binocular imaging system. For establishing the correspondence, the same entity in both versions of the image is detected.

In the absence of occlusion and image noise, let for an object point O, u is the point in left image L and v is the corresponding point in right image R (Fig. 9.11). This correspondence boils

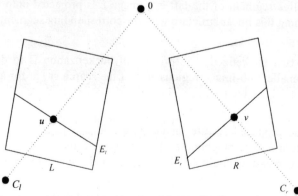

Fig. 9.11   Illustrates the stereo imaging geometry for object point O. u and v are the image points on left and right eye images, L and R respectively. C_l and C_r are optical centres of L and R and E_r and E_l are epipoles of image points u and v, respectively.

down to a search problem between a point and a 2D plane. However, the constraints of stereo geometry reduces the search problem to 1D search space. To see this, let us re-examine the stereo geometry in Fig. 9.11. Let C_l and C_r are the two optical centres of the left and right images L and R, respectively. Now consider the projection of image point of u at the right image plane R. The line joining u and the optical centre C_r intersects the right image plane R at E_r. This point E_r is the *epipole* of the image point u in the right image plane R. The line joining E_r and v is the *epipolar line* of the image point u in L. Note that the corresponding point of u in the right image plane R will always lie on the epipolar line of u. This property being symmetric, there will be similar epipolar line of the image point v on the left image plane L. Therefore, this constraint reduces the search space for correspondence from 2D image plane to 1D epipolar line.

As detailed in Section 9.2.2, considering typical graylevel image, the two most important aspects of the image function that could be used to exploit correspondence are:

- *Brightness pattern of the image function*: This is a grayvalue similarity based measure between the pair of stereo images. We have already explained correlation-based approaches in Section 9.2.2 while discussing registration of satellite images.

- *Feature sets extracted from the image*: Such features could be different geometrical patterns embedded in the image, for example, detection of corresponding edges, corners or domain specific shapes in a pair of stereo images. In the following section, we present one such feature matching based approach.

Feature based correspondence approach

As noted earlier, these features could be edges, corners or any domain specific shape detected in stereo image pair. Let the transformation between the left eye image to that of right eye is given by[3]:

$$\mathbf{M}_R = \mathbf{R}\mathbf{M}_L + \mathbf{T} \tag{9.16}$$

$\mathbf{M}_R$ is the corresponding point in the right eye image and $\mathbf{M}_L$, of the left eye image. The rotation matrix $\mathbf{R}$ and the translation vector $\mathbf{T}$ project one image onto the other. A feature-based correspondence can utilize this transformation provided $\mathbf{R}$ and $\mathbf{T}$ are known through camera calibration.

Let us consider the case of linear structures present in the stereo image pair. Using Equation (9.16), a line segment of the left eye image L is projected onto the right eye image R. The steps for matching this linear structure with the corresponding segment of the right eye image are as follows:

- Images are first bucketized. The process of bucketization is to divide the entire image space into smaller sub-image regions so that the search space for any projected feature is reduced. Only those buckets in and around the one onto which the feature is projected is searched.

- Let f_p be the projected feature on the image R, and in this case it is a linear structure projected from L. The neighbours of the projected line and their distances are tabulated. The distance measure could be the Euclidean distance between middle points of line

---

[3]See Chapter 4 for more detail description.

segments. Instead of simple Euclidean distance Mahalanobis distance may be used in order to account for the error associated in the process of stereo projection from the left eye image to the right eye one. The Mahalanobis distance can be interpreted as the square of Euclidean distance weighted by the sum of covariance matrices. For a pair of feature sets S_1 and S_2, the Mahalanobis distance is given by:

$$D(S_1, S_2) = (S_1 - S_2)^t (\Lambda_1 + \Lambda_2)^{-1} (S_1 - S_2) \qquad (9.17)$$

The parameters Λ_1 and Λ_2 are the covariance matrices for feature sets S_1 and S_2 respectively.

- A confidence factor is defined for each pair of match. It is defined as a function of the relative distance of the projected segment to its first and second nearest neighbours. Suppose that S_2 and S_3 are respectively the first and second nearest neighbours of S_1. The confidence factor c is defined as:

$$c = \frac{D(S_1, S_3) - D(S_1, S_2)}{D(S_2, S_3)} \qquad (9.18)$$

The smaller magnitude of confidence factor implies that there is an ambiguity in matching and the correspondence between the candidates are rejected even if the nearest neighbours are close to the projected candidate.

- The matching hypothesis thus generated (in the above step) is verified through the epipolar constraint mentioned in the last section. To illustrate this, the epipolar line of the midpoint of one segment (say, from the left camera image) is checked for intersection with the corresponding segment in the right camera image.

9.3.2   Algorithms to Recover Depth

Refer to Fig. 9.12 and assume that the correspondence is established between the stereo image pair. Let the disparity between two cameras are $2d$. Disparity is the distance of separation between the left and the right camera. With the stereo arrangement as in Fig. 9.12, two separate images of the point $p(x, y, z)$ are formed at $(x + d)$ and $(x - d)$ locations along x-axis.

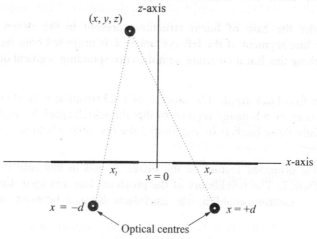

Fig. 9.12 The stereo pair images are formed at $(x + d)$ and $(x - d)$ locations along x-axis. Note that the distance of separation between the two cameras is $2d$.

If f is the focal length of the pinhole camera system and x_l and x_r are the left and right camera images respectively, then

$$x_l = \frac{(x - d)f}{f - z} \quad \text{and} \quad x_r = \frac{(x + d)f}{f - z} \tag{9.19}$$

Equivalently,

$$z = f - \frac{2df}{x_r - x_l} \tag{9.20}$$

Therefore, for a given binocular camera model with known focal length and disparity of camera pair, the depth of the object could be recovered once the correspondence between the left and the right eye images are solved.

Summary

In this chapter both image-to-image and image-to-map registrations are discussed. In case of image-to-image registration, images may be taken at certain time interval, (e.g. for analyzing motion of some objects) or may be taken from different view points (e.g. stereo imaging). Registration is done basically by means of geometric transformation. Various types of geometrical transformation are presented along with their invariants. Parameters of transformation functions are estimated using correspondence points that are identified as local features. Various methods of establishing the correspondence are discussed. Some problems related to discrete coordinate systems are mentioned and their solutions by means of reverse mapping and graylevel interpolation are presented. The methods are described with some practical examples. Correspondence problem relevant to stereo imaging is also discussed.

Problems

1. How many degrees of freedom are there in a plane projective transformation? Name the properties that are preserved under such transformation. What simplification need to be imposed on plane projective transformation to arrive at plane affine transformation? Give physical interpretation of parameters of plane affine transformation.

2. List the properties that are preserved under the following plane transformations:

   (i) Affine transformation

   (ii) Similarity transformation

   (iii) Euclidean transformation.

3. Given two sets of ground control points. $\{(x_i, y_i) \mid i = 0, 1, 2, ..., n - 1\}$ and $\{(u_i, v_i) \ i = 0, 1, 2,..., n - 1\}$ in two-dimensional image plane such that (x_i, y_i) corresponds to (u_i, v_i). Consider the mapping

   $$x_i = au_i + bv_i + c \quad \text{and} \quad y_i = du_i + ev_i + f$$

   Estimate the parameters a, b, c, d, e and f in least-square sense where $n > 6$.

4. Take a good quality image and do the following operations:

(a) Rotate the image by 45° using the reverse mapping technique. Call the output image as 'OUT1'.

(b) Rotate the image by 45° using the forward mapping technique. Call the output image as 'OUT21'. Then close 'OUT21' with a 2×2 structuring element to obtain the final image 'OUT22'.

Compare 'OUT22' with 'OUT1'.

Bibliography

Banerjee, S., Mukherjee, D.P. and Dutta Majumder, D., 'Point landmarks for registration of CT and MR images', *Patt. Recog. Letters*, **16**:1033–1042, 1995.

Brown, L.G., 'A survey of image registration', *ACM Computing Survey*, **24**:325–376, 1992.

Collignon, A., Vandermeulen, D., Seutens, P. and Marchal, G., 'Registration of 3d multimodality medical imaging using surface and point landmarks', *Patt. Recog. Letters*, **15**:461–467, 1994.

Elsen Van den, P.A., Pol, E.J.D. and Viergever, M.A., 'Medical image matching—a review with classification', *IEEE Trans. on Engg. Med. Biol*, **7**:26–39, 1993.

Goshtasby, A., 'Template matching in rotated images', *IEEE Trans. on Patt. Anal. and Mech. Intell*, PAMI-**7**:338–344, 1985.

Horn, B.K.P., *Robot Vision*, MIT Press, Cambridge, Massachusetts, 1986.

Mukherjee, D.P., *On Detection and Use of Reflectional Symmetry in Computer Vision*, PhD thesis, Indian Statistical Institute, 1994.

Mukherjee, D.P. and Dutta Majumder, D., 'Implementing wave propagation on transputers for symmetry detection', in *Proc. 3rd Intl. Conf. on Advances in Pattern Recognition and Digital Techniques*, pp. 149–158, Calcutta, 1993.

Mundy, J.L. and Zisserman, A. (Ed.), *Geometric Invariance in Computer Vision*, MIT Press, Boston, 1992.

Pelizzary, C.A., Chen, G.T.Y., Spelbring, D.R., Weichselbaum, R.R. and Chen, C.T., 'Accurate 3d registration of CT, PET and/or MR images of the brain', *J. Comp. Asst. Tomography*, **13**:20–26, 1989.

Preparata, F.P. and Shamos, M.I., *Computational Geometry: An introduction*, Springer-Verlag, New York, 1985.

Richards, J.A., *Remote Sensing Digital Image Analysis: An introduction*, Springer-Verlag, New York, 1986.

Rosenfeld, A. and Kak, A.C., *Digital Picture Processing*, 2nd ed., Vols. 1 and 2, Academic Press, New York, 1982.

Rothwell, C.A., Zisserman, A., Mundy, J.L. and Forsyth, D.A., 'Canonical frames for planar object recognition', in *Proceedings of the 2nd European Conf. on Computer Vision (ECCV2)*, pp. 757–772, 1992b.

Rothwell, C.A., Zisserman, A., Mundy, J.L. and Farsyth, D.A., 'Efficient model library access by projectively invariant indexing', in *Proc. Intl. Conf. on Computer Vision and Patt. Recog.* pp. 109–114, 1992a.

Thompson, M.M., *Manual of photogrammetry*, American Society of Photogrammetry, Falls Chuch, Virginia, 1966.

Wong, R.Y. and Hall, E.L., 'Scene matching with invariant moments', *Computer Graphics and Image Processing*, **8**:16–24, 1978.

Chapter 10

Multi-valued Image Processing

So far we are familiar with grayscale image where a pixel value at any image point can be represented by a *single-valued* function within a range of 0 to 255 in an 8-bit system. At the same time, the intensity distribution in an image depends on the properties of sensors and measuring devices used in imaging the object where different physical properties of the object contribute differently while generating intensity map of the object. Such images are usually represented by a multi-valued function. That means, if more than one measurements are made at the object point, the pixel value at the corresponding image point is multivariate (see Section 1.2). These could be grouped into following two major areas:

1. *Multi-spectral:* As the name suggests, measurements correspond to different spectral bands of frequencies (or wavelengths) of electromagnetic waves. For example, different spectral bands correspond to red, blue and green lights in colour images.

2. *Multi-modal:* The measurement of different physical properties of any single object or its parts are the concept of multi-modal imaging. Different sensors are employed to extract multi-modal characteristics. For example, X-ray, computed tomography (CT) scan, magnetic resonance imaging (MRI), ultrasonography (USG), positron emission tomography (PET), single photon emission computed tomography (SPECT), etc., are examples of imaging systems of various modalities.

In case of multi-temporal images, that is an image sequence captured at different time intervals, pixel value at any particular location may also be considered multivariate. It could be tracking of moving object(s) in consecutive image frames or capturing images of objects from a moving sensor. The time interval could be seconds to years depending on application. Devices like automated guided vehicle to satellites generate multi-temporal images. However, discussion on multi-temporal image processing is beyond the scope of this text.

The algorithms developed and employed for multi-spectral and multi-modal image processing depend very much on the application area as well as the imaging system used to capture the images; so we prefer to discuss them with reference to some practical examples. In this chapter, we first discuss the colour image processing as it is the most common example of multi-spectral images. Figure 10.1 shows the colour image of a scene and its representation in three visible bands, viz., red, green and blue. Colour image processing is followed by discussion on one of the most useful multi-spectral image processing—The processing of satellite images. In order to present multi-modal image processing methodologies we consider an example of medical image processing. Modern medical diagnostic system includes images from different sensor modalities in order to increase the information content present in comparison to any single modality. This would be presented in Section 10.3.

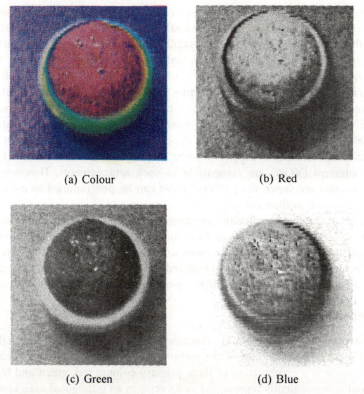

(a) Colour   (b) Red

(c) Green   (d) Blue

Fig. 10.1 An example of colour image and its three visible bands.

10.1 Processing of Colour Images

The perception and display of colour has three specific aspects. The first is obviously the generation of colours. It is well known that light is an electromagnetic wave and the visible spectrum of light is limited by the wavelengths from 0.4 to 0.7 μm. Within this range, different colours correspond to different wavelengths. While indigo and violet stay at the shortwave end, the generation of colour red is at the opposite extreme. Therefore, the generation of colour is basically the generation of different wavelengths within the visible spectrum of electromagnetic waves.

10.1.1 Display of Colour on Cathode Ray Tube

But, how is actually the colour source realized in the display monitor? Similar to a monochrome cathode ray tube (CRT), the colour CRT has three electron guns. Each of them generates stream of electrons corresponding to red, green and blue of perceptual intensity. The CRT face plate on which the electron beams are colliding has, in turn, three phosphor dots each sensitive to red, green and blue wavelengths [Hearn and Baker (1992)]. Once hit by the respective electron beams, these dots are excited to higher energy states. The colour is perceived when these dots start emitting energy in order to come back to the normal state. These dots are so closely packed that the perceptual mix of different intensity levels creates the sensation of a particular colour. Similar to grayscale arrangements, if the intensity of individual colour is represented in an 8-bit system, as many as 256 different shades of a colour, say red, could be realized. Therefore, in the three primary colour (red, green and blue) system, a total of $256 \times 256 \times 256$ combinations of colour shades are possible. Obviously, such a wide possibility of colour is closer to real life applications but at the same time it is well beyond the perceptual limit of any human observer. The possibility once again increases in a 10-bit system when 2^{30} colour possibilities are theoretically achieveable. In an ordinary colour display system, every frame buffer location where the pixel description is stored is 8-bit long. Therefore at any point of time, only 256 different colours are realized through video hardware out of more than 16 million possibilities. A colour look up table (CLUT) is maintained to select these 256 different colours depending on the application. Most of the modern programming language compilers support routine to program the content of CLUT. Standard video graphics adapters (VGA) are compatible to such arrangements. However, most of the modern VGA monitors are super VGA (SVGA) and can be programmed to colour beyond 256 levels and even up to 16 million colours.

The final issue in the context of colour perception is the human biological aspects. Our retina consists of cone cells which are sensitive to colours of specific wavelength. Some cone cells respond to wavelength of red colour while some to blue or green one. For a derived colour like yellow, cone cells sensitive to wavelengths of both red and green colours are energized to appropriate extent. If there are equal sensation in all three types of cone cells, the colour perception is gray.

10.1.2　Representation of Colour

Various colour representation schemes are discussed in Chapter 3. Here we briefly recapitulate some of them for easy understanding of the section. So far we have observed that any specific perception of a colour is a combination of three primary colours red, green and blue. Therefore, a particular colour is conveniently represented as a vector in an orthogonal axes system. The three axes represent the *true* red, green and blue colours, commonly known as RGB space. The term 'true' points to the purity or saturation of the particular colour. This means, a point on the red axis represents a certain colour value with only red component and no green or blue components.

Therefore, a colour (r, g, b) denotes a vector from the origin to a point (r, g, b) in the RGB coordinate space. The origin with $r = 0$, $g = 0$ and $b = 0$ are conveniently considered as 'black'. Similarly, considering a unit cube with a corner on the origin, the diagonally opposite corner (with respect to the origin) represents the colour 'white'. For super video graphics adapters, each primary colour is represented in 8 bits. Therefore, in a 24-bit 'true' colour system, the length of each side of the colour cube is 256 units. However, as mentioned earlier, for most applications a set of 256 or 16 colours are selected out of more than 16 million possible sheds in the colour cube. There is an interesting set of algorithms available to find the best 256 colours out of 24-bit colourcube [Ashdown (1995)].

10.1.3　Colour Interpolation

In the RGB space, we can interpolate between two colours, or to be precise, two vectors say, (r_1, g_1, b_1) and (r_2, g_2, b_2) in a colour cube by finding a new vector, which is a weighted average of their primary components in the colour space as under:

$$\{r_m, g_m, b_m\} = \left\{ \frac{r_1 + r_2}{2}, \frac{g_1 + g_2}{2}, \frac{b_1 + b_2}{2} \right\} \tag{10.1}$$

The same goes for weighted average and the weighting function is applied to each component of the colour separately as follows:

$$r_w = \frac{w_1 r_1 + w_2 r_2}{w_1 + w_2}, \qquad g_w = \frac{w_1 g_1 + w_2 g_2}{w_1 + w_2}, \qquad b_w = \frac{w_1 b_1 + w_2 b_2}{w_1 + w_2} \qquad (10.2)$$

Detecting the values of weights (w_1, w_2) depend on the domain and the application developer. Even though, the weights w_i are strictly problem dependent, the difficulty lies in selecting the colour vector closest to the calculated one. This is particularly a plague when we are working with a colour palette of fixed size, say, 256 colours. For the palette colour for which its distance from the blended colour is minimum, the particular palette colour is chosen as a 'trade-off'. The common distance measures are Euclidian or weighted absolute distance.

10.1.4 An Enhancement Scheme for a Class of Colour Images

The ability to visually discriminate between various objects is dependent, to a large extent, on our capability of colour perception. The power to discriminate between objects of different colours suffers if the scene is poorly lit, or if the objects display low contrast. Following Gupta and Chanda (1996), a scheme is presented to enhance the contrast between two objects in a colour image. Their model of colour formation is in line with the Phong's illumination model and the colour enhancement scheme is based on the specular reflection model.

The structures (or regions) observed can be modelled as rough surfaces illuminated by ambient light, as well as, a point light source. Both the light source and the viewer are assumed to be far enough so that incident and reflected beams are considered to be parallel. Since the object is rough, the facet model provides a good approximation of the surface. With these assumptions on the illumination and the reflecting body, the intensity at any point has five possible components— the direct effect of the ambient light, the diffuse reflection component, the specular spike due to appropriately aligned facets, the forescatter lobe around the direction of reflected light and the backscatter lobe around the direction of the incident light. In most real cases, observation of the specular spike is least likely. Insignificant backscattering is also assumed, since backscattering needs scatterers located in a plane parallel to the mean surface normal to the object surfaces. In the physical problem, the presence of such scatterers is not expected. These simplifications reduce two of the five terms in the observed intensity. The third component, the forescatter lobe, needs closer attention. There are at least three different models to explain the form of the forescatter radiance, the most popular being the Torence–Sparrow model [Foley et al. (1992)]. According to this model, the specular lobe is the product of a Fresnel reflection term, an inter-facet shadowing term, and a term to represent a Gaussian fall-off function of the angle between the viewer and the reflected light. It is assumed that the product of the first two terms is a constant. That means within the range of incidence angle, the Gaussian fall-off function can be well approximated by a power-of-cosine function. Then this model reduces to the Phong illumination model.

Derivation of the model

Let us first write Phong's model of reflected light as

$$C^x(\lambda_n) = E_a(\lambda_n)T_a S^x(\lambda_n) + f_{att}E_p(\lambda_n) \left[T_d S^x(\lambda_n) \cos\theta + T_s \cos^m\alpha \right] \qquad (10.3)$$

where

λ_n, the n-th sample of wavelength range

x, position of a point on the surface

$C^x(\lambda_n)$, intensity of emitting light in the direction of the viewer

$S^x(\lambda_n)$, surface reflectance at x

$E_a(\lambda_n)$, intensity of ambient light

$E_p(\lambda_n)$, intensity of a point light source

T_a, ambient reflection coefficient

T_d, diffuse reflection coefficient

T_s, specular reflection coefficient

θ, angle of incidence

α, angle of viewer with respect to angle of specular reflection, and

m, constant (≥ 1)

Let us also suppose that $R_k(\lambda_n)$ is the spectral sensitivity of the k-th receptor and $\rho_k^x(\lambda_n)$ is the intensity recorded by the k-th receptor at the point x. Using these definitions in Equation (10.3), we get

$$\rho_k^x(\lambda_n) = \sum_{n=1}^{N} \{E_a(\lambda_n)\, T_a\, S^x(\lambda_n)\, R_k(\lambda_n) + f_{att}\, E_p(\lambda_n)\, [T_d S^x(\lambda_n)\cos\theta$$

$$+ T_s \cos^m\alpha]\, R_k(\lambda_n)\} \tag{10.4}$$

$$= \sum_{n=1}^{N} E_a(\lambda_n)\, T_a\, S^x(\lambda_n)\, R_k(\lambda_n) + \sum_{n=1}^{N} f_{att}\, E_p(\lambda_n)\, T_d\, S^x(\lambda_n)\cos\theta\, R_k(\lambda_n)$$

$$+ \sum_{n=1}^{N} f_{att}\, E_p(\lambda_n)\, T_s\, \cos^m\alpha\, R_k(\lambda_n) \tag{10.5}$$

$$= \rho_{a_k}^x(\lambda_n) + \rho_{d_k}^x(\lambda_n) + \rho_{s_k}^x(\lambda_n) \tag{10.6}$$

Following Wandell (1987), and Ho et al. (1990) all the terms that appear as functions of wavelength λ_n, can be decomposed into a set of orthogonal basis functions such as the Fourier or Lagrange basis of a suitable dimensionality. Thus,

$$E_a(\lambda_n) = \sum_{i=1}^{D(E_a)} \varepsilon_{a_i} \mathcal{E}_{\rangle}(\lambda_n) \tag{10.7}$$

where $D(E_a)$ is the dimensionality of expansion and $\mathcal{E}_{\rangle}(\lambda_n)$ represents the i-th basis function. If N samples are taken from the visible spectrum, then n (the subscript of λ) ranges from 1 to N, leading to an $N \times D(E_a)$ expansion matrix **E**. Similarly there are $D(E_a)$ terms of ε_{a_i} constituting the vector $\hat{\varepsilon}_a$. Then

$$E_p(\lambda_n) = \sum_{i=1}^{D(E_p)} \varepsilon_{p_i} \mathcal{E}_{\rangle}(\lambda_n) \tag{10.8}$$

$$S^x(\lambda_n) = \sum_{i=1}^{D(S)} \sigma_i^x \, S_i(\lambda_n) \tag{10.9}$$

Likewise, the matrix S (the basis function for the surface reflectance) and the vectors $\hat{\varepsilon}_p$ and $\hat{\sigma}$ are defined. Also, for notational simplicity denote $D(E_a) = D(E_p) = M$ and $D(S) = L$. Now,

$$\rho_{a_k}^x = \sum_{n=1}^{N} E_a(\lambda_n) T_a S^x(\lambda_n) \, R_k(\lambda_n)$$

$$= T_a \sum_{n=1}^{N} E_a(\lambda_n) S^x(\lambda_n) \, R_k(\lambda_n)$$

$$\hat{\rho}_a^x = T_a \, \Omega_{E_a} \hat{S}^x \tag{10.10}$$

where $\hat{\rho}_a^x$ is a K-vector for K sensors, and Ω_{E_a} is a $K \times N$ matrix, whose kj-th term stands for $E_a(\lambda_j)$ $R_k(\lambda_j)$. Similarly, from the other two terms of Equation (10.6)

$$\hat{\rho}_d^x = \gamma_1^x \Omega_{E_p} \hat{S}^x \tag{10.11}$$

$$\hat{\rho}_s^x = \gamma_2^x \Omega_{E_p} \hat{u} \tag{10.12}$$

where γ_1^x stands for $f_{att}^x T_d \cos\theta$, γ_2^x stands for $f_{att}^x T_s \cos^m\alpha$ and $\hat{u}$ is the transpose of a vector whose elements are all 1. Therefore,

$$\hat{\rho}^x = \hat{\rho}_a^x + \hat{\rho}_d^x + \hat{\rho}_s^x \tag{10.13}$$

$$= T_a \Omega_{E_a} \hat{S}^x + \gamma_1^x \Omega_{E_p} \hat{S}^x + \gamma_2^x \Omega_{E_p} \hat{u}$$

$$= T_a \Omega_{E_a} S \hat{\sigma}^x + \gamma_1^x \Omega_{E_p} S \hat{\sigma}^x + \gamma_2^x \Omega_{E_p} \hat{u}$$

$$= T_a \Lambda_{E_a} \hat{\sigma}^x + \gamma_1^x \Lambda_{E_p} \hat{\sigma}^x + \gamma_2^x \Lambda_{E_p} \hat{u} \tag{10.14}$$

In reality, the ambient light component E_a is not a completely different source of light and can be considered to have reached the object after multiple reflections of the point light source from different reflectors in the environment. This implies that $\Lambda_{E_a} = \delta\Lambda_{E_p}$, where δ is a constant. Let us drop the subscript from E_p, the last equation becomes

$$\hat{\rho}^x = \delta T_a \Lambda_E \hat{\sigma}^x + \gamma_1^x \Lambda_E \hat{\sigma}^x + \gamma_2^x \Lambda_E \hat{u}$$

$$= (\delta T_a + \gamma_1^x) \Lambda_E \hat{\sigma}^x + \Lambda_2^x \Lambda_E \hat{u}$$

$$= \gamma_3^x \Lambda_E \hat{\sigma}^x + \gamma_2^x \Lambda_E \hat{u} \tag{10.15}$$

Now, let us consider the ideal case considered in Wandell (1987) where the object is illuminated by ambient light alone and there is no attenuation of the incident light from the surface. The observed intensity in this case is given by

$$\hat{I}^x = \Lambda_E \hat{\sigma}^x \tag{10.16}$$

Equating Equations (10.15) and (10.16), we get

$$\hat{\rho}^x = \eta_1^x \hat{I}^x + \hat{\eta}_2^x \tag{10.17}$$

where $\eta_1^x = \gamma_3^x$ and $\hat{\eta}_2^x = \gamma_2^x \Lambda_E \hat{u}$. Since the second term of Equation (10.17) is constant for a specific imaging condition, it reveals that the recorded intensity $\hat{\rho}^x$ can be interpreted as the ideal intensity $\hat{I}^x$ corrupted by both additive and multiplicative position-dependent noise.

The contrast enhancement problem

With the above interpretation of recorded colour intensity, our objective is to restore I^x up to a multiplicative constant given ρ^x and some knowledge about the noise. In other words, given ρ^x, η_1^x and η_2^x, we have to find $\bar{I}^x$, an estimate of I^x, multiplied by a constant m. Naturally, our solution would be a family of estimates depending on the choice of m. Here, we choose that m which maximises the *difference in colour appearance* keeping the hue unaltered. Let the difference in colour appearance be defined by the expression

$$\Delta(I) = \sum_{k=1}^{K} (I_k^{x_1} - I_k^{x_2})^2 \tag{10.18}$$

where $\hat{I}$ denotes the intensity vector, and x_1 and x_2 denote positions. Then maximisation of the expression implies that we would maximally increase this difference if the colour of the two pixels are different and reduce their difference to zero if their colour is the same. However, in doing so, the hue, represented by the proportions of the colour responses, would be preserved. This idea may be viewed as an extension of graylevel stretching. For example, suppose for two points x_1 and $x_2, I_i^{x_1} > I_k^{x_1}$ for $k = 1, 2, 3, ..., K$ where $i \neq k$ and $I_j^{x_2} > I_k^{x_2}$ for $k = 1, 2, 3, ..., K$ where $j \neq k$. Now if $i \neq j$, then the dominating sensors for the two positions are different. In this case, their intensity difference $\Delta(I)$ is made as large as possible. On the other hand, if

$$\frac{I_1^{x_1}}{I_1^{x_2}} = \frac{I_2^{x_1}}{I_2^{x_2}} = \frac{I_3^{x_1}}{I_3^{x_2}} = \cdots = \frac{I_K^{x_1}}{I_K^{x_2}} \tag{10.19}$$

then $\Delta(I)$ is made equal to zero. All other cases map between these two extremes.

Secondly, it is obvious from Equation (10.17) that we have to subtract $\hat{\eta}_2^x$ from the measurement $\hat{\rho}^x$. It has been assumed that $\gamma_2^x \hat{c}_k = p\hat{\rho}_k^x$. where $0 < p < 1$. That means, $\hat{\eta}_2^x$, the constant term in Equation (10.17), can be represented as a fraction p of $\hat{\rho}^x$. Now,

$$\gamma_2^x \sum_{k=1}^{K} c_k = p \sum_{k=1}^{K} \rho_k^x$$

$$p = \frac{\gamma_2^x \Sigma_{k=1}^K c_k}{\Sigma_{k=1}^K \rho_k^x}$$

$$= \frac{\gamma_2^x \Sigma_{k=1}^K c_k}{\eta_1^x \Sigma_{k=1}^K I_k^x + \gamma_2^x \Sigma_{k=1}^K c_k}$$

$$= 1 - \frac{\eta_1^x \Sigma_{k=1}^K I_k^x}{\eta_1^x \Sigma_{k=1}^K I_k^x + \gamma_2^x \Sigma_{k=1}^K c_k} \tag{10.20}$$

Let us denote $\Sigma_{k=1}^K \rho_k^x = I^x$. Then Equation (10.20) suggests that p is a monotonically decreasing function which asymptotically tends to zero as I^x tends to infinity. The above discussion leads to the following transformation from ρ_k^x to $\bar{I}_k^x$:

$$\bar{I}_k^x = \frac{m}{\eta_1^x} \left\{ \rho_k^x - p(I^x) \rho_k^x \right\} \tag{10.21}$$

for $k = 1, 2, 3, \ldots, K$, where m is a constant.

Algorithm and results

The algorithm treats chromatic and achromatic pixels separately. The conceptual treatment is, however, the same for both the cases, because colour contrast has been interpreted as an extension of graylevel contrast. Therefore, the algorithm first determines if a pixel is achromatic by checking if the relative proportions of red, green and blue responses are all around 0.33. If it is so, its intensity value is simply stretched, otherwise, it is subjected to the transformation proposed in the previous section. Here, the constant m is the maximum allowable value in the system, and η_1^x is taken to be max{Red, Green, Blue}. The function $p(I^x)$ is given by

$$p(I^x) = c_1 e^{-I^x} + c_2 \tag{10.22}$$

where c_1 and c_2 are experimentally determined constants. Figure 10.2 presents the results produced by this algorithm.

10.1.5 Pseudo- and False Colouring

The process of assigning different colour to every intensity value available in a grayscale image is known as *pseudo-colour processing*. In other words, it is yet another image intensity representation technique similar to grayvalue distribution. Many image features and their comparisons could readily be done using pseudo-colours; for example, interpretation of a grayscale satellite image of land use map is easy assigning one colour to the intensity emanating from the land while a different colour to the river and yet another colour to vegetation, and so on. However, pseudo-colouring may not be suitable for such images where we are accustomed to see them in graylevel, for example, an image of a human face. Obviously, the extent of colour assignment depends on the hardware support. Almost all the modern display monitors support 256 colour levels and most image processing systems support 16 million colour as demonstrated in the colour cube described in Section 10.1.2 as well as in Chapter 3. For any 8-bit (i.e. 256 level) gray image, assigning maximum 256 different colours in an 8-bit colour monitor is a straightforward proposition.

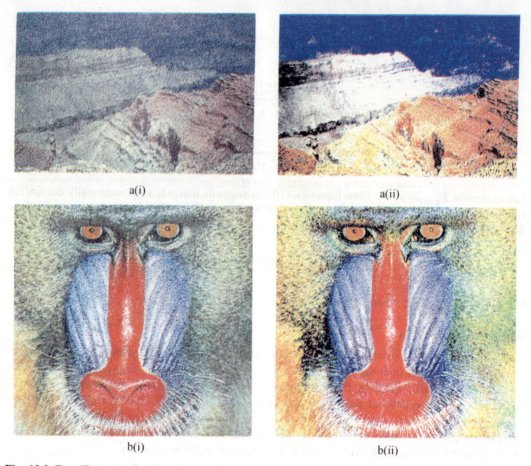

a(i)   a(ii)

b(i)   b(ii)

Fig. 10.2 Two illustrations of the colour enhancement scheme: a(i) and b(i), original images, a(ii) and b(ii) enhanced images.

Figure 10.3 shows a scheme for pseudo-colouring. Colour coordinate transformation block takes as input a graylevel image and gives out colour triplet (red, green and blue, in this case) suitable for display. So we have three mapping functions each of which produces a primary colour value based on input graylevel. An example of such mapping functions may be given as:

$$g_R(r, c) = \begin{cases} \dfrac{1}{1 - t_R}\{g(r, c) - t_R\} & \text{if } g(r, c) \geq t_R \\ 0 & \text{otherwise} \end{cases}$$

$$g_G(r, c) = \begin{cases} 1 - \dfrac{1}{t_{G'}} \, |\, g(r, c) - t_G\, | & \text{if } t_G - t_{G'} \leq g(r, c) \leq t_G + t_{G'} \\ 0 & \text{otherwise} \end{cases} \tag{10.23}$$

$$g_B(r, c) = \begin{cases} \dfrac{1}{t_B} \{t_B - g(r, c)\} & \text{if } g(r, c) \leq t_B \\ 0 & \text{otherwise} \end{cases}$$

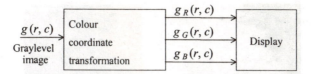

Fig. 10.3   A simple scheme for pseudo-colouring.

for $0 \le t_R, t_G, t_{G'}, t_B \le 1$. That means both graylevel and colour intensity range are in $[0, 1]$. The graphical representation of these functions are shown in Fig. 10.4 for $t_R = t_G = t_B = 0.5$ and $t_{G'} = 0.25$ The functions can easily be written for 256 levels.

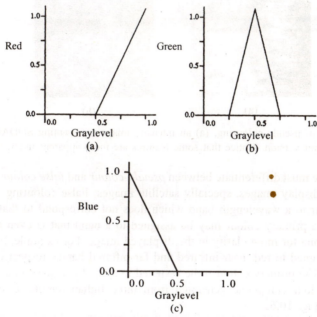

Fig. 10.4   An example of mapping functions for colour coordinate transformation.

However, assigning 256 different colours to a gray image with more than 256 intensity levels requires algorithms to find out the 256 best possible colours. The problem could be equivalently posed as to find m intensity levels (in this case 256), which best represents n different intensity levels where typically $n \gg m$. Several algorithms exist to this effect. The term *density slicing* is associated with generating pseudo-colour. Consider the intensity distribuion of a gray-scale image as a function $f(x, y)$. If there are n number of planes $s_1, s_2, \ldots, s_n$ such that the intensity map $f(x, y)$ is divided into $n + 1$ numbers of graylevels, then each of this level is known as density slice of intensity. Such slicing is particularly necessary when the number of intensity level for which pseudo-colours are to be produced are much higher compared to the available number of colours either in the display device or hardcopiers.

Not only grayscale images, but also non-optical or non-intensity images can be represented using pseudo-colouring. For example, temperature profile over a region, or altitude of a surface, or any other 3D information can be displayed on a 2D plane using pseudo-colouring. An example of pseudo-colouring is shown in Fig. 10.5 using the mapping functions as shown in Fig. 10.4.

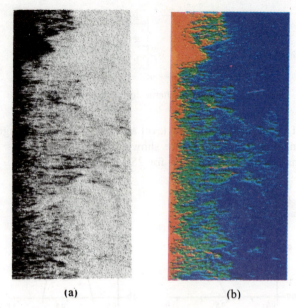

(a)   (b)

Fig. 10.5 Illustration of pseudo-colouring: (a) an intensity image representing SODAR signal and (b) its pseudo-colour version. Notice that some features are more apparent in (b) than (a).

At this stage, we must differentiate between *pseudo-colour* and *false colour composites* (FCC) frequently used to display images, specially satellite images. False colouring, as its name goes, assigns a true colour to a wavelength band which does not correspond to that colour in reality. As a consequence, a primary colour may be assigned to a band that is even outside the visible spectrum. This is done for more clarity in the displayed image. For example, blue, green and red colours may be assigned to red, near-infrared and far-infrared bands, respectively for displaying this 3-band image. The primary colour to be assigned to a band is chosen in a completely ad hoc manner. A false colour composite generated from three Indian remote-sensing satellite (IRS) bands is shown in Fig. 10.6.

10.2 Processing of Satellite Images

Satellites and airborne sensors are a constant source of images catering a wide range of needs from land-use resource mapping to weather prediction and from target identification to environmental monitoring. The techniques of digital image processing discussed so far are widely applicable in processing satellite images. The two major issues involved in satellite image processing are (a) the early processing techniques specific to the image acquisition systems of satellite and airborne sensors and the atmospheric medium through which remotely sensed images are captured and (b) the computer-based interpretation [Bernstein (1978), Siegel and Gillespie (1980), Paine (1981), Richards (1986)]. The latter, however, involves integration of information extracted from the images with the land-based information and groundtruths such as land-use maps, toposheets, vegetation information and so on. Since the digital image processing techniques necessary for the second goal are discussed in depth throughout the book, only the portion relevant to satellite image processing related to low-level error correction of satellite images are discussed in this section.

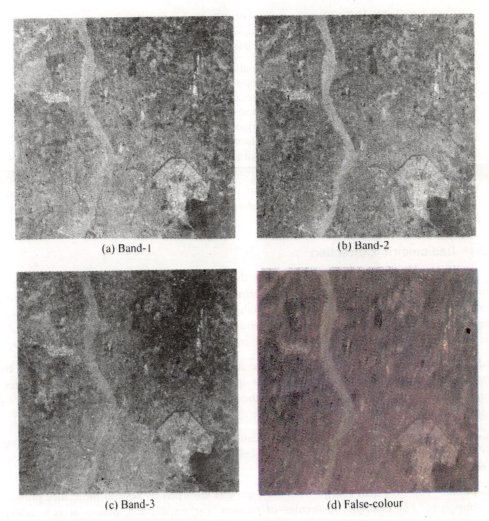

(a) Band-1　　　　　　　　　　　　　(b) Band-2

(c) Band-3　　　　　　　　　　　　　(d) False-colour

Fig. 10.6　An example of false-colour composite generated from three bands.

Satellite-based remote sensing devices are a constant source of multi-spectral images and at the same time cluster of satellites provides multi-source images depending on data used from Landsat, NOAA, SPOT, INSAT, IRS, etc. This immediately gives rise to a problem while registering images from different sensors with different pixel resolution. Resolution, in case of satellite imagery, refers to the size of region on the earth surface represented by a pixel. For example, multi-spectral scanner (MSS) boarded on Landsat has a resolution of 79 m × 79 m; while that of SPOT is 10 m and Indian remote-sensing satellite (IRS) has a spatial resolution of 37 m × 37 m. Processing of satellite imagery takes a major share of entire image processing activities because of many important applications such as natural resources management, crop estimation, rescue planning and monitoring, environment monitoring. For example, different bands of *thematic mapper* data, another scanning device boarded on Landsat, are used for the various applications (Table 10.1).

Table 10.1 Thematic mapper of different bands and their uses

Band	Wavelength range	Application (μ m)
1	0.45 – 0.52	Soil analysis, water-depth studies
2	0.52 – 0.60	Vegetation
3	0.63 – 0.69	Vegetation discrimination
4	0.76 – 0.90	Different types of land-water discrimination
5	1.55 – 1.75	Crop type, water content in crop, soil moisture
6	2.08 – 2.35	Rock formation
7	10.40 – 12.50	Thermal conditions

We start with the most important issues of low-level satellite image processing, known as *radiometric correction*. This is specific to any remote-sensing device and it includes errors introduced due to the atmospheric medium.

10.2.1 Radiometric Correction

The pixel value recorded at an image point is the average reflected brightness from a specific region on the earth. There always exists an atmospheric medium through which the reflected intensity travels and the consequent distortion in the pixel value is termed as *radiometric* distortion. Before we see how such distortion could be removed from the image, let us define some of the basic terms related to radiometric correction. Some of these terms are redefined from Chapter 4.

Irradiance. Given a source of electromagnetic energy, for example, the Sun, the radiation from the source follows the inverse square law. This specifies the radiated energy from the source to the unit surface area (of a sphere surrounding the energy source). The measurement unit is watts per square metre.

Radiance. The amount of incident energy scattered back to the atmosphere is the 'radiance' from a given object point. The power density scattered back from the point is measured in watts per square metre per steradian.

Absorption. The irradiated energy from the source is absorped by several molecules present in the atmosphere. For example, molecules of oxygen, carbon dioxide, ozone. It is a selective process and depending on the absorption medium, certain wavelengths got trapped in the medium while the rest is transmitted through it.

Scattering. The 'scattering' in the radiated energy is due to the presence of microparticles in the atmosphere. If air molecules themselves participate in scattering, the phenomenon is known as *Rayleigh scattering*. If the size of the particles is bigger due to the presence of suspended aerosols in smoke, fume or haze, the type of scattering is known as *Mie* or *aerosol scattering*.

Transmittance. The amount of solar irradiance reaches the earth after atmospheric absorption and scattering is the transmittance. Hence, in the absence of atmosphere, the transmittance is 100%. Clearly, it depends on the path the energy travels.

In addition, energy incident on a pixel is subjected to secondary irradiance either from the suspended particles in the atmosphere or from the neighbouring pixels. They are collectively called *sky irradiance*. On the other hand, radiation from the neighbouring pixels contribute to radiance towards the centre along the path of radiance from the pixel under consideration to the sensor. This is called *path radiance*. Therefore, the total irradiance reaching the earth can be modelled as:

$$E_T = E_\lambda T_I \cos\theta \, \Delta\lambda + E_S \tag{10.24}$$

where E_λ is the spectral irradiance of the Sun, T_I is the transmittance of the atmosphere and θ is angle of incidence. T_I depends on the path from the source to the pixel. The total irradiance is summed over a wavelength band $\Delta\lambda$. The secondary sky irradiance is taken care of with the term E_S. In a similar note, radiance model due to the total irradiance as in Equation (10.24) is given by:

$$L_T = \frac{R}{\pi} T_R E_T + L_p \tag{10.25}$$

Since, radiance is a portion of the incident energy depending on the reflectance of the surface, R in Equation (10.25) denotes the reflectance of the surface. The reflected energy is scattered in the upper atmosphere which forms a hemisphere around the point of reflection. This hemisphere forms a solid angle π. The path radiance is given by L_p, and T_R is the transmittance associated with the path from the earth surface to the sensor. It is this radiance value some scaling of which gives the digital value of a pixel usually in the range of 0 to 255 in an 8-bit imaging system.

The effect of scattering, both primary and secondary, and absorption mechanism in the atmosphere contribute to error and affect the imaging detail. These come under the purview of radiometric errors. In the next section we will see how such errors could be tackled.

Correction of atmospheric effects

Looking at the analysis in the last section, it is reasonable to assume that the correction of atmospheric effects depends on the quality of modelling of scattering and absorption phenomena. A method for removing the effect of cloud cover from satellite imagery [Chanda and Dutta Majumder (1991)] is already described in Chapter 7. A number of researchers [Schowengerdt (1997)] have worked in this area exploiting various other atmospheric conditions prevailing during overpass of the satellite. For example, Forster (1984) calculated the transmittance of the atmosphere in the following steps:

1. Calculate the equivalent mass of water vapour in atmosphere from temperature and humidity information.

2. Visibility of the medium is determined from water vapour percentage.

3. Mie scattering effect is calculated from the visibility while Rayleigh scattering at the particular wavelength of the sensor is known. These together gives a term known as *normal optical thikness, τ_o.*

4. The transmittance is calculated from $T = e^{-\tau_o \sec\theta}$, where θ accounts for the angle of incidence. Note that, $\sec\theta$ gives the measure of path through the atmospheric medium on which the transmittance depends.

Forster also detailed the methodology for measuring solar irradiance per square metre under 100% transmittance condition.

The problem however comes from the non-availability of data related to atmospheric conditions at the time of satellite overpass. The model for correction depends on precise information of temperature, relative humidity, atmospheric pressure and visibility. As a compromise, frequently bulk correction of atmospheric effects are performed. It is assumed that due to such effects, especially due to path radiance, histogram of intensity value is shifted towards higher end of intensity spectrum. That is, some sort of constant value is added to the brightness and as a result, intensity values at the lower end close to zero may not be present at all in the image. The crude correction is performed by subtracting the amount by which the histogram is shifted toward the higher end of the brightness spectrum, that is toward 255 in the case of 8-bit system.

10.2.2 Other Common Errors

The quality of satellite image products are degraded with at least two major factors. Like any other sensing devices, satellite and airborne sensors suffer from instrumentation errors. Instrument output or signal out are expected to perform linearly with respect to the radiation incident on it. However, non-linearity is frequently introduced in the system. Also, sensing devices in the satellite are collection of similar CCD sensors. It is natural that the transfer characteristics of such devices will be slightly different. This gives rise to band-to-band errors and even more significant within band instrument error.

There are a family of imaging distortion that degrades the quality of satellite images. They are grouped under the following geometric distortions:

- Error due to earth rotation: As the sensing device captures the image frame, due to rotation of the earth in a particular direction (say west to east), the earth's location shifts in the same direction with respect to every scan line. Therefore, before a scan line is completely digitized, the target pixel points on the earth surface changes place resulting in distortion as shown in Fig. 10.7(a).

- Field of view error: For remote-sensing devices, the angular field of view[1] is constant throughout the scan line. As a result, the pixel size at extreme ends of the scan line appears larger compared to that at nadir [Fig. 10.7(b)]. Such error is referred to as *panoromic distortion*.

- Error due to earth curvature: The satellite sensing devices with wide swath[2] and having constant field of view look at the planar patch on the earth surface, but at the boundaries of swath, pixels undergo stretching and contraction due to earth curvature; as a result, the image gets distorted.

- Error due to variations in altitude and velocity of airborne devices: During motion or during atmospheric turbulence remote-sensing platforms may change its position in terms of variation in the elevation or altitude. This alters the pixel resolution and the digitized image undergoes transformation similar to scaling.

Exact mathematical model and the associated parameters may not be available for all the errors described above. Second, even if they are available, many a time they lead to very complicated processing of data resulting in significant computational error and cost. Therefore, enhancement techniques that manipulate radiometric values become a reasonable choice for improving the quality/appearance of multi-spectral image. Moreover, such processing sometimes brings out some features that are not readily seen in the images.

---

[1]Field of view is the scan angle at either side of the nadir over which data is recorded.
[2]The sweeping width of the scanner.

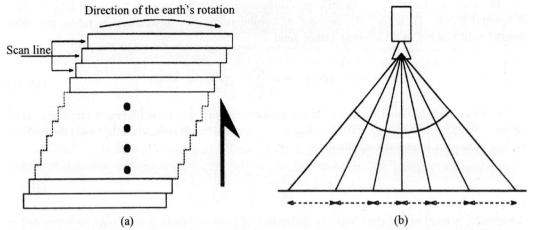

Fig. 10.7   Error introduced in a satellite image due to (a) the earth's rotation and (b) field of view.

10.2.3   Enhancement of Multi-spectral Image

Enhancement procedures are often performed on multi-spectral images of a scene in order to accentuate salient features to assist subsequent human interpretation or machine analysis. These procedures include, as discussed earlier, individual image plane enhancement techniques such as contrast enhancement, histogram modification, etc., [see Chapter 6 for detail]. Other methods, considered in this section, involve the joint processing of multi-spectral image planes. Suppose we are dealing with image data corresponding to four bands, value at each position (r, c) is represented by a vector of four elements, i.e. $g(r, c) = [g_1(r, c)\ g_2(r, c)\ g_3(r, c)\ g_4(r, c)]$. Here these four elements correspond to brightness in four different bands. That means $g_m(r, c)$ denotes brightness at (r, c) due to band m.

Multi-spectral images are often subtracted in pairs according to the relation

$$f_{m,n}(r, c) = |\, g_m(r, c) - g_n(r, c) \,| \qquad (10.26)$$

in order to accentuate reflectivity variations between the multi-spectral planes. $f_{m,n}(r, c)$ is called the *difference image*. An associated advantage is the removal of any unknown but common luminance bias components that exist.

Another simple, but highly effective, means of multi-spectral image enhancement is the formation of ratios of the image planes. The *ratio image* between the m-th and n-th multi-spectral planes is defined as

$$f_{m,n}(r, c) = \frac{g_m(r, c)}{g_n(r, c)} \qquad (10.27)$$

It is assumed that the image planes are adjusted to be non-zero. In many multi-spectral imaging systems, the image plane $g_m(r, c)$ can be modelled by the product of an object reflectivity function $r_m(r, c)$ and an illumination function $I_m(r, c)$ that is nearly identical for all multi-spectral planes. Ratio of such imagery provides an automatic normalization or compensation of the illumination factor. But, there is one problem with this method is that the accentuation of the gray-scale quantization error is associated with each plane.

There are a total of $N(N-1)$ different 'difference' or 'ratio' pairs that may be formed from N spectral bands. To reduce the number of combinations, the differences or ratios are often formed with respect to an average image field

$$\bar{g}(r,\ c) = \frac{1}{N}\sum_{m=1}^{N} g_m(r,\ c)$$

(10.28)

It may be argued that both the above mentioned corrections can be achieved if ratios are taken on the difference between data corresponding to two spectral bands rather than the bands themselves, i.e. the enhanced image is computed as

$$f'(r,c) = \frac{|\,g_k(r,c) - g_l(r,c)\,|}{|\,g_m(r,c) - g_n(r,c)\,|}$$

(10.29)

Sometimes, instead of the ratio between difference of pairs of bands, people may be interested in the ratio of sum of any two bands with sum of two other bands. For example,

$$f'(r,c) = \frac{g_k(r,c) + g_l(r,c)}{g_m(r,c) + g_n(r,c)}$$

(10.30)

Results of band combination in various ways are shown in Fig. 10.8. Convex combination among the multi-spectral planes has also been employed as a means of enhancement. A popular transformation of this kind is the principal component analysis or K–L transform as given in Chapter 2. The comparison of Fig. 10.6(d) with Figs. 10.8(g) and 10.8(h) reveals that the band combination brings out certain features that are not readily visible in original image.

10.3 Medical Image Processing

One of the successful applications of image processing technique is in the area of medical imaging or medical image processing. Introduction to sophisticated imaging devices coupled with advances in algorithms specific to medical image processing both for diagnostics and therapeutic planning is the key to wide popularity of image processing in this field. The earlier applications involve computer processing of X-rays, chromosome karyotyping, blood cell analysis and similar other computer analysis technique for laboratory testing, especially which involves human observation under microscopes. From early 1970s, there was considerable advancement in radiographic imaging technique. This is an important tool for diagnostics and also for pre-operative planning. Similar to remotely-sensed images, the methodologies discussed so far in the book are equally applicable for medical images. The specific algorithms which are of special interest for medical diagnostics are related to enhancement, restoration, noise filtering and segmentation process. In fact, detection and localization of certain regions of interest (ROI) are of prime importance. Relatively, less stress is focussed for low-level image processing algorithms as most of the images are captured in controlled environment. However, contrast enhancement techniques offer help in manual interpretation of medical images. Even though final interpretation solely depends on medical professionals, several advisory expert systems have been developed combining expert knowledge and interactive image processing of medical images [Besl and Mekay (1992)].

Lately, there has been extensive focus in multi-modal medical image processing. With the

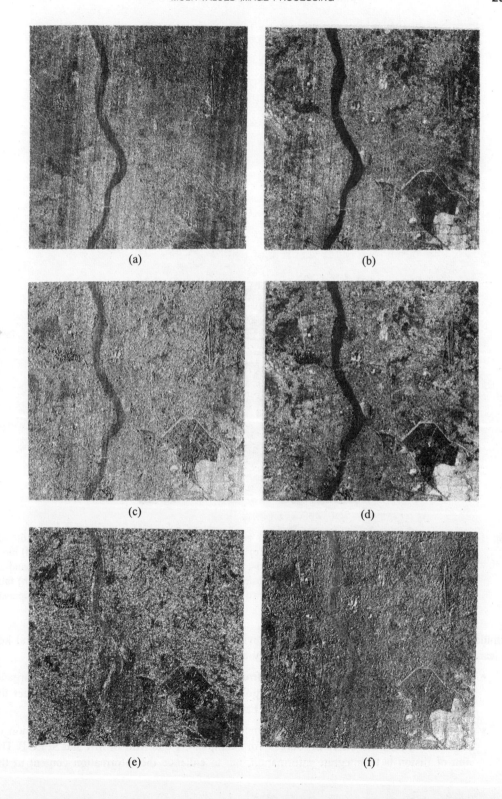

(a)

(b)

(c)

(d)

(e)

(f)

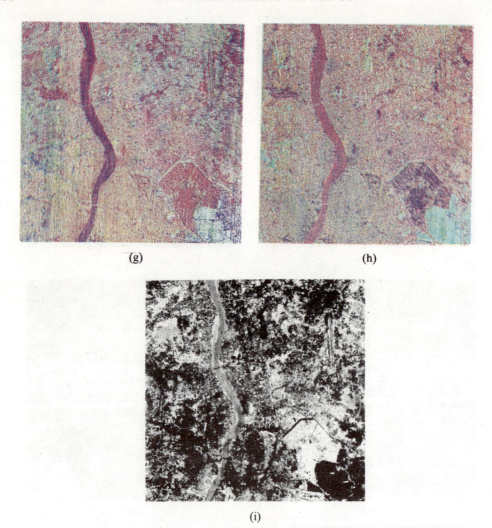

Fig. 10.8 Results of band combination. Original bands are the same as shown in Figs. 10.6(a–c). (a) |band-1 – band-2|, (b) band-1/band-2, (c) differences of band-1 from the average one, (d) ratios of band-1 with the average one, (e) |band-1 – band-2|/|band-2 – band-3|, (f) (band-1 + band-2)/ (band-2 + band-3), (g) false colour composite with red = (a), green = (b) and blue = (c), (h) false colour composite with red = (f), green = (d) and blue = (e), and (i) most dominant component of K–L transform of three bands.

popularization and sophistication of imaging devices like CT, MR, SPECT or PET, several key research issues are emerging in this field. They are specifically:

- displaying volume rendered 3D images from the planar sectional images of human organs. Such display requires information interpolation from the image plane to reconstruct the organ. [Interested readers may refer to Faugeras (1993) for details].

- The important emerging area in multi-modal medical image processing is the fusion of medical images from different sources, for example, CT and MR, or MR and SPECT. The aim of fusion is to integrate information, i.e. to enhance the information content in the fused image frame. Several approaches in this regard are detailed in Section 10.3.1. Any such fusion process must be preceded by registration of multi-modal images. This has been thoroughly discussed in Chapter 9.

10.3.1 Multi-modal Medical Image Fusion

The clinical diagnosis and treatment of radiotherapeutic patients usually require exhaustive exploration of biomedical images with varieties of signal modalities. However, images of a single modality do not provide a complete set of information. The inadequacy of clinical information makes the biomedical image of a single modality insufficient for use in the clinical interpretation and diagnosis of disease. In general, information acquired from images resulting from different modalities are complementary in nature. A computed tomography (CT) image, for example, is suitable for visualization of ventricular systems, and skull and bone-like hard structures; whereas, a magnetic resonance (MR) image, due to its exceptional soft-tissue contrast, is more suitable for visualizing cerebral tissues accurately. Therefore, an accurate interpretation and diagnosis of disease requires a thorough inspection of the regions of interest in the images of biological organs using both the image modalities. However, viewing several such images individually and separately is clinically too inconvenient. This situation is overcome if it is possible to realize a composite image which consists of all object features visualized in all the image modalities. Such an image is constructed by fusing the constituting images of different modalities subject to some geometrical and biomedical constraints. Thus a successfully fused image contains all the features that are visualized in at least one of the constituting modalities, and the inconvenience of exploring all the image modalities is avoided.

A number of researchers have been working in the field of image fusion. Generally, data fusion in multi-modal images [Abidi and Gonzalez (1992), Clark and Yuille (1990), Luo et al. (1989)] is partly redundant as some regions are depicted in all the modalities and is partly complementary as each modality highlights certain features that are absent in images of other modalities. There are many methods that are based on the classification of pixel [Bloch (1996)]. In this direction, Hurn et al. (1995) have suggested a Bayesean probabilistic method for biomedical image fusion. Mukherjee et al. (1998) have developed an algorithm for fusing CT and MR images based on entropy. A hierarchical scheme for fusion of MR and CT brain images by constructing multi-resolution morphological pyramids has been devised by Matsopoulos et al. (1994)]. We also choose the same problem here to describe fusion technique given below as discussed by Chanda et al. (1998).

Image fusion using multi-scale morphological operations

The top-hat transformation originally proposed in [Meyer (1978)] provides an excellent tool for extracting bright (respectively, dark) features smaller than a given size from an uneven background. It relies on the fact that by gray-scale opening one can remove the brighter areas, i.e. features, that cannot hold the structuring element, from an image. Subtracting the open image from the original one yields an image where the features that have been removed by opening, clearly stand out. Similarly it is true for closing operation as well. That means using a closing instead of an opening and subtracting the original image from the closed one allows us to extract dark features against a brighter background. It is called a *black top-hat* transformation as opposed to *white top-hat* transformation in case of opening. The structuring element used in both opening and closing is a disk or, more specifically, a discrete approximation of disk. An ordered sequence of morphological filtering (i.e. opening or closing) of both the image modalities with a convex structuring element at different scales extracts scale-specific features from both the images. These scale-specific features resulting from various image modalities are then compared to select the best for subsequent construction of the fused image. The proposed method is described elaborately in the following subsections.

Construction of morphological towers.   The CT as well as the MR image are made to undergo a sequence of morphological opening and closing operations. Here we consider a 3×3 set as structuring element B. We then construct two sets of morphological towers for multi-scale opening and multi-scale closing operations. In each set, we have two different towers corresponding to MR and CT images. A tower basically comprises of a stack of images produced after morphological opening or closing operations on the CT or MR image for different values of the scale factor i of the structuring element as shown in Fig. 10.9. As the value of scaling parameter increases, the size of the remaining features in the resulting image also increases and the images are found to contain large flat plateaus (in case of opening) and valleys (in case of closing). However, the prime objective is a sequential separation of scale-specific features from the images. Thus, the

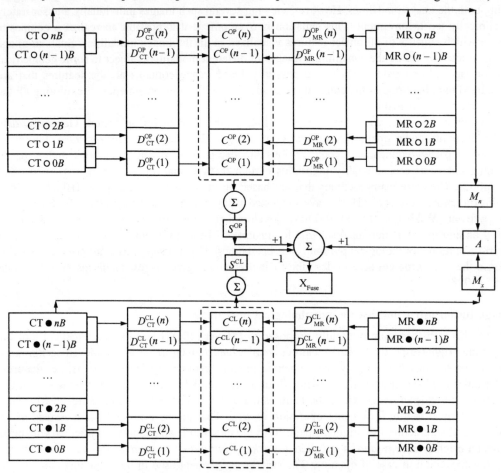

Fig. 10.9   Morphological towers for image fusion.

i-th entry in the multi-scale opening tower of the CT/MR image contains the image produced by opening the CT/MR image with a structuring element iB. So, altogether, there are four such towers of height n for multi-scale opening and closing operations of the CT and the MR images as under:

$$\text{CT} \circ iB = (\text{CT} \ominus iB) \oplus iB$$
$$\text{MR} \circ iB = (\text{MR} \ominus iB) \oplus iB$$
$$\text{CT} \bullet iB = (\text{CT} \oplus iB) \ominus iB$$
$$\text{MR} \bullet iB = (\text{MR} \oplus iB) \ominus iB$$

for $i = 1, 2, \ldots, n$. Multi-scale opening and closing are discussed in Chapter 2.

Construction of difference towers. As stated earlier, the image, resulting after morphological opening operation using a structuring element iB, contains only those features of the original image (CT or MR) which are equal to or larger than the size of the structuring element. Likewise, the resultant image after a morphological opening operation using a structuring element $(i + 1)B$ contains all those features of the original image (CT or MR) which are equal to or larger than the size of the structuring element. Thus, a difference of these two resulting images gives rise to another image which contains only those features of the original image which have size exactly equal to that of the structuring element iB. This holds good also for the multi-scale closing operations of the images.

With such views, we construct four difference towers for opening and closing operations of the CT and the MR images by carrying out difference operations between all successive pairs of images resulting after morphological opening (closing) operations using the structuring elements corresponding to two successive scales. Figure 10.9 shows four such *difference towers*. The difference towers are constructed by taking the difference between all successive pairs of the images in the morphological towers constructed in the immediate previous step. Thus the i-th entries in the difference tower for morphological operations are defined as

$$D_{\text{CT}}^{\text{op}}(i) = [\text{CT} \circ (i - 1)B] - (\text{CT} \circ iB)$$
$$D_{\text{MR}}^{\text{op}}(i) = [\text{MR} \circ (i - 1)B] - (\text{MR} \circ iB)$$
$$D_{\text{CT}}^{\text{cl}}(i) = (\text{CT} \bullet iB) - [\text{CT} \bullet (i - 1)B]$$
$$D_{\text{MR}}^{\text{cl}}(i) = (\text{MR} \bullet iB) - [\text{MR} \bullet (i - 1)B]$$

for $i = 1, 2, \ldots, n$.

Construction of combined tower. The scale-specific features from both the image modalities are now available in the difference towers constructed in the previous step. For constructing the fused image from the CT and the MR images, features from both of them should be combined. At each scale, the feature present in at least one image modality should be collected for fusion. With such views, we extract the scale-specific features from difference towers for opening (closing) operation by taking pixel-wise max of two images as shown in Fig. 10.9. The set of images obtained through max operation results in two more towers called the *combined towers*. The i-th entries of the combined tower corresponding to the opening and closing operations are basically the images produced respectively by

$$C^{\text{op}}(i) = \max\{D_{\text{CT}}^{\text{op}}(i),\ D_{\text{MR}}^{\text{op}}(i)\}$$
$$C^{\text{cl}}(i) = \max\{D_{\text{CT}}^{\text{cl}}(i),\ D_{\text{MR}}^{\text{cl}}(i)\}$$

for $i = 1, 2, \ldots, n$. Here 'max' stands for a pixel-wise maximum of two images.

Reconstruction.   For reconstructing the final image we do the following steps:

- Sum up all the entries in the combined tower corresponding to the opening operation. This results in an image consisting of bright features of all possible scales that are present in at least one modality. Therefore,

$$S^{\text{op}} = \sum_{i=1}^{n} C^{\text{op}}(i) \tag{10.31}$$

The summation, here, denotes pixel-wise sum of n images.

- We perform the same operation on the combined tower corresponding to the closing operation. This results in an image consisting of dark features of all possible scales that are present in at least one modality. Hence,

$$S^{\text{cl}} = \sum_{i=1}^{n} C^{\text{cl}}(i) \tag{10.32}$$

- We take the pixel-wise min (max) operation between the CT and the MR images after opening (closing) them with nB. Then we take the average of these two resulting images. That is,

$$M_x = \max\{\text{CT} \bullet nB, \text{MR} \bullet nB\}$$

$$M_n = \min\{\text{CT} \circ nB, \text{MR} \circ nB\}$$

$$A = \text{average } (M_x, M_n)$$

Here 'average' denotes the pixel-wise average of two images. Finally, Fused image is obtained by combining the three images as given by

$$X_{\text{Fuse}} = A + S^{\text{op}} - S^{\text{cl}} \tag{10.33}$$

The '+' and '−' operations are applied between corresponding pixels of the three different images

Justification of strategy.   The rationale behind such a fusion scheme is as follows:

The *difference tower* corresponding to opening contains a series of images of the same size each having scale-specific bright features. The i-th layer image contains bright features that are larger than or equal to size corresponding to scale $(i-1)$, but smaller than that corresponding to scale i. The i-th layer of the *max tower* corresponding to opening contains an image consisting of all bright features coming from both the modalities and are of size between scales $(i-1)$ and i. The image formed by summing all the images of max tower pixel-wise corresponding to opening contains all bright features of all scales. Similar operations related to closing do the same kind of things for the dark features.

Now CT $\circ$ nB (respectively CT $\bullet$ nB) is the background image with respect to scale n. Since we superpose feature image on (by adding it to) the background image, we take minimum of MR $\circ$ nB and CT $\circ$ nB to avoid intensity clipping as much as possible. In case of closing, it is the maximum of MR $\bullet$ nB and CT $\bullet$ nB as we subtract the feature image from the background one. Finally, we take the average of maximum of open and minimum of closed images because of the same reason. The bright and dark feature images are then added to and subtracted from the average image to obtain the final fused image.

The original CT and MR images and the fused image produced by the above method are shown in Fig. 10.10. B is a 3×3 point set and $n = 31$. The fused image is found to comprise of features that are present in either/both the modalities without any appreciable distortion. The fused image is found to be clinically more informative as compared to the individual constituting images. The fusing ability of the algorithm is measured quantitatively by means of, say, pixel-graylevel correlation between two images.

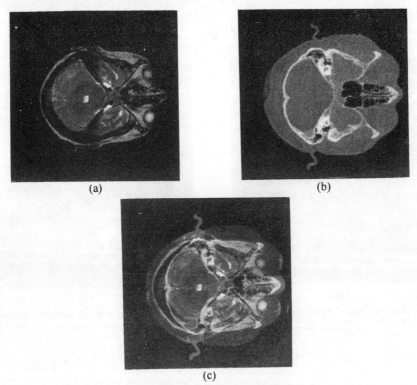

(a)

(b)

(c)

Fig. 10.10 (a) MR image of brain, (b) affine transformed CT image of brain used in the experiment and (c) the resultant image after fusing registered CT and MR images using morphological tower.

Image fusion by averaging

Although the method described in previous section is very effective and useful; it is computationally very expensive too. Among some of the less expensive methods, *averaging* is the simplest technique of fusing multi-modal images in which the fused image is formed by a pixel-wise averaging of the constituting images. This method is crude and does not hold good in many cases. The fused image usually does not contain all the salient features of the individual images. As a result, there may be a huge loss of information at the time of blending the multi-modal images. An alternative approach may be weighted averaging. One of the approaches to determine the weights is K–L transform.

Image fusion employing K–L transform

For constructing the fused image employing K–L transform, we form N vectors $\mathbf{f}_1, \mathbf{f}_2, \ldots, \mathbf{f}_N$ where $\mathbf{f}_j = \{f_{1j}, f_{2j}\}$ and N is the number of pixels in both the images. The first element of the vector is a pixel value of the first image while the second one is the value at corresponding pixel of the second image. We then construct the *mean* vector and the *variance-covariance matrix* from these N vectors. The fused image $F(r, c)$ is constructed from the individual images $F_1(r, c)$ and $F_2(r, c)$ using the following relation

$$F(r, c) = \phi_1 F_1(r, c) + \phi_2 F_2(r, c) \qquad (10.34)$$

where $\Phi = \{\phi_1, \phi_2\}$ is the normalized *eigenvector* of the variance-covariance matrix corresponding to its largest *eigenvalue*. Thus this method is nothing but a weighted averaging technique where the weights are determined by the K–L transform. Results are shown in Fig. 10.11.

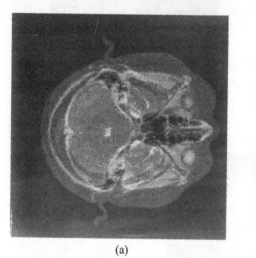 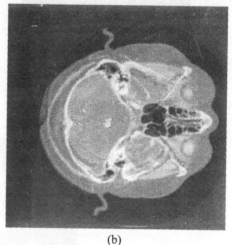

(a)   (b)

Fig. 10.11   The resultant fused image obtained by (a) simple averaging and (b) weighted averaging (K–L transform). These images are same as in Fig. 10.10.

Summary

Usually, gray-scale images are considered single-valued functions. There are some cases where an image is represented by a multi-valued function. That means pixels of the image are vector valued and elements of the vector come from various measurements at the same location of scene or object. Multi-spectral and multi-modal images are two major classes of such images. In this chapter, processing of these two classes of images are described with reference to real-life applications. Processing of colour images, a special case of multi-spectral images, is also discussed. A brief idea of pseudo-colouring and false-colour composite representation of images are given in this context. Various problems related to processing of satellite imagery as well as various methods are presented. In multi-modal image processing, only medical image processing techniques are discussed, however in detail, with emphasis to image fusion.

Problems

1. Suppose a colour image is represented by three graylevel images corresponding to three primary colours: red, green and blue. Show that if each graylevel image is enhanced independently by histogram equalization technique, hue is, in general, not preserved.

2. Given a graylevel image with 256 levels. Convert it to a pseudo-colour image such that for all colour shades (i) value = 127, and (ii) saturation = 50% and (iii) graylevel 0 gets the hue of colour blue, graylevel 128 gets the hue of colour green and graylevel 255 gets the hue of colour red.

3. Fuse two images using bright top-hat transform (i.e. original minus open image) only. Compare the result with that using both opening and closing as described in Section 10.3.1.

4. Fuse .two images using dark top-hat transform (i.e. close minus original image) only. Compare the result with that using both opening and closing as described in Section 10.3.1.

Bibliography

Abidi, M.A. and Gonzalez, R.C., *Data Fusion in Robotics and Machine Intelligence*, Academic Press, Boston, 1992.

Ashdown, I., 'Octree color quantization', *C, C++ Users' Journal*, **3**: 31–44, 1995.

Bernstein, R. (Ed.), *Digital Image Processing for Remote Sensing*, IEEE Press, New York, 1978.

Besl, P.J. and Mekay, N.D., 'A method for registration of 3d shapes', *IEEE Trans. on Patt. Anal. and Mach. Intell*, PAMI-**14**:239–256, 1992.

Bloch, I., 'Information combination operators for data fusion: a review with classification', *IEEE Trans. on Systems Man and Cybern. Part A: Systems and Humans*, **26**:52–67, 1996.

Chanda, B. and Dutta Majumder, D., 'An iterative algorithm for removing the effect of thin cloud cover from landsat imagery', *Mathematical Geology*, **23**:853–860, 1991.

Chanda, B., Mukherjee, S. and Ghosh, P., 'Multiscale morphological fusion of MR and CT images', in *Proc. ICVGIP'98*, pp. 21–26, New Delhi, 1998.

Clark, J.J. and Yuille, A.L., *Data Fusion for Sensory Information Processing Systems*, Kluwer Academic, Boston, 1990.

Faugeras, O., *Three-dimensional Computer Vision: A Geometric Viewpoint*, MIT Press, Cambridge, 1993.

Foley, J., Van Daam, A., Feiner, S. and Hughes, J., *Computer Graphics: Principles and Practice*, Addison-Wesley, Reading, Massachusetts, 1992.

Forster, B.C., 'Derivation of atmospheric correction procedures for landsat mss with particular reference to urban data', *Int. J. Remote Sensing*, **5**:799–817, 1984.

Gupta, A. and Chanda, B., 'A hue preserving enhancement scheme for a class of color images', *Patt. Recog. Letters*, **17**:109–114, 1996.

Hearn, D. and Baker, M.P., *Computer Graphics*, Prentice-Hall of India, New Delhi, 1992.

Ho, J., Funt, B.V. and Drew, M.S., 'Separating a color signal into illumination and surface reflectance components: theory and applications', *IEEE Trans. on Patt. Anal. Mach. Intell.*, PAMI-**12**:966–977, 1990.

Hurn, M.A., Mardia, K.V., Hainsworth, T.J., Kirkbride, J. and Berry, E., 'Bayesian fused classification of medical images', *Technical Report STAT/95/20/C*, University of Leeds, 1995.

Luo, R.C., Lin, M. and Scherp, R.S., 'Multisensor integration and fusion in intelligent systems', *IEEE Trans. on Systems Man and Cybern*, SMC-**19**:901–931, 1989.

Matsopoulos, G.K., Marshall, S. and Brunt, J.N.H., 'Multiresolution morphological fusion of MR and CT images of the human brain', *IEEE Proc.-Vis. Image Signal Process.*, **141**:137–142, 1994.

Meyer, F., 'Contrast feature extraction', in Chermant, J.L. (Ed.), *Quantitative Analysis of Microstructure in Material Sciences, Biology and Medicine*, Riederer Verlag, Stuttgart, Germany, 1978.

Mukherjee, D.P., Dutta, P. and Dutta Majumder, D., 'Entropy theoretic fusion of multimodal medical images', *Technical Report ECSU/2/98, Electronics and Communication Sciences Unit*, Indian Statistical Institute, Calcutta, 1998.

Paine, D.P., *Aerial Photography and Image Interpretation for Resources Management*, John Wiley and Sons, New York, 1981.

Richards, J.A., *Remote Sensing Digital Image Analysis: An Introduction*, Springer-Verlag, New York, 1986.

Schowengerdt, R.A., *Remote Sensing: Models and Methods for Image Processing*. Academic Press, New York, 1997.

Siegel, B.S. and Gillespie, A.R. (Eds.), *Remote Sensing in Geology*, John Wiley and Sons, New York, 1980.

Wandell, B.A., 'The synthesis and analysis of color images', *IEEE Trans. on Patt. Anal. Mach. Intell.*, PAMI-**9**:2–13, 1987.

Part–III

Image Analysis

Part—III

Image Analysis

Chapter 11

Segmentation

11.1 Introduction

Image processing techniques—enhancement and restoration—take a digital image as input and gives out another image that is of improved quality. On the other hand, in image analysis technique, the same input gives out somewhat detail description of the scene whose image is being considered. Most of the image analysis algorithms perform *segmentation* as a first step towards producing the description. Here input and output are 'still' images, but output is an abstract representation of the input. Segmentation technique basically divides the spatial domain, on which the image is defined, into 'meaningful' parts or regions. This meaningful region may be a complete object or may be a part of it. The segmentation algorithms try to make systematic use of some physically measured image features, but its performance is measured based on the 'meaning' associated with the extracted regions. So we may consider segmentation as a *psycho-physical* problem. Secondly, the requirement that the extracted region must have some meaning with respect to the given scene or objects in it makes the problem mathematically ill-posed. As a result, there exists no general segmentation algorithm which can work reasonably well for all images. Users have to choose or develop a segmentation algorithm suitable for the problem in hand. So, all the segmentation algorithms are ad hoc in nature. This algorithm may be incorporated explicitly or implicitly, or even in the form of various parameters. These algorithms are based on one of the two following approaches [Chanda (1988)]:

1. Satisfying homogeneity property in image feature(s) over a large region.

2. Detecting abrupt change in image feature(s) within a small neighbourhood.

The first approach extracts the regions as a whole over which some measure shows the presence of homogeneity in feature value, while the second one detects the border between two regions and is commonly known as *edge detection*. Figure 11.1 shows the results of these two approaches. Original graylevel image is shown in Fig. 11.1(a). The result of the first approach and that of the second approach are shown in Fig. 11.1(b) and Fig. 11.1(c), respectively. Edge-detection techniques will be discussed in the next chapter. In this chapter, we present segmentation algorithms that are based on the first approach. Because of the type of output they may be grouped under the heading of *region extraction*.

Fu and Mui (1981) and Pal and Pal (1993) have presented good surveys on segmentation methodologies.

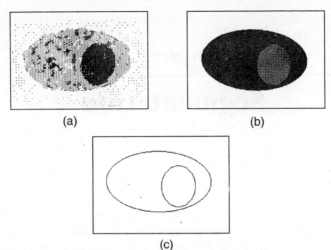

Fig. 11.1   Outputs of various segmentation techniques: (a) input image, (b) expected result of the region-extraction techniques and (c) expected result of edge detection techniques.

11.2   Region Extraction

Suppose the spatial domain on which the image is defined [see Section 5.5] is denoted by $\mathcal{D}$. Then image segmentation technique divides $\mathcal{D}$ into, say, n regions denoted by R_i ($i = 1, 2, \ldots, n$) such that

1. $\displaystyle\bigcup_{i=1}^{n} R_i = \mathcal{D}$

2. $R_i \cap R_j = \emptyset$

3. Prop (R_i) = True

4. Prop $(R_i \cup R_j)$ = False, if R_i and R_j are adjacent.

where Prop (R) represents some property defined in terms of feature values over the region R. Secondly, the regions R_i and R_j are said to be adjacent if a pixel (or a point) of R_i is a neighbour of some pixels of R_j and vice versa. The first condition says that every pixel of the image domain is mapped to one region or the other. The second condition ensures that a pixel is mapped to only one region. Third condition indicates that the regions are defined based on some property. Finally, maximality of each region is assured by the fourth condition.

11.3   Pixel-based Approach

An image contains various regions corresponding to different objects or their parts in the scene. The pixels comprising a region receive information from points of corresponding object or its part. Since different objects or different parts of the same object have different characteristics (e.g. reflectance of material, surface orientation and texture), feature values recorded at pixels belonging to various regions should be different. If we map the feature values at every pixels to a feature space, we expect to find distinct clusters formed corresponding to types of regions in the image.

Now an appropriate set of boundary functions can isolate each cluster from the others. Consequently, pixels in the image are classified[1] into various regions. Thus the image is segmented. If we consider a single feature then the distribution of pixel values in the feature space is degenerated to a *feature histogram* and the boundary function to a *threshold*. One of the simplest kind of features in graylevel image is gray value at a pixel. Thus, image can be segmented by simple graylevel thresholding method.

11.3.1 Feature Thresholding

Consider an image that contains two types of regions, and the distinctness of the regions is reflected by the feature value at the pixels belonging to them. Suppose there exists a threshold t such that feature values of all pixels that actually belong to regions of first type are less than or equal to t and gray values of all pixels that actually belong to regions of the second type are greater than t. In this case the segmented image is obtained as

$$b(r, c) = \begin{cases} 1 & \text{if } p(r, c) \le t \\ 0 & \text{if } p(r, c) > t \end{cases} \tag{11.1}$$

where $p(r, c)$ is the feature value at pixel (r, c). If graylevel is the feature then $p(r, c) = g(r, c)$ for all (r, c). Note that, here 1 and 0 represent labels and not values. They can be replaced by any other symbols. However, assigning 0s and 1s to the pixels of segmented image helps in data storing and the subsequent processing. Hence, pixels are basically classified into one of the two different classes—first type regions and the second type regions. The threshold can be treated as the class boundary. The idea can be extended to multi-class problem and can be applied on the images that contain more than two types of regions. Evidently, the number of thresholds is equal to the number of classes minus one. Figure 11.2 shows some examples of graylevel thresholding.

It should be noted that though feature thresholding is the simplest method of image segmentation, usually it precedes the selection of appropriate feature to obtain a useful result. Secondly, the selection of threshold is also a non-trivial task. Any inappropriate threshold would incur significant and non-acceptable error of classification. Thus, the use of thresholding techniques for image segmentation needs to solve the following two problems:

1. Choice of features/properties to achieve desired segmentation

2. Selection of optimum threshold that would incur the least classification error.

The feature or property is usually computed over a small neighbourhood around the candidate pixel. As said earlier, the simplest feature may be graylevel. However, to get a useful result other features need to be computed from the pixel values as discussed with examples in the next section.

11.3.2 Choice of Feature

Let us consider some examples. Figure 11.3 shows three images where there is a disk at the centre against a uniform background. Suppose our objective is to segment the image into two distinct regions: The central disk and the background. Graylevel of the background in all the three images is 127. In Fig. 11.3(a), all the pixels of the central disk have graylevel 255. Hence, any threshold

---

[1]A detail description of classification methodologies is given in Chapter 15.

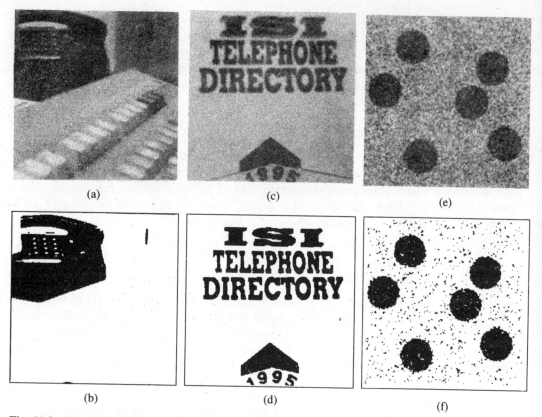

Fig. 11.2   Examples of different class of images and their segmentation by graylevel thresholding: The left column shows some graylevel images containing two types of regions, and the corresponding segmented images are shown in the right column.

between 128 and 254 inclusive can solve the purpose. However, the central disk of Fig. 11.3(b) contains 25% pixels with graylevel 127, 50% pixels with graylevel 191 and 25% pixels with graylevel 255, and these pixels are spatially uniformly distributed. Since both background and the disk contain pixels with graylevel 127, we cannot achieve the desired segmentation just by graylevel thresholding. However, applying a mean filter to the image shown in Fig. 11.3(b) we get an image where the pixels of the central disk have graylevels around 191 and that of background is still 127. Hence, an appropriate threshold between 128 and 190 can segment the image into desired regions. Finally, the central disk of Fig. 11.3(c) contains 25% pixels with graylevel 0, 50% pixels with graylevel 127 and 25% pixels with graylevel 254, and these pixels are spatially uniformly distributed. Here again both background and the disk contain pixels with graylevel 127, and moreover, simple mean filter would result in the graylevels of the pixels of central disk 127. Suppose, we apply a gradient operator (see Chapter 12 for detail) followed by a mean filter to the image shown in Fig. 11.3(c). In the resultant image, the pixels of the central disk have graylevels around 169 and that of the background is now 0. Hence, an appropriate threshold between 1 and 168 can segment the image into desired regions. In the first case graylevel is the feature, while in the second case average graylevel over a neighbourhood is the feature, and in the third case average gradient over a neighbourhood is the feature. Hence, we see from the above

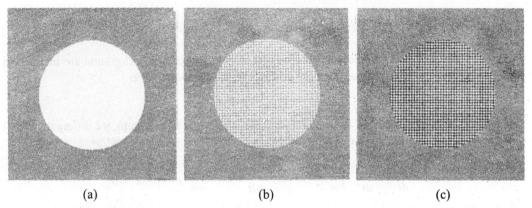

(a)   (b)   (c)

Fig. 11.3 Three examples of graylevel images, each of which contains a disk at the centre of a uniform background. All these images can be segmented using feature thresholding. However, the features are different in each case (see text).

examples that even for such simple images, features are different in each case. Thus, one can realize why no single algorithm can segment all kinds of images. In the next section, we show how one can determine the value of optimum threshold.

11.3.3 Optimum Threshold

Let us determine an optimum threshold for graylevel thresholding. Suppose an image contains two types of regions R_1 and R_2 with mean graylevels μ_1 and μ_2, respectively. Variation in graylevel is due to additive noise with zero mean and standard deviation σ. The a priori probability that a pixel of the image belongs to region R_1 is P_1 and that for region R_2 is P_2. Note that $P_1 + P_2 = 1$. Then the optimum threshold for image segmentation may be determined as follows.

Suppose graylevel in the image is denoted by z. The probability density function (p.d.f.) of graylevel in R_1 is

$$p_1(z) = \frac{1}{\sqrt{2\pi}\sigma} \exp\left[\frac{-(z - \mu_1)^2}{2\sigma^2}\right]$$

and that in R_2 is

$$p_2(z) = \frac{1}{\sqrt{2\pi}\sigma} \exp\left[\frac{-(z - \mu_2)^2}{2\sigma^2}\right]$$

Hence, p.d.f. of graylevel for the entire image, i.e. normalized graylevel histogram is $p(z) = P_1p_1(z) + P_2p_2(z)$. Without loosing generality, let us assume $\mu_1 < \mu_2$. Then the threshold t, that maps a pixel to R_1 (if $z \le t$) or to R_2 (if $z > t$), must satisfy $\mu_1 < t < \mu_2$. Now the probability of erroneously classifying a pixel (that actually belongs to R_2) to R_1 is

$$E_1(t) = \int_{-\infty}^{t} p_2(z)\, dz$$

Similarly, the probability of erroneously classifying a pixel (that actually belongs to R_1) to R_2 is

$$E_2(t) = \int_t^\infty p_1(z) \, dz = 1 - \int_{-\infty}^t p_1(z) \, dz$$

Figures 11.2(e) and 11.2(f) reveals such errors where some pixels of background are mapped to the class of disk and vice versa. Total error due to the said threshold is

$$E(t) = P_2 E_1(t) + P_1 E_2(t)$$

To find the optimum threshold, i.e. the threshold for which $E(t)$ is minimum, we differentiate $E(t)$ with respect to t and equate the result to zero, i.e.

$$\frac{dE}{dt} = \frac{d}{dt} P_2 \int_{-\infty}^t p_2(z) \, dz + \frac{d}{dt} P_1 [1 - \int_{-\infty}^t p_1(z) \, dz] = 0$$

or

$$P_2 p_2(t) - P_1 p_1(t) = 0$$

or

$$P_2 = \frac{1}{\sqrt{2\pi}\sigma} \exp\left[\frac{-(t - \mu_2)^2}{2\sigma^2}\right] = P_1 = \frac{1}{\sqrt{2\pi}\sigma} \exp\left[\frac{-(t - \mu_1)^2}{2\sigma^2}\right]$$

or

$$\frac{P_2}{P_1} \exp\left[\frac{-(t - \mu_2)^2}{2\sigma^2}\right] = \exp\left[\frac{-(t - \mu_1)^2}{2\sigma^2}\right]$$

Taking logarithm on both sides, we get

$$\ln \frac{P_2}{P_1} - \frac{(t - \mu_2)^2}{2\sigma^2} = -\frac{(t - \mu_1)^2}{2\sigma^2}$$

$$2\sigma^2 \ln \frac{P_2}{P_1} = (t - \mu_2)^2 - (t - \mu_1)^2$$

$$= -2t\mu_2 + \mu_2^2 + 2t\mu_1 - \mu_1^2$$

$$= 2t(\mu_1 - \mu_2) - (\mu_1 + \mu_2)(\mu_1 - \mu_2)$$

$$\frac{2\sigma^2}{\mu_1 - \mu_2} \ln \frac{P_2}{P_1} = 2t - (\mu_2 + \mu_1)$$

Hence, the optimum threshold is

$$t = \frac{\mu_1 + \mu_2}{2} + \frac{\sigma^2}{\mu_1 - \mu_2} \ln \frac{P_2}{P_1} \tag{11.2}$$

Assuming two different values of standard deviations of graylevels in R_1 and R_2 results in a more general expression for the optimum threshold. Suppose σ_1 and σ_2 are the standard deviations of graylevels associated with R_1 and R_2, respectively. Then

$$t = \frac{b \pm \sqrt{b^2 - 4ac}}{2a} \tag{11.3}$$

where

$$a = \sigma_1^2 - \sigma_2^2$$

$$b = 2(\mu_1\sigma_2^2 - \mu_2\sigma_1^2)$$

$$c = \sigma_1^2\mu_2^2 - \sigma_2^2\mu_1^2 + 2\sigma_1^2\sigma_2^2 \ln \frac{\sigma_1 P_2}{\sigma_2 P_1}$$

and plus or minus sign is selected with the view that t satisfies the constraint: $\mu_1 < t < \mu_2$. In practice, optimum threshold is seldom computed using Equations (11.2) and (11.3). This is because estimating the parameters P_1, P_2, μ_1, μ_2 and σ (or, σ_1 and σ_2) from a given graylevel histogram is a non-trivial task. Therefore, in almost all the cases, the threshold is determined heuristically. However, the selection of heuristic is implicitly guided by the above analysis. An example of such strategy is described in the next section.

11.3.4 Threshold Selection Methods

In general, the threshold can be chosen as the relation, $t = t(r, c, p(r, c))$, where $p(r, c)$ is the feature value at the pixel (r, c). In case of graylevel thresholding, $p(r, c) = g(r, c)$ for all (r, c) within the image domain. If t depends on the feature $p(r, c)$ only, it is called *local threshold*, if t depends on the pixel position (r, c) as well as on the feature $p(r, c)$ at that pixel, it is called *dynamic threshold*, otherwise it is *global* or *position-independent threshold*. Weszka (1978) presented a good survey on various threshold selection methods.

Using histogram

Our objective is to segment an image $g(r, c)$ of size $M \times N$ that contains, say, two types of regions R_1 and R_2 by graylevel thresholding. The methods may be generalized for the images containing more than two types of regions. Secondly, the method is also valid for features other than graylevel. Let us denote graylevel histogram of the image as n_i for $i = 0, 1, 2, ..., L - 1$. So that,

$$\sum_{i=0}^{L-1} n_i = MN$$

Threshold can be selected using the information contained by graylevel histogram of the image. Doyle (1962) suggested *p-tile* method. Suppose graylevel of pixels belonging to R_2-type regions are, in general, greater than that of R_1, and the number of pixels contained in R_2-type region is $p\%$ of total number of pixels present in the image. Therefore, threshold t should be such that

$$\sum_{i=t+1}^{L-1} n_i = \frac{pMN}{100} \tag{11.4}$$

The problem of this method is that it cannot be applied to unknown class of images, i.e. where p is not known a priori.

One of the most popular methods of threshold selection using information contained in histogram is the *mode method* [Prewitt and Mandelsohn (1966), Chanda (1988)]. This method selects the threshold corresponding to the bottom of valley between the two peaks of the histogram. This method needs the histogram to be bimodal. Since the image contains two distinct types of regions, R_1 and R_2, the graylevel (or feature) histogram n_i contains two distinct peaks or modes at $z = k$ and $z = l$ (say) corresponding to graylevels of pixels belonging to those regions. The graylevels between the regions R_1 and R_2 usually seldom occur in the image. Thus we expect a deep valley at, say, $z = m$ between the peaks giving the histogram a bimodal shape. Now the bimodality of the histogram may be measured as follows [Chanda (1988)]. Suppose s_1 and s_2 are magnitude of slopes of lines joining bottom of valley and each of the peaks, i.e.

$$s_1 = \left| \frac{n_k - n_m}{k - m} \right|$$

$$s_2 = \left| \frac{n_l - n_m}{l - m} \right|$$

Therefore, the histogram is said to

1. be bimodal if $s_1 > t_{sl}$ and $s_2 > t_{sl}$, or
2. have peak and shoulder if $s_1 > t_{sl}$ and $s_2 \leq t_{sl}$ or vice versa, or
3. be flat if $s_1 \leq t_{sl}$ and $s_2 \leq t_{sl}$.

where t_{sl} is a pre-defined threshold. It should be noted that the values of s_1 and s_2 depend on the number of pixels in the image. So, before computing them n_is may be normalized with respect to MN. Finally, the strength of the bimodality may be measured as

$$S_b = s_1 s_2 \tag{11.5}$$

If the histogram is strongly bimodal, graylevel corresponding to the bottom of this valley can be taken as a near optimum (see Section 11.3.3) threshold. However, in real images, because of noise and blurring variance of graylevels of pixels belonging to a region becomes large. As a result, graylevel distributions corresponding to different regions overlap and the histogram may not have the bimodal shape. Figure 11.4 shows some examples of a histogram. According to the measure defined above Figs. 11.4(a) and 11.4(d) are bimodal, while Fig. 11.4(b) have peak and shoulder form and Fig. 11.4(c) is flat. Secondly, the strength of bimodality of the histogram shown in Fig. 11.4(a) is more than that of Fig. 11.4(d). It should be noted that the intermediate graylevels occur more frequently in the vicinity of the border between two regions than in the interior of the regions. Finally, due to discreteness of graylevels envelope of the histogram, unlike those shown in Fig. 11.4, are jagged. This makes locating peaks and valley a non-trivial task. The problem may be surmounted by taking local average of frequencies in the histogram. The following example gives an idea how peaks and valley in a histogram are located.

Example Our objective is to detect two peaks and a bottom of valley in the graylevel histogram of an image. Suppose n_i for $i = 0, 1, 2, \ldots, 255$ denotes the frequency of occurrence of pixels with graylevel i. To avoid the problem caused due to jaggedness in the histogram let us compute local average of bar-heights as

$$\bar{n}_i = \frac{1}{2q + 1} \sum_{k=-q}^{q} n_{i+k}$$

for $i = q, q + 1, \ldots, 255 - q$. Boundary values of the smooth histogram will be computed in appropriate way. Value of q usually is a small integer. Now select local maxima at $z_1, z_2, \ldots, z_K$ such that n_{zl} is the greatest over a neighbourhood of size, say, $2s + 1$, i.e.

$$n_{zl} \geq n_{zl+k} \quad \text{for} \quad -s \leq k \leq s$$

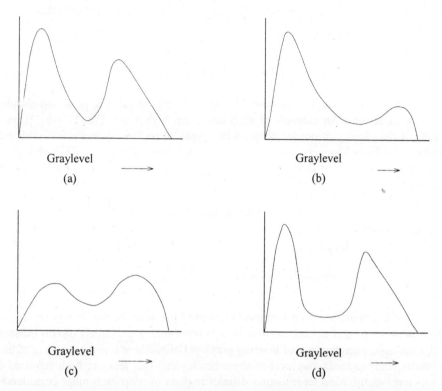

Fig. 11.4 Examples of histogram: (a) strongly bimodal, (b) peak and shoulder, (c) flat and (d) weakly bimodal. Envelope of bar-heights are drawn for simplicity in representation.

Then select bottom of valley at v such that n_v as minimum between two extreme local maxima, i.e.

$$n_v < n_i \quad \text{for} \quad z_1 \le i \le z_K$$

Finally, two distinct peaks (or modes) $n_{z'}$ and $n_{z''}$, say, are detected as

$$n_{z'} \ge n_i \quad \text{for} \quad z_1 \le i < v$$

$$n_{z''} \ge n_i \quad \text{for} \quad v > i \ge z_K$$

This procedure may be followed by computing slopes and strength of bimodality.   ■

Detecting graylevel threshold using histogram, the histogram be, at least, fairly bimodal. This is necessary to detect the peaks and the bottom valley in the histogram reliably. Unfortunately, as stated earlier, in many cases histograms do not take bimodal form though there exist two distinctly different types of regions in the image. To bring out those hidden peaks, histogram may be computed in a different fashion. Many algorithms for the said job is reported. We describe below just two of them. To realize the difference we first present a procedure to compute a graylevel histogram in traditional way.

Algorithm 11.1

```
for all i set n_i = 0
for all (r, c) begin
   i = g(r, c)
   n_i = n_i + 1
end
```

If $P_1 \ll P_2$ or vice versa (see Section 11.3.3) the histogram takes a 'peak-and-shoulder' form rather than bimodal one. An example of such histogram is shown in Fig. 11.4(b). If we consider pixels only at the vicinity of border between two types of regions, then a priori probabilities are comparable. This leads histogram to take fairly bimodal shape. The pixels at the vicinity of border usually have high *gradient*[2] values. Let us denote gradient at the pixel (r, c) by $g'(r, c)$. Hence we have Algorithm 11.2.

Algorithm 11.2

```
for all i set n_i = 0
for all (r, c) begin
   i = g(r, c)
   if g'(r, c) > threshold then n_i = n_i + 1
end
```

Here threshold is a predefined constant used to identify pixels in the border regions. Now suppose difference between μ_1 and μ_2 (see Section 11.3.3) representing graylevels of two distinct regions is not high enough. Then because of blurring graylevel of pixels of one region lying in the vicinity of the border tends towards graylevel of the other region. This leads to high standard deviation σ and graylevel distribution representing distinct regions overlap each other considerably. Thus intermediate graylevels have significant frequency of occurrences. As a result, we get a histogram whose strength of bimodality is low. An example of such histogram is shown in Fig. 11.4(c). In such cases, we may adopt a method, in principle, complimentary to Algorithm 11.2. Here we consider a window W around each pixel. Rather than incrementing the frequency count of graylevel of the candidate pixel by one, we increment the count by number of pixels having the same graylevel as the candidate pixel within the window [Chanda (1988)]. As a result, graylevels of the pixels interior to regions are counted heavily compared to those lying in the vicinity of the border. The method is described in Algorithm 11.3.

Algorithm 11.3

```
for all i set n_i = 0
for all (r, c) begin
   i = g(r, c)
   count = 0
   for all (j, k) ∈ W begin
      if i = g(r + j, c + k) then count = count + 1
   end
   n_i = n_i + count
end
```

---

[2]The detail treatment of gradient is presented in Chapter 12.

Example histograms computed using Algorithms 11.1 and 11.3 are shown in Fig. 11.5.

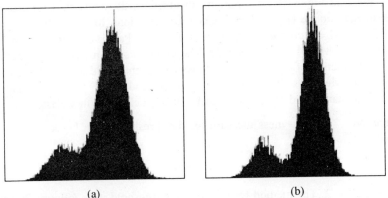

(a)   (b)

Fig. 11.5   Graylevel of histogram of Fig. 11.2(c) computed by two different methods: (a) due to Algorithm 11.1, (b) due to Algorithm 11.3.

Using graylevel co-occurrence matrix

Let the discrete variables m_1 and m_2 represent the graylevel of pixels (r, c) and $(r + d \cos \theta, c - d \sin \theta)$ respectively of a L-level gray-tone image $g(r, c)$ of size $M \times N$. So $m_1, m_2 \in \{0, 1, 2, ..., L - 1\}$. We are interested in considering the co-occurrence of graylevels in pairs of pixels where one is lying at a distance of d in the direction θ with respect to the other [Haralick (1973)]. Let us take the value of d equal to 1 and θ as an integer multiple of $\frac{1}{2}\pi$. So we have the graylevel co-occurrence matrix $\mathbf{C}$ as defined in Section 6.2.5, where $\mathbf{C} = \{c_{m_1,m_2}\}$.

Let t be the graylevel threshold that maps the original image into two distinct types of regions R_1 and R_2. This mapping consequently divides the graylevel co-occurrence matrix into four non-overlapping blocks as shown in Fig 11.6. The respective blocks of $[C]$ represent:

1. the co-occurrence of graylevels in region R_1, i.e. those c_{m_1, m_2} for which $m_1 \le t$ and $m_2 \le t$ (shaded area W),

2. the co-occurrence of graylevels in region R_2, i.e. those c_{m_1, m_2} for which $m_1 > t$ and $m_2 > t$ (shaded area Z) and

3. the co-occurrence of graylevel in the border region of R_1 and R_2, i.e. those c_{m_1, m_2} for which either $m_1 \le t$ and $m_2 > t$ (shaded area X) or $m_1 > t$ and $m_2 \le t$ (shaded area Y).

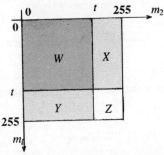

Fig. 11.6   Partition of a graylevel co-occurrence matrix with respect to a threshold t.

The methods of threshold selection using the co-occurrence matrix can be divided into two classes. One, the threshold for which the number of pairs of border pixels, i.e. sum of c_{m_1, m_2} over the blocks X and Y in Fig. 11.6, is minimum. In other words, it searches for a threshold which segments the image into the largest possible connected regions. Measures like *Busyness* [Weszka and Rosenfeld (1978)], *conditional probability* [Deravi and Pal (1983)] and *entropy* [Chanda and Dutta Majumder (1988)] belong to this class. The other class of methods for threshold selection defines a suitable function of c_{m_1, m_2} and then looks for the threshold for which the function attains an optimum value. Measures like *average contrast* [Chanda et al. (1985)], *Weber contrast* and *average entropy* [Chanda and Dutta Majumder (1988)] belong to this class.

Busyness measure.   The Busyness measure for the threshold t can be defined as

$$\text{Busy}(t) = \sum_{m_1=0}^{t} \sum_{m_2=t+1}^{L-1} c_{m_1, m_2} + \sum_{m_1=t+1}^{L-1} \sum_{m_2=0}^{t} c_{m_1, m_2} \tag{11.6}$$

for $t = 0, 1, 2, ..., L-2$. The method for selecting the threshold is as follows: Search for minima in Busy(t) and then select the value of t as the threshold which corresponds to a minimum among these minima.

Conditional probability measure.   Deravi and Pal (1983) measured the probability of pixel $(r + \cos\theta, c - \sin\theta)$ lying in R_2 when (r, c) is known to lie in R_1 and that of pixel $(r + \cos\theta, c - \sin\theta)$ lying in R_1 when (r, c) is known to lie in R_2. So this conditional probability for a threshold t may be expressed as

$$\text{Conditional probability}(t) = P\{g(r + \cos\theta, c - \sin\theta) > t \mid g(r, c) \le t\}$$

$$+ P\{g(r + \cos\theta, c - \sin\theta) \le t \mid g(r, c) > t\}$$

$$= \frac{P\{g(r + \cos\theta, c - \sin\theta) > t, g(r, c) \le t\}}{P\{g(r, c) \le t\}}$$

$$+ \frac{P\{g(r + \cos\theta, c - \sin\theta) \le t, g(r, c) > t\}}{P\{g(r, c) > t\}}$$

Hence, from the co-occurrence matrix we can write

$$\text{Conditional probability}(t) = \frac{\sum_{m_1=0}^{t}\sum_{m_2=t+1}^{L-1} P_{m_1, m_2}}{\sum_{m_1=0}^{t}\sum_{m_2=0}^{L-1} P_{m_1, m_2}} + \frac{\sum_{m_1=t+1}^{L-1}\sum_{m_2=0}^{t} P_{m_1, m_2}}{\sum_{m_1=t+1}^{L-1}\sum_{m_2=0}^{L-1} P_{m_1, m_2}} \tag{11.7}$$

for $t = 0, 1, 2, ..., L-2$, where $p_{m_1, m_2} = \dfrac{c_{m_1, m_2}}{MN}$. The method for selecting the threshold is similar to that using the Busyness measure.

Entropy measure.   Here we measure the entropy or information content of border pixels as

$$\text{Entropy}(t) = -\sum_{m_1=0}^{t} \sum_{m_2=t+1}^{L-1} P_{m_1, m_2} \log(P_{m_1, m_2}) - \sum_{m_1=t+1}^{L-1} \sum_{m_2=0}^{t} P_{m_1, m_2} \log(P_{m_1, m_2}) \tag{11.8}$$

for $t = 0, 1, 2, ..., L - 2$. Since $\log (p_{m_1,m_2})$ is a monotonic increasing function of p_{m_1,m_2}, the method for selecting the threshold is similar to that using the Busyness measure.

Average contrast measure.   It is known that, in an image, contrast is the maximum at the regions where different types of regions meet. So those c_{m_1,m_2}, where pixel having graylevel m_1 and pixel having graylevel m_2 lie in different regions, are responsible for the maximum contrast and the magnitude of contrast is an even function of difference in graylevels, i.e. $(m_1 - m_2)$. Average contrast per pixel in the border region for the threshold t can be defined as:

$$\text{Average contrast } (t) = \frac{\sum_{m_1=0}^{t} \sum_{m_2=t+1}^{L-1} (m_1 - m_2)^2 c_{m_1,m_2}}{\sum_{m_1=0}^{t} \sum_{m_2=t+1}^{L-1} c_{m_1,m_2}}$$

$$+ \frac{\sum_{m_1=t+1}^{L-1} \sum_{m_2=0}^{t} (m_1 - m_2)^2 c_{m_1,m_2}}{\sum_{m_1=t+1}^{L-1} \sum_{m_2=0}^{t} c_{m_1,m_2}} \tag{11.9}$$

for $t = 0, 1, 2, ..., L - 2$. The method for selecting the threshold based on this measure is as follows: Search for maxima in Av. cont.(t) and then select the value of t as threshold which corresponds to the maximum among these maxima.

Weber contrast measure.   Average contrast of an image can also be defined incorporating human visual response, specifically logarithmic response to brightness (Weber's law). Here, instead of squared difference of graylevels, the contrast is defined as the ratio of the difference of graylevels of neighbouring pixels to the minimum of them. Then the average contrast, we call it here Weber contrast, is given as

$$\text{Weber contrast } (t) = \frac{\sum_{m_1=0}^{t} \sum_{m_2=t+1}^{L-1} \frac{|m_1 - m_2|}{\min\{m_1,m_2\}} c_{m_1,m_2}}{\sum_{m_1=0}^{t} \sum_{m_2=t+1}^{L-1} c_{m_1,m_2}}$$

$$+ \frac{\sum_{m_1=t+1}^{L-1} \sum_{m_2=0}^{t} \frac{|m_1 - m_2|}{\min\{m_1,m_2\}} c_{m_1,m_2}}{\sum_{m_1=t+1}^{L-1} \sum_{m_2=0}^{t} c_{m_1,m_2}} \tag{11.10}$$

for $t = 0, 1, 2, ..., L - 2$. The method for selecting the threshold based on this measure is the same as that in the average contrast measure.

Average entropy measure.   It is observed that boundary pixels play the most important role in detecting and interpreting an object in an image by a human observer. So one may argue that average entropy per pixel in the border region should be maximum. Average entropy per pixel for a threshold t may be defined as

$$\text{Average entropy } (t) = - \frac{\sum_{m_1=0}^{t} \sum_{m_2=t+1}^{L-1} p_{m_1,m_2} \log (p_{m_1,m_2})}{\sum_{m_1=0}^{t} \sum_{m_2=t+1}^{L-1} c_{m_1,m_2}}$$

$$- \frac{\sum_{m_1=t+1}^{L-1} \sum_{m_2=0}^{t} p_{m_1,m_2} \log (p_{m_1,m_2})}{\sum_{m_1=t+1}^{L-1} \sum_{m_2=0}^{t} c_{m_1,m_2}} \tag{11.11}$$

for $t = 0, 1, 2, ..., L - 2$. The approach to select the graylevel threshold is similar to that using average contrast.

Example Consider a graylevel image of size 16×16 as shown in Fig. 11.7(a). The number of graylevels present in the image is 8. Figure 11.7(b) shows its graylevel co-occurrence matrix $\{c_{m_1,m_2}\}$. We compute busyness measure for a threshold 3 as follows:

$$\text{Busy}(3) = \sum_{m_1=0}^{3} \sum_{m_2=4}^{7} c_{m_1,m_2} + \sum_{m_1=4}^{7} \sum_{m_2=0}^{3} c_{m_1,m_2}$$

$$= c(0, 4) + c(0, 5) + c(0, 6) + c(0, 7) + c(1, 4) + c(1, 5) + c(1, 6) + c(1, 7)$$

$$+ c(2, 4) + c(2, 5) + c(2, 6) + c(2, 7) + c(3, 4) + c(3, 5) + c(3, 6) + c(3, 7)$$

$$+ c(4, 0) + c(4, 1) + c(4, 2) + c(4, 3) + c(5, 0) + c(5, 1) + c(5, 2) + c(5, 3)$$

$$+ c(6, 0) + c(6, 1) + c(6, 2) + c(6, 3) + c(7, 0) + c(7, 1) + c(7, 2).+ c(7, 3)$$

$$= 0 + 0 + 0 + 0 + 0 + 0.5 + 0 + 0 + 1.25 + 2.5 + 0 + 0 + 3.5 + 0.25 + 0 + 0$$

$$+ 0 + 0 + 0.25 + 3.5 + 0 + 0 + 2.5 + 1.25 + 0 + 0 + 0.5 + 0 + 0 + 0 + 0 + 0$$

$$= 16$$

Busyness measures for other values of threshold can be computed in a similar way. Finally, other measures can similarly be computed. Figure 11.7(c) presents values of aforementioned measures for $t = 0, 1, 2, ..., 6$.

■

```
2  2  2  2  2  1  2  2  4  4  5  5  5  5  5  5
2  2  2  2  1  1  2  2  4  4  5  5  5  5  5  5
2  2  2  2  2  1  2  2  4  4  5  5  5  5  5  5
2  2  2  2  2  1  2  2  4  4  4  5  5  5  5  5
2  2  2  2  2  2  2  3  4  5  5  5  5  5  5  5
2  2  2  2  2  2  2  3  4  4  4  4  5  5  5  5
1  1  2  2  2  2  3  3  4  5  5  5  5  5  5  5
1  2  2  2  2  2  3  3  4  4  4  4  5  5  5  5
2  2  2  2  2  2  3  3  4  4  4  4  5  5  5  5
2  2  2  2  2  2  3  3  4  4  4  4  5  5  5  5
2  2  2  2  2  2  2  3  4  4  5  5  5  5  5  5
2  2  2  2  2  2  2  3  4  4  5  5  5  5  5  5
3  3  2  2  2  2  2  3  4  5  5  5  5  5  5  5
3  3  2  2  2  2  2  3  4  5  5  5  5  5  5  4
3  3  2  2  2  2  2  3  4  5  5  5  5  4  5  4
2  3  2  2  2  2  3  3  4  5  5  5  5  4  4  4
```

(a)

Fig. 11.7 (Contd.)

t	0	1	2	3	4	5	6	7
0	0.00	0.00	0.00	0.00	0.00	0.00	0.00	0.00
1	0.00	3.00	4.50	0.00	0.00	0.50	0.00	0.00
2	0.00	4.50	81.00	6.75	1.25	2.50	0.00	0.00
3	0.00	0.00	6.75	13.50	3.50	0.25	0.00	0.00
4	0.00	0.00	1.25	3.50	25.50	10.75	0.00	0.00
5	0.00	0.50	2.50	0.25	10.75	73.00	0.00	0.00
6	0.00	0.00	0.00	0.00	0.00	0.00	0.00	0.00
7	0.00	0.00	0.00	0.00	0.00	0.00	0.00	0.00

(b)

t	Busy (t)	Conditional probability (t)	Entropy (t)	Average entropy (t)	Average contrast (t)	Weber contrast (t)
0	0.00	0.00	0.00	0.00	0.00	0.00
1	10.00	0.65	0.24	0.02	1.25	0.65
2	22.00	0.18	0.85	0.04	1.92	0.85
3	16.00	0.13	0.69	0.04	2.50	1.00
4	28.00	0.24	0.76	0.03	1.51	0.74
5	0.00	0.00	0.00	0.00	0.00	0.00
6	0.00	0.00	0.00	0.00	0.00	0.00

(c)

Fig. 11.7 (a) An 8-level image of size 16×16, (b) its graylevel co-occurrence matrix, (c) various measures for threshold t, where $0 \leq t < 7$.

11.4 Multi-level Thresholding

In fact, all the thresholding methods described so far can be extended to multi-level thresholding. Suppose an image contains n (where $n > 2$) types of regions. The feature (e.g. graylevel) histogram of the image is expected to contain n number of peaks (or modes) each of which corresponds to distinct type of regions. Thus we have $(n - 1)$ valleys in the histogram and select graylevels corresponding to the bottom of these valleys as threshold for image segmentation (Figure 11.8).

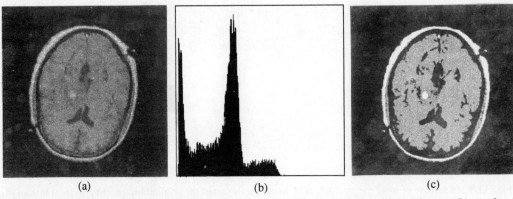

(a) (b) (c)

Fig. 11.8 Examples of image segmentation by multi-level thresholding: (a) original image, (b) graylevel histogram, and (c) segmented image.

shows an example of image segmentation by multilevel thresholding. Instead of histogram we may use other measures, like Busyness or average contrast, and follow the similar procedure.

11.5 Local Thresholding

Consider Fig. 11.9(a), where due to variation in illumination overall brightness of the image varies widely from one corner to the other. However, the object, which is a 'key' being seen at the centre

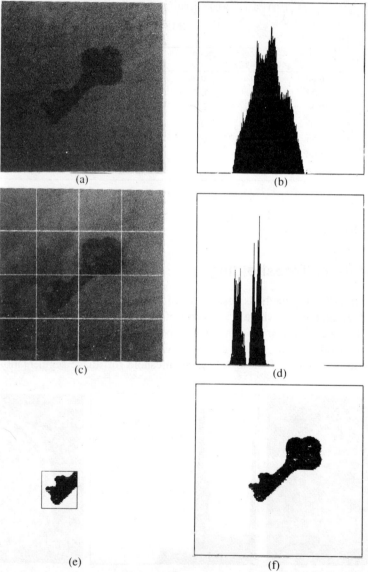

(a)

(b)

(c)

(d)

(e)

(f)

Fig. 11.9 Example of image segmentation by local thresholding: (a) original image, (b) graylevel histogram, (c) subdivisions of the original image, (d) histogram of sub-image located at the 2nd row and the 2nd column, (e) segmented image of the said subdivision and (f) segmented original image.

of the image, maintains a good local contrast against the background. In this case, the graylevel distributions for the object as well as for the background overlap each other significantly. Hence no single graylevel threshold can segment the image properly. This problem may be surmounted by dividing the whole image into smaller ones so that the variation in illumination over each of these sub-images is negligible. Finally, each sub-image is segmented independently, and the segmented sub-images are put together in appropriate order to get segmented version of the original image. Figure 11.9(c) is divided into 16 images (where 4 divisions in the horizontal direction and 4 divisions along the vertical) and is segmented by the said method.

11.6 Region-based Approach

Image segmentation algorithms described so far are parallel in nature, i.e. every pixel is treated independently. In other words, all the pixels can be processed simultaneously and the result at any pixel position does not depend on the results at other positions. Moreover, the decision that a pixel belongs to some region, once taken, is final and is not updated. In this section, we describe some algorithms that are sequential and/or iterative in nature.

11.6.1 Region Growing

Let us pick up an arbitrary pixel (r, c) from the domain of the image to be segmented. This pixel is called *seed pixel* and this pixel belongs to some other region. Now examine the nearest neighbours (4- or 8-neighbours depending on the connectivity assumed) of (r, c) one by one, and a neighbouring pixel is accepted to belong to the same region as (r, c) if they together satisfy the homogeneity property of a region. Once a new pixel is accepted as a member of the current region the nearest neighbours of this new pixel are examined. This process goes on recursively until no more pixel is accepted. All the pixels of the current region are marked with a unique label. Then another seed pixel is picked up and the same procedure is repeated. We go on labelling the regions until every pixel is assigned to some region or the other.

Main problems of this approach in addition to large execution time are (i) the selection of the property to be satisfied and (ii) the selection of seed points. Suppose the smooth regions in an image corresponds to the planer surfaces of the scene or objects. Accordingly, one may assume that the variance in graylevel of pixels within a region should be small [Pavlidis (1982)]. This leads to a property, or more specifically *homogeneity* property, to be satisfied by the graylevels of pixels lying within a region. Let us denote this property by Prop (R), where

$$\text{Prop } (R): \frac{1}{\text{Card}(R)} \sum_{(r,c) \in R} \{g(r,c) - \bar{g}\}^2 \leq th \qquad (11.12)$$

where Card (R) is the number of pixels in the region R and $\bar{g}$ is the mean graylevel of pixels lying in that region, i.e.

$$\bar{g} = \frac{1}{\text{Card}(R)} \sum_{(r,c) \in R} g(r, c)$$

and *th* is a predefined threshold. If *th* be very small, many tiny regions would come up. On the other hand, if *th* is large many regions would merge to a single region. Another problem of this measure of homogeneity is as the region grows, i.e. more and more pixels are included in the region the pixels having graylevels with higher variations are accepted because of averaging [see Equation (11.12)]. To avoid this problem, we take the 'homogeneity' property for a small range of graylevels of pixels lying in a region and define the property as

$$\text{Prop } (R): \max_{(r,c)\in R} \{g(r,c)\} - \min_{(r,c)\in R} \{g(r,c)\} \le th \tag{11.13}$$

The problem of seed point selection may be explained with the help of the following example:

Example   Consider an 8×8 image as shown in Fig. 11.10(a). Graylevels in the image are ranging from 0 to 7. Suppose we like to segment the image using region growing technique. Property to be satisfied by each region is given by Equation (11.13) where $th = 3$. Result is shown in Fig. 11.10(b). The pixels encircled served as the seed points. One could start from either of them and would arrive at the same result. Problem that arises due to selection of seed points is illustrated in Fig. 11.10(c). Here we have started with the seed points that are shown encircled. Clearly the image is segmented into three distinct regions. Thus the result is completely different from that shown in Fig. 11.10(b). ∎

5	6	6	6	7	7	6	6
6	7	6	7	5	5	4	7
6	6	4	4	3	2	5	6
5	4	5	4	2	3	4	6
1	3	2	3	3	2	4	7
0	0	1	0	2	2	5	6
1	1	0	1	0	3	4	4
1	0	1	0	2	3	5	6

(a)   (b)   (c)

Fig. 11.10 Example of pixel based region growing technique: (a) original image, (b) and (c) segmented images. Seed points are encircled in respective images.

Assigning one pixel at a time as a member of the current region is the simplest approach to region growing. This is one of the slowest methods as well. A better approach is to consider a small region at a time instead of single pixel. Depending on the property to be satisfied this region-based approach is more robust to noise than the pixel-based approach. Such techniques may again be grouped as *region splitting* and *region merging* [Pavlidis (1977)].

11.6.2 Region Splitting

Suppose we try to satisfy the homogeneity property over a rectangular region. If the graylevels (or, in general, the features measured) present in the region do not satisfy the property, we divide the region into four equal quadrants. If the property is satisfied, we leave the region as it is. This is done recursively until all the regions satisfy the property. In terms of graph theory let us call a region a *node*. Then a node is split into four *children* if the node does not satisfy the given property; otherwise the node is left unaffected. The former node is called a *parent node* and the latter a *leaf node*. This method is applicable to images whose number of rows and number of columns are some integer power of 2. We start the method taking the whole image. That means the image is taken as the *root node* and a *quad tree* is formed where each leaf node represents a rectangular homogeneous region.

Example Consider an 8 × 8 image as shown in Fig. 11.11(a). Graylevels in the image are ranging from 0 to 7. The image is same as that shown in Fig. 11.10(a). Property to be satisfied by each region is given by Equation (11.13) where *th* = 3. Results of region splitting are shown in Figs. 11.11(b) and 11.11(c) in two steps. ∎

Fig. 11.11 Example of region splitting technique: (a) original image, (b) image after the first step of splitting, and (c) image after the second step of splitting.

11.6.3 Region Merging

This method is exactly opposite to the region splitting method. In fact, we may call the region splitting method a *top-down* method, while the present one is a *bottom-up* method. Like region splitting, this method also is applicable to images whose number of rows and number of columns are some integer power of 2. Here, we start from the pixel level and consider each of them a homogeneous region. At any level of merging we check if four adjacent homogeneous regions arranged in a 2 × 2 fashion together satisfies the homogeneity property. If yes, we merge those regions to a single homogeneous region; otherwise the regions are left as they are. Hence, in terms of graph theory, child nodes are removed if the parent node satisfies the homogeneity property; otherwise child nodes are declared as leaf node. We repeat this operation recursively until there are no more regions that can be merged. As before, a quad tree is formed with the image as the root node and each leaf node represents a rectangular homogeneous region.

Example Consider an 8 × 8 image as shown in Fig. 11.12(a). Graylevels in the image are ranging from 0 to 7. The image is same as that shown in Fig. 11.10(a). Property to be satisfied by each region is given by Equation (11.13) where *th* = 3. Results of region merging are shown in Figs. 11.12(b) and 11.12(c) in two steps. ∎

Fig. 11.12 Example of region merging technique: (a) original image, (b) image after first step of merging, and (c) image after second step of merging.

11.6.4 Split and Merge

It is stated above that the split technique starts with the whole image as one region and splits a region into four sub-regions until the sub-regions satisfy the predefined homogeneity property. On the other hand, merge technique starts by taking each pixel a region and merge small regions into a larger region if the latter satisfies the predefined homogeneity property. So it is clear that if most of the homogeneous regions are small, then split technique is inferior to merge technique in terms of time requirement. Reverse is true if most of the regions are large. Hence, if no a priori knowledge is available about the size of the regions a hybrid of above two approaches are employed. The method is known as *split-and-merge* technique [Pavlidis (1977)].

Split-and-merge technique starts somewhere at the middle level. Suppose we start with rectangular regions of size $m \times m$ pixels. To each region homogeneity property is tested. If the test fails, the region is split into four quadrants each of size $\frac{m}{2} \times \frac{m}{2}$, and this process is carried on recursively. If the region satisfies the homogeneity property then the merging process is followed to form a region of size $(2m) \times (2m)$. Finally, the method terminates with homogeneous regions as before. Exact implementation of the method and its time complexity depends on the data structure used.

Region formation

As discussed in the preceding section, split or merge, or split-and-merge technique results in non-overlapping rectangular homogeneous regions that satisfy conditions 1, 2 and 3 of the definition of segmentation (see Section 11.2). Figure 11.11(c) or 11.12(c) shows such homogeneous regions. To satisfy the fourth condition, i.e. no two adjacent regions can have similar attributes or features based on which segmentation is performed, some extra processing is needed. In other words, if the predicate is satisfied over the union of adjacent regions then adjacent regions are grouped and labelled as a single region by some post-processing. Let us describe this post-processing method based on a data structure of special type called *region adjacency graph* (RAG) [Pavlidis (1977)]. Suppose each rectangular region resulted in by the above methods is represented by a node of a graph. If two regions share a common border, they are said to be *adjacent* and corresponding nodes in the graph are connected by an edge. The graph constructed this way is called a RAG. Figure 11.13(a) shows regions of an image and Fig. 11.13(b) represents corresponding RAG. Now the homogeneity property is tested over every pair of regions whose corresponding nodes in the RAG is directly connected by edge. If the test fails, edge between corresponding nodes is removed.

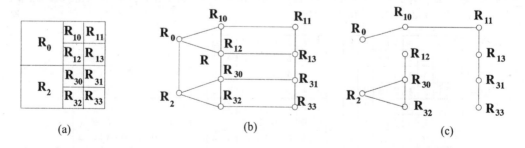

(a)   (b)   (c)

Fig. 11.13 Illustrates region adjacency graph (RAG): (a) rectangular regions of an image as in Fig. 11.11(c), (b) RAG representing regions of (a), (c) sub-graphs representing maximal homogeneous regions of Fig. 11.11(c).

As a result, a set of disconnected graphs are formed. Each of these sub-graphs represents a maximal region that is homogeneous. Thus condition 4 is satisfied. Figure 11.13(c) shows sub-graphs corresponding to maximal homogeneous regions of Fig. 11.11(c) or Fig. 11.12(c). The problem of this approach is that resultant sub-graphs depend on the order in which node pairs are examined for homogeneity. RAG may also be used to merge small regions to adjacent large regions obtained from other segmentation techniques.

Summary

Image segmentation is an essential step in almost all image analysis systems. These techniques partition image domain into meaningful regions. The partitioning is exhaustive as well as non-overlapping. The image domain is partitioned into regions either by extracting whole regions (called region extraction) or by identifying the contours separating the regions (called edge detection). In this chapter, image segmentation techniques based on region extraction are discussed. Both parallel and sequential methods are presented. The basic idea is to classify each pixel to one region or another based on the feature values at that pixel as well as at its neighbour. Edge detection techniques are presented in the next chapter.

Problems

1. Define image segmentation. In terms of this definition, state the property satisfied by the pixels in each region obtained by graylevel thresholding technique. Elaborate the terms 'global', 'local' and 'dynamic' threshold.

2. Suppose an image contains two types of regions, R_1 and R_2. The a priori probability that a pixel belongs to R_1 is P_1 and to R_2 is P_2. Probability density functions of intensity in R_1 and R_2 are Gaussian with mean μ_1 and μ_2 and standard deviations σ_1^2 and σ_2^2, respectively. Determine the optimum threshold for image segmentation by the graylevel thresholding technique.

3. Consider similar situation as described in Problem 2 except that standard deviation $\sigma_1^2 = \sigma_2^2 = \sigma^2$. Determine the optimum threshold for image segmentation by the graylevel thresholding technique.

4. Suppose an image contains two types of regions, R_1 and R_2. The a priori probability that a pixel belongs to R_1 is 0.4 and to R_2 is 0.6. Probability density functions of intensity in R_1 and R_2 are denoted by $p_1(z)$ and $p_2(z)$, respectively, where

$$p_1(z) = 0.2 - 0.04 \, |\, 5 - z\,| \qquad \text{for } 0 \le z \le 10$$

$$p_2(z) = 0.2 - 0.04 \, |\, 10 - z\,| \qquad \text{for } 5 \le z \le 15$$

Determine the optimum threshold for image segmentation by the graylevel thresholding technique.

5. Extend the idea of busyness measure to optimum select thresholds, say t_1 and t_2, when three types of regions are present in the image.

6. Describe the region growing technique for image segmentation and mention the problems associated with it.

7. Explain, why Property (R): $\text{variance}_{(r,c) \in R}\{g(r, c)\} \leq th$ cannot be a good property for image segmentation using region-growing or splitting or merging technique.

8. Describe, how an image is segmented using the split-and-merge technique in association with the region adjacency graph.

Bibliography

Chanda, B., 'On preprocessing techniques for image analysis', PhD thesis, University of Calcutta, 1988.

Chanda, B., Chaudhuri, B.B. and Dutta Majumder, D., 'On image enhancement and threshold selection using graylevel co-occurrence matrix', *Pattern Recognition Letters*, **3**:243–251, 1985.

Chanda, B. and Dutta Majumder, D., 'A note on use of graylevel cooccurrence matrix in threshold selection', *Signal Processing*, **15**:149–167, 1988.

Deravi, F. and Pal, S.K., 'Graylevel thresholding using second-order statistics', *Pattern Recognition Letters*, **1**:417–422, 1983.

Doyle, W., 'Operations useful for similarity invariant pattern recognition', *J. Association of Computing Machine*, **9**:259–267, 1962.

Fu, K.S. and Mui, J.K., 'A survey on image segmentation' *Pattern Recognition*, **13**:3–16, 1981.

Haralick, R.M., 'Textural features for image classification', *IEEE Trans. on System, Man, and Cybern.*, SMC-**3**:610–621, 1973.

Pal, N.R. and Pal, S.K., 'A review on image segmentation', *Pattern Recognition*, **26**:1277–1294, 1993.

Pavlidis, T., *Structural Pattern Recognition*, Springer-Verlag, New York, 1977.

Pavlidis, T., *Algorithms for Graphics and Image Processing*, Computer Science Press, Rockville, Maryland, 1982.

Prewitt, J.M.S. and Mandelsohn, M.L., 'The analysis of cell images', *Trans. of N.Y. Academy of Science*, **128**:1035–1053, 1966.

Weszka, J.S., 'A survey of threshold selection techniques', *Computer Graphics and Image Processing*, **7**:259–265, 1978.

Weszka, J.S. and Rosenfeld, A., 'Threshold evaluation technique', *IEEE Trans. on System, Man, and Cybern.*, SMC-**8**:622–629, 1978.

Chapter 12

Edge and Line Detection

12.1 Introduction

Contours of images of objects or, in other words, *edges* in the paradigm of image processing and computer vision, provide valuable information towards human image understanding. Probably the most important image processing step in human picture recognition system consists of edge-detection process. Naturally, edge-detection has become a serious challenge to the image processing scientists, and since the last two decades, in particular, numerous publications have been detailing methodologies for edge detection.

How do edges come in an image? Probably, the answer to this question provides the early important clue for locating edges in an image. The variations of image features, usually brightness, give rise to edges. More objectively, the edges are the representations of the discontinuities of image intensity function. There could be various reasons, such as lighting conditions, object(s) geometry, type of material, surface texture, etc., as well as their mutual interactions, for the discontinuities. Therefore, *edge-detection* algorithm is essentially a process of detection of these discontinuities in an image as mentioned in Section 11.1.

Since the abrupt change in brightness level indicates edge, its detection in binary or segmented image (i.e. the result of the methods described in Chapter 11) is quite straightforward.[1] However, the process of edge localization is quite complex in the case of graylevel or intensity level images. The transition in intensity in gray-scale image is relatively smooth in nature rather than abrupt as in the case of segmented or binary images. The nature of intensity variation points to the application of derivative operators for detecting edges. Application of derivative operators on intensity image produces another image, usually called *gradient image* as it reveals the rate of intensity variation. This image is made to undergo thresholding and/or edge linking in order to yield contours. Thus, the image is decomposed into various regions resulting in another kind of segmentation.

12.2 Edge Detection

In a grayscale image, the *edge* is a local feature that, within a neighbourhood, separates two regions in each of which the graylevel is more or less uniform with different values on the two sides of the edge. So, an ideal edge has a step like cross-section as shown in Fig. 12.1(a). Figure 12.1(b) exemplifies the cross-section of a more realistic edge which has a shape of ramp function corrupted with noise. The process of edge detection are broadly classified into two categories:

---

[1]Such edges are called *border* or *boundary*. Detail treatment is given in Chapter 11.

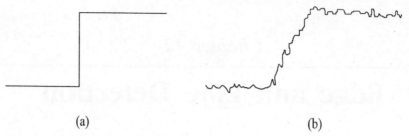

(a)   (b)

Fig. 12.1 Cross-section or intensity profile along a scanline of (a) a step edge, (b) a ramp edge corrupted with noise.

- **Derivative approach.** Edge pixels or *edgels* are detected by taking derivative followed by thresholding (e.g. Roberts operator and 4-neighbour operator). They occasionally incorporate noise cleaning scheme (e.g. Prewitt operator and Sobel operator). Two-dimensional derivatives are computed by means of what we call *edge masks*.

- **Pattern fitting approach.** A series of edge approximating functions in the form of *edge templates* over a small neighbourhood are analysed. Parameters along with their properties corresponding to the best fitting function are determined. Based on these information, whether or not an edge is present, is decided. We also call them *edge filters*.

Both the approaches have advantages and disadvantages. However, it is our common experience that the second approach gives better result as compared to the derivative approach. The reason could be followed from the primary aim of the latter which is (i) to detect derivatives of image intensity, and at the same time (ii) to make the process robust to noise. But as Faugeras (1993) has rightly pointed out, these properties are self-contradictory in nature and a desired result is always a trade-off between them. Suppose the resultant $S(x)$ of a signal $s(x)$ perturbed by a sinusoidal noise is given by

$$S(x) = s(x) + \eta \sin (\omega x) \qquad (12.1)$$

Taking derivatives with respect to x,

$$S'(x) = s'(x) + \eta \omega \cos (\omega x) \qquad (12.2)$$

If η is small then $s(x)$ is close to $S(x)$ while, if ω is large, the noise can predominate the resultant signal specially when the derivative is of interest. A thorough and lucid discussion in this respect is given in [Faugeras (1993)].

However, following either of the approaches, the complete process of generation of edge map may involve some or all of the steps:

- Noise smoothing
- Edge localization
- Edge enhancement
- Edge linking
- Edge following
- Edge extraction

Many edge-detection algorithms incorporate some of these steps without mentioning them explicitly. One of the main reasons of this is that these steps are not always too easy to be distinguished mutually from one another.

Let us try to understand these steps of edge detection. We have already mentioned that a 'significant' intensity differential represents an edge. Given the uncontrolled illumination in and around the scene, a digital image should have intensity differential at almost every point. However, it may be straightaway understood that not all of these differentials are edges. So, it is needed to smoothen some of these insignificant intensity differentials which correspond to false edges in the image. Hence, the step is known as *noise smoothing*.

Filtering for noise smoothing obviously would have a blurring effect to some extent on the intensity map of the image. Even the sharp edges corresponding to step change in intensity are going to be averaged out and the peaks of the differentials become flattened. Given this, the *edge localization* process marks the edge pixels by placing them as faithfully as possible

Even after localization, depending on the degree of change in intensity, edge value corresponding to edge strength is determined along with the orientation of edge pixel. Weak edges correspond to weak changes in intensity value while strong edges correspond to significant intensity gradient. The process of *edge enhancement* filters out edgels due to noise pixels by looking around the particular edgel for orientation and continuity. Obviously, stray strong edgels with no spatial coherence in magnitude and orientation are noisy edges and need to be eliminated. The operations like edge strength thresholding or non-maximal suppression perform a satisfactory job in this respect.

Finally, *edge linking* and *edge following* operations are the fundamental steps in any image understanding system. Edge linking process takes an unordered set of edge pixels produced by an edge detector as an input to form an ordered list of edgels. Local edge information are utilized by edge linking operation; while the edge following process takes the entire edge strength or gradient image. The output of this step is in the form of geometric primitives such as lines or curves.

There are numerous algorithms describing the edge-detection process. We discuss only some of the widely used operators. As the earlier discussion suggests, the significant gradient of intensity represents edge, the backbone of many algorithms is the discrete approximation of derivative operation. We consider here only two groups of such algorithms:

- first order derivative
- second order derivative

The process of noise smoothing and edge enhancement is discussed along with the respective algorithm.

12.3 Derivative (Difference) Operators

The derivative, or, in discrete domain, difference operators, which yield high values at places where graylevel changes rapidly, are used to find gradient of an image as shown in Fig. 12.2. In continuous domain, if $\partial g/\partial x$ and $\partial g/\partial y$ are the rates of change of two-dimensional function $g(x, y)$ along x- and y-axes, respectively, the rate of change in any direction θ (measured from the x-axis) is given as

$$\frac{\partial g}{\partial u} = \frac{\partial g}{\partial x} \cos\theta + \frac{\partial g}{\partial y} \sin\theta$$

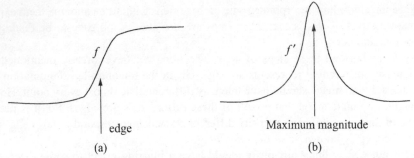

edge   Maximum magnitude

(a)   (b)

Fig. 12.2 Cross-section of (a) a ramp edge and (b) its first derivative.

where u is a variable in the direction θ. Moreover, the direction in which this rate of change has the greatest magnitude is

$$\tan^{-1}\left(\frac{\partial g/\partial y}{\partial g/\partial x}\right)$$

and magnitude of which is

$$\sqrt{\left(\frac{\partial g}{\partial x}\right)^2 + \left(\frac{\partial g}{\partial y}\right)^2}$$

The vector having this magnitude and direction is called the gradient of $g(x, y)$ and is denoted by $g'(x, y)$.

For a digital image, analogously, we could use first differences instead of first derivative, e.g.

$$\nabla_r\, g(r, c) = g(r, c) - g(r - 1, c) = d_1 \text{ (say)}$$
$$\nabla_c\, g(r, c) = g(r, c) - g(r, c - 1) = d_2 \text{ (say)}$$

The magnitude $g'(r, c)$ of gradient is then given by

$$g'(r, c) = \sqrt{\frac{1}{2}(d_1^2 + d_2^2)} \tag{12.3}$$

and the direction of the greatest steepness is

$$\theta(r, c) = \tan^{-1}\left(\frac{d_2}{d_1}\right) \tag{12.4}$$

Equations (12.3) and (12.4) represent a simple difference operator. To reduce the computational cost, $g'(r, c)$ is sometimes defined as

$$g'(r, c) = \frac{1}{2}[|d_1| + |d_2|] \tag{12.5}$$

or, as

$$g'(r, c) = \max\{|d_1|, |d_2|\} \tag{12.6}$$

From now on $g'(r, c)$ will be called, simply, gradient in root mean square (rms) sense, average magnitude sense or maximum sense according to which Equations (12.3), (12.5) and (12.6) are used to obtain it. Equations (12.3), (12.5) and (12.6) can be summarized by a point operator 0_p, such that $g'(r, c) = 0_p (d_1, d_2)$. Hence, obtaining the gradient image $g'(r, c)$ from the input image $g(r, c)$ can be expressed as a transformation such that

$$g'(r, c) = \nabla g(r, c) \qquad (12.7)$$

where ∇ includes both the difference operator and the point operator in itself. An edge element is deemed present at (r, c) if $g'(r, c)$ exceeds a predefined threshold. Quite a few gradient operators are available in the literature. Below we describe some of them.

12.3.1 Roberts, 4-Neighbour, Prewitt and Sobel Operators

For brevity, let $g(r, c)$ be written as g_0 and the graylevels of its neighbouring pixels $g(r - 1, c)$, $g(r - 1, c - 1)$, $g(r, c - 1)$, $g(r + 1, c - 1)$, $g(r + 1, c)$, $g(r + 1, c + 1)$, $g(r, c + 1)$ and $g(r - 1, c + 1)$ be written as $g_1, g_2, ..., g_8$, respectively as shown in Fig. 12.3.

g_2	g_1	g_8
g_3	g_0	g_7
g_4	g_5	g_6

Fig. 12.3 Neighbours of the candidate pixel g_0.

Then various gradient operators using first-order difference can be defined as follows.

Ordinary operator. Equation (12.8) can be implemented as convolution of the following masks with image intensity.

$$d_1 = g_0 - g_1 \text{ and } d_2 = g_0 - g_3 \qquad (12.8)$$

0	−1
0	1

0	0
−1	1

Roberts operator [Roberts (1965)]. Equivalent masks are then given by Equation (12.9)

$$d_1 = g_0 - g_2 \quad \text{and} \quad d_2 = g_1 - g_3 \qquad (12.9)$$

−1	0
0	1

0	1
−1	0

Note that the differential along the diagonals of a 2×2 mask is used and the edge value after the convolution corresponds to the central point $(r - 1/2, c - 1/2)$.

4-Neighbour operator [Chaudhuri and Chanda (1984)]. Instead of calculating edge strength at the point $(r - 1/2, c - 1/2)$, it is desired to calculate it at the point (r, c). To take care of this, 3×3 mask are used as against 2×2 mask in Roberts operator. Then

$$d_1 = g_5 - g_1 \quad \text{and} \quad d_2 = g_7 - g_3 \qquad (12.10)$$

The corresponding masks are given by

0	−1	0
0	0	0
0	1	0

0	0	0
−1	0	1
0	0	0

Prewitt operator [Prewitt (1970)]. In Prewitt operator while approximating the first derivative, similar weights are assigned to all the neighbours of the candidate pixel whose edge strength is being calculated.

$$d_1 = \frac{1}{3}[(g_4 + g_5 + g_6) - (g_2 + g_1 + g_8)]$$

$$d_2 = \frac{1}{3}[(g_8 + g_7 + g_6) - (g_2 + g_3 + g_4)]$$

(12.11)

The corresponding masks are given by

−1	−1	−1
0	0	0
1	1	1

−1	0	1
−1	0	1
−1	0	1

Sobel operator [Duda and Hart (1973)]. On the other hand, in Sobel operator higher weights are assigned to the pixels close to the candidate pixel.

$$d_1 = \frac{1}{4}[(g_4 + 2g_5 + g_6) - (g_2 + 2g_1 + g_8)]$$

$$d_2 = \frac{1}{4}[(g_8 + 2g_7 + g_6) - (g_2 + 2g_3 + g_4)]$$

(12.12)

Thus the corresponding 3 × 3 masks are given by

−1	−2	−1
0	0	0
1	2	1

−1	0	1
−2	0	2
−1	0	1

Finally, the gradient $g'(r, c)$ at pixel (r, c) is obtained by a point operator 0_p applying on $d_i(i = 1, 2)$. Because of the nature of point operator, d_1 and d_2 in the above equations can be defined interchangeably without affecting the value of $g'(r, c)$. Note that among these operators, the ordinary operator is not symmetric. Prewitt operator can detect vertical edges better than that by Sobel operator; while Sobel operator is superior to Prewitt operator in detecting diagonal edges. Third, ordinarily, Roberts and 4-neighbour operators are sensitive to noise. Effect of noise is reduced in case of Prewitt and Sobel operators by inherent averaging of neighbouring pixels. Therefore, to achieve the desired result, gradient operators are usually preceded by noise cleaning. The results of these operators are shown in Fig. 12.4. Gradient image is thresholded to display the edge map.

This suggests that if $[f(r, c)]$ and $[F(u, v)]$ respectively denote the two-dimensional arrays or matrices of size $M \times N$ of numbers and its Fourier transform components then

$$[F(u, v)] = \mathbf{W}_M [f(r, c)] \, \mathbf{W}_N$$

8. *Periodicity:*

$$F(u + M, v + N) = F(u, v)$$

9. *Parsival theorem:*

$$\sum_{c=0}^{N-1} \sum_{r=0}^{M-1} f^2(r, c) = \frac{1}{MN} \sum_{v=0}^{N-1} \sum_{u=0}^{M-1} |F(u, v)|^2$$

As stated earlier, Fourier transform is most widely used in image processing and it can diagonalize (block) circulant matrix. However, straightforward method takes N^2 multiplications and $N(N-1)$ additions to compute one-dimensional discrete Fourier transform of N data points. A fast version of this algorithm developed by Cooley and Tukey (1965), called *FFT algorithm*, takes only $\frac{1}{2}$ ($N \log N$) multiplications and ($N \log N$) additions to do the same job. However the algorithm is applicable when the number of data points is 2 raised to an integer power (i.e. $N = 2^n$). So, if the number of data points does not satisfy the criterion, required number of zeros may be appended with the given data. Fourier transform represents a function by a set of orthogonal sinusoidal functions. A specific type of linear transformation in which basic linear operations are exactly invertible and the operator kernel satisfies certain orthogonality conditions is called *unitary transforms* [Pratt (1991)]. Hence, Fourier transform is an unitary transform. Amongst other unitary transform that utilize sinusoidal functions as their orthogonal basis are *discrete cosine and sine* and *Hartley* transforms.

2.4.2 Discrete Cosine and Sine Transform

The discrete cosine transform (DCT) is not simply the real part of the discrete Fourier transform as we will see later. However, Fourier transform coefficients of a real symmetric function are real corresponding to the cosine term of the transform. Thus, DCT can be defined in terms of DFT by imposing symmetry in the given function [Ahmed et al. (1974), Means et al. (1974)].

Suppose a sequence $\{f(r) \mid r = 0, 1, ..., M-1\}$ represents a digital signal. A symmetrical digital signal can be formed by reflecting it about its edge according to the relation

$$f_s(r) = \begin{cases} f(r) & \text{for } 0 \le r \le M - 1 \\ f(-r - 1) & \text{for } -M \le r \le -1 \end{cases} \tag{2.59}$$

Thus $f_s(r)$ is symmetric about $r = -1/2$. Taking the Fourier transform of $f_s(r)$ about the point of symmetry, we get

$$F_s(u) = \frac{1}{\sqrt{2M}} \sum_{r=-M}^{M-1} f_s(r)\omega^{u(r+\frac{1}{2})/2M} \tag{2.60}$$

$$= \frac{1}{\sqrt{2M}} \sum_{r=-M}^{M-1} f_s(r) \exp\left[-\sqrt{-1} \frac{2\pi}{2M} u\left(r + \frac{1}{2}\right) \right] \tag{2.61}$$

for $u = -M, ..., -1, 0, 1, ..., M-1$. Since $f_s(r)$ is real and symmetric, the imaginary part of the $F_s(u)$ is zero. Then

$$F_s(u) = \sqrt{\frac{2}{M}} \sum_{r=0}^{M-1} f(r) \cos\left[\frac{\pi}{M}u\left(r + \frac{1}{2}\right)\right] \tag{2.62}$$

So, in terms of Fourier transform of $f(r)$, we can define $F_s(u)$ as

$$F_s(u) = \sqrt{\frac{2}{M}} \ \text{Real}\left\{\exp\left[\sqrt{-1}\frac{\pi u}{2M}\right] \sum_{r=0}^{M-1} f(r) \exp\left[-\sqrt{-1}\frac{2\pi}{2M}ur\right]\right\} \tag{2.63}$$

Hence, the forward discrete cosine transform is defined as [Ahmed et al. (1974)]

$$F(u) = \sqrt{\frac{2}{M}}C(u) \sum_{r=0}^{M-1} f(r) \cos\left[\frac{\pi}{M}u\left(r + \frac{1}{2}\right)\right] \tag{2.64}$$

$$= \sum_{r=0}^{M-1} f(r) \frac{1}{\sqrt{M}}C(u)\sqrt{2} \cos\left[\frac{\pi u(2r + 1)}{2M}\right] \tag{2.65}$$

The basis vectors of DCT are related to a class of Chebyshev polynomials [Ahmed and Rao (1975)] and the transform can also be represented by

$$\mathbf{F} = \mathbf{Cf} \tag{2.66}$$

where $\mathbf{C} = \dfrac{1}{\sqrt{M}}[c_{ru}]$ is a $M \times M$ matrix whose elements are

$$c_{ru} = \begin{cases} 1 & \text{for } u = 0 \\ \sqrt{2} \cos\left[\dfrac{\pi u(2r + 1)}{2M}\right] & \text{for } 1 \leq u \leq M - 1 \text{ and } 0 \leq r \leq M - 1 \end{cases} \tag{2.67}$$

The inverse transform is defined by

$$\mathbf{f} = \mathbf{C}^{\mathrm{T}}\mathbf{F} \tag{2.68}$$

The two-dimensional DCT and its inverse transform may be defined as

$$[F(u, v)] = \mathbf{C}[f(r, c)]\mathbf{C}^{\mathrm{T}} \tag{2.69}$$

and

$$[f(r, c)] = \mathbf{C}^{\mathrm{T}}[F(u, v)]\mathbf{C} \tag{2.70}$$

It should be noted that M coefficients of DCT can be computed by using a $2M$ point FFT. Secondly, the rows of the matrix $\mathbf{C}$ closely approximate the eigenvectors of Toeplitz matrix [Ahmed and Rao (1975)]. The DCT is interrelated to a similar type of unitary transform, called *discrete sine transform* (DST) in a sense that both of them diagonalize a family of tridiagonal matrix [Jain and Angel (1974)]. One-dimensional DST and its inverse transform can be defined likewise.

$$\mathbf{F} = \mathbf{Sf} \tag{2.71}$$

and

$$\mathbf{f} = \mathbf{S}^{\mathrm{T}}\mathbf{F} \tag{2.72}$$

where $\mathbf{S} = \sqrt{\dfrac{2}{M + 1}}[s_{ru}]$ is a $M \times M$ matrix whose elements are

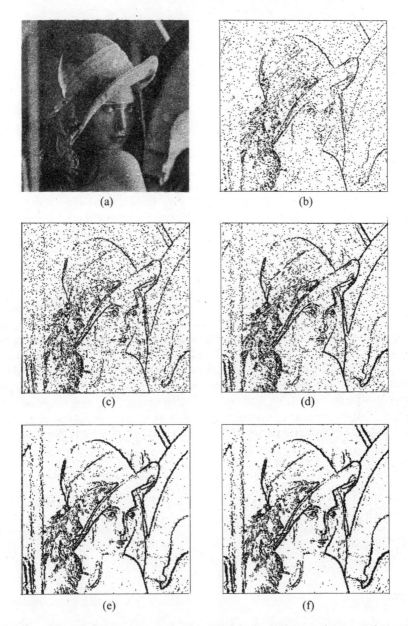

Fig. 12.4 Results of first-derivative operators: (a) original image. Various edge maps due to (b) ordinary, (c) Roberts, (d) 4-neighbour, (e) Prewitt and (f) Sobel edge detector.

Instead of computing contrast (d_1 and d_2) in two orthogonal directions only and then taking some sort of average, maximum of contrast computed along all directions keeping candidate pixel at the centre may also be taken as a measure of edge strength. This may be implemented by convolving the intensity image with following edge masks and then taking the maximum of response:

0	−1	0
0	0	0
0	1	0

−1	0	0
0	0	0
0	0	1

0	0	0
−1	0	1
0	0	0

0	0	1
0	0	0
−1	0	0

0	1	0
0	0	0
0	−1	0

1	0	0
0	0	0
0	0	−1

0	0	0
0	0	−1
0	0	0

0	0	−1
0	0	0
1	0	0

The operator is known as *compass oprator* [Chanda et al. (1985)] and is very useful in detecting weak edges. The method is, as expected, very sensitive to noise. The given masks are designed from 4-neighbour operator. Compass operator corresponding to other symmetric operators, such as Sobel and Prewitt, can also be designed in a similar way.

12.3.2 Canny Edge Detector

This is also based on first-derivative coupled with noise cleaning. We put this operator in a separate section as it has become the most popular derivative operator for edge detection nowadays. As discussed earlier, the detection of step edges are influenced by the presence of noise. Therefore, the noise smoothing improves the accuracy of edge detection while adding uncertainty in localizing the edge. Canny edge detector tries to achieve an optimal trade-off between the two by approximating the first derivative of the Gaussian. Notice the similarity between the shape of the first derivative of Gaussian [Fig. 12.5(e)] and the second derivative [Fig. 12.5(c)] of the intensity corresponding to a ramp edge [Fig. 12.5(a)]. The derivative of the bell shape of the Gaussian function [Fig. 12.5(d)] approximates second-derivative or zero crossing operator. Canny (1986) has considered the following criteria for localizing edges:

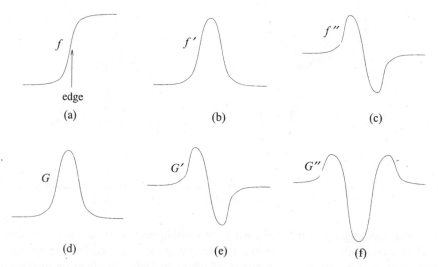

Fig. 12.5 (a) A ramp edge, (b) first derivative of ramp edge, (c) second derivative of ramp edge, (d) Gaussian function, (e) first derivative of Gaussian function, and (f) second derivative of Gaussian function.

- *Good detection:* There should be a low probability of failing to detect a real edge point and, equivalently, low probability of falsely marking non-edge points. That is to maximize the signal to noise ratio (SNR).

- *Good localization:* The point marked by the operator as edge points should be as close as possible to the real edge point. That is minimizing the variance σ^2 of the zero crossing position.

- *One response to one edge:* The detector should not generate multiple outputs in response to a single edge. That is, there should be low probability of number of peaks to a given edge response.

Given the good detection, localization and uni-response to a true edge, the algorithmic steps for Canny edge detection are as follows:

1. Convolve the image $g(r, c)$ with a Gaussian function (select appropriate σ) to get smooth image $g'(r, c)$, i.e.

$$\bar{g}(r, c) = g(r, c) * G(r, c; \sigma) \tag{12.13}$$

2. Apply first difference gradient operator to compute edge strength.

$$d_1 = \frac{1}{2}\{g'(r, c) - g'(r, c - 1) + g'(r - 1, c) - g'(r - 1, c - 1)\}$$

$$\tag{12.14}$$

$$d_2 = \frac{1}{2}\{g'(r, c) - g'(r - 1, c) + g'(r, c - 1) - g'(r - 1, c - 1)\}$$

Then edge magnitude and direction are obtained as before.

3. Apply non-maximal suppression to the gradient magnitude. This is achieved by suppressing the edge magnitudes not in the direction of the gradient. In fact, in Canny's approach, the edge direction is reduced to any one of the four directions. To perform this task for a given point, its gradient is compared with that of points of its 3×3 neighbourhood. If the candidate magnitude is greater than that of neighbourhood, the edge strength is maintained, else it is discarded.

4. Apply threshold to the non-maxima suppressed image. Similar to any other edge-detection process, the edge magnitudes below a certain value are discarded. However, the Canny's approach employs a clever double thresholding commonly referred to as *hysteresis*. In this process, two thresholds, upper and lower thresholds are set by the user so that for a given edgel chain if the magnitude of any one edgel of the chain is greater than the upper threshold, all edgels above the lower thresholds are selected as edge points. Canny has not provided any basis for selecting upper and lower thresholds and similar to many such applications, selection of the thresholds are application dependent.

The result of applying Canny edge detector is shown in Fig. 12.6.

Fig. 12.6 The results of Canny edge detector. Original image is same as in Fig. 12.4(a).

12.3.3 Second Order Derivative

We have seen in Chapter 6 that edge can be sharpened/enhanced by taking second derivative of image intensity. Edge detection by second derivative operator corresponds to the detection of zero-crossing. The widely used second derivative operator is the Laplacian edge detector. In one of its useful variations, Laplacian is preceded by the noise smoothing operation commonly known as *Laplacian of Gaussian* (LoG) or Marr-Hildreth [Marr and Hildreth (1980)] operator.

Laplacian edge detector

Given an image matrix, the Laplacian of the image function is the second order partial derivatives along x and y directions.

$$\nabla^2 g = \frac{\partial^2 g}{\partial x^2} + \frac{\partial^2 g}{\partial y^2} \qquad (12.15)$$

In the digital approximation of the second order, partial derivative in x direction is

$$\frac{\partial^2 g}{\partial x^2} = \frac{\partial \{g(r, c) - g(r, c - 1)\}}{\partial x}$$

$$= \frac{\partial g(r, c)}{\partial x} - \frac{\partial g(r, c - 1)}{\partial x}$$

$$= g(r, c) - g(r, c - 1) - g(r, c - 1) + g(r, c - 2)$$

$$= g(r, c) - 2g(r, c - 1) + g(r, c - 2) \qquad (12.16)$$

Similarly, the second order derivative along y direction is given by

$$\frac{\partial^2 g}{\partial y^2} = g(r, c) - 2g(r - 1, c) + g(r - 2, c) \qquad (12.17)$$

Both the approximating Equations (12.16) and (12.17) are centred around the point $(r - 1, c - 1)$. Conveniently, this pixel could be replaced by (r, c). The corresponding Laplacian masks for convolution are given by

0	1	0
1	−4	1
0	1	0

It may be necessary to add higher weights at the centre pixel. The restriction is that the sum of all the weights of the mask must add to zero.

Laplacian of Gaussian edge detector

We have already observed [in Chapter 6] that the weight distribution in a Laplacian mask evokes strong response to stray noise pixels. It indicates that some sort of noise cleaning preceded by Laplacian should provide a better result. For noise cleaning, one may employ Gaussian smoothing. Then the resultant algorithm is *Laplacian of Gaussian* (LoG) [Fig. 12.5(f)] edge operator.

The algorithmic steps are given as follows:

1. Smooth the image intensity $g(r, c)$ by convolving it with a digital mask corresponding to Gaussian function.

2. Apply the Laplacian mask as in Section 12.3.3 on the smooth image intensity profile.

3. Find the zero-crossings in the image subjected to Laplacian second-derivative operator.

Mathematically,

$$g''(r, c) = \nabla^2 \{g(r, c) * G(r, c)\} \tag{12.18}$$

which, following the rule of convolution, becomes

$$g''(r, c) = g(r, c) * \{\nabla^2 G(r, c)\} \tag{12.19}$$

Extracting edge points or edgels by detecting zero-crossing in the second derivative still suffers from the problem of *false alarm*, i.e. a non-edge pixel may be marked as edge pixel. This is because even a small non-linear variation in intensity profile (due to quantization error and other negligible reasons) gives rise to zero-crossing in second-order derivative. The problem may be surmounted by considering both first- and second-order derivatives. In that case, an edgel is said to be present if there exists a zero-crossing in second derivative and if magnitude of the first derivative exceeds a threshold at the same location.

12.4   Pattern Fitting Approach

In this approach a gray-scale image is considered a topographic surface where altitude at a point is given by its intensity or graylevel. The main objective, here, is to fit a pattern over the neighbourhood of the pixel at which edge strength is being calculated. Parameters corresponding to the best fit of the pattern are estimated locally. Finally, properties of edge points are determined based on these parameters and edgels are marked accordingly.

12.4.1 Hueckel Operator

The pattern used is a model of step-edge making an angle α with the x-axis [Hueckel (1971)]. Graylevel on one side of the edge be 'a' and that on the other side is '$a + b$'. In other words, the model $h(x, y)$ can be described as [see Fig. 12.7]

$$h(x, y) = \begin{cases} a & \text{if } x \sin \alpha - y \cos \alpha < 0 \\ a + b & \text{if } x \sin \alpha - y \cos \alpha \geq 0 \end{cases} \qquad (12.20)$$

where (x, y) is a point in a finite symmetric window W around the origin. Hence, one has to estimate 'b', the change in intensity and the 'α', the edge orientation, corresponding to best fit of this model over the intensity surface.

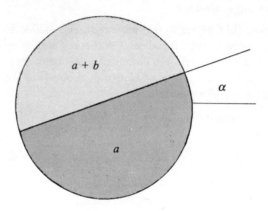

Fig. 12.7   A model of a step edge used to derive Hueckel's operator.

12.4.2 Best-plane Fit Gradient (bpf)

Obtaining gradient by the bpf technique is a bit different from the previous approach. In this method, graylevels of the neighbours of the pixel under consideration are intended to fit with a plane $v = a_1 r + a_2 c + a_3$. An error of fit is defined and the error is minimized with respect to a_1, a_2 and a_3. Then the slope of the plane gives the gradient at the said pixel. For example, let g_0, g_1, g_2 and g_3 be the graylevels of the pixels over a 2×2 neighbourhood to be fitted with the plane. Let the error be 'squared difference', which is given by

$$\varepsilon = [a_1 r + a_2 c + a_3 - g_0]^2 + [a_1(r - 1) + a_2 c + a_3 - g_1]^2$$
$$+ [a_1(r - 1) + a_2(c - 1) + a_3 - g_2]^2 + [a_1 r + a_2(c - 1) + a_3 - g_3]^2$$

Setting the partial derivatives of ε with respect to a_1, a_2 and a_3 equal to zero, we get

$$a_1 = \frac{g_0 + g_3}{2} - \frac{g_1 + g_2}{2}, \qquad a_2 = \frac{g_0 + g_1}{2} - \frac{g_2 + g_3}{2} \qquad (12.21)$$

It is seen that a_1 and a_2 are similar to d_1 and d_2, respectively. The gradient $g'(r, c)$ is, here, given by a slightly different point operator O_p' that signifies square root of squared sum (rss), i.e.

$$g'(r, c) = O_p'(a_1, a_2) = \sqrt{a_1^2 + a_2^2} \qquad (12.22)$$

It can be shown that bpf gradient is equivalent to Roberts', Prewitt's and Sobel's gradient for different mask sizes and different weightages to the neighbouring pixels [Chaudhuri and Chanda (1984)].

The equivalence of bpf gradient with Roberts' gradient

1. The bpf gradient in rss sense is the same as Roberts' gradient in rms sense.

2. The bpf gradient in sum of magnitude sense is the same as Roberts' gradient in maximum sense.

3. The bpf gradient in maximum sense is the same as Roberts' gradient in average magnitude sense.

Rosenfeld and Kak (1982) showed that Roberts' gradient with max operator is the same as Hueckel's gradient. Hence, it can be readily said that the bpf gradient in sum of magnitude sense is the same as Hueckel's gradient defined over a 2×2 window.

The equivalence of bpf gradient with Prewitt's gradient

Consider now that the plane is estimated using the graylevels $g_i (i = 0, 1, 2, ..., 8)$ as shown in Fig. 12.3. In a similar manner, as above, it can be shown that

$$a_1 = \frac{1}{2} \left[\frac{g_4 + g_5 + g_6}{3} - \frac{g_1 + g_2 + g_8}{3} \right]$$

$$a_2 = \frac{1}{2} \left[\frac{g_6 + g_7 + g_8}{3} - \frac{g_2 + g_3 + g_4}{3} \right]$$

(12.23)

Then

1. The bpf gradient in rss sense is the same as $\dfrac{1}{\sqrt{2}}$ times Prewitt's gradient in rms sense.

2. The bpf gradient in sum of magnitude sense is the same as Prewitt's gradient in average magnitude sense.

3. The bpf gradient in maximum sense is the same as 1/2 times Prewitt's gradient in maximum sense.

The equivalence of bpf gradient with Sobel's gradient

A similar relationship between the bpf gradient and Sobel's gradient can also be found, if the graylevels g_1, g_3, g_5 and g_7 are weighted by 2 and the rests are weighted by 1. In that case by fitting the plane over the graylevels g_i $(i = 1, 2, ..., 8)$ we have

$$a_1 = \frac{g_4 + 2g_5 + g_6}{6} - \frac{g_2 + 2g_1 + g_8}{6}$$

$$a_2 = \frac{g_6 + 2g_7 + g_8}{6} - \frac{g_2 + 2g_3 + g_4}{6}$$

(12.24)

Then

1. The bpf gradient of weighted graylevels in rss, sense is the same as $(2\sqrt{2}/3)$-times Sobel's gradient in rms sense.

2. The bpf gradient of weighted graylevels in sum of magnitude sense is the same as $(4/3)$-times Sobel's gradient in average magnitude sense.

3. The bpf gradient of weighted graylevels in maximum sense is the same as $(2/3)$-times Sobel's gradient in maximum sense.

   Therefore, it is seen that the bpf gradient technique is quite general and is equivalent to other operators except, sometimes, for the constant factors that may be absorbed in the threshold for edge detection. However, a more generalized technique in this direction is due to *facet model* where a bi-cubic surface is fit over a 5×5 neighbourhood of the candidate pixel [Haralick and Shapiro (1992)].

12.5 Morphologic Edge Detection

A simple method of performing gray-scale edge detection in morphology is to take the difference between an image and its erosion/dilation image by a structuring element. This may be preceded by preprocessing or followed by postprocessing or both. The difference image is an image of edge strength. Most popularly used structuring element for edge detection is rod shaped with flat top. To define the gray-scale rod structuring element having flat top and rod shaped domain, let $(0, 0)$ denotes the centre of local neighbourhood and a point by (r, c) at an offset of r along row direction and c along column direction. Then the domain of rod structuring element, say, of radius 1 (using *city-block distance*) is denoted by D_{rod1} and is defined as

$$D_{\text{rod1}} = \{(0, -1), (0, 1), (0, 0), (-1, 0), (1, 0)\}$$

and its value is a mapping $b: D_{\text{rod1}} \rightarrow \{0 \ldots 255\}$. Since rod is flat on the top, the gray-scale value of $b(r, c) = 0$, $\forall~(r, c) \in D_{\text{rod1}}$. This is represented diagrammatically as

$$0$$
$$0 \quad * \quad 0$$
$$0$$

Also, $D_{\text{rod1}} = $ Domain of rod structuring element of radius one. And, '*' indicates the origin. Hence, D_{rod1} is nothing but the 4-neighbour of the origin including it. Let us denote it also by N_4. Similarly, 8-neighbour of the origin including it is denoted by N_8.

   The edge strength image due to *dilation residue edge detector* is given by

$$G_d(r, c) = (f \oplus b)(r, c) - f(r, c)$$
$$= \max_{(i, j) \in D_{\text{rod1}}} \{f(r - i, c - j) - f(r, c)\} \qquad (12.25)$$
$$= \max_{(i, j) \in N_4(r, c)} \{f(i, j) - f(r, c)\}$$

The edge strength image due to *erosion residue edge detector* is given by

$$G_e(r, c) = f(r, c) - (f \ominus b)(r, c)$$
$$= f(r, c) - \min_{(i, j) \in D_{\text{rod1}}} f(r - i, c - j) \qquad (12.26)$$
$$= \max_{(i, j) \in N_4(r, c)} \{f(r, c) - f(i, j)\}$$

Both dilation residue edge detector and erosion residue edge detector are noise sensitive. Moreover, these are biased in the sense that the former gives the edge strength to that side of an edge which has low value while the latter gives to the high value side. A position unbiased operator can be obtained by the combination of the operators $G_d(r, c)$ and $G_e(r, c)$. Three such combinations are defined using pixel-wise minimum, maximum and sum. They are denoted by G_{min} (r, c), $G_{max}(r, c)$ and $G_{sum}(r, c)$, respectively and are defined as

$$G_{min}(r, c) = min\{G_d(r, c), G_e(r, c)\} \tag{12.27}$$

$$G_{max}(r, c) = max\{G_d(r, c), g_e(r, c)\} \tag{12.28}$$

$$G_{sum}(r, c) = G_d(r, c) + G_e(r, c) \tag{12.29}$$

G_{max} and G_{sum} are still sensitive to noise. G_{max} is same as the 4-neighbour compass gradient in max sense [Chanda et al. (1985b)]. G_{sum} results in thick edges, and strength of detected edge is less than actual edge strength. G_{min} (r, c) is less sensitive to noise but cannot detect ideal step edges.

Lee et al. (1987) suggested the following improved edge detectors which were less sensitive to noise but yet could detect ideal step edge. Before describing these operators we need to define the structuring elements. Consider four structuring elements which have flat top and have domains denoted by D_1, D_2, D_3, D_4 and D, and are defined as

$$\begin{aligned} D_1 &= \{(-1, 0), (0, 0), (0, 1)\} \\ D_2 &= \{(0, -1), (0, 0), (1, 0)\} \\ D_3 &= \{(-1, 0), (0, 0), (0, -1)\} \\ D_4 &= \{(0, 1), (0, 0), (1, 0)\} \\ D &= \{(-1, -1), (-1, 1), (0, 0), (1, -1), (1, 1)\} \end{aligned} \tag{12.30}$$

Hence, $D_1 \cup D_2 \cup D_3 \cup D_4 = N_4$ and $D = N_8/N_4 \cup (0, 0)$, where the binary operator '/' represents set subtraction such that $A/B = \{x \mid x \in A \text{ and } x \notin B\}$.

Suppose dilation and erosion of $f(r, c)$ by the flat top structuring element whose domain is a, are denoted by $\text{dilation}_a(r, c)$ and $\text{erosion}_a(r, c)$, respectively. Then the *improved dilation residue operator* is defined as

$$\begin{aligned} G_d'(r, c) = min\{&\text{dilation}_{D_{rod1}}(r, c) - f(r, c), \\ &\text{dilation}_D(r, c) - f(r, c), G_d''(r, c)\} \end{aligned} \tag{12.31}$$

where $G_d''(r, c)$ is defined as

$$\begin{aligned} G_d''(r, c) = max\{&|\text{dilation}_{D_1}(r, c) - \text{dilation}_{D_2}(r, c)|, \\ &|\text{dilation}_{D_3}(r, c) - \text{dilation}_{D_4}(r, c)|\} \end{aligned}$$

and the *improved erosion residue operator* is defined as

$$\begin{aligned} G_e'(r, c) = min\{&f(r, c) - \text{erosion}_{D_{rod1}}(r, c), \\ &f(r, c) - \text{erosion}_D(r, c), G_e''(r, c)\} \end{aligned} \tag{12.32}$$

where $G_e''(r, c)$ is defined by

$$\begin{aligned} G_e''(r, c) = max\{&|\text{erosion}_{D_1}(r, c) - \text{erosion}_{D_2}(r, c)|, \\ &|\text{erosion}_{D3}(r, c) - \text{erosion}_{D4}(r, c)|\} \end{aligned}$$

These improved operators are biased for ideal step edges and a natural resolution is to consider their sum. This leads to a new edge detector G'_{sum} defined as

$$G'_{sum}(r, c) = G'_d(r, c) + G'_e(r, c) \tag{12.33}$$

The shortcoming of this detector is that its capability to reduce effects of noise is limited.

Now recall that the minimum of dilation residue and erosion residue as given by Equation (12.27) is a good detector of ramp edge and is less sensitive to noise, but it cannot detect step edge. So, before applying this operator if we blur the image by, say, simple mean filter, our achievement is twofold: effect of noise is further reduced and step edges are converted to ramp edges which can now be detected by the said operator. The resultant operator is what we call *blur-minimum edge detector* [Lee et al. (1987)].

Even though blur-minimum operator is less sensitive to noise, the edge strength assigned to the edge pixel is less than edge contrast. This is due to the blurring of input image which diffuses the edge peaks over the blur neighbourhood area. Hence weak edge points may be undetected. Secondly, the thickness of the edge detected by blur-minimum operator increases as the slope of ramp edge decreases. This decreases the ability of the blur-minimum operator to localize edges correctly.

12.5.1   Multi-scale Morphological Edge Detector

The goal of edge detection is to detect and localize edge points even under noisy condition. All edges with various fineness regarding spectral contrast and spatial geometry cannot be detected by a single operator. In fact, some detail that seems to be freak and noisy in one scale may become relevant in other scale. Hence, edges of different fineness are detected using operators at different scale, and then they are judiciously combined to produce all the edges of interest in an image.

The *multi-scale morphological edge detector* is able to differentiate these fine variations of graylevel surface, and also can remove noise. As the name implies, this is based on multi-scaling approach. Structuring elements of different sizes are used to extract features at different scales. The smaller the size of structuring element, lesser is the noise removing capacity and more the ability to detect fine edges. By using large-size structuring element one can remove more noise, but at the same time the thickness of edge increases causing smearing of closely spaced edges. Hence to overcome these problems one can combine judiciously different edge maps obtained with different size structuring elements. True edge points are extracted from this combined edge map. The following are the different steps involved:

1. Obtain edge strength maps using structuring elements of different size.

2. Combine edge strength maps/images obtained in Step 1.

3. Extract the edge points lying on the ridge of the edge strength surface using non-maximal suppression technique.

The following paragraphs give a detailed description of each of the three steps of multi-scale morphologic edge detection method:

Step 1: Obtain edge maps. Consider four flat top structuring elements whose domains are nD_1, nD_2, nD_3 and nD_4 that are same as D_1, D_2, D_3 and D_4, respectively [defined by Equation (12.30)] but have size n and $nD = (nN_8)/(nN_4)$. Similarly, the domain of a flat top rod structuring element of radius n, denoted by D_{rodn}, is defined as $D_{rodn} = nD_{rod1}$. Thus the

edge strength map at scale n may be given as

$$G_d^n(r, c) = \min\{\text{dilation}_{nD_{\text{rod1}}}(r, c) - f(r, c),$$

$$\text{dilation}_{nD}(r, c) - f(r, c), G_d^{n'}(r, c)\} \qquad (12.34)$$

where $G_d^{n'}(r, c)$ is defined as

$$G_d^{n'}(r, c) = \max\{|\text{dilation}_{nD_1}(r, c) - \text{dilation}_{nD_2}(r, c)|,$$

$$|\text{dilation}_{nD_3}(r, c) - \text{dilation}_{nD_4}(r, c)|\}$$

A close examination of Equation (12.34) reveals that this is similar to improved dilation residue operator [as defined in Equation (12.31)] at scale n. So we may also define the edge strength by an operator similar to improved erosion residue operator. Sometimes edge strength is defined as the sum of responses due to improved dilation residue and improved erosion residue operators.

Step 2: *Combining edge strength.* Suppose edge strength at scale n due to an image $f(r, c)$ is denoted by $f_n'(r, c)$. Thus according to the operator presented in Step 1, $f_n'(r, c) = G_d^n(r, c)$. Now we combine these edge strengths of different scales, most naturally, by simple pixel-wise summation, i.e.

$$f'(r, c) = \sum_{n=k}^{l} w_n f_n'(r, c)$$

where $[k, l]$ represents the range of scale that explicit the edges of interest, and w_i's are respective weights that are supplied by the user. Note that other kinds of combination are also possible. Secondly, the edge strength map $f'(r, c)$ appears to contain long range of mountains and true edge lies along its ridge.

Step 3: *Non-maximal suppression.* As stated earlier, true edge corresponds to the ridges of hilly terrain of the result of Step 2. Therefore, to get the edge points and subsequently the edges we employ non-maxima suppression technique. However, to extract ridges one may also employ edge-following or line-detection (see Section 12.9) technique.

The results of morphological edge detectors are shown in Fig. 12.8.

12.6 Edge Linking and Edge Following

In order to extract meaningful information from the edge map of an image, it needs to be approximated using appropriate geometric primitives. Edge linking and edge following act as a bridge between the process of edge detection and subsequent edge approximation and recognition. By edge linking we basically label edgels to make them belong to a continuous line or curve segment. In other words, by this method we form a continuous line segment from individual and, occasionally, sparse edgels. The process of edge linking gets complicated because of false alarm and misdetection primarily due to noise.

Edge-linking methods usually operate on edge image, i.e. where edgels are extracted by thresholding (see Section 12.7) or by other means. On the other hand, edge following is always applied on edge strength or gradient image. If we consider a gradient image as a topographic

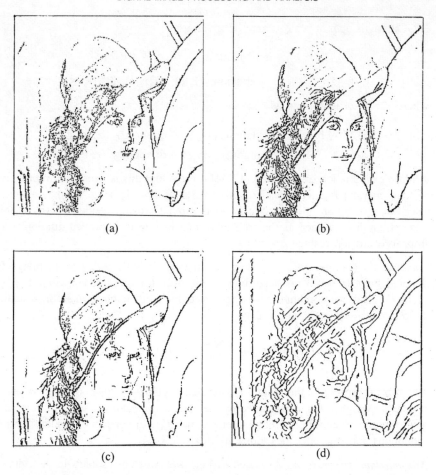

Fig. 12.8 Results of morphological edge detectors: edge map due to (a) dilation residue edge detector, (b) erosion residue edge detector, (c) blur-minimum edge detector and (d) multi-scale morphological edge detector. Original image is same as in Fig. 12.4(a).

surface then edges that are present in the original intensity image correspond to ridges of chains of mountains. Usually, altitude of these ridges vary due to variation in contrast between different regions. Edge-following techniques basically labels the edge points by tracking these ridges.

In the following sections, we briefly cover a couple of edge-linking and edge-following algorithms.

12.6.1 Hough Transform

This method of edge linking determines whether or not a set of edgels lie on a line (or a specified curve) [Hough (1962)]. This method then links the edgels by producing the line or curve. To understand the method, let us consider the simple problem of detecting line passing through a given set of points. Suppose in the xy-plane (Euclidean space) using Cartesian coordinate system equation of a line L passing through two points (x_1, y_1) and (x_2, y_2) is given by $y = m'x + b'$. In the mb-plane (also called *parameter space*) the line is represented by a point (m', b') as shown in Fig. 12.9. On the other hand, infinite number of lines pass through the point (x_1, x_2) in the xy-plane which correspond to a line $b = x_1m - y_1$ in the mb-plane. One of these infinite lines is the line L. Same is true for (x_2, y_2) also, and the equation of the corresponding line in the parameter space is $b = x_2m - y_2$. However, these two lines in the parameter space intersect at the point (m', c'). If we have n points that lie on the line L, then in the parameter space there are n concurrent lines passing through the point (m', c'). Therefore, the problem of detecting line passing through a given set of points reduces to finding the point of intersection, of the lines in the parameter space, each of which corresponds to a point in the Euclidean space.

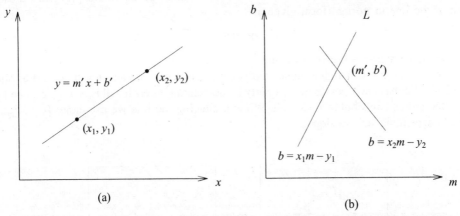

(a)   (b)

Fig. 12.9   Hough transform of line and points: (a) xy-plane and (b) parameter space.

To implement the method in the discrete domain, mc-plane is approximated by a two-dimensional array $A(m, b)$ where each element of array is an accumulator for the discrete values m and b as shown in Fig. 12.10. Thus the algorithm for n given points (r_i, c_i) goes like

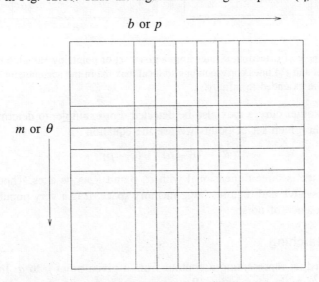

Fig. 12.10   Accumulator array.

```
for  each  (r_i, c_i),  (i = 1, 2, ..., n)
for  every  m
   compute  b  =  r_i m  +  c_i
   increment  A(m, b)
```

It is expected that the accumulator $A(m', b')$ corresponding to the point of intersection (m', b') would be incremented more rapidly than any other cell. Hence, local maxima in $A(m, b)$ gives the parameters of a line in the (r, c) plane on which relatively large number of points lie.

It should be noted that m $(= \tan \theta$, where θ is the angle that the line makes with r-axis) and b approaches infinity as the line approaches a vertical position. To avoid this problem we use the equation of the line in normal form given as

$$p = r \cos \theta + c \sin \theta \qquad (12.35)$$

and the parameter space is the (p, θ)-plane.

Second, Hough transform determines the parameters of the line and not its extent as shown in Fig. 12.11. We may incorporate this property by associating to each cell r_{min}, r_{max}, c_{min} and c_{max} based on the points contribute to that cell. While producing the line we use either $[r_{min}, c_{max}]$ or $[c_{min}, c_{max}]$ depending on the slope.

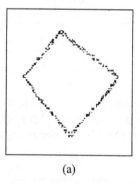
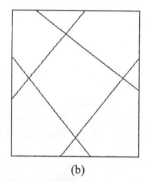

(a)   (b)

Fig. 12.11   An example of detection of lines from a given set of points by Hough transform: (a) given set of points and (b) lines corresponding to local maxima in the accumulator array. Note that lines drawn are extended to infinity.

Similar to lines other curves may also be detected. For example, to determine the circle that may pass through the given set of points we use the equation

$$R^2 = (r - \alpha)^2 + (c - \beta)^2 \qquad (12.36)$$

where parameter space is three-dimensional with α, β and R as its axes. Though the method is computationally expensive and requires large memory space, it is a very popular one because of its robustness in presence of noise.

12.6.2 Graph Searching

Let a collection of edgel representing a contour from a given point p to q. In case of a closed contour, both p and q are the same points. Representing the edge chain as a graph G with terminal nodes as p and q, the path between p and q could be through one or a set of nodes n_k for $k =$ 1, 2, ... Let $\Phi(n_k)$ be the *cost function* for the path from p to q passing through the intermediate node n_k. Therefore, in context of edge linking, for an edgel node n_i, the objective is to optimize the cost $\Phi(n_k)$ in order to decide the potential edgel at the immediate neighbourhood of n_i. A possible objective (or reciprocal of cost) function could be the maximization of overall edge gradient magnitude between two consecutive edgels. The algorithm terminates when all the intermediate nodes between p and q are searched and the optimum path or edge chain is established [Martelli (1972)]. Alternately, if q is not known, the search starts from p and $\Phi(n_k)$ is the cost function for the path from p to n_k. In this case, search technique picks up the minimum cost path and terminates when overall cost exceeds a predefined threshold. A set of linkage rules could be defined for an edgel with respect to its eight neighbours. Detail algorithms are given in Section 12.9 where we deal with a similar problem, i.e. detecting lines in graylevel image.

12.6.3 Local Analysis of Proximity

Two nearby (but not connected) pixels possessing similar edge properties may be joined together and thereby a long continuous contour can be formed. We consider two basic properties—gradient magnitude and edge direction. Thus, two edgels (r, c) and (r', c') would be joined if

(i) $d((r, c), (r', c')) < t_d$

(ii) $| g'(r, c) - g'(r', c') | < t_g$ and

(iii) $| \theta(r, c) - \theta(r', c') | < t_\theta$

where d denotes distance measure, and t_d, t_g and t_θ are three thresholds. The first condition assures the spatial proximity, second one gives their edge-likeness similarity and the third condition preserves smoothness of the contour by putting constraint on edge direction. These two pixels may be joined either (i) by simply generating a straight line connecting them or (ii) by establishing a minimum cost path between them using graph search method as described in Section 12.6.2. The method can be extended to connect short segments instead of individual pixels as discussed in Section 12.9.

12.6.4 Relaxation Labelling

A labelling problem can be solved by assigning a set of labels to a set of entities (or units) such that assigned labels are consistent subject to given constraints. Such labelling has many applications and includes the problem of graph matching (see Section 15.8) where labels are assigned to nodes of the graphs. Rosenfeld et al. (1976) have described an iterative scheme for computing consistent labels.

In relaxation labelling method too, gradient image is taken as input to locate edge along the ridges of chain of mountains. In this process the likelihood of a potential edgel is updated considering all the edgels in and around the candidate edgel [Zucker et al. (1977)]. Each edgel is classified into one of the $(m + 1)$ labels—the m different labels correspond to m different directions. The $(m + 1)$-th label correspond to a pixel without any edge. For a given problem, the parameter m could be typically 4 or 8. Also, each edgel has a confidence value assigned to it. This confidence value may be probability or fuzzy membership that the edge belongs to an edge. Accordingly, we call it *probabilistic-relaxation* or *fuzzy-relaxation* technique. As noted earlier, the process of relaxation labelling updates this confidence value iteratively with respect to the confidence values of its neighbours. Initially, this confidence value is assigned from the normalized edge strength (gradient) magnitude. One of the major problems of this approach is in defining a *compatibility function C(r, c)* that updates the confidence values. This is similar to linkage rules described in case of graph search based edge linking. In this case, compatibility means likelihood of edge direction for two consecutive edgels. A typical formulation of compatibility function for a particular problem is strictly domain dependent. This problem can partially be solved by means of artificial neural network technique [Basak et al. (1994)].

12.7 Edge Elements Extraction by Thresholding

Most of the edge detection techniques have two steps: (i) finding the rate of change of graylevels, i.e. the gradient of the image and (ii) extracting the edge elements where gradient exceeds a predefined threshold. In the previous sections, we have described methods for obtaining the gradient $g'(r, c)$. Now, we like to have an image whose value $e(r, c)$ at the pixel (r, c) is obtained as

$$e(r, c) = \begin{cases} 1 & \text{if } g'(r, c) > t(r, c) \\ 0 & \text{if } g'(r, c) \leq t(r, c) \end{cases} \tag{12.37}$$

So, $e(r, c)$ is a binary image where the image subset S_e contains only edge elements of $g(r, c)$. Here $t(r, c)$ is the threshold at the pixel (r, c) and can be found out using the relation:

$$t(r, c) = \Phi''_{th}(r, c, Q_p(r, c))$$

where $Q_p(r, c)$ denotes the set of features at pixel (r, c). Depending on the variables to determine $t(r, c)$, the threshold is called *global* (or space-invariant), *local* (or space-variant) and *dynamic*. In brief, the edge extraction technique then reduces the selection of threshold that transforms the gradient image onto the edge image, i.e.

$$T_{th}: \ g'(r, c) \rightarrow e(r, c)$$

The operator T_{th} satisfies the following two conditions:

1. T_{th} is not invertible since it is not one-one.

2. T_{th} can take any value $t(r, c)$ as threshold from the interval $[\min_{r, c}\{g'(r, c)\}, \max_{r, c} \{g'(r, c)\}]$.

The threshold that extracts edges between the regions can be found in three different ways:

1. If the shape of the ideal edge in the image is known (that means, the shape or type of the regions whose edges are to be extracted are known) a priori, then $t(r, c)$ can be chosen in an interactive way so that the subset S_e of edge image represents the nearest approach to the ideal edge.

2. If the threshold $t(r, c)$ (or simply, t) is known a priori, then the image subset S_e, obtained by the thresholding operation, gives the edges of the objects whatever they might be. This approach is used when the threshold is estimated based on a large number of training images with proper ground-truth.

3. If neither the shape of S_e nor the threshold $t(r, c)$ is known a priori, then the threshold is chosen such that S_e satisfies the following criteria:

$\{t_i, i = 1, 2, 3, \ldots, n_1\} \leftarrow$ A non-empty set of threshold values

$\{P_j, j = 1, 2, 3, \ldots, n_2\} \leftarrow$ A non-empty set of properties those an ideal edge should possess

$\varepsilon_{P_j}(t_i) \leftarrow$ An error function characterizing how loosely S_e satisfies the property P_j for the threshold t_i

$\varepsilon(t_i) \leftarrow$ Some convex combination of $\varepsilon_{P_1}(t_i), \varepsilon_{P_2}(t_i), \ldots, \varepsilon_{P_{n_2}}(t_i)$

Hence, t_o can be taken as optimum threshold if $\varepsilon(t_o) = \min_i \{\varepsilon(t_i)\}$ and the image subset S_e is accepted as an optimum edge. Usually, the measurement of error incorporates defects that occur in edges extracted by thresholding. Various types of errors introduced during edge extraction are shown in Fig. 12.12.

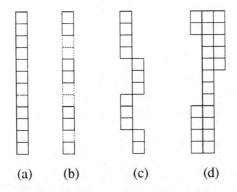

(a)   (b)   (c)   (d)

Fig. 12.12   Various types of defects that occur in extracted edges: (a) ideal, (b) fragmented, (c) offset, and (d) smeared.

12.8   Edge Detector Performance

For evaluating performance of an edge detector we need to study variation in its response due to variation in orientation and location of edge, edge type such as step or ramp or some other, and its noise sensitivity. For example, let us consider a model of step edge centred at pixel (r, c) as shown in Fig. 12.13. One side of the edge has graylevel E and the other side $E + e$.

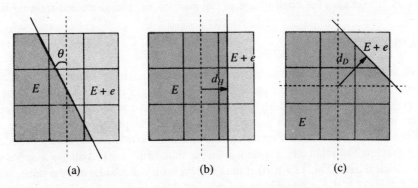

(a)   (b)   (c)

Fig. 12.13   Models of step edge used to evaluate edge-detector performance.

12.8.1 Edge Orientation Response

Suppose the edge is a straight line that makes an angle θ with the vertical ($c-$) axis. Figure 12.13(a) shows the model we use in the study. We need to compute gradient or slope $g'_\theta(r, c)$ for all possible values of θ at the centre of the model. For an ideal, or in other words, rotation-insensitive gradient, operator $g'_\theta(r, c)$ should be constant for all θ.

12.8.2 Edge Position Response

An important property of an edge detector is its ability to localize an edge. We investigate this property of the edge detector usually for two extreme cases—vertical (or horizontal) edge and (left or right) diagonal edge. Suppose the vertical edge is displaced from the centre by an amount d_H and the diagonal edge by d_D. Figures 12.13(b) and 12.13(c) show the models that are used to study this property. For an ideal edge finder, both $g'_{d_H}(r, c)$ and $g'_{d_D}(r, c)$ should fall sharply as magnitudes of d_H and d_D increase, respectively.

12.8.3 Noise Sensitivity

The three types of errors associated with edge detection are: (i) missing valid edge points (i.e. misdetection), (ii) classification of noise fluctuations as edge points (i.e. false alarm) and (iii) failure to localize edge points. Pratt (1991) has introduced a figure of merit defined as

$$R = \frac{1}{I_m} \sum_{i=1}^{I_a} \frac{1}{1 + wd^2} \qquad (12.38)$$

where

I_i = Number of ideal edge map points

I_a = Number of actual edge map points

I_m = $\max\{I_i, I_a\}$

w = Scaling constant, adjusted to penalize edge points that are detected but offset from true position

d = Separation distance of an actual edge point along a line normal to a line of ideal edge points

This measure is taken on the edge image in comparison to ground-truthed training image.

12.9 Line Detection

Line detection is an important step in image processing and analysis. Lines and edges are features in any scene, from simple indoor scenes to noisy terrain images taken by satellite. If the algorithm to detect these features is not properly designed then we have to introduce the intermediate step of line/edge completion in between feature extraction and interpretation, which serves to join the disrupted segments. To avoid this step an optimized feature extraction algorithm is necessary. For a line, the graylevel is relatively constant along a thin strip. There will be a spike-like cross-section in the ideal case [Fig. 12.14(a)] if the graylevels on either sides are the same, which looks like an uneven spike if the graylevels on either sides differ [Fig. 12.14(b)]. When combined with noise and blurring, the cross-section may look like a roof in one dimension [Fig. 12.14(c)].

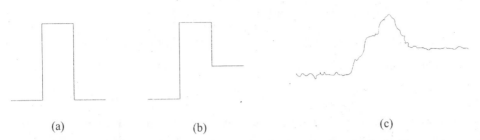

(a)   (b)   (c)

Fig. 12.14 Cross-section of (a) an ideal line, (b) a line when graylevel on the both sides are not equal and (c) a noisy line.

12.9.1 An Overview of Early Works

Most of the earlier methods for detecting lines were based on pattern matching. The patterns directly followed from the definition of a line. These pattern templates are designed with suitable coefficients and are applied at each point in an image. A set of such templates is shown in Fig. 12.15. A line pixel is deemed to be present if the absolute value of response of one of the templates exceeds a threshold. These linear operators have the serious shortcoming that they also respond, although weakly, at points near a line and edge-like patterns. To overcome this drawback, non-linear operators have been introduced [Rosenfeld and Kak (1982)]. A non-linear operator for vertical lines is defined as

$-\dfrac{1}{2}$	1	$-\dfrac{1}{2}$
$-\dfrac{1}{2}$	1	$-\dfrac{1}{2}$
$-\dfrac{1}{2}$	1	$-\dfrac{1}{2}$

$\dfrac{1}{2}$	$\dfrac{1}{2}$	$\dfrac{1}{2}$
1	1	1
$-\dfrac{1}{2}$	$-\dfrac{1}{2}$	$-\dfrac{1}{2}$

1	$-\dfrac{1}{2}$	$-\dfrac{1}{2}$
$-\dfrac{1}{2}$	1	$-\dfrac{1}{2}$
$-\dfrac{1}{2}$	$-\dfrac{1}{2}$	1

$-\dfrac{1}{2}$	$-\dfrac{1}{2}$	1
$-\dfrac{1}{2}$	1	$-\dfrac{1}{2}$
1	$-\dfrac{1}{2}$	$-\dfrac{1}{2}$

     (a)   (b)   (c)   (d)

Fig. 12.15 Templates for line detection: (a) vertical line, (b) horizontal line, (c) left-diagonal line and (d) right-diagonal line.

$$h_v = g(r, c + 1) + g(r, c) + g(r, c - 1) - \frac{1}{2}\{g(r - 1, c + 1) + g(r - 1, c) \quad (12.39)$$

$$+ g(r - 1, c - 1) + g(r + 1, c + 1) + g(r + 1, c) + g(r + 1, c - 1)\}$$

if the following conditions are satisfied:

$$g(r, c + 1) > g(r - 1, c + 1), g(r, c + 1) > g(r + 1, c + 1),$$

$$g(r, c) > g(r - 1, c), g(r, c) > g(r + 1, c),$$

$$g(r, c - 1) > g(r - 1, c - 1), \text{ and } g(r, c - 1) > g(r + 1, c - 1)$$

Otherwise, $h_v = 0$.

Similar operators are defined for the other directions. These non-linear operators do not respond to patterns other than lines. However, lines are detected only if they are very clear. To overcome this sensitivity problem, some semi-linear operators have been designed. For example, a semi-linear operator for bright vertical lines may be defined as

$$h_v = \{g(r, c + 1) + g(r, c) + g(r, c - 1)\} - \frac{1}{2}\{g(r - 1, c + 1) + g(r - 1, c)$$

$$+ g(r - 1, c - 1) + g(r + 1, c + 1) + g(r + 1, c) + g(r + 1, c - 1)\} \quad (12.40)$$

if the following conditions are satisfied:

$$g(r - 1, c + 1) + g(r, c + 1) + g(r + 1, c + 1) < g(r, c) + g(r - 1, c) + g(r + 1, c),$$

$$g(r - 1, c - 1) + g(r, c - 1) + g(r + 1, c - 1) < g(r, c) + g(r - 1, c) + g(r + 1, c)$$

Otherwise, $h_v = 0$. This is also not perfect in the presence of noise and responds to patterns other than lines. Results of line detection operators are shown in Fig. 12.16.

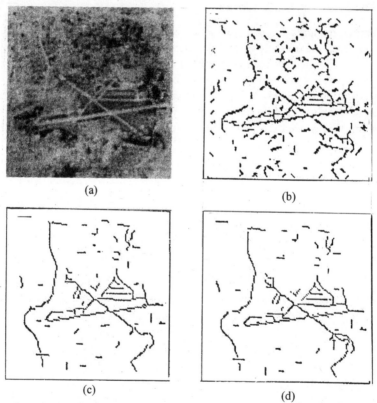

(a)

(b)

(c)

(d)

Fig. 12.16 Results of line detection operators: (a) original image, and results due to (b) linear, (c) non-linear, and (d) semi-linear operators.

A set of four performance goals for extraction of lines in graylevel image by tracking has been formulated by Fischler et al. (1981):

1. No point on a track should be outside the line when the feature is clearly visible.

2. The track should be smooth when the feature is straight or smoothly curved.

3. If a linear feature is partly occluded, the portions of the continuous track should be labelled identically.

4. In areas where a linear feature is partly occluded, the track should follow the actual centre of the feature.

To detect continuous lines some assumptions are usually made. For example:

1. The width of a line does not exceed three pixels.

2. Not more than $p\%$ of a line being tracked is occluded by other objects.

3. The contrast between a line and its background exceeds a given and constant threshold value.

4. We detect only one type of line (bright or dark) at a time.

Disadvantages of conventional methods

The line segments in an image may not be fully extracted using conventional methods. The linear features can be detected from another angle by merit of a confidence measure.

When linear features are extracted using a conventional method, the presence of a line is stated with a confidence measure 'C' equal to 1. Suppose we use the operator h_v [Equation (12.39)], then the presence of a line is confirmed only if all the six neighbours as shown in Fig. 12.17(a) have intensity values less (or greater) than that of the candidate pixel. Once this condition is satisfied, we can state that the a's form a line segment with confidence measure equal to 1. However, this procedure causes the following problems:

1. Consider a curve, as shown in Fig. 12.17(b), with only two pixels in the curvature part. Here only the horizontal line segment will be detected and neither the right curve nor the vertical segment of the line will be judged as being part of a continuous line. Had the vertical line been longer it would have been detected—but the curved part will never appear in the result, thus disconnecting different parts of a continuous line.

2. The second problem is encountered when an image is corrupted by noise, see Fig. 12.17(c). When the h_v operator is applied to this image, it will not detect this line since the gray value of all the six neighbours are not strictly less (or greater) than that of the candidate pixel. In this case the vertical line segment of length more than three pixels (including pixels above and below) will be lost. Hence, discontinuities in the linear features may occur at many places.

The first problem stated above can be overcome by testing and marking only two pixels at a time rather than three (which again may give rise to many small spurious line segments all over the image and these have to be dealt with separately). A solution to the second problem requires a somewhat more complicated procedure.

```
        1  1  1
 b  a  b                    b  a  c
                 1
 b  a  b                    b  a  b
                 1
 b  a  b                    c  a  b
        1  1  1

   (a)          (b)            (c)
```

Fig. 12.17   (a) Line pixels (where $a < b$ or $a > b$) that can be detected by linear, semi-linear and non-linear operators, (b) a curved line with two pixel on the curved part that cannot be detected by a conventional operator of size 3×3 or more, (c) a line that cannot be detected by a non-linear operator.

A possible solution

The above problems are due to the fact that a line is accepted only if the corresponding confidence measure is 1. By accepting features with a smaller confidence as well, the discontinuity can be removed to a certain extent. In this context, the use of confidence has the following advantages over the use of mask responses:

1. We need not know the actual gray values in the image, and some confidence threshold can be fixed depending on the strength (e.g. weak or strong or moderate) of line we intend to extract.

2. When the image has lines with widely varying contrasts from the background, their responses to the detection operators vary considerably. This excludes using only one threshold. Multiple thresholds can be used, but the selection of a suitable threshold for the line being examined involves the evaluation of other local characteristics.

3. As already mentioned, the use of a confidence measure may lead to a good detection of lines in the presence of noise.

We may employ search techniques for tracking line segments of varying contrast in noisy images. Basic idea of graph searching technique for this kind of problem is given in Section 12.6.2. To this end, a best-first search and a depth-first search techniques are used.

12.9.2 Confidence Measure

We use four masks in order to compute the confidence measure at every line segment consisting of a pair of neighbouring pixels. These masks are shown in Fig. 12.18. Suppose that we are interested in detecting bright (higher gray values) lines consisting of the pixels marked by 'a' in the figure at this moment, and that the numbers of pixels b and c that satisfy the conditions

$$[a - b] > th \quad \text{and} \quad [a - c] > th$$

are n_1 and n_2, respectively; where th stands for threshold. A confidence measure based on these numbers should attend a value 1 if $n_1 = n_2 = 6$, and 0 if $n_1 = n_2 = 0$. The confidence measure should increase monotonically with n_1 and n_2. Two examples of such function are given below:

$$C = \frac{1}{12}\sqrt{2 \times (n_1 + n_2) \times \min(n_1, n_2)}$$

and

$$C = \frac{1}{6}\sqrt{n_1 \times n_2}$$

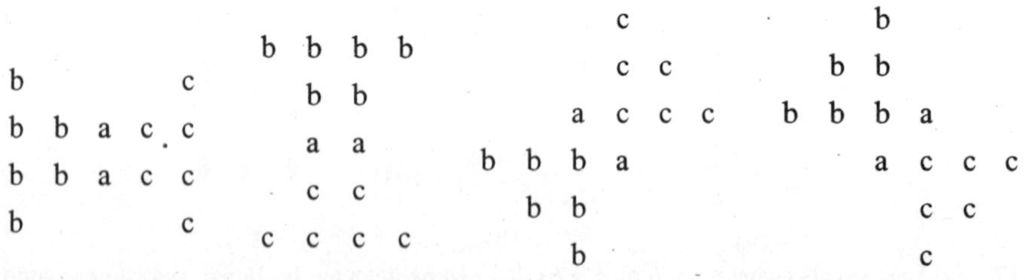

Fig. 12.18 Neighbourhood to be considered to compute the confidence of a line segment: a = line pixel; b, c = neighbors to be considered: (a) vertical line, (b) horizontal line, (c) left-diagonal line and (d) right-diagonal line.

12.9.3 Search Methods

For detecting lines, either of the above mentioned confidence measure functions may be selected. The selected function is used to compute the confidence at every line segment consisting of two adjacent pixels. The computed confidence values thus form a matrix of size equal to that of the input image. Each element of this matrix is a vector with 4 elements, each of which represents the confidence that a line two pixels long—is present in one of the 4 different directions. So, the matrix may be viewed as a graph with weighted edges and each pixel represents a node of the graph. Now a search[2] is conducted through this matrix. However, the search algorithms need a slightly different interpretation in the present context. In the matrix, each node (element or pixel) that has a confidence value greater than a given threshold can be considered to be root node; the search can be initiated at all such nodes. Next, there is no specific goal node. The search through the entire matrix is continued until the average accumulated confidence falls below a threshold value. Thus the criterion for expanding one of the children of the root node is that the confidence in that direction is greater than the threshold, and that for expanding children of an intermediate node is that the average composite confidence accumulated so far should be greater than the threshold minus a tolerance. The average confidence is equivalent to the reciprocal of average cost per unit length incurred so far. For the 'depth-first' search, the number of alternatives is constrained by considering only those nodes which have a confidence measure greater than a second threshold. The advantage of a depth-first search becomes clear when the confidences at a given pixel in more than one direction exceed the threshold. In such cases, the 'best-first' search goes into the direction corresponding to the greatest confidence, whereas the depth-first technique searches along all those directions. As a consequence, the bifurcation of lines can be detected easily by the depth-first search. An example that how search proceeds through pixels is shown in Fig. 12.19.

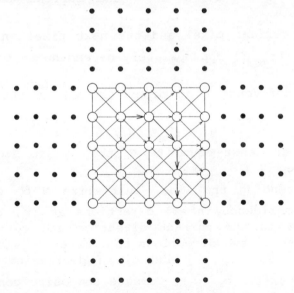

Fig. 12.19 Illustrates the progress of search through pixels marked by 'O'. '●' is the root node and thin lines are links connecting a node with its children. Thick lines represent path along which the search proceeds (i.e. the extracted line segment).

[2]Details on search techniques can be found in Chapter 15.

Detailed algorithms are presented below. Before presenting the algorithms let us define the following terms:

Parameters to be supplied. C_m = minimum confidence required at a point, L = minimum length of a line segment, C_t = tolerance for confidence, M_c = minimum contrast for line with respect to the background and E = maximum extension of the line allowed.

Important variables. D indicates direction currently being tracked/searched. Value of D is assumed 1 for vertical, 2 for horizontal, 3 for left diagonal and 4 for right diagonal direction. N is number of pixels by which line can be extended.

Algorithm 12.1 (using the depth-first search)

Step 1: Fix values of M_c, C_m, C_t, L and E.

Step 2: Initialize $r \leftarrow$ starting row and $c \leftarrow$ starting column.

Step 3: If gray value at (r, c) is greater than M_c go to Step 4 else go to Step 9.

Step 4: Compute confidence in all four directions at that point. Initialize $D \leftarrow 1$.

Step 5: If confidence in current direction is at least C_m then go to Step 6 else go to Step 8.

Step 6: Start tracking the line in direction D as follows:

6(a): Initialize $r' \leftarrow r$, $c' \leftarrow c$ and current length of line $L' \leftarrow 0$.

6(b): Mark the current pixel and the next pixel in direction D.

6(c): Increment (r', c') appropriately depending on D and increment length L'.

6(d): Compute confidence C at point (r', c') in the direction D. Update C_c as

$$C_c = (L' \times C_c + C)/(L' + 1)$$

If C_c is at least equal to C_m then go to Step 6 (b) else go to Step 7.

Step 7: Start extending the line. Initialize N to zero.

7(a): Compute confidence in all directions at (r', c'). Let c_1 is confidence in the current direction and c_2 and c_3 be the confidences in two directions that make 45° with the current direction. Sort c_1, c_2 and c_3 in decreasing order.

7(b): Set $C \leftarrow \max\{c_1, c_2, c_3\}$. Compute composite confidence C_c as

$$C_c = (L' \times C_c + C)/(L' + 1)$$

7(c): If $C_c \geq (C_m - C_t)$ and $N \leq E$ then mark the pixels and increment N. Increment r' and c' appropriately and go to Step 7 (a). If C_c does not satisfy the condition or if $N > E$ or if $C \geq C_m$ then go to Step 7 (d).

7(d): If $C \geq C_m$ then keep the last point marked or else erase it and repeat steps from 7(a) in the other two directions till all the directions for all the points have been covered.

Step 8: Set $D \leftarrow D + 1$. If $D \leq 4$ go to Step 5 else go to Step 9.

Step 9: Increment (r, c). If all the points are not covered go to Step 3 else stop.

Algorithm 12.2 (using the breadth-first search)

Step 1: Fix values of M_c, C_m, L.

Step 2: Initialize $r \leftarrow$ starting row and $c \leftarrow$ starting column.

Step 3: If gray value at (r, c) is greater than M_c go to Step 4 else go to Step 9.

Step 4: Compute confidence in all the four directions at the point (r, c) Initialize $D \leftarrow 1$.

Step 5: If the confidence in current direction D is at least C_m and the current direction at this point has not been explored then go to Step 6, else go to Step 8.

Step 6: Start searching the line as follows:

6(a): Initialize $r' \leftarrow r$, $c' \leftarrow c$, length of the line $L' \leftarrow 0$, direction $D_t \leftarrow D$ and composite confidence $C_c \leftarrow C$, where C is the confidence at (r, c) in current direction D_t.

6(b): Mark this pixel and the next one in direction D_t.

6(c): Set flag of (r', c') in current direction to TRUE and $L' \leftarrow L' + 1$. Increment (r', c') in the current direction.

6(d): Compute confidence in all directions at (r', c'). Let $c_1 = $ confidence in current direction, and c_2 and $c_3 = $ confidences in directions that make $45°$ with current direction D

6(e): Set $C \leftarrow \max\{c_1, c_2, c_3\}$. Compute composite confidence C_c as

$$C_c = (L' \times C_c + C) / (L' + 1)$$

6(f): If C_c is at least equal to C_m then set $D_t \leftarrow$ direction with confidence C and go to Step 6b.

Step 7: If $L' < L$ then unmark all pixels marked in Step 6.

Step 8: Set $D \leftarrow D + 1$. If $D \leq 4$ go to Step 5.

Step 9: Increment (r, c). If all pixels are not covered go to Step 3 else terminate.

The first algorithm employs a simple tracking technique followed by the depth-first search. The starting points for the lines are ones where confidence value in that particular direction is at least equal to the threshold. The line is tracked as long as the accumulated confidence (composite confidence) is greater than or equal to a threshold. If the line cannot be tracked any further, the depth-first search is initiated at that point. All the points starting from the end point are searched for the presence of line segment (if any) in a depth-first manner so that the line already found can be continued. If the search is successful the extended points are accepted or else they are rejected. The best-first search discussed above can effectively be used to obtain the lines in the images satisfying user-specified parameters like confidence and length.

In the list processing technique, emphasis is laid not only on further simplification in parameter selection, but also on the reduction of search space. The idea behind this method is that, if a reasonable number of segments of the linear feature can be found in the image, they can be joined using suitable method. For joining the line segments a higher level representation of these segments based on their characteristics is used. The characteristics of each line include the starting and the end points, slope and direction of the line at the beginning and at the end, are stored in the form of a record. A list of all the segments is maintained.

Any pair of line segments are joined if they satisfy two conditions, viz., spatial proximity and edge proximity. The two lines can be spatially proximate if out of the four end points distance between any two be less than some threshold. Secondly, more than one line segments can be proximate to a given segment. Proper care must be taken to check all the possibilities. Joining two lines, which satisfy both the proximity conditions, by a straight line is simple but not always acceptable. Instead, an optimal path is found between them for which the principle of A* algorithm is used.

Algorithm 12.3 (using the list processing)

Step 1: Find the line segments using the best-first search, with simple parameters. Obtain the output as a binary image.

Step 2: Extend the line by a few pixels (say, a fixed percentage of the line length) at both ends in the direction last taken by the line at that end. If any non-zero pixel is encountered during extension then leave the marked pixels or else erase them. This procedure will help in filling small gaps in the line as well as will possibly join the branches.

Step 3: Examine the lines in the resultant image and form a list of characteristics of the lines. Each element in the list contains various details of the line as already explained in the previous section.

Step 4: Until all the lines in the list covered, peak one line at a time and repeat Steps 5 and 6.

Step 5: For each line in the list check the spatial proximity and angular proximity with respect to the current line. If both the conditions are satisfied then go to Step 6 else go to Step 4.

Step 6: Join two lines as follows:

6(a): Compute the confidence and response in all the eight directions from the end point of the current line.

6(b):   Award score to each of the directions depending on confidence and response.

6(c):   Compute distance of each pixel to the end point of the other line. Award score to each direction so that higher score is assigned to the direction with smaller distance. This helps in guiding the path towards the goal, so that the path does not deviate greatly from the correct direction.

6(d):   Mark the pixel in the direction with maximum total score obtained as the sum of those assigned in Steps 6(b) and 6(c).

6(e):   Repeat the Steps from 6(a) to 6(d) until the other end point is reached or a maximum limit on the number of points in the path is reached. If the goal is not reached erase the marked pixels or else retain the markings.

Results of the said algorithms are shown in Fig. 12.20. The method can also be used for edge tracking or edge following.

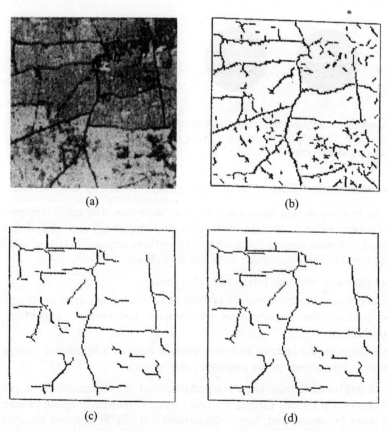

(a)   (b)

(c)   (d)

Fig. 12.20   Results of line detection by search techniques: (a) original image, and results due to (b) Algorithm 1, (c) Algorithm 2 and (d) Algorithm 3.

12.10   Corner Detection

A corner provides another major shape feature used in object matching and registration. Thus corner detection is an important step in many image analysis and object recognition procedure. Simply speaking, a corner is an image point with high contrast along all the directions. That means all the corner points are also edge points. This directional contrast is measured with respect to a symmetric neighbourhood centred around the concerned pixel. Figure 12.21 shows some examples of corners. This simple intuitive definition of corner suggests that corner detector can be designed using compass operator (see Section 12.3.1) except 'min' should be considered instead of 'max'. According to this operator, except in Fig. 12.21(a) all other centre points are corner points. However, response of this operator is same for all the corner points shown in Figs. 12.21(b), 12.21(c) and 12.21(d); though sharpness at the centre point of Figs. 12.21(c) and 12.21(d) are much more than that of Fig. 12.21(b). This problem may be surmounted by considering the area of the regions distinguished by their graylevels as shown in the figure. The corner-detection techniques can be classified into two major groups:

1. Curvature- or contour-based techniques
2. Operator-based techniques

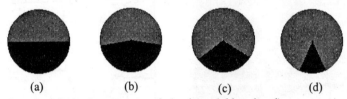

(a)   (b)   (c)   (d)

Fig. 12.21   Examples of corner points (centres of circular neighbourhood):
Note that all are edge points too. (a) not a corner point, (b) weak corner, (c) sharp corner, (d) very sharp corner.

12.10.1   Contour-based Corner Detection

This is more or less the earliest approach for corner detection. The method relies on extraction of contours of regions either (i) straightway by edge detection or (ii) by segmenting the image into regions followed by border finding.[3] A good survey on these techniques is available in Rutkowski and Rosenfeld (1977). The algorithmic steps are as follows:

1. Extract contours from the image and label them.
2. For each contour, traverse along the contour and at each point, compute slope (or curvature) of the contour. For discrete case, we compute k-slope (or k-curvature) as given in Section 13.4.4.
3. Label a point on the contour as corner point if there is a significant change in slope (or curvature) with respect to the previous point visited.

Performance of this method, thus, largely depends on that of contour extraction process. Hence, the approach observes a limited success for noisy images. However, abrupt change in slope (or curvature) of possible contour and, hence, the corners can also be detected straightway from the intensity image using facet model [Zuniga and Haralick (1983)].

---

[3]Detail of border or boundary extraction is given in Chapter 13.

12.10.2 Operator-based Corner Detection

The operators are designed, based on the pattern of the neighbourhood of corner points. For example, for detecting top-right corner of binary object we can apply binary hit-and-miss transform with the structuring elements as shown in Fig. 12.22.

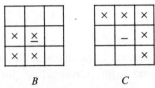

B   C

Fig. 12.22 Structuring elements for detecting top-right corner by hit-and-miss transform.

Designing operator for detecting corners in graylevel image gets complicated due to variation in its contrast, sharpness and orientation. However, the intuitive definition of corner, as given in the literature, leads to the following measure of *strength of cornerty*.

Let us consider a line passing through the pixel (r, c) at which the strength of cornerty is being measured. Suppose the line intersects the boundary of a circular neighbourhood (or window) of (r, c) at $(r + m, c + n)$ and $(r - m, c - n)$, respectively (see Fig. 12.23). Thus, the corner response function can be defined as [Trajkovic and Hedley (1998)]:

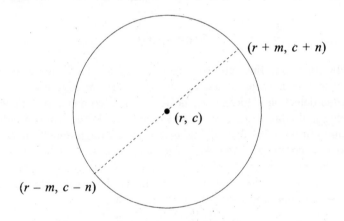

Fig. 12.23 Neighbourhood for computing corner response.

$$c_R(r, c) = \min_{m, n} \left[\{g(r, c) - g(r + m, c + n)\}^2 + \{g(r, c) - g(r - m, c - n)\}^2 \right] \quad (12.41)$$

This is the minimum contrast along any direction at (r, c). Equation (12.41) is similar to minimum of response due to compass operator [Chanda et al. (1985)]. Suppose $\bar{g}_w(r, c)$ is the average graylevel of pixels within the neighbourhood centred at (r, c). Let us count the number of pixels with graylevels less than $\bar{g}_w(r, c)$ and that greater than or equal to $\bar{g}_w(r, c)$. Suppose these numbers are A_d and A_b, respectively. Then sharpness of corner at (r, c) may be given by

$$c_S(r, c) = \frac{|A_d - A_b|}{A_d + A_b} \quad (12.42)$$

For a straight edge $c_S(r, c) = 0$ and it increases with sharpness of the corner. For example, c_S for Fig. 12.21(d) is greater than c_S for Fig. 12.21(c) which is again greater than that for Fig. 12.21(b). The measure c_S may be made robust to noise by discarding $p/2$ percentile pixels with higher and lower graylevels during computation of $\overline{g}_w(r, c)$ and A_d and A_b, where $p\%$ noise is present in the image. Finally, the *strength of cornerty* is given by

$$S_c(r, c) = c_R(r, c) * c_S(r, c) \tag{12.43}$$

A pixel (r, c) is labelled as corner point if $S_c(r, c)$ exceeds a predefined threshold. Since, this procedure gives reasonably high response at points near the actual corner points, it is desired to perform non-maximum suppression before thresholding. Result of this approach is shown in Fig. 12.24.

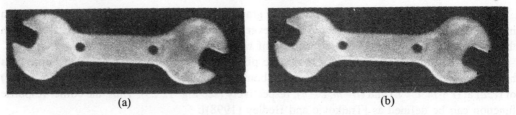

(a)   (b)

Fig. 12.24 Result of corner detection: (a) original image and (b) detected corners.

Summary

Linear features like edges and lines are important information for image analysis and computer vision. In this chapter, we have presented various techniques of edge and line detection. Major steps of a good edge detection algorithm are noise cleaning, computation of edge strength, edge linking or following and edge extraction. Edge strength can be determined either by derivative operator or by pattern fitting. For edge linking methods like Hough transform, relaxation labelling and graph searching are commonly used. And edge extraction can be done by simple thresholding. We use search techniques for edge following and line detection. Properties of a good edge detector and method to evaluate them are described. Finally, detection of corner, another important feature for image registration and recognition, are presented.

Problems

1. Prove that gradient of image intensity due to Prewitt operator along horizontal direction can be obtained by convolving the image by $[1 \ \ 1 \ \ 1]$ followed by $[-1 \ \ 0 \ \ 1]^T$ and then scaling the result by 1/3.

2. Prove that the gradient of an image intensity due to Sobel operator along horizontal direction can be obtained by convolving the image by $[1 \ \ 1]$ followed by $[1 \ \ 1]$ followed by $[-1 \ \ 0 \ \ 1]^T$ and then scaling the result by 1/4.

3. Derive an expression of gradient in terms of pixel graylevels using the best-plane fit approach.

4. Prove the following:

(a) The bpf gradient in root-sum-square (rss) sense is the same as Roberts' gradient in root-mean-square (rms) sense.

(b) The bpf gradient in sum of magnitude sense is the same as Roberts' gradient in maximum sense.

(c) The bpf gradient in maximum sense is the same as Roberts' gradient in average magnitude sense.

(d) The bpf gradient in rss sense is the same as $1/\sqrt{2}$ times Prewitt's gradient in rms sense.

(e) The bpf gradient in sum of magnitude sense is the same as Prewitt's gradient in average magnitude sense.

(f) The bpf gradient in maximum sense is the same as 1/2 times Prewitt's gradient in maximum sense.

(g) The bpf gradient of weighted graylevels in rss sense is the same as $2\sqrt{2}/3$ times Sobel's gradient in rms sense.

(h) The bpf gradient of weighted graylevels in sum of magnitude sense is the same as 4/3 times Sobel's gradient in average magnitude sense.

(i) The bpf gradient of weighted graylevels in maximum sense is the same as 2/3 times Sobel's gradient in maximum sense.

5. Take an image containing only an octagon at the centre. Suppose the graylevel of the octagon is 50 and that of background is 200. Add zero mean symmetric noise having a range [−100, 100] to it. Then compute the edge strength as dilation minus erosion with a 3×3 structuring element.

6. Suggest a way to determine the extent of line segment whose parameters are estimated through Hough transform. Extract edge pixels by thresholding the gradient obtained in Problem 5. Use Hough transform to obtain close contour of the octagon.

7. State the problems associated with Hough transform when slope-intercept form of equation of straight line is considered. Why is the problem reduced when normal form is considered?

8. Using graph search technique extract the close contour in the gradient image obtained in Problem 5.

9. Apply various line detection algorithms on the gradient image obtained in Problem 5 to extract close contour. Compare the performance of different algorithms.

10. Take an image containing a polygonal object with many concave as well as convex corners. Compute a new image by taking close minus open with a circular structuring element. Check how many corners are correctly detected. Explain the reason of failures, if any.

Bibliography

Basak, J., Chanda, B. and Dutta Majumder, D., 'On edge and line linking with connectionist models', *IEEE Trans. on Systems, Man and Cybern.*, SMC-**24**:413–428, 1994.

Canny, J., 'A computational approach to edge detection', *IEEE Trans. on Patt. Anal. and Mach. Intell.*, PAMI-**8**:679–698, 1986.

Chanda, B., Chaudhuri, B.B. and Dutta Majumder, D., 'A differentiation/enhancement edge detector and its properties', *IEEE Trans. on System, Man and Cybern.,* SMC-**15**:162–168, 1985.

Chanda, B., Kundu, M.K. and Padmaja, Y.V., 'A multi-scale morphologic edge detector', *Pattern Recognition,* **31**:1469–1478, 1998.

Chaudhuri, B.B. and Chanda, B., 'The equivalence of best plane fit gradient with Roberts', Prewitt's and Sobel's gradient for edge detection and a 4-neighbour gradient with useful properties', *Signal Processing,* **6**:143–151, 1984.

Duda, R.O. and Hart, P.E., *Pattern Classification and Scene Analysis,* Wiley-Interscience, New York, 1973.

Faugeras, O., *Three-dimensional Computer Vision: A Geometric Viewpoint,* MIT Press, Cambridge, 1993.

Fischler, M.A., Tenenbaum, J.M. and Wolf, H.C., 'Detection of roads and linear structures in low-resolution aerial imagery using multisource knowledge integration technique', *Computer Vision, Graphics and Image Processing,* **15**:201–223, 1981.

Haralick, R.M. and Shapiro, L.G., *Computer and Robot Vision,* Vols. 1 and 2. Addison-Wesley, Reading, Massachusetts, 1992.

Hough, P.V.C., 'Methods and means for recognizing complex patterns', *U.S. Patent,* 3069654, 1962.

Hueckel, M., 'An operator which locates edges in digitized pictures', *J. Assoc. Comput.,* **18**: 113–125, 1971.

Koundinya, K.N.V.L.N. and Chanda, B., 'Detecting lines in graylevel images using search techniques', *Signal Processing,* **37**:287–299, 1994.

Koundinya, K.N.V.L.N. and Chanda, B., 'On detection of lines using search techniques and list processing', *Int. J. Syst. Sc.,* **26**:1053–1077, 1995.

Lee, J.S.J., Haralick, R.M. and Shapiro, L.G., 'Morphologic edge detection', *IEEE Trans. on Robotics Automat.,* **3**:140–156, 1987.

Marr, D.C. and Hildreth, E., 'Theory of edge detection', *Proc. Royal Soc. Lond.,* **B**:187–217, 1980.

Martelli, A. 'Edge detection using heuristic search method', *Computer Graphics and Image Processing,* **1**:169–182, 1972.

Pratt, W.K., *Digital Image Processing,* 2nd ed., Wiley-Interscience, New York, 1991.

Prewitt, J.M.S., 'Object enhancement and extraction', in Lipkina, B.S. and Rosenfeld, A. (Eds), *Picture Processing and Psychopictorics,* Academic Press, New York, 1970.

Roberts, L.G., 'Machine perception of three dimensional solids', in Tippet, J.T. (Ed)., *Optical and Electro-optical Information Processing,* MIT Press, Cambridge, Massachusetts, 1965.

Rosenfeld, A., Hummel, R.A. and Zucker, S.W., 'Scence labelling by relaxation operations', *IEEE Trans. on System, Man and Cybern.,* **6**: 420–433, 1976.

Rosenfeld, A. and Kak, A.C., *Digital Picture Processing,* 2nd ed., Vols. 1 and 2, Academic Press, New York, 1982.

Rutkowski, W.S. and Rosenfeld, A., 'A comparison of corner detection techniques for chain-coded curves', *Technical Report* 623, Computer Science Center, University of Maryland, 1977.

Trajkovic, M. and Hedley, M., 'Fast corner detection', *Image and Vision Computing*, **16**:75–87, 1998.

Zucker, S.W., Hummel, R. and Rosenfeld, A., 'An application of relaxation labelling to line and curve enhancement', *IEEE Trans. on Computer*, C-**26**:394–403, 1977.

Zuniga, O. and Haralick, R.M., 'Corner detection using facet model', in *Proc. IEEE Conf. on CVPR*, pp. 30–37, IEEE Press, 1983.

Chapter 13

Feature Extraction

13.1 Introduction

In a scene analysis or any visual pattern recognition problem, the camera takes a picture of the scene and passes the picture to a *feature extractor*, whose purpose is data reduction by measuring certain *features* or properties that distinguish objects or their parts. Feature extraction, usually, is associated with another method called *feature selection* detailed analysis of which is beyond the scope of this chapter. The *pattern space* is, in general, a space of high dimensionality. The objective of the feature selection and extraction techniques is to reduce this dimensionality. During this process, only the salient features necessary for the recognition are retained. As a result, classification methodologies can be implemented in a space with vastly reduced dimension and, consequently, need reasonable time.

In the previous chapter, we have seen that segmentation techniques divide an image into a set of meaningful regions each of which is either an object or a part of an object. To generate the description of the scene or for image understanding, we usually need to recognize each of these regions. One of the prerequisites of identification and recognition is *feature extraction*. By the term *feature extraction* we mean determining various attributes as well as properties associated with a region or object. Suppose a segmentation technique divides image domain $\mathcal{D}$ into n regions $R_1, R_2,..., R_n$. Note that (i) R_i is a set of connected pixels, (ii) R_i and R_j are disjoint for all i and j and (iii) the union of all R_i covers the entire image domain. Let us consider two sets R and S. The elements of first set are R_is and the second set is a union of elements of a proper subset of the first one, i.e.

$$R = \{R_1, R_2,..., R_n\} \tag{13.1}$$

$$S = S_1 \cup S_2 \cup \cdots \cup S_m \tag{13.2}$$

where $m < n$ and for each i there exists a j such that $S_i = R_j$. Therefore,

1. S is a set of pixels and need not be connected
2. The *complement* of S, denoted by S^c, is defined as

$$S^c = \left(\bigcup_{R_i \in R} R_i \right) / S = \mathcal{D} / S$$

Let us call the process of defining S over $\mathcal{D}$ via R as *image abstraction*. Feature extraction methodologies, mainly, operate on abstracted image information obtained through segmentation. Applicability of a feature extraction methodology depends on how abstracted information is represented. Finally, it should be noted that objective of feature extraction is to represent an object in a compact way that facilitates image analysis task in terms of algorithmic simplicity and computational efficiency. Therefore, representing object in terms of its features differs from the representation schemes we have discussed in Chapter 8, because we are no longer interested in reconstructing the image or object from the representation.

13.2 Representation

The simplest way of representing the abstracted image information is by a two-dimensional *indicator function* whose size is same as that of the original input image. Let us denote the indicator function of S by $b_S(r, c)$ and define it as

$$b_S(r, c) = \begin{cases} 1 & (r, c) \in S \\ 0 & \text{otherwise} \end{cases} \tag{13.3}$$

Thus $b_S(r, c)$ is a binary image where 1-pixels (or the pixels belonging to S) constitute foreground or objects of interest and 0-pixels constitute the background. (We may visually distinguish foreground from background in 3D scene as the former is closer and better organized than the latter.) For brevity, sometimes we may drop the subscript S and denote the abstracted image simply by $b(r, c)$. It can be readily seen that abstracted and segmented images are same when number of region types is two. S is also called *domain of support* and is defined as

$$S = \{(r, c) \mid b_S(r, c) = 1\} \tag{13.4}$$

It should be noted that Equations (13.3) and (13.4) define indicator function and digital objects in terms of the other. Secondly, equivalence of Equations (13.2) and (13.4) is established by means of Equation (13.3). Once the objects are represented this way, value of pixels of the binary image (i.e. indicator function) $b_S(r, c)$ no longer remains important and only (relative) positions of pixels get involved in the subsequent processing. However, for simplicity in presenting the algorithms later we continue with these values.

Some other methods of representing the abstracted image information are by (i) run-length code, (ii) maximal block, (iii) binary tree, (iv) quad tree, (v) contour code, etc., as described in Chapter 8. It becomes sometimes necessary to have methods to convert one form of representation to another. Usually, it is sufficient to have methods that convert a representation to and from indicator function. For example, representing S by chain code or crack code of its contour is facilitated by detection of boundary of S.

13.2.1 Boundary

Boundary of an object may be an *interior boundary* or an *exterior boundary*. Interior boundary consists of pixels that belong to the object(s) itself and pixels of exterior boundary belong to the background (S^c). That means the exterior boundary of an object is same as the interior boundary of the background. In the following discussion, by the term *boundary* we mean interior boundary. Secondly, boundary can be 4-connected or 8-connected depending on the connectivity of the object. Thus the boundary of S, denoted by S', may be obtained as

$$S' = S/S \ominus K \tag{13.5}$$

where K is a binary structuring element as shown in Fig. 13.1(a) for 8-connected boundary and in Fig. 13.1(b) for 4-connected boundary. Similarly, indicator function $b_{S'}(r, c)$ of S' may be obtained from $b_S(r, c)$ as

for 4-connectivity:

$$b_{S'}(r, c) = b_S(r, c) \wedge \neg\ [(b_S(r-1, c-1) \wedge b_S(r-1, c) \wedge b_S(r-1, c+1)$$
$$\wedge\ b_S(r, c-1) \wedge b_S(r, c+1) \wedge b_S(r+1, c-1) \wedge b_S(r+1, c) \wedge b_S(r+1, c+1)] \quad (13.6)$$

for 8-connectivity:

$$b_{S'}(r, c) = b_S(r, c) \wedge \neg\ [b_S(r-1, c) \wedge b_S(r, c-1) \wedge b_S(r, c+1) \wedge b_S(r+1, c)] \quad (13.7)$$

	X	
X	X	X
	X	

X	X	X
X	X	X
X	X	X

(a)   (b)

Fig. 13.1 Examples of two simple structuring elements (SE) used to detect boundary of digital objects: (a) SE used to detect 8-connected boundary and (b) SE used to detect 4-connected boundary, by erosion residue. The pixel marked with underline indicates the origin of the SE. These structuring elements may be used for other purposes as well (see text).

Sequential algorithm for finding boundary, known as *boundary following* or *boundary tracking* may be found in Rosenfeld and Kak (1982), Pavlidis (1982). Finally, given the boundary information explicitly in terms of pixel coordinates or its chain code or crack code representation one can reconstruct the original object without error. From the given chain code or crack code (see Section 8.4.5) coordinates of the boundary pixels are computed sequentially based on the indicator pixel (i.e. the starting pixel of the contour/boundary) and a look-up table. Once the boundary pixels are known, boundary is drawn on the image domain. Finally, objects are reconstructed by polygon filling method [Foley et al. (1992)].

13.2.2 Medial Axis Transform

According to the block coding scheme described in Chapter 8, a binary image can be represented by a set of ordered triples: $\{(r_i, c_i, n_i) \mid i = 0, 1, 2, ...\}$, where (r_i, c_i) represents the coordinate of, say, top-left corner of the i-th maximal square of 1-pixels only and n_i represents the number of 1-pixels on each side of that square. Now, instead of being the coordinate of the top-left corner pixel of maximal block, let (r_i, c_i) represent the coordinate of the centre pixel of a maximal disk. Secondly, n_i is replaced by the radius ρ_i of the disk [Ahuja et. al. (1978)]. Let us denote the disk of 1-pixels with radius ρ centred at (r, c) by $B(r, c, \rho)$, where

$$B(r, c, \rho) = \{(k, l) \mid d((r, c), (k, l)) \le \rho\}$$

and d stands for distance measure. Now if, instead of Euclidean distance (d_e), chess-board distance (d_8) or city-block distance (d_4) is considered, then $B(r, c, \rho)$ takes the shape of a square or a diamond, respectively. Now $B(r, c, \rho)$ is called a maximal disk contained in S at (r, c) if both the following conditions are true:

1. $B(r, c, \rho) \subseteq S$

2. There exists no other (r', c') and $\rho' > \rho$ such that $B(r', c', \rho') \supseteq B(r, c, \rho)$.

Hence, representation of S by the ordered triplet: $\{(r_i, c_i, \rho_i) \mid i = 0, 1, 2,...\}$ is called the *medial axis* (MA) or *symmetric axis* of *S* [Blum (1967), Pfaltz and Rosenfeld (1967)] or *skeleton*. Medial axis transformed (MAT) image of a binary image $b_S(r, c)$ may be defined as

$$\text{MAT}_S(r, c) = \begin{cases} \rho & \text{if } B(r, c, \rho) \text{ is a maximal disk} \\ 0 & \text{otherwise} \end{cases} \tag{13.8}$$

Generation of medial axis

Let us first detect the pixels that lie on the MA of the object *S*. Recall multi-scale opening as described in Chapter 2. Suppose *K* is a disk of radius one centred at $(0, 0)$. Then ρK defined as

$$\rho K = \underbrace{K \oplus K \oplus K \oplus \cdots \oplus K}_{\rho - 1 \text{ times}}$$

represents a disk of radius ρ, i.e. $\rho K = B(0, 0, \rho)$ [Maragos (1989), Chen and Yan (1989)]. Now $S \ominus \rho K$ is the maximal set of (r, c) such that $B(r, c, \rho) \subseteq S$, or in other words, $S \ominus \rho K$ is the maximal set of centres of disks of radius ρ contained in *S*. Similarly, $S \ominus (\rho + 1) K$ is the maximal set of centres of disks of radius $(\rho + 1)$ contained in *S*. So, a pixel belonging to the set $\{S \ominus (\rho + 1) K\} \oplus K$ has at least one neighbour which is the centre of disk of radius $(\rho + 1)$ contained in *S*. Therefore, the set of pixels comprising the MA of *S* is given by

$$\text{MA} = \bigcup_{\rho=0}^{s} (S \ominus \rho K)/\{(S \ominus (\rho + 1) K) \oplus K\}$$

where *s* is the radius of the largest disk that can fit in *S*, i.e. $S \ominus (s + 1) K = \emptyset$. Finally, medial axis transformed image $\text{MAT}_S(r, c)$ of $b_S(r, c)$ is given as

$$\text{MAT}_S(r, c) = \{\sum_{\rho=0}^{s} b_s(r, c) \ominus \rho K\} \times b_{\text{MA}}(r, c) \tag{13.9}$$

for all (r, c) where $b_{\text{MA}}(r, c) = 1$ if $(r, c) \in \text{MA}$, and 0 otherwise. Note that if (r, c) is an element of MA then $\text{MAT}_S(r, c) \geq 1$. Secondly, $\text{MAT}_S(r, c) \geq 1$ implies that the value of $\text{MAT}_S(r, c)$ is the radius of the disk plus 1. So the value of $\text{MAT}_S(r, c)$ is the distance of $(r, c) \in S$ from S^c. In the right-hand side of Equation (13.9), $\{\sum_{\rho=0}^{s} b_s(r, c) \ominus \rho K\}$ computes distance of all $(r, c) \in S$ from S^c and the second part keeps only those pixels whose distances from S^c are locally maximum. Hence, MAT can also be obtained in two steps—first computing distance transform and then detecting local maxima in distance transform values. Distance transform values $\text{DT}(r, c)$ of $b_S(r, c)$ may be given as

$$\text{DT}_S(r, c) = \sum_{\rho=0}^{s} b_s(r, c) \ominus \rho K \tag{13.10}$$

where value of *s* is such that $S \ominus (s + 1) K = \emptyset$. The structuring element *K* for d_4 and d_8 disks are shown in Figs 13.1(a) and (b), respectively. Example of $\text{DT}_S(r, c)$ for d_4 and d_8 distance measures are shown in Figs. 13.2(b) and 13.2(c), respectively. However, computing $\text{DT}_S(r, c)$ using Equation (13.10) is expensive on sequential machines. A faster computation is possible by repeated erosion by *K* instead of erosion by ρK in Equation (13.10), since

```
000000000000000        000000000000000        000000000000000
011111111111100        011111111111100        011111111111100
011111111111000        012222222221000        012222222211000
011111111110000        012333333210000        012333322110000
011111111100000        012222222100000        012222221100000
011111111000000        011111111000000        011111111000000
000000000000000        000000000000000        011111110000000
```
      (a)   (b)   (c)

Fig. 13.2 Example of distance transform: (a) binary image, (b) distance transform using d_4 metric, and (c) distance transform using d_8 metric.

$$S \ominus \rho K = S \ominus \underbrace{(K \oplus K \oplus K \oplus \cdots \oplus K)}_{(\rho - 1)\text{-times}}$$

$$= S \ominus K \underbrace{\ominus K \ominus K \ominus \cdots \ominus K}_{(\rho - 1)\text{-times}}$$

$$= [S \ominus K \underbrace{\ominus K \ominus K \ominus \cdots \ominus K]}_{(\rho - 1)\text{-times}} \ominus K$$

$$= [S \ominus \underbrace{(K \oplus K \oplus K \oplus \cdots \oplus K)]}_{(\rho - 2)\text{-times}} \ominus K$$

$$= [S \ominus (\rho - 1)K] \ominus K$$

A less expensive algorithm for sequential machine is given in Rosenfeld and Kak (1982). In this algorithm pixels are considered sequentially according to raster-scan order starting from top-left corner of the image. Let us decompose the neighbourhood of a pixel (r, c) into two parts—K_1 consists of pixels top and left to (r, c), and K_2 consists of remaining pixels of neighbourhood. That means when we consider (r, c) pixel

for 4-neighbourhood:

$$K_1 = \{(r - 1, c), (r, c - 1)\}, \; K_2 = \{(r, c + 1), (r + 1, c)\}$$

for 8-neighbourhood:

$$K_1 = \{(r - 1, c - 1), (r - 1, c), (r - 1, c + 1), (r, c - 1)\}$$

$$K_2 = \{(r, c + 1), (r + 1, c - 1), (r + 1, c), (r + 1, c + 1)\}$$

Based on K_1 and K_2, the distance transform is computed in two steps as

$$DT'_S(r, c) = \begin{cases} 0 & \text{if } b_S(r, c) = 0 \\ \min_{(\alpha, \beta) \in K_1} \{DT'_S(\alpha, \beta)\} + 1 & \text{otherwise} \end{cases} \quad (13.11)$$

$$DT_S(r, c) = \min_{(\alpha, \beta) \in K_2} \{DT_S(\alpha, \beta) + 1, DT'_S(r, c)\} \quad (13.12)$$

r and c vary from 0 to their largest values sequentially, i.e. the exactly the raster-scan order is followed during computation of Equation (13.11). On the other hand, the exactly reverse raster-scan is followed during computation of Equation (13.12). Figure 13.3 illustrates the algorithm with an example using the chess-board distance measure.

```
00000000000000000000    00000000000000000000    00000000000000000000
01111110000000000000    01111110000000000000    01111110000000000000
01111110000000000000    01222210000000000000    01222210000000000000
01111110000000001110    01233210000000001110    01222210000000001110
01111110000000001110    01233210000000001210    01111210000000001210
00001111111111111110    00001211111111111210    00001211111111111110
00001111111111110000    00001222222222220000    00001222222222210000
00001111111111110000    00001233333333310000    00001233333333210000
00001111111111110000    00001234444444210000    00001222222222210000
00001111111111110000    00001234555553210000    00001111111111110000
00000000000000000000    00000000000000000000    00000000000000000000
         (a)                     (b)                     (c)
```

Fig. 13.3 Example of computing distance transform of a binary image by sequential algorithm for d_8 metric: (a) binary image, (b) intermediate values obtained by using Equation (13.11), (c) distance transform obtained by applying Equation (13.12) on (b).

Now $MAT_S(r, c)$ is obtained from $DT_S(r, c)$ as

$$MAT_S(r, c) = \begin{cases} DT_S(r, c) & \text{if } DT_S(r, c) = \max_{(\alpha, \beta) \in K} \{DT_S(\alpha, \beta)\} \\ 0 & \text{otherwise} \end{cases} \tag{13.13}$$

where K is $B(r, c, 1)$.

Reconstruction from medial axis transform

Since block coding is a loss-less representation technique (see Chapter 8) and since MAT is just another form of block coding, original binary image can exactly be reconstructed from the corresponding MAT as follows:

$$b_S(r, c) = \begin{cases} 1 & \text{if } (r, c) \in S \\ 0 & \text{otherwise} \end{cases} \tag{13.14}$$

where

$$S = \bigcup_{MAT_S(r, c) > 0} B(r, c, MAT_S(r, c) - 1) \tag{13.15}$$

Obviously, the disk of 1-pixels $B(r, c, \rho)$ is generated using the same metric used in generating the MAT. A faster algorithm for sequential machine is as follows. Similar to the sequential algorithm given for generating $DT_S(r, c)$ from $b_S(r, c)$, we present below a two-pass algorithm for computing $DT_S(r, c)$ from $MAT_S(r, c)$. Then $b_S(r, c)$ is obtained from $DT_S(r, c)$ by thresholding. First, we compute $DT_S(r, c)$ from $MAT_S(r, c)$ as

$$DT'_S(r, c) = \max_{(\alpha, \beta) \in K_1} \{MAT_S(r, c), DT'_S(\alpha, \beta) - 1\} \tag{13.16}$$

$$DT_S(r, c) = \max_{(\alpha, \beta) \in K_2} \{DT_S(\alpha, \beta) - 1, DT'_S(r, c)\} \tag{13.17}$$

r and c vary from 0 to their largest values sequentially, i.e. the exactly raster-scan order is followed during computation of Equation (13.16). On the other hand, the exactly reverse raster-scan is followed during computation of Equation (13.17). Figure 13.4 illustrates the algorithm with an example using the chess-board distance measure.

```
000000000000000          000000000000000          000000000000000
010000000001100          010000000001100          011111111111100
002000000220000          002100000221000          012222222221000
000333333000000          001333333110000          012333333210000
002000000000000          002222222100000          012222221100000
010000000000000          011111111000000          011111111000000
000000000000000          000000000000000          000000000000000
```

       (a)   (b)   (c)

Fig. 13.4 Example of computing distance transform from medial axis transform by sequential algorithm for d_8 metric: (a) medial axis transform matrix, (b) intermediate values obtained from Equation (13.16), (c) distance transform obtained by applying Equation (13.17) on (b).

Now $b_S(r, c)$ is obtained from $DT_S(r, c)$ as

$$b_S (r, c) = \begin{cases} 1 & \text{if } DT_S(r, c) > 0 \\ 0 & \text{otherwise} \end{cases} \qquad (13.18)$$

where K, K_1 and K_2 are the same as before and correspond to the metric used to compute distance transform.

    Pixels that belong to the medial axis or skeleton of a connected component or object may not, in general, be connected. An example of such a skeleton of a connected component is shown in Fig. 13.5. Thus, though from medial axis transform, original image may be reconstructed, it apparently loses some important shape information that is very useful for image analysis. Secondly,

```
00000000000000000000000
00000000000000000000000
00222200000000000000000
00222200000000000000000
00000020000000000000200
00000020000000000000000
00000000000000000000000
00000033333333333000000
00000000000000000000000
00000000000000000000000
00000000000000000000000
```

Fig. 13.5   Medial axis transform matrix of the binary image shown in Fig. 13.3.

thickness of medial axis may be two at some places as shown in Fig. 13.5. So, below we present another method, called *thinning*, for extracting single pixel thick connected skeleton that preserves basic (not all) shape information. Such skeletons faithfully represent shape of objects that are mainly composed of ribbon-like structures. Some examples of such objects are shown in Fig. 13.6.

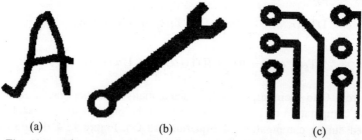

      (a)   (b)   (c)

Fig. 13.6   Objects that are mainly composed of ribbon-like structures.

13.2.3 Thinning

As the requirement suggests, *thinning* is basically a *search and delete* process that removes (from S) only those boundary pixels whose deletion

1. do not change connectivity of their neighbours locally, and

2. do not reduce the length of an already thinned curve.

The pixel whose deletion changes the connectivity of its neighbourhood locally is called *critical pixel*. The pixel whose deletion reduces the length of an already thinned curve is called an *end pixel*. Number of neighbouring pixels (that are in S) of an end pixel is less than two. In the following discussion we assume that S is 8-connected. Figure 13.7 shows some examples of boundary pixels. Depending on the connectivity assumed, let us see whether the boundary pixel of interest (marked with underline) is a critical pixel or an end pixel, or none of them. We observe in the said examples that centre pixels of the windows shown in (b), (c) and (d) are critical pixels, but that in (a), (e), (f) and (g), are not. Again, centre pixels of the windows shown in (f) and (g) are end pixels. Thus we can delete the centre pixels shown in (a) and (e) without affecting local connectivity of the neighbourhood or reducing the length of the arc. If we consider 4-connectivity for object then (a) is a critical pixel and (b) is not.

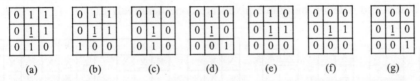

(a)   (b)   (c)   (d)   (e)   (f)   (g)

Fig. 13.7 Examples of boundary pixels of interest (marked with *underline*) relevant to thinning process.

The deletion of all boundary pixels that satisfy the above criteria should be done simultaneously to ensure symmetry in the resultant skeleton. However, such strategy may delete completely a curve segment of thickness two as shown below.

1 1 1 1 1 1 1 1
1 1 1 1 1 1 1 1

In this example, all the pixels satisfy the above criteria and have the same possibility of being deleted. So the entire curve would vanish. To avoid this problem we apply the deletion process simultaneously to all boundary pixels of a particular side, such as north, east, south and west at a time. Secondly, to make the skeleton as close to the medial axis as possible, pixels are deleted from all sides alternately, i.e. north, east, south, west, north, and so on. Now a pixel $(r, c) \in S$ is called a *north-boundary pixel* if $(r - 1, c) \in S^c$. Boundary pixels of other sides are defined in similar way.

Let us call the boundary pixels, that are neither critical pixels nor end pixels, as *simple pixel*. Hence, basic strategy for thinning algorithm [Arcelli et al. (1975), Pavlidis (1980), Rosenfeld (1975)] may be described as follows:

Algorithm 13.1

```
repeat (until no change takes place) begin
    for sides: north, east, south and west begin
        for all boundary pixels begin
        detect and delete simple pixel
        end
    end
end
```

A fast algorithm for sequential machine is proposed by Saha et al. (1993). Main problem in devising a thinning algorithm is detecting simple pixels. We know morphological hit-and-miss operator can detect spatial feature in an object. Suppose ψ_1 and ψ_2 are two structuring elements that can detect simple pixel on a particular side of the boundary. Then thinning of S by the structuring element pair $\psi = \{\psi_1, \psi_2\}$ is defined as

$$S \odot \psi = S/(S \otimes \psi) = S/[(S \ominus \psi_1) \cap (S^c \ominus \psi_2)] \qquad (13.19)$$

Let us consider a set of structuring element pairs as shown in Fig. 13.8. The set of structuring elements is almost similar to that suggested by Jang and Chin (1990). Based on these structuring elements search and deletion of simple pixels are done iteratively as

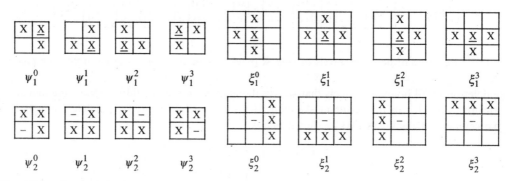

Fig. 13.8 Structuring elements used in thinning algorithm (see text). Pixel marked with underline is the origin.

$$S^{(k)} = [(S^{(k-1)} \odot \psi^{(k-1) \bmod 4}) \cap (S^{(k-1)} \odot \psi^{k \bmod 4}) \cap (S^{(k-1)} \odot \xi^{(k-1) \bmod 4})] \qquad (13.20)$$

for $k = 1, 2, \ldots$, where $S^{(0)} = S$. There exists an m such that $S^{(m)} = S^{(m+1)}$. Thus $S^{(m)}$ is the desired skeleton which is connected, one pixel thick and more or less symmetric with respect to the object.

Example Figure 13.9 illustrates the steps of the thinning process based on Equation (13.20). Pixels belonging to S are marked with 'x' and others are blank. Pixels deleted from S are marked with black rectangle (■). Results after deleting boundary pixels from north, east, south, west, north, etc. are shown in (b), (c), (d), (e), (f) and so on respectively. Finally the skeleton is shown in (j).   ■

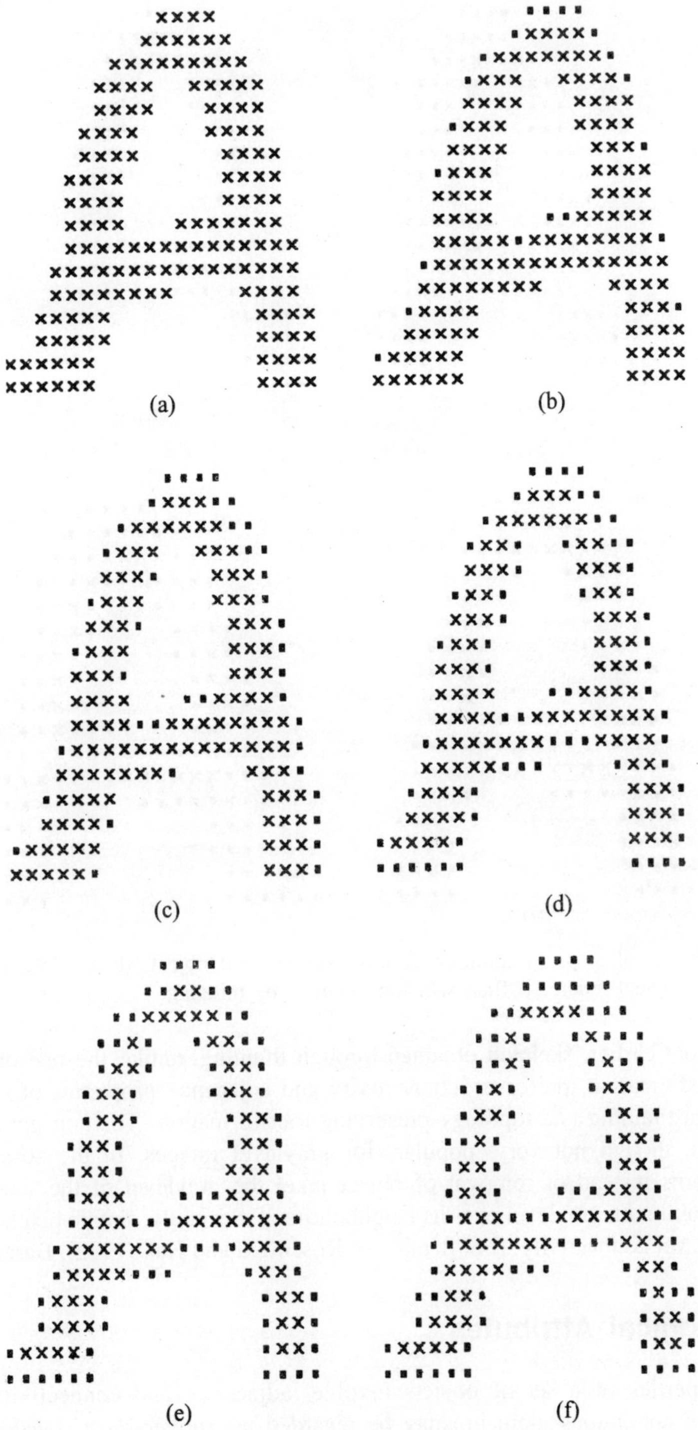

(a)

(b)

(c)

(d)

(e)

(f)

Fig. 13.9   (Contd.)

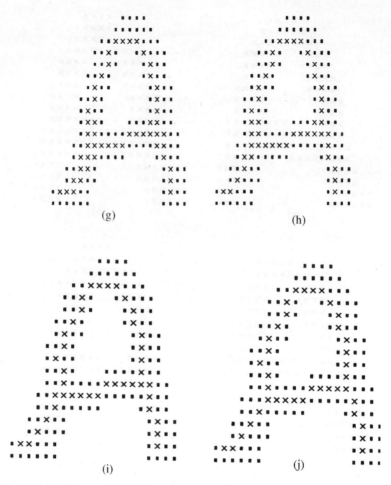

Fig. 13.9   Illustraion of steps of thinning process: (a) original object, (b)–(i) intermediate results in chronological order, (j) final skeleton obtained by thinning.

As pointed out earlier, skeleton obtained through thinning, unlike the one obtained through medial axis transformation, preserves connectivity and adjacency properties of original objects. Thus, we see that thinning is a topology preserving transformation. The concept of thinning has been generalized, though not very popular, for graylevel images. In the so-called graylevel thinning algorithms instead of removal of object pixel the graylevel of the candidate pixel is replaced by the minimum graylevel over its neighbourhood. Secondly, simple pixels are determined in terms of graylevel connectivity. [For detail, see Rosenfeld and Kak (1982), Basak et al. (1996).]

13.3   Topological Attributes

Topological properties of a set of objects involve adjacency and connectivity. Topological transformation, in continuous domain, may be regarded as *rubber-sheet* transformation where shape and size of the objects may change but not their connectivity.

13.3.1 Connectivity Number

Connectivity numbers are assigned to the pixels which belong to the domain of support. Purpose of this number is to show how a pixel of domain of support is connected to its like neighbours. Though we call it *connectivity number*, it is actually a label and has no arithmetic property. Connectivity number operator associates with each pixel belonging to domain of support one of the six different values: 5 values for boundary pixels and 1 value for interior pixels. Here we adopt the definition of connectivity number as was given in [Haralick (1981)]. Accordingly labels are shown in Fig. 13.10 with an example. Suppose domain of support is represented by S and $C(r, c)$ is the connectivity number assigned to the pixel $(r, c) \in S$. Two different definitions of connectivity number are considered here.

```
XXXXX   X              13221    0
  X                      2
  X                      2
XXXXXXXX               12422222
  X     X                2       2
  X     X                2       1
XXXX                    1211
XXXX                    1551
XXXX  X                 1551  0
XXXX                    1111
```

Binary object	Connectivity number
(a)	(b)

Key:	Number	Class	Meaning
	0	Boundary pixel	Isolated
	1	Boundary pixel	Edge
	2	Boundary pixel	Connecting
	3	Boundary pixel	Branching
	4	Boundary pixel	Crossing
	5	Interior pixel	Interior

Fig. 13.10 Connectivity numbers assigned to pixels of a binary object: (a) original object, (b) connectivity numbers of the pixels.

Yokoi connectivity number

This definition was originally suggested by Yokoi et al. (1975). This definition is slightly different depending on whether the object is 4-connected or 8-connected as given below:

4-connectivity case:

$$C(r, c) = \max\left\{\sum_{i=2}^{5} (b_S \ominus K_i)(r, c) - \sum_{i=10}^{13} (b_S \ominus K_i)(r, c), 5(b_S \ominus K_1)(r, c)\right\} \quad (13.21)$$

8-connectivity case:

$$C(r, c) = \max\left\{\sum_{i=2}^{9} (b_S \ominus K_i)(r, c) - \sum_{i=10}^{17} (b_S \ominus K_i)(r, c), 5(b_S \ominus K_1)(r, c)\right\} \quad (13.22)$$

where K_is are structuring elements as shown in Fig. 13.11 [Chanda and Haralick (1990)]. In both cases, max may be replaced by the sum of arguments.

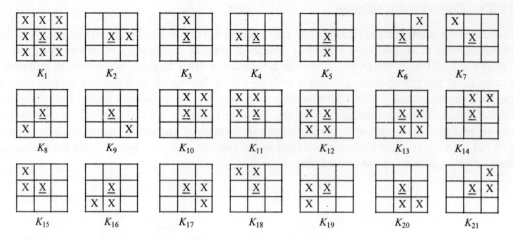

Fig. 13.11   Structuring elements for connectivity number labelling.

Rutovitz connectivity number

This definition was originally suggested by Rutovitz (1966). This number is also called 'crossing number' and is defined as the number of transitions from domain of support to its complement if we travel around 8-neighbourhood of a candidate pixel belonging to boundary of object, and is just 5 if candidate pixel is an interior pixel. According to this definition, connectivity number at pixel (r, c) of domain of support is

$$C(r, c) = \max\left\{ \sum_{i=2}^{9} (b_S \ominus K_i)\right\}(r, c) - \sum_{i=14}^{21} (b_S \ominus K_i)(r, c), 5(b_S \ominus K_1)(r, c)\right\} \quad (13.23)$$

Determining topological attributes helps in computing other properties too. For example, to measure geometric properties of an object it needs to be isolated from the other objects present in the image. And to isolate the object we primarily use connectivity and mark a maximal connected component with a unique label. The method is called *component labelling*.

13.3.2   Component Labelling

Suppose S is a set of connected components and is represented by a two-dimensional array $b_S(r, c)$, where $b_S(r, c) = 1$ if $(r, c) \in S$, and 0 if $(r, c) \in S^c$. We need to mark each connected component of S by a unique label so that the components can be identified by the label. Below we describe an iterative algorithm for assigning unique label to each connected component.

Algorithm 13.2

```
i = 1
for all (r, c) begin
    if (bₛ(r, c) = 1)  bₛ(r, c) = i
    i = i + 1
end
k = 1
```

```
repeat (until no change takes place) begin
    for all (r, c) begin
```
if ($b_S^{(k-1)}(r, c) > 0$) $b_S^{(k)}(r, c)$ = $\max_{(\alpha, \beta) \in B(r, c, 1)} b_S^{(k-1)}(\alpha, \beta)$
```
    end
k = k + 1
end
```

Here $B(r, c, 1)$ is a disk of radius 1. Number of iterations required to converge may be as large as the maximum of lengths of the shortest paths connecting any two pixels of the object minus 1. And this can be very large in many cases. A more efficient algorithm for sequential machines [Rosenfeld and Kak (1982)] is described below. The method starts with an empty *equivalence table*. Binary image is scanned in raster order from left to right and from top to bottom. Once a 1-pixel is found, its top-left neighbours [as given by K_1 in Equation (13.11)] are checked. If all these neighbours are 0-pixels, assign a new label to the candidate pixel. If a unique label exists in this neighbourhood, assign that label to the candidate pixel. And, if more than one label exist in this neighbourhood, assign one of these labels to the candidate pixel and enter these labels as equivalent in the equivalence table. The labelled image is scanned again, and in consultation with the equivalence table, equivalent labels are replaced by a unique label. So, every connected component is marked with a unique label. Thus the method needs only two raster scan, to label all the connected components. A concise algorithm is presented below.

Algorithm 13.3

```
equiv_table   = Null
i = 0
for all (r, c) begin
    Ψ = ∅
    if (bₛ(r, c) ≠ 0){
        if (bₛ(r, c - 1) ≠ 0)  Ψ = Ψ ∪ bₛ(r, c - 1)
        if (bₛ(r - 1, c - 1) ≠ 0)  Ψ = Ψ ∪ bₛ(r - 1, c - 1)
        if (bₛ(r - 1, c) ≠ 0)  Ψ = Ψ ∪ bₛ(r - 1, c)
        if (bₛ(r - 1, c + 1) ≠ 0)  Ψ = Ψ ∪ bₛ(r - 1, c + 1)
        if (Card {Ψ} = 0)  bₛ(r, c) = new_label
        if (Card {Ψ} = 1)  bₛ(r, c) = element of Ψ
        if (Card {Ψ} > 1)  bₛ(r, c) = last element entered in Ψ
                and if (Ψ ∉ equiv_table) equiv_table(i) = Ψ and i = i + 1
        }
end
Process equiv_tables to group equivalent labels.
for all (r, c) begin
    if (bₛ(r, c) ≠ 0)   {
        use equiv_table and
            bₛ(r, c) = unique_label
    }
end
```

Figure 13.12 illustrates the steps of the component labelling process (Algorithm 13.3). The pixels not belonging to S are blank.

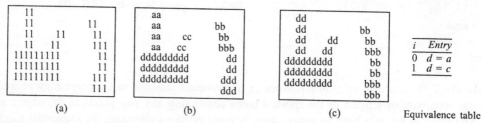

(a)   (b)   (c)   Equivalence table

Fig. 13.12 An example of component labelling algorithm: (a) original binary image, background is blank, (b) result after the first pass, (c) final result after the second pass using the equivalence table shown at the bottom-right corner.

13.3.3 Component Counting

If we have an image with connected components labelled properly, then the number of non-zero labels present is the number of components in the image. However, below we describe a morphology-based iterative algorithm [Lavialdi (1972)] that can count the number of components by operating directly on the binary image. The algorithm uses erosion and hit-and-miss operation with the structuring elements shown in Fig. 13.13. The erosion operation shrinks a connected component gradually towards north–west to a single isolated pixel and hit-and-miss operation detects that

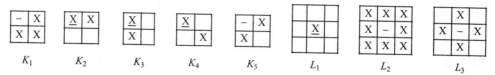

Fig. 13.13 Structuring elements used in connected component counting (see text).

isolated pixel before it vanishes in the next iteration. Suppose $b^{(0)}$ is the given binary image $b_S(r, c)$ and c_n is the number of isolated pixel after n iterations. Therefore, after n iterations we have

$$b^n = \bigcup_{i=k}^{m} b^{(n-1)} \ominus K_i$$

$$c_n = c_{n-1} + \text{Card } \{b^n \otimes (L_1, L_{1+l})\} \tag{13.24}$$

for $n = 1, 2, \ldots$ where $c_0 = \text{Card } \{b^{(0)} \otimes (L_1, L_{1+l})\}$. There exists an N such that $b^N = \emptyset$ and c_N is the number of connected components in $b_S(r, c)$. Note that $k = 2$, $m = 5$ and $l = 1$ for 8-connected objects, and for 4-connected objects $k = 1$, $m = 3$ and $l = 2$.

13.3.4 Computing Genus

A *Genus* of an image is defined as the number of connected components (or objects) minus number of holes in the entire image. Suppose the set S represents entire domain of support, and the indicator function is $b_S(r, c)$. Minsky and Papert (1969) defined the genus $G(b_S)$ of the image as follows:

$$G(b_S) = \Sigma \alpha_1 b_S(r, c) + \Sigma \alpha_2 b_S(r, c) b_S(r, c + 1) + \Sigma \alpha_3 b_S(r, c) b_S (r + 1, c)$$

$$+ \Sigma \alpha_4 b_S(r, c) b_S(r + 1, c) b_S(r, c + 1) b_S(r + 1, c + 1) \qquad (13.25)$$

where summations are taken over all (r, c), and $\alpha_1 = \alpha_4 = 1$ and $\alpha_2 = \alpha_3 = -1$. The first term of the right-hand side gives the sum of value of all pixels or the number of object (foreground) pixels since the value of the foreground pixel is 1. The second and the third terms give the number of pairs of object pixels that are adjacent horizontally and vertically, respectively. Finally, the fourth term gives the number of 2×2 blocks of object pixels. Instead of taking sum of products as suggested in Equation (13.25), we can compute these numbers by counting the elements of the sets S, $S \ominus K_1$, $S \ominus K_2$ and $S \ominus K_3$, respectively, where the structuring elements K_1, K_2 and K_3 are shown in Fig. 13.14(a). Adjacency of pair of pixels and the 2×2 block of this approach reminds us the 4-connectivity of object. So in 4-connectivity case, genus $G(b_S)$ of the binary image with indicator function $b_S(r, c)$ can be computed as [Chanda and Haralick (1990)]

$$G(b_S) = \#(S) - \#(S \ominus K_1) - \#(S \ominus K_2) + \#(S \ominus K_3) \qquad (13.26)$$

where, $\#(S)$ means the number of elements in set S. The structuring elements K_is are shown in Fig. 13.14(a).

Now if we imagine a 4-connected object as a web-type collection of polygons formed by the most closely situated pixels, then each pixel of domain of support may be viewed as a vertex of these polygons. So each pair of horizontally or vertically adjacent pixels represents an edge, and a 2×2 block represents a face. Hence, the right-hand side of Equation (13.26) may be written as *number of vertices – number of edges + number of faces*. This is, again, well known *Euler Polygon Formula*. Minsky and Papert (1969) have shown that the genus and the number computed by this formula exactly agree to each other in 4-connectivity case.

When the object is considered as 8-connected, along with horizontally and vertically adjacent pairs of pixels, diagonally adjacent pairs of pixels also constitutes edge. The number of edges can be obtained by counting the elements of the sets $S \ominus K_1$, $S \ominus K_2$, $S \ominus K_3$, $S \ominus K_4$, where the structuring elements K_i $(i = 1, ..., 4)$ are shown in Fig. 13.14(b). Secondly, the polygons formed by the most closely situated pixels, in this case, are right-angled triangles consisting of three pixels and 2×2 squares. Since we are dealing with objects in two-dimensional space, sides of polygons should not cross each other. So during counting faces, we count only the non-overlapping triangular faces and the square faces. Now it can be readily seen that the number of non-overlapping triangular faces plus the number of square faces is equal to the number of all triangular faces minus the number of square faces. The number of all triangular faces can be obtained by counting the elements of the sets $S \ominus K_5$, $S \ominus K_6$, $S \ominus K_7$ and $S \ominus K_8$, and the number of square faces can be obtained by counting the elements of the set $S \ominus K_9$, where the structuring elements K_i $(i = 5, ..., 9)$ are shown in Fig. 13.14(b). Hence, the polygonal formula for 8-connected objects is *number of vertices – number of edges + number of triangular faces – number of square faces*. Thus in 8-connectivity case, genus $G(b_S)$ of the binary image with indicator function $b_S(r, c)$ can be computed as [Chanda and Haralick (1990)]

$$G(b_S) = \#(S) - \sum_{i=1}^{4} \#(S \ominus K_i) + \sum_{i=5}^{8} \#(S \ominus K_i) - \#(S \ominus K_9) \qquad (13.27)$$

where, $\#(S)$ means number of elements in set S. The structuring elements K_is are shown in Fig. 13.14(b).

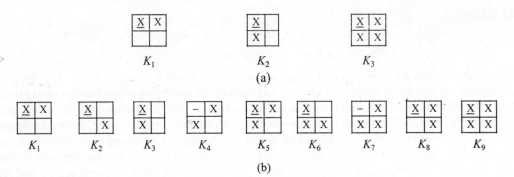

Fig. 13.14 Structuring elements for computing genus for (a) 4-connectivity and (b) 8-connectivity (see text).

13.4 Geometrical Attributes

Once the connected components or objects in an image are labelled each object can be isolated by its label. Thus geometrical attributes such as perimeter, area may be measured for individual object. Algorithms for measuring these attributes depend on the representation scheme used. For example, Rosenfeld and Kak (1982) and Kitchin and Pugh (1983) used crack code of the object boundary for computing these attributes. Here we describe algorithms for computing geometrical attributes where objects are represented by run-length coded 4-chain code of its boundary.

Obtaining chain code [Freeman (1974)] of boundary is a trivial task. Suppose that the boundary is 4-connected and the object boundary is traversed anti-clockwise starting from any boundary pixel. The chain code due to a pixel p_0 is 0 or 1 or 2 or 3 depending on the previous pixel encountered during traversal of boundary is p_5, p_7, p_1, p_3, respectively as shown in Fig. 13.15. Thus the chain code of the boundary is a sequence of integers ranging from 0 to 3. It is observed that in many places of this sequence, the same code is repeated several times at a

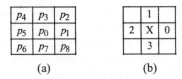

Fig. 13.15 (a) Neighbours of pixel p_0, (b) chain code for the 4-connected boundary of an object.

stretch. A *run* of chain code is a maximal subsequence of the sequence of codes such that in the subsequence the value of the code does not change. The number of codes in the run is called the run-length (see Chapter 8). Hence, run-length coded chain code of an object is a sequence of ordered pairs $\{(l_i, n_i) \mid i = 0, 1, 2, \ldots, m-1\}$, where n_i is the value of chain code of the i-th run and $n_i \in \{0, 1, 2, 3\}$, and l_i is the run-length and is cyclic, i.e. $(l_{m+i}, c_{m+i}) = (l_i, c_i)$. So n_i is a member of 4-chain code. If $n_i \in \{0, 1, \ldots, 8\}$ we would call it a member of 8-chain code and is used to represent 8-connected boundary. A *corner* of an object S is a pixel on the boundary of S where the value of the chain code changes. This definition of corner is very crude, and the number of pixels labelled as corner using this definition may be large compared to the number of actual corners of the object. It is also seen that even and odd codes (i.e. n_is) usually occur alternately. If it does not do so, an extra code n_i is inserted with $l_i = 0$, where

$$n_i = \begin{cases} 3 & \text{if } n_{i+1} = 0 \\ n_{i+1} - 1 & \text{otherwise} \end{cases}$$

For simplicity, it is assumed that n_0 is even. It is guaranteed by selecting appropriate starting pixel (indicator pixel) for boundary tracking.

13.4.1 Perimeter

The perimeter P of an object, i.e length of contour is defined as

$$P = \sum_{i=0}^{m-1} l_i + \left(\sqrt{2} - 2\right)n_d \tag{13.28}$$

where n_d is the number of occurrences of code pairs (0, 1), (1, 2), (2, 3) and (3, 0).

On the other hand, if the boundary of the object is 8-connected and run-length coded 8-chain code is used to represent it, then

$P = $ sum of all l_i (if n_i is even) $+ \sqrt{2} \times$ sum of all l_i (if n_i is odd)

13.4.2 Diameter of the Enclosing Circle

Diameter of the circle that encloses the object S is equal to the largest distance between two pixels belonging to S. Suppose s_i denotes the sequence of pixels comprising the i-th run, i.e. $\mathbf{s}_i = \langle s_{i,1}, s_{i,2}, \ldots, s_{i,l_i} \rangle$. Thus $s_{i,k}$ is the k-th pixel of the sequence. Then it may be verified that

1. the distance $d(p, s_{i,k})$ between any arbitrary pixel p and any pixel $s_{i,k}$ of a run $\mathbf{s}_i$ is maximum if $k = 1$ or $k = l_i$.

2. then the maximum distance between any two pixels of the sequence can be given by

$$\max\{\max_j(r_j + c_j) - \min_j(r_j + c_j), \max_j(r_j - c_j) - \min_j(r_j - c_j)\}$$

where $\{(r_j, c_j) \mid j = 1, 2, 3, \ldots \}$ is a sequence of pixels.

Note that the distance measure we consider here is *city-block* distance or d_4 distance measure. These two statements suggest that (i) only corner pixels may be considered for computing the diameter and (ii) only sum and difference of the coordinate values of the corner pixels are sufficient to compute maximum distance or diameter. Therefore, we compute the diameter as follows.

Algorithm 13.4

```
h(-1)  =  v(0)  =  0
for  j  =  0,  1,  2,  ...,  (m - 1)/2 begin
    h(2j)  =  h(2j + 1)  =  (1 - n2j) l2j + h(2j - 1)
    v(2j + 1)  =  v(2j + 2)  =  (n2j+1 - 2) l2j+1 + v(2j)
end
```

```
for j = 0, 1, 2, ..., m - 1 begin
    M₁(j) = h(j) + v(j)
    M₂(j) = h(j) - v(j)
end
Diameter = max[max_j{M₁(j)} - min_j{M₁(j)}, max_j{M₂(j)} - min_j{M₂(j)}]
```

In this algorithm $h(j)$ and $v(j)$ are r and c values of coordinate of j-th corner pixel, respectively. So M_1 and M_2 are the sum and difference of coordinate values.

13.4.3 Area

Area of an object S is defined as the number of pixels comprising the object. The basic idea behind the algorithm presented here for computing the area of an object is to decompose the object into a set of rectangles. An example of decomposing a polygon into rectangles is shown in Fig. 13.16. Sides of these rectangles are represented by the runs of 4-chain code. Actual lengths of the sides are computed based on values of the previous, the present and the next chain codes. Depending

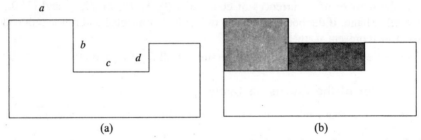

(a)   (b)

Fig. 13.16 Example of convex (marked with 'a'), step (marked with 'b') and concave (marked with 'c') sides of a polygon. Secondly, area of the rectangle with sides 'a' and 'b' is added and area of the rectangle with sides 'c' and 'd' is subtracted, etc., to compute the area of the polygon.

on these chain codes, a side may be regarded as (i) convex, (ii) concave and (iii) step. Consequently, lengths of the sides are run-length plus 1, run-length minus 1 and the run-length, respectively. Secondly, the area of a rectangle may be added or subtracted to compute the area of the object depending on its position in the polygon representing the object. This addition and subtraction of area is taken care of by assigning a plus or minus sign to the length of the sides.

Algorithm 13.5

```
for i = 0, 1 2, ..., m - 1 begin
    if (nᵢ = 0)
        if (nᵢ₊₁ = 1) lᵢ' = lᵢ - 0.5|nᵢ₊₁ - nᵢ₋₁|
        else lᵢ' = lᵢ + 0.5|nᵢ₊₁ - nᵢ₋₁|
    if (nᵢ = 1)
        if (nᵢ₊₁ = 2) lᵢ' = -lᵢ + 0.5|nᵢ₊₁ - nᵢ₋₁|
        else lᵢ' = -lᵢ - 0.5|nᵢ₊₁ - nᵢ₋₁|
    if (nᵢ = 2)
        if (nᵢ₊₁ = 1) lᵢ' = -lᵢ - 0.5|nᵢ₊₁ - nᵢ₋₁|
        else lᵢ' = -lᵢ + 0.5|nᵢ₊₁ - nᵢ₋₁|
```

```
if (nᵢ = 3)
    if (nᵢ₊₁ = 2) lᵢ′ = lᵢ + 0.5|nᵢ₊₁ - nᵢ₋₁|
    else lᵢ′ = lᵢ - 0.5|nᵢ₊₁ - nᵢ₋₁|
```

end

$l_0'' = l_i'$

for $i = 1, 2, \ldots, (m/2 - 1)$ **begin**

$\quad l_{2i}'' = l_{2i}'' + l_{2i-2}''$

end

Finally,

$$\text{Area} = \sum_{i=0}^{(m/2)-1} l_{2i}'' l_{2i+1}'$$

Given below is an example for better understanding of the algorithms presented above for computing geometrical features.

Example Consider a binary object as shown in Fig. 13.17. Run-length coded 4-chain code of the object boundary is given by

i	0	1	2	3	4	5	6	7	8	9	10	11	12	13	14	15	16	17
n_i	0	3	0	3	2	3	0	3	2	1	2	3	2	1	0	1	2	1
l_i	7	3	3	5	3	4	5	9	4	5	4	2	6	9	6	5	4	4

Fig. 13.17 Example of a binary object that is used to illustrate computation of geometric features (see text).

We have to compute perimeter, diameter of the enclosing circle and area of the object. Let us first complete the following table using the Algorithms 13.4 and 13.5.

i	0	1	2	3	4	5	6	7	8	9	10	11	12	13	14	15	16	17
$h(i)$	7	7	10	10	7	7	12	12	8	8	4	4	-2	-2	4	4	0	0
$v(i)$	0	3	3	8	8	12	12	21	21	16	16	18	18	9	9	4	4	0
$M_1(i)$	7	10	13	18	15	19	24	<u>33</u>	29	24	20	22	16	7	13	8	4	<u>0</u>
$M_2(i)$	<u>7</u>	4	7	2	-1	-5	0	-9	-13	-8	-12	-14	<u>-20</u>	-11	-5	0	-4	0
l'_i	8	3	3	6	-3	3	5	10	-5	-5	-3	2	-7	-10	6	-4	-4	-5
l''_i	8		11		8		13		8		5		-2		4		0	

Here n_d is equal to 6. So perimeter of the object is

$P = 7 + 3 + 3 + 5 + 3 + 4 + 5 + 9 + 4 + 5 + 4 + 2 + 6 + 9 + 6 + 5 + 4 + 4 + (1.414 - 2)6$
$= 88 - 3.5 = 84.5$ unit

From the table, we see

$$\max\{M_1(i)\} = 33 \quad \text{and} \quad \min\{M_1(i)\} = 0$$

as underlined. Similarly

$$\max\{M_2(i)\} = 7 \quad \text{and} \quad \min\{M_2(i)\} = -20$$

Therefore, the diameter of the circle enclosing the object is

$$\text{Diameter} = \max\{33 - 0, 7 - (-20)\} = 33 \text{ unit}$$

Finally, we compute the area of the object as

Area $= 8 \times 3 + 11 \times 6 + 8 \times 3 + 10 \times 13 - 8 \times 5 + 5 \times 2 + 2 \times 10 - 4 \times 4 - 0 \times 5$

$= 24 + 66 + 24 + 130 - 40 + 10 + 20 - 16 - 0 = 218$ sq. unit. ∎

13.4.4 Slope, Curvature and Straightness

The objects we have considered so far are of blob types, i.e. objects having significant numbers of interior pixels. There are another kind of objects where all pixels belonging to the object are boundary pixels. Objects of this class are usually single pixel thick. Some important examples of this kind of objects are: thin linear structures, such as roads or streams, in satellite imagery, strokes and characters in document images. Even skeleton and boundary of blob-type regions also belong to this class. So, most of the objects of this type are *digital arcs*.

An 8-connected finite set S of pixels is an *open digital arc* if all but two of the pixels have exactly two neighbours in S, and each of exceptional two pixels (the end pixels) has exactly one neighbour in S [Rosenfeld (1973)]. If all pixels have exactly two neighbours in S, then it is a *closed digital arc*. A slope at any pixel p_i of the digital arc is defined as the slope of the line segment connecting p_i and the next pixel p_{i+1}. Thus, its value is an integer multiple of $45°$ if the arc is 8-connected and is an integer multiple of $90°$ if the arc is 4-connected, respectively. Suppose the slope at any pixel is denoted by θ and $-180 < \theta \le 180$. If the arc is represented by 8-chain code then slope τ_i at p_i may be given as

$$\tau_i = \begin{cases} 45n_i & \text{if } n_i \le 4 \\ 45(n_i - 8) & \text{otherwise} \end{cases} \tag{13.29}$$

However, this measure gives one of a few discrete values and, thus, does not reflect the actual slope at that part of the object. Secondly, it depends on sampling resolution and is sensitive to noise. So, to get a more realistic measure of slope reasonably free from the aforementioned problems, we take the average of unit slopes [as defined in Equation (13.29)] at k pixels on either sides. Let us call such measure as *k-slope* and define it as

$$\tau_i^k = \sum_{j=i-k}^{i+k} \tau_j \qquad (13.30)$$

However, k-slope cannot be defined for the pixels that are not at least k pixels away from the end pixels. Secondly, because of similar reasons, just like determining the size of window in mean filtering, determining the value of k is also a non-trivial task.

Since, by definition, the *radius of curvature* of a curve is the rate of change of slope, at any point it can be computed by taking derivative of the slope. Hence, the radius of curvature ρ_i at the pixel p_i can be defined as

$$\rho_i = \tau_{i+1} - \tau_i \qquad (13.31)$$

However, to surmount the problems similar to those due to Equation (13.29), the radius of curvature is defined as

$$\rho_i^k = \tau_{i+1}^k - \tau_{i-1}^k \qquad (13.32)$$

This measure is called *k-curvature* [Rosenfeld and Johnston (1973)]. Note that, k-curvature is not the average of ρ_i at k pixels on the either sides of p_i as is in the case of k-slope [see Equation (13.30)]. A *digital arc* of interest is said to be a *digital straight line* segment if it has chord property. In fact, in many applications curvilinear arcs are approximated by and decomposed into digital straight line segments.

Let p, q be any two pixels in S. The straight line segment $\overline{pq}$, connecting p and q, is said to lie near S if for any real point (x, y) of $\overline{pq}$ there exists a point (r, c) of S such that $\max\{|r - x|, |c - y|\} < 1$. We say that S has the chord property if, for every p, q in S, the line segment $\overline{pq}$ lies near S [Rosenfeld (1974)].

Now for analyzing and decomposing digital arcs into straight line segments we need to check the straightness (or chord property) of the arc. If the arc is represented by run-length coded chain code, digital straight line segment should satisfy the following three conditions:

1. At most two codes may occur in the string of codes, and if two codes occur they must differ by one.

2. All the run-lengths for at least one code must be one.

3. At most two different run-lengths may occur for the other code, and if there are two different run-lengths they must differ by one.

The last condition may be relaxed at the end of the arc.

13.4.5 Convexity

In continuous domain $\mathbf{R}^2$, a convex object may be defined as follows:

Let $\mathbf{A}$ be a figure in $\mathbf{R}^2$. $\mathbf{A}$ is said to be *convex* if for every pair of points p and q belonging to $\mathbf{A}$ and for every real $\gamma \in [0, 1]$ we have

$$\gamma p + (1 - \gamma) q \in \mathbf{A}$$

However, this definition cannot be straightaway translated to discrete domain. As a result, quite a few definitions of digital convexity have been suggested in the literature [Kim and Rosenfeld (1980), Chassery (1983)]. Some of them are described here. Before stating these definitions we need following preliminary notion. Suppose sampling intervals in both x and y directions are same, i.e. $\Delta x = \Delta y = h$ (say). For each point $p \in \mathbb{Z}^2$ consider a closed square of size $2l \times 2l$ centred at p and denote it by $s(p, l)$. Then

$$s(p, l) = \{q \in R^2 \mid d_8(p, q) \le 1\}$$

Now if the value of l is greater than or equal to $h/2$ then

$$\bigcup_{p \in Z^2} s(p, l) = \mathbf{R}^2$$

Let S be a digital object and S' be the set of all points of all the squares $s(p, h/2)$, where p is in S. Suppose $\delta(S')$ denotes boundary of S', and $P(S; p, q)$ denotes a set of polygons in $\mathbf{R}^2$ whose boundaries consist of parts of line segment $\overline{pq}$ and parts of $\delta(S')$, and whose interiors are subset of complement of S'. $P(S; p, q)$ may be empty for some p and q. Based on this notion some definitions of digital convexity may be given as follows.

Digitally convex

(1) A digital object S is *digitally convex* if and only if there exists at least one convex figure $\mathbf{S}$ in $\mathbf{R}^2$ of which the given digital object S is an image [Sklansky (1970)].

This definition suggests an indirect test for digital convexity, though searching for such an $\mathbf{S}$ is not practically feasible.

(2) A digital object S is *digitally convex* if and only if for every pair of pixels $p, q \in S$ and for every real $\gamma \in [0, 1]$ there exists a pixel centre $t \in S$ [Freeman and Shapira (1975)] such that

$$\gamma p + (1 - \gamma)q \in s(t, h/2)$$

The main problem with this definition of digital convexity is that the digital straight line segments that constitute the boundary of a convex object should have slopes equal to integer multiple of $\pi/4$ only. This kind of convexity is, more popularly, known as *ramp-convexity*.

(3) A digital object S is *digitally convex* if and only if for every pair of pixels $p, q \in S$, $P(S; p, q)$ does not contain any pixel centre of S^c, the complement of S [Kim and Rosenfeld (1980)]

(4) Chanda and Haralick (1994) have proposed another definition of digital convexity based on the morphological concept. Determining whether or not an object is convex based on these definitions is an extremely time consuming task. To have a simpler method for determining convexity let us, first, define the *convex hull*.

Convex hull

The minimal convex polygon that contains an object is known as the *convex hull* of that object.

Several algorithms are available for generating convex hull [Arcelli and Levialdi (1971), Rutovitz (1975)]. A morphological algorithm for generating convex hull S^H of the object S may be described as follows:

$$S^H = \bigcup_{0 \le \theta < \pi} S \bullet l_\theta \tag{13.33}$$

where l_θ is a digital straight line segment of orientation θ and of length equal to the diameter of the circle enclosing the object. In case of ramp-convex hull, $\theta = 0$, $\pi/2$, π, and $3\pi/4$ are sufficient. The ramp-convex hull can also be obtained in a single step by closing the object by an octagon whose sides are equal to diameter of the object. Based on the convex hull we may define digital convex object.

Digital convex

A digital object S is said *digital convex* object if and only if it is same as its *convex hull* S^H.
Thus, a measure of convexity may be given by

$$\text{Convexity} = 1 - \frac{\Psi(S^H/S)}{\Psi(S)} \tag{13.34}$$

Therefore, convexity $\in (0, 1]$ and higher the value closer to the convex hull. Finally, if S is convex then convexity $= 1$. However, generating convex hull is still a costly process. A less expensive method to decide whether or not a digital object is convex may be suggested based on the following property. Suppose a shape in two-dimensional continuous domain $\mathbf{R}^2$ is represented by a compact set $S \subseteq \mathbf{R}^2$. If B has size one, then

$$\rho S = \{\rho p \mid p \in S\} \tag{13.35}$$

defines an object of size ρ that has same shape as S. One can also define the larger shape by repetitive dilation, i.e.

$$S^\rho = \underbrace{S \oplus S \oplus S \oplus \cdots \oplus S}_{(\rho-1)\text{-times}}$$

Now $\rho S = S^\rho$ if and only if S is convex [Maragos (1989), Serra (1982)]. We can use this property in determining digital convexity. Since, straightforward implementation of Equation (13.35) in discrete domain disintegrates the resultant object, we say S is convex if

$$S = \frac{1}{\rho} S^\rho \tag{13.36}$$

Equation (13.34) may be modified accordingly.

13.5 Some Other Properties

A large number of properties other than topological and geometrical properties may be defined over an image or a region of image. Each measurable property highlights some specific characteristics of the image region and is useful for some recognition strategies. Here we present only a few properties that are well known and are widely used in many image analysis tasks. A property may be (i) position (or translation) invariant, (ii) size (or scale) invariant and (iii) orientation (or rotation) invariant. Such invariant properties relieve recognition algorithm from the registration. For example, area of an object is position and orientation invariant; convexity is position, size and orientation invariant; etc.

13.5.1 Spatial Moments

The idea is borrowed straightaway from physics. The graylevel at a pixel is considered as the mass at a point of an object. Thus (i, j)-th moment of an image $f(r, c)$ is defined as

$$m(i, j) = \sum_c \sum_r r^i c^j f(r, c) \tag{13.37}$$

$m(0, 1)$ and $m(1, 0)$ are simply called *moments* with respect to r-axis and c-axis, respectively. We see $m(0, 0)$ is the mass of the object represented by f, and

$$\left\{ \frac{m(1, 0)}{m(0, 0)}, \frac{m(0, 1)}{m(0, 0)} \right\}$$

is the coordinate of the centroid of that object. Similarly, $m(0, 2)$ and $m(2, 0)$ are moments of inertia of object f about r-axis and c-axis, respectively. Let us define m_0 as $m(0, 2) + m(2, 0)$. Then m_0 is the moment of inertia of f about the origin. It may be verified that m_0 is rotation invariant and is also invariant to scaling up to a scaling factor. If we define moment $\overline{m}(i, j)$ about the centroid it is called *central moment*. Central moments are invariant to translation. $m(i, j)$ can also be used as an indicator of symmetry. Substituting r by $-r$ in Equation (13.37) we get

$$m(i, j) = \sum_c \sum_r (-r)^i c^j f(-r, c)$$

$$= (-1)^i \sum_c \sum_r r^i c^j f(-r, c)$$

$$= (-1)^i \sum_c \sum_r r^i c^j f(r, c) \qquad [\text{if } f(-r, c) = f(r, c)]$$

$$= (-1)^i m(i, j)$$

$$= - m(i, j) \qquad\qquad\qquad [\text{if } i \text{ is odd}]$$

or

$$m(i, j) = 0$$

In other words, if $f(r, c)$ is symmetric about c-axis and if i is odd, then $m(i, j)$ is 0. Similarly, if $f(r, c)$ is symmetric about r-axis and if j is odd, then $m(i, j)$ is 0. Finally, if $f(r, c)$ is symmetric about r-axis as well as about c-axis and if $i + j$ is odd, then $m(i, j)$ is 0. For every object, i.e. image, there exists at least one straight line about which its moment of inertia is minimum. Let us call this straight line the *principal axis* of the object. It can be shown that the principal axis passes through the centroid of the object and its slope $\tan \theta$ with respect to r-axis is a root of the following quadratic equation [Rosenfeld and Kak (1982)]:

$$\tan^2 \theta + \frac{\overline{m}(2, 0) - \overline{m}(0, 2)}{\overline{m}(1, 1)} \tan \theta - 1 = 0$$

Another root of this equation is the slope of the line perpendicular to the principal axis.

Example Consider the following table showing pixel values in a small block (4×4) of a graylevel image where coordinates (r, c) of pixels are also given.

$$
\begin{array}{c|cccc}
 & \multicolumn{4}{c}{c} \\
f(r, c) & 1 & 2 & 3 & 4 \\
\hline
1 & 3 & 1 & 2 & 0 \\
2 & 2 & 0 & 3 & 1 \\
3 & 2 & 3 & 1 & 0 \\
4 & 1 & 3 & 0 & 2 \\
\end{array}
$$

$$m(0, 0) = \sum_c \sum_r r^0 c^0 f(r, c) = \sum_c \sum_r f(r, c) = 24$$

$$m(1, 0) = \sum_c \sum_r r^1 f(r, c) = \sum_r r \sum_c f(r, c)$$

$$= 1 \times 6 + 2 \times 6 + 3 \times 6 + 4 \times 6 = 60$$

$$m(0, 1) = \sum_c \sum_r c^1 f(r, c) = \sum_c c \sum_r f(r, c)$$

$$= 1 \times 8 + 2 \times 7 + 3 \times 6 + 4 \times 3 = 52$$

$$m(1, 1) = \sum_c \sum_r rc \, f(r, c)$$

$$= 1 \times 3 + 2 \times 1 + 3 \times 2 + 4 \times 0 + 2 \times 2 + 4 \times 0 + 6 \times 3$$
$$+ 8 \times 1 + 3 \times 2 + 6 \times 3 + 9 \times 1 + 12 \times 0 + 4 \times 1 + 8 \times 3$$
$$+ 12 \times 0 + 16 \times 2$$
$$= 134$$

$$m(2, 0) = \sum_c \sum_r r^2 f(r, c) = \sum_r r^2 \sum_c f(r, c)$$

$$= 1 \times 6 + 4 \times 6 + 9 \times 6 + 16 \times 6 = 180$$

$$m(0, 2) = \sum_c \sum_r c^2 f(r, c) = \sum_c c^2 \sum_r f(r, c)$$

$$= 1 \times 8 + 4 \times 7 + 9 \times 6 + 16 \times 3 = 138$$

$$m_0 = m(2, 0) + m(0, 2) = 180 + 138 = 318 \qquad \blacksquare$$

13.5.2 Texture

Texture analysis is one of the most important techniques used in analysis and classification of images where repetition or quasi-repetition of fundamental image elements occur. Such characteristics can easily be seen in remote sensing images obtained from an aircraft or a satellite platform, or in biomedical images of cells and tissues. Texture is evaluated by one or more properties such as coarseness, smoothness, granulation, randomness and regularity. The spatial organization of the tonal primitives characterizes a texture fairly well.

Generally, by the term *texture* we mean roughness of the surface of the object imaged. Textural features corresponding to human visual perception are very useful for parameterization of appearance of object and its subsequent recognition [Tamura et al (1978)]. Textural features can also be used to estimate orientation and depth of object surface [Horn (1986)]. In an intensity image this roughness is recorded as tonal or intensity variation over a neighbourhood. In most cases this variation appears as a repetitive arrangement of some basic pattern. Basic patterns of large size are indicative of coarser texture. Similarly basic patterns of small size are indicative of finer texture. Again, repetition may or may not be random. However, randomness in textural pattern may occur due to randomness in the basic pattern or due to randomness in repetition nature. Thus texture analysis and classification (also called *texture segmentation*) involve determining the basic pattern(s) as well as regularity/randomness in repetition. All the methods reported in the literature are based on one of the following two approaches:

1. Spectral approach

2. Statistical approach and

3. Structural approach

Spectral techniques (optical transforms and digital transforms) are based on the properties of Fourier spectrum. The image is analysed globally by identifying the percentage energy in the peak. Calculation of discrete Laplacian of the peak, area of the peak, angle of the peak, squared distance of the peak from the origin and angle between the two highest peaks are involved. Among the statistical approaches are autocorrelation functions, texture edgeness, structural elements, spatial moments, spatial graylevel co-occurrence probabilities, graylevel run-length and autoregressive models which are commonly used. Structural approaches deal with the primitives and their spatial relationships. A primitive is usually defined as a connected set of pixels characterized by attributes. The attributes may be gray tone, shape or connected region and/or homogeneity of the local properties. In texture analysis, we try to determine the size of the basic pattern and the periodicity with which it is repeated. It is known that auto-correlation may be used to measure presence and periodicity of subpattern within a signal. So, this may be used for texture analysis as well. Let $g(r, c)$ is the original graylevel image of size $M \times N$ that contains some textured regions. Now we obtain a zero-mean image function corresponding to this image as

$$g^o(r, c) = g(r, c) - \overline{g} \tag{13.38}$$

for all (r, c), where

$$\overline{g} = \frac{1}{MN} \sum_{r=0}^{M-1} \sum_{c=0}^{N-1} g(r, c) \tag{13.39}$$

Auto-correlation at a spatial coordinate (r, c) is computed as the sum of pixel-wise product of the given function with itself translated to (r, c). Therefore, auto-correlation function, or simply auto-correlation matrix, $R(r, c)$ may be defined as

$$R(r, c) = \frac{1}{(M-r)(N-c)} \frac{\sum_{i=0}^{M-r-1}\sum_{j=0}^{N-c-1} g^o(i, j)g^o(i+r, j+c)}{\sum_{i=0}^{M-1}\sum_{j=0}^{N-1} g^o(i, j)g^o(i, j)} \tag{13.40}$$

for $r = 0, 1, 2, ..., M - 1$ and $c = 0, 1, 2, ..., N - 1$. Nature of $R(r, c)$ indicates the presence of basic pattern and its periodicity of repetition. To the extent that basic primitives are spatially periodic, auto-correlation function falls off and rises with distance in periodic manner. If the basic pattern is small the period is small. On the other hand, the period is large if the basic pattern is large.

Since basic patterns are formed by certain arrangements of graylevels, co-occurrence of graylevels at predefined relative positions may be an indication of presence and periodicity of basic pattern. From this point of view graylevel co-occurrence matrix are used in texture analysis and classification. Let us denote the graylevel co-occurrence matrix by $\mathbf{C} = \{e_{i,j}\}$, where i and j are graylevels at pixels at predefined relative positions. So, $0 \leq i, j \leq L - 1$ for an L-level image. For definition and properties of co-occurrence matrix see Chapters 6 and 8. For large M and N, the relative frequency of co-occurrence $P_{i,j} = C_{i,j}/MN$ represents approximately the joint probability mass of the discrete variables i and j. Some statistics based on graylevel co-occurrence matrix that are commonly used in texture analysis are [Haralick et al. (1973), Haralick and Shanmugam (1974), Haralick (1986)]:

$$
\text{Energy:} \qquad \sum_{i=0}^{L-1} \sum_{j=0}^{L-1} P_{i,j}^2 \qquad\qquad (13.41)
$$

$$
\text{Entropy:} \qquad -\sum_{i=0}^{L-1} \sum_{j=0}^{L-1} P_{i,j} \log P_{i,j} \qquad\qquad (13.42)
$$

$$
\text{Contrast:} \qquad \sum_{i=0}^{L-1} \sum_{j=0}^{L-1} (i - j)^2 P_{i,j} \qquad\qquad (13.43)
$$

$$
(m, n)\text{-th Moment:} \qquad \sum_{i=0}^{L-1} \sum_{j=0}^{L-1} i^m j^n P_{i,j} \qquad\qquad (13.44)
$$

$$
\text{Homogeneity:} \qquad \sum_{i=0}^{L-1} \sum_{j=0}^{L-1} \frac{P_{i,j}}{1 + |i - j|} \qquad\qquad (13.45)
$$

These features are used to quantify spatial variation of pixel graylevel or intensity that forms the textural pattern. Finally, these are used for texture classification. Apart from these statistical measures, structural approaches are also employed to describe texture. One such measure of textural property or surface roughness may be provided by, so called, *pattern spectrum*.

13.5.3 Pattern Spectrum

Let us first consider a two-dimensional binary object and establish the physical significance of pattern spectrum. Then we will extend the notion to graylevel image for texture analysis. We know that opening of an object by a structuring element retains only those portions of object where the structuring element can fit in. Thus the number of pixels in the set obtained by subtracting the opened object from the original one gives the area of portion of the object that cannot contain the structuring element. If shape of the structuring element is chosen to preserve the smoothness then the above mentioned number represents the amount of roughness in the object shape. Secondly, if a set of structuring elements is chosen that are of same shape but of various sizes then we correspondingly have a series of numbers representing object roughness at various scale. Suppose S is a binary object and K is a structuring element. Then *pattern spectrum* or *size distribution* may be defined as

$$
PS(n) = \# [S/S \circ nK] \qquad\qquad (13.46)
$$

or, more commonly, as

$$PS(n) = \#\,[(S \circ nK)/(S \circ (n+1)K)] \tag{13.47}$$

for $n = 0, 1, 2, \ldots$ where

$$nK = \underbrace{K \oplus K \oplus K \oplus \cdots \oplus K}_{(n-1)\text{-times}}$$

defines the same pattern K but of size n. By convention, $nK = \{(0, 0)\}$ if $n = 0$. Usually, any regular shape such as circle, square, hexagon, octagon, straight line, etc., is chosen as K. Secondly, size of K is taken to be one, e.g. circle of radius one or straight line of unit length. It may be observed that in Equations (13.46) and (13.47) pattern spectrum is defined in terms of multi-scale opening. Pattern spectrum may also be defined in terms of multi-scale closing and multi-scale erosion [Haralick and Shapiro (1992)]. Figure 13.18 shows an example of residue objects obtained through multi-scale opening by an octagonal structuring element. Figure 13.18(a) is the original image containing an object S. Figures 13.18(b) and 13.18(c) are $S \circ K$ and $S \circ 2K$, respectively. Suppose we intend to use Equation (13.47) to compute the pattern spectrum. Accordingly, the residue objects, i.e. $S/(S \circ K)$ and $(S \circ K)/(S \circ 2K)$ are shown, respectively in Figs. 13.18(d) and 13.18(e). Hence, the number of black pixels in Figs. 13.18(d) and (e) are PS(0) and PS(1),

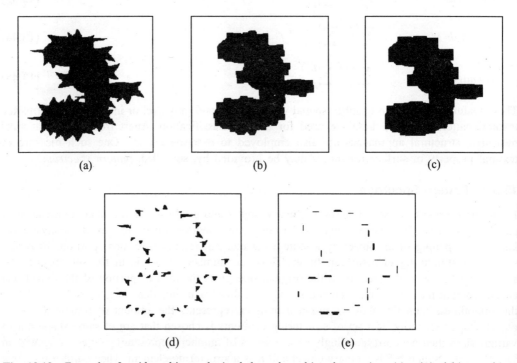

(a)   (b)   (c)

(d)   (e)

Fig. 13.18   Example of residue objects obtained through multi-scale opening: (a) original binary object. Same object after opening: (b) $S \circ K$ and (c) $S \circ 2K$, where K is an octagon. Residual objects are (d) $S/(S \circ K)$ and (e) $(S \circ K)/(S \circ 2K)$.

respectively.

A graylevel image may be viewed as a 3D binary object where size of the image defines the length and width of the object while height at every point is defined by the graylevel at that pixel. Thus, the textural pattern is described as roughness of the top-surface of this 3D object. So, the texture may be quantified through 3D multi-scale opening as is in the case of 2D binary object. Using graylevel morphological operation [Sternberg (1986)] we may rewrite Equation (13.47) in terms of graylevel image $f(r, c)$ and graylevel structuring function $h(r, c)$ as

$$PS(n) = \sum_{(r, c)} [(f \circ nh)(r, c) - \{f \circ (n + 1)h\}(r, c)] \qquad (13.48)$$

for $n = 0, 1, 2, \ldots$, where

$$nh(r, c) = \underbrace{h(r, c) \oplus h(r, c) \oplus h(r, c) \oplus \cdots \oplus h(r, c)}_{(n-1)\text{-times}}$$

Usually $h(r, c)$ is chosen to be a concave function. Thus values of $PS(n)$ for different values of n may form a vector which represents structural properties of texture. In case of fine texture, value of $PS(n)$ is relatively large for low value of n, while $PS(n)$ is higher for high value of n in case of coarse texture.

Summary

In this chapter, various methods for extracting features associated with image regions are described. Various representation schemes suitable for computing image features are also presented. Among the image features the important ones are topological features (e.g. Euler number), geometrical features (e.g. area), structural features (e.g. skeleton) and surface features (e.g. texture). Other features, such as moment, straightness, etc., are also discussed. These features correspond to various attributes of an object or its parts. Each of them is suitable for a specific type of application. So, decomposition and recognition methodologies (as discussed in the following chapters) use these features to classify and recognize the objects in a scene and, subsequently, generate the description of the scene.

Problems

1. Define medial axis. How can medial axis be formed from the distance transform of an object? Give an example.

2. Describe sequential algorithm for computing distance transform. Show that there exists a minimal subset of distance transform from which original object can be reconstructed, and that the medial axis is usually a superset of this minimal set.

3. Describe a morphological algorithm for thinning. State the differences between medial axis and the skeleton obtained through thinning.

4. Consider the following figure where 'X' represents object pixel, and the blank pixels belong to the background.

X	X	X	X	X	X	X
			X			
	X		X		X	
			X			
X	X	X	X	X	X	X
X			X			X
X			X			X
X			X			X
X	X	X	X	X	X	X
X	X	X	X	X	X	X
X	X	X	X	X	X	X
X	X	X	X	X	X	X

Assign (i) Yokoi and (ii) Rutovitz connectivity number to each object pixel.

5. Suggest a sequential method for counting connected components in a binary image.

6. Suppose an object in a binary image is represented by run-length coded chain code (c_i, n_i) of its boundary as given below.

$$(0, 5) \ (3, 6) \ (0, 6) \ (1, 4) \ (0, 5) \ (3, 9) \ (2, 16) \ (1, 11)$$

where c_i is the code and n_i is its run-length. Calculate (i) diameter of the circle enclosing this object and (ii) area of the object.

7. Given a 4×4 image whose graylevels, ordered lexicographically, are as follows:

$$2 \ 3 \ 0 \ 1 \ 1 \ 3 \ 1 \ 2 \ 0 \ 2 \ 0 \ 3 \ 1 \ 1 \ 2 \ 3$$

Calculate the spatial moments up to the second order.

8. Show how moments can be used to determine symmetry in an image.

9. Derive the equation of principal axis of a binary object. Justify the existence of two solutions of slope parameters.

10. Suggest some measures of textural properties based on graylevel co-occurrence matrix. State which textural properties can be determined by investigating pattern spectrum.

Bibliography

Ahuja, N., Davis, L.S. Milgram, D.L., and Rosenfeld, A., 'Piecewise approximation of pictures using maximal neighbourhood', *IEEE Trans. on Computer.*, C-27:375–379, 1978.

Arcelli, C., Cordella, L. and Lavialdi, S., 'Parallel thinning of binary pictures', *Electronic Letters*, 11:148–149, 1975.

Arcelli, C. and Lavialdi, S., 'Concavity extraction by parallel processing', *IEEE Trans. on System, Man and Cybern.*, SMC-1:394–396, 1971.

Basak, J., Pal, N.R. and Patel, P.S., 'Thinning in binary and gray images: A connectionist approach', *J. Inst. Electronics and Tele-commn. Engrs.*, 42:305–313, 1996.

Blum, H., 'A transformation for extracting new descriptor of shapes' in Wathen-Dunn, W., (Ed.), *Models for the Perception of Speech and Visual Forms*, MIT Press, Cambridge, Massachusetts, 1967.

Chanda, B. and Haralick, R.M., 'Mathematical morphology and topological properties of digital objects', Technical Report EE–ISL–90–02, Univ. of Washington, Seattle, 1990.

Chanda, B. and Haralick, R.M., 'Studies on the properties of digital objects using mathematical morphology', *Indian J. Pure and Applied Mathematics*, **25**:181–203, 1994.

Chassery, J.M., 'Discrete convexity: definition, parameterization, and compatibility with continuous convexity', *Comp. Vision, Graphics, and Image Proc.*, **21**:326–344, 1983.

Chen, M. and Yan, P., 'A multiscaling approach based morphological filtering', *IEEE Trans. on Pattern Anal. and Mechine Intell.* PAMI-**11**:694–700, 1989.

Foley, J., Van Daam, A., Feiner, S. and Hughes, J., *Computer Graphics: Principles and Practice.* Addison-Wesley, Reading, Massachusetts, 1992.

Freeman, H., 'Computer processing of line drawing images', *ACM Computing Survey*, **6**:57–97, 1974.

Freeman, H. and Shapira, R., 'Determining the minimum-area encasing rectangle for an arbitrary closed curve', *Commn. of the ACM*, **18**:409–413, 1975.

Haralick, R.M., 'Some neighborhood operators', in Onoe, M., Preston K. Jr. and A. Rosenfeld, (Ed.), *Real Time Parallel Computing Image Analysis*, Plenum, New York, 1981.

Haralick, R.M., 'Statistical image texture analysis, in Young T.Y. and Fu, K.S. (Ed.), *Handbook of Pattern Recognition and Image Processing*. Academic Press, San Diego, California, 1986.

Haralick, R.M. and Shanmugam, K., 'Combined spectral and spatial processing of ERTS image data', *J. Remote Sensing Environment*, **3**:3–13, 1974.

Haralick, R.M., Shanmugam, K. and Dinstein, I., 'Textural features for image classification', *IEEE Trans. on Syst., Man, and Cybern.*, SMC-**3**:610–621, 1973.

Haralick, R.M. and Shapiro, L.G., *Computer and Robot Vision*, Vols. 1 and 2, Addison-Wesley, Reading, Massachusetts, 1992.

Horn, B.K.P., *Robot Vision*, MIT Press, Cambridge, Massachusetts, 1986.

Jang, B. and Chin, R.T., 'Analysis of thinning algorithms using mathematical morphology', *IEEE Trans. on Pattern Anal. and Machine Intell.*, PAMI-**12**:541–551, 1990.

Kim, C.E. and Rosenfeld, A., 'Digital straight lines and convexity of digital regions', Technical Report TR-876, Dept. of Comp. Science, University of Maryland, College Park, Maryland, 1980.

Kitchin, W. and Pugh, A., 'Processing of binary images', in A. Pugh, (Ed.), *Robot Vision*, 1983.

Lavialdi, S., 'On shrinking binary picture patterns', *Commn. ACM*, **15**:7–10, 1972.

Maragos, P., 'Pattern spectrum and multiscale shape representation', *IEEE Trans. on Pattern Anal and Machine Intell.*, PAMI-**11**:701–716, 1989.

Minsky, M. and Papert, S., *Perceptrons*, MIT Press, Cambridge, Massachusetts, 1969.

Pavlidis, T., 'A thinning algorithm for discrete images', *Computer Graphics and Image Processing,* **13**:142–157, 1980.

Pavlidis, T., *Algorithms for Graphics and Image Processing,* Computer Science Press, Rockville, Maryland, 1982.

Pfaltz, J.L. and Rosenfeld, A., 'Computer representation of planer regions by their skeletons', *Commn. ACM,* **10**:119–122, 1967.

Rosenfeld, A., 'Arcs and curves in digital pictures', *Journal Assoc. of Comp. Mach.,* **20**:81–87, 1973.

Rosenfeld, A., 'Digital straight line segments', *IEEE Trans. on Computer,* C-**23**:1264–1269, 1974.

Rosenfeld, A., 'A characterization of parallel thinning algorithm', *Inform. Contr.,* **29**:286–291, 1975.

Rosenfeld, A. and Johnston, E., 'Angle detection on digital curves', *IEEE Trans. on Computer,* C-**22**:875–878, 1973.

Rosenfeld, A. and Kak, A.C., *Digital Picture Processing,* 2nd ed., Vols. 1 and 2, Academic Press, New York, 1982.

Rutovitz, D., 'Pattern recognition', *J. Royal Statistics Soc.,* **129(A)**:504–530, 1966.

Rutovitz, D., 'An algorithm for in-line generation of a convex cover', *Comp. Graphics and Im. Proc.,* **4**:74–78, 1975.

Saha, P., Chanda, B. and Dutta Majumder, D., 'A single scan boundary removal thinning algorithm for 2d binary object', *Pattern Recognition Letters,* **14**:173–179, 1993.

Serra, J., *Image Analysis and Mathematical Morphology,* Academic Press, London, 1982.

Sklansky, J., 'Recognition of convex blobs', *Pattern Recognition,* **2**:3–10, 1970.

Sternberg, S.R., 'Grayscale morphology', *Comp. Vision, Graphics, and Image Proc.,* **35**:333–355, 1986.

Tamura, H., Mori, S. and Yamawaki, T., 'Textural features corresponding to visual perception', *IEEE Trans. on Syst. Man, and Cybern.,* SMC-**8**:460–473, 1978.

Weszka, J.S., Dyer, C. and Rosenfeld, A., 'A comparative study of texture measures for terrain classification', *IEEE Trans. on Syst., Man, and Cybern.,* SMC-**6**:269–285, 1976.

Yokoi, S., Toriwaki, J. and Fukumura, T., 'An analysis of topological properties of digitized binary pictures using local features', *Comp. Graphics and Image Processing,* **4**:63–73, 1975.

Chapter 14

Description

14.1 Introduction

Apart from a variety of methods for extracting various kinds of information from pictorial data discussed different aspects of segmentation have also been dealt with in some detail in Chapters 11 and 12. The objective of describing meaningful segments of a scene resulting at the output of segmentation process and their relationship, will be the key concern of this chapter. In order to perceptually distinguish an object, the description should be powerful enough to store the intricate details. On the other hand, the process of description in the form of data function and information contained therein should not be computationally prohibitive. A given shape could be represented either through its boundary information or using its different regions. Description schemes should be chosen accordingly. In short, description of an object involves a collection of features or attributes. In Chapter 13, we have described various feature extraction techniques. Features usually are computed independent of one another. However, a sufficiently large collection of such features along with their inter-relationship (if any) provide a complete and distinctive description of an object.

There are many different ways in which the notion of description can be interpreted even in traditional pattern recognition problems. When the extracted features are amenable to measurements we can take recourse to statistical classificatory analysis using supervised or unsupervised, parametric or non-parametric, and their combination of approaches. In this approach, describing an object or a scene means assigning it to one of the predetermined number of classes or outside them. This is a very useful approach in many practical situations. However, there are other important and interesting real-life problem domains in which it is not the natural one. For example, where there are abundance of structural information, but the methods are not easily amenable to measurements, the aforementioned methods by themselves are inadequate. In such situations, syntactic or shape theoretic methods that deal explicitly with structural information are needed. In those domains, we are interested in a discursive description rather than in a mere classification.

In a given scene, object(s) and its components described separately have intrinsic relationship of their own. This has perceptual relevance both in identifying and also in discriminating among a cluster of objects. Thus representing such relationship is also an important step in describing an object or a scene. Any shape or pattern description technique must satisfy both the criteria of local and global feature representation. The local features are confined to points or a small neighbourhood around it. For example, the corner points or points with sharp change in curvature and junctions are the local features. The global features are more concerned with large regions rather than certain points of interests or neighbourhoods around them. The contiguous cluster of pixels of identical properties represent a region and parameters like moment, texture, orientation of principal axis and area, are some examples of global feature specified for a region.

14.2   Boundary-based Description

Boundary-based description is the most common medium of depicting a shape and is capable of storing the local features more authentically. Boundaries encompass regions and they are often decomposed to smaller and regular regions which are easy to represent. *Boundary* is a collection of pixels at least one of whose neighbours belong to either background or any other region. There are different ways to represent a boundary. These are boundary as a sequence of (a) connected points, (b) chain codes, (c) connected line segments and (d) Fourier components.

14.2.1   Boundary as a Sequence of Connected Points

The point list representing a boundary of an object in a binary image is an output of the border or boundary following algorithm Pavlidis (1982), [Rosenfeld and Kak (1982)] to generate ordered list of boundary points. Considering 8-connectedness for the object the algorithmic steps are as follows:

Algorithm 14.1

Step 1:   Start rastar scanning (row-wise) from the top-left corner of the image matrix.

Step 2:   As soon as an object pixel (1-pixel or black pixel) is obtained, mark it as start pixel. Do the following steps until we came back to this start pixel.

Step 3:   Based on the pixel last visited (let us call it *previous pixel*) and the pixel being visited currently (let us call it *current pixel*), find the *next pixel* on the boundary.

Note that the *next pixel* of the *current pixel* 'c' is found by searching latter's neighbourhood anti-clockwise, starting from position 's' up to *the previous pixel* 'p' as shown in Fig. 14.1.

Step 4:   Mark the *current pixel* as the *previous pixel* and the *next pixel* as the *current pixel*. Go to Step 3.

This algorithm will follow the boundary in anti-clockwise direction for any closed contour. The boundary point list gives the necessary representation for any closed contour. Obviously, it keeps a lot of information (all edge points) which may not be necessary for cognition or shape discrimination point of view. For each region and each hole, the algorithm has to be repeated accordingly.

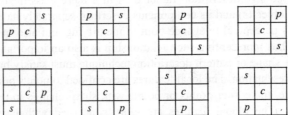

Fig. 14.1   Shows start 's' and end 'p' position of anti-clockwise search for boundary following for different *previous pixel* positions. The *current pixel* is denoted by 'c' and the *previous pixel* by 'p'.

14.2.2 Boundary as a Set of Chain Codes

Chain code due to Freeman (1974) has the advantage of incorporating information regarding local direction. This may be generated from the list of connected point sequence of the boundary. Depending on the previous pixel in the list the current pixel can be represented by one of the eight codes between 0 and 7, in case of 8-connected boundary, or by one of the four codes between 0 and 3, in case of the 4-connected boundary [see Section 8.4.5]. The efficiency and detailed representation of a shape through chain code depends on the resolution and length of chain. Various local features such as high curvature points, corners and shape attributes like convexity could be determined from the chain code. The perimeter, area and many other attributes of the enclosed shape can also be computed from the chain code of the boundary as discussed in Chapter 13.

14.2.3 Boundary as a Sequence of Connected Line Segments

This is more commonly known as *polygonal approximation*. The output of boundary extraction techniques is post-processed to determine a set of control points which are points of interest and marks a significant change of curvature. Then boundary is approximated by a set of straight line segments whose terminal points are pairs of consecutive control points. This results in a polygon which is an approximate description of the given shape or object. Thus, a digital boundary can be approximated by a polygon with arbitrary accuracy. For a closed curve, the approximation is exact when the number of segments in the polygon is equal to the number of points in the boundary so that each pair of adjacent points define a segment of the polygon. However, the goal of a polygonal approximation is to describe the boundary of shape with the fewest possible polygonal segments. It certainly needs less number of bytes to store the entire boundary. A proper threshold has to be selected that makes an optimum trade-off between accuracy of description and the storage requirement. Several methods for polygonal approximation are available in the literature [Fu et al. (1987)]. Below we describe some methods involving *split* and *merge* techniques.

Split

This technique basically *decomposes* the boundary into a set of small segments and, then, represent each segment by a straight line segment. So the main concern here is how to decompose a (closed) curve. One approach is to successively subdivide a segment into two parts until a given criterion is satisfied. Most widely used criterion is that the perpendicular distance between any point on the segment and the line joining segment's end-points should not exceed a preset threshold. If it does, the initial segment is divided into two subsegments the farthest point from the said line. Thus the method is expected to divide the boundary or curve at the points of high curvature. Therefore, vertices of the approximated polygon should be very close to the prominent inflection points of the curve. For an open curve one can start decomposing it trivially based on straight line segment joining its two end-points. However, for a closed curve or object boundary, the best starting pair of points are usually the two farthest points in the boundary or two points farthest along x- or y-direction or crossings of the principal axis with the boundary.

Example An example is shown in Fig. 14.2. Figure 14.2(a) shows an object boundary, and Fig. 14.2(f) shows the approximated polygon obtained by the splitting technique. Figures 14.2(b)–14.2(e) show different steps of splitting. For example, Fig. 14.2(b) shows the first subdivision of the boundary about its furthest points. The point marked 'u' has the largest perpendicular distance from the top segment to line '*pq*'. Similarly, point '*v*' has the largest distance in the bottom segment. [Note that the line '*pq*' is supposed to be two lines coinciding perfectly: one for the top segment and another for the bottom segment.

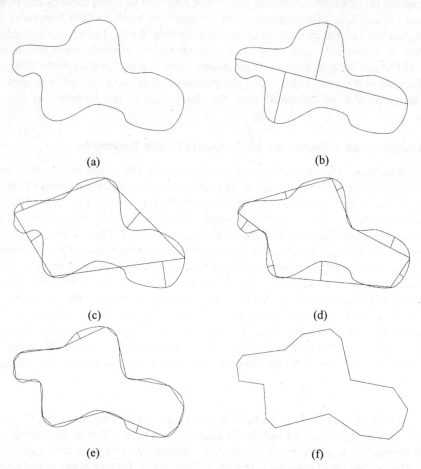

(a)

(b)

(c)

(d)

(e)

(f)

Fig. 14.2 Different steps of polygonal approximation of object boundary by splitting: (a) original boundary, (b)–(e) results of different steps in order, (f) approximated polygon.

Merge

This technique works in a direction opposite to that of splitting method. The method starts at pixel level and grows into a straight line segment by merging connecting pixels to it until a given criterion is satisfied. A commonly used criterion is to check if the least-squares error line fit of the points, merged thus far, exceeds a preset threshold. If it does, the line is terminated and its end-points are stored. The next line starts from the last end-point recorded, and the procedure is repeated until the entire curve is approximated by line segments. Criterion used for splitting may also be used for merging and vice versa. At the end of the procedure, the end points of adjacent line segments form the vertices of the approximated polygon.

Split and merge

One of the major disadvantages of both the 'split' and 'merge' methods is that vertices of polygon do not, in general, correspond to points of inflections (such as corners) in the boundary. This is because a line does not terminate, in case of merging, (or is not divided, in case of splitting) until the error exceeds the threshold. For example, if a long straight line on the boundary were being tracked, it would have turned into a corner and a number (depending on the threshold) of points past the corner would be absorbed before the threshold is exceeded [Fig. 14.3(a)]. Similarly, the distance of corner point from the line joining the end points of boundary segment can be less than the threshold avoiding any further split as shown in Fig. 14.3(b). It is possible, however, to use splitting along with merging to alleviate this difficulty. A comprehensive discussion of this method is given by Pavlidis (1977).

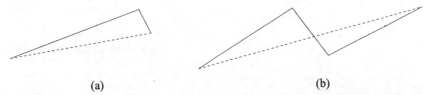

(a)   (b)

Fig. 14.3   Illustrates problems of polygonal approximation by (a) merge technique and (b) split technique. Solid lines are parts of original boundary of object and dotted lines are sides of approximated polygon. Note that end-points of the sides, i.e. vertices of polygon may not always correspond to corners of the boundary.

Lines and arcs

If a boundary has many curvilinear portions then polygonal approximation technique produces (i) either many short line segments or (ii) a crude approximation of the boundary leaving behind many important features. The problem may be surmounted by approximating as much portion of the boundary as possible with straight line segments and the remaining portions with circular or parabolic or elliptical arcs. Secondly, if we have a unit length for a particular type of segment (e.g. straight line of different orientation or arc) then each segment can be viewed as a concatenation of a number of unit segments. Such unit segments are called *structural primitives* or, simply, *primitives*. Now, if we have a code for each distinct primitive then the boundary can be described as a sequence of these codes. Figure 14.4 shows an example of describing boundary by primitives. This kind of representation is suitable for *syntactic recognition*[1].

14.2.4   Boundary as a Sequence of Fourier Components

Let us consider continuous domain where boundary of an object is defined as a closed curve. Then the boundary b may be parameterized as

$$b(t) = [x(t), y(t)], \qquad 0 \le t \le L$$

where L is the arc length of the closed curve. If we view this boundary as being in the complex plane, then each two-dimesnional boundary point is reduced to the one-dimensional complex number. Therefore, the complex function, equivalent to the curve description, is given by

---

[1]Syntactic pattern recognition techniques is described in Section 15.6.

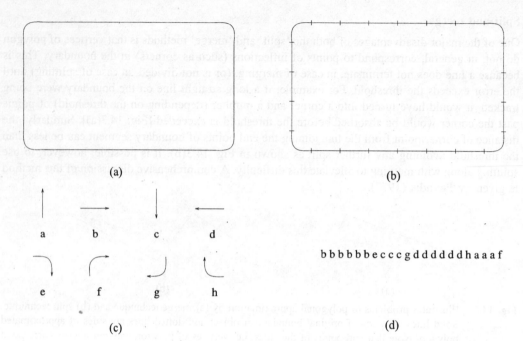

Fig. 14.4 Boundary description by structural primitives: (a) original boundary, (b) decomposed boundary, (c) primitives and their codes, (d) description of the boundary shown in (a) using the codes.

$$b(t) = x(t) + jy(t) \tag{14.1}$$

where $j = \sqrt{-1}$. The Fourier series for $b(t)$ will be given by

$$b(t) = \sum_{n=-\infty}^{\infty} a_n \exp\left(\frac{2\pi j}{L} nt\right) \tag{14.2}$$

and Fourier descriptors are the coefficients $\{a_n\}$ which is given by

$$a_n = \frac{1}{L}\int_0^L b(t) \exp\left(-\frac{2\pi j}{L} nt\right) dt \tag{14.3}$$

One-dimensional discrete Fourier transform can be used to describe a two-dimensional boundary [Persoon and Fu (1977)]. Suppose that N points on a boundary are available. In contrast to representing the entire boundary by a list of points $\{(x_i, y_i) \mid i = 0, 1, 2, ..., N-1\}$ it may be described by a sequence of N complex numbers as given by

$$b(i) = x(i) + j\, y(j) \tag{14.4}$$

The Fourier representation of $b(i)$ is

$$b(i) = \frac{1}{L}\sum_{u=0}^{N-1} B(u) \exp\left(\frac{2\pi j}{L} iu\right) \tag{14.5}$$

for $i = 0, 1, 2,..., N-1$; where $B(u)$ is the Fourier transform of $b(i)$, is given by

$$B(u) = \sum_{i=0}^{N-1} b(i) \exp\left(-\frac{2\pi j}{L}iu\right) dt \qquad (14.6)$$

for $u = 0, 1, 2, \ldots, N-1$. If N is an integer power of 2, $B(u)$ can be computed using FFT algorithm [Cooley and Tukey (1965)]. Secondly, the description of boundary using Fourier transform can easily be normalized, translated (i.e. position of starting point), rotated and sized. For example, to change the size of a contour one can simply multiply the components of $B(u)$ by an appropriate constant; because this is equivalent to multiplying the contour by the same factor. Again, rotation by an angle θ is equivalent to multiplying the elements of $B(u)$ by $\exp(j\theta)$. Finally, shifting the starting point of the contour in the spatial domain corresponds to multiplying the k-th component of $B(u)$ by $\exp(jkT)$, where T is the angular shift of the starting point, and $0 \le T \le 2\pi$. Thus the motivation for this approach is that only the first few components of $B(u)$ are generally required to describe an object in terms of its boundary which can easily be normailzed [Fu et al. (1987)].

14.3   Region-based Description

The region-based description of a shape relies on the global features associated with a particular region. Spatial moments, textures, geometrical attributes like perimeter, area, convexity are some examples of global features and are already discussed in Chapter 13. Some ways for describing regions are given in the folowing sections:

14.3.1   Projection

In general, horizontal projection of an image is a function of row coordinate. Thus the *horizontal projection* $P_f(r)$ of the image $f(r, c)$ may be defined as

$$P_f(r) = \sum_c f(r, c) \qquad (14.7)$$

for all r. The *vertical projection* can also be defined in a similar way as

$$P_f(c) = \sum_r f(r, c) \qquad (14.8)$$

for all c. These are also called horizontal and vertical *signatures*, respectively. Thus, by definition, projection does not preserve enough information enabling reconstruction. In case of binary image, horizontal projection means number of black pixel or foreground pixel or 1-pixel in each row. Figure 14.5 shows an example of projection of binary image or shape. However, projection can be taken along any direction. For example, projection of $f(r, c)$ along a direction θ measured with respect to r-axis can be given by

$$P_{f,\theta}(d) = \sum_r f(r, r, (\tan \theta) + d) \qquad (14.9)$$

for all d. Projection techniques are extensively used in document image analysis and computed tomography.

14.3.2   Minimum Bounding Rectangle

A region can simply be described in terms of the smallest rectangle that encompasses it. For a

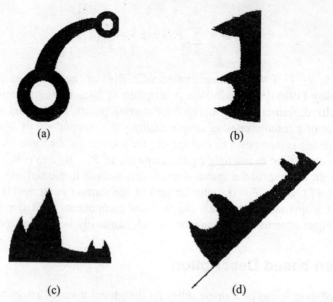

Fig. 14.5   Illustrates projection of object: (a) original binary image containing an object, (b) horizontal projection, (c) vertical projection, (d) diagonal projection.

binary image function $f(r, c)$ a region may be described as a set S of points or pixels such that $S = \{(r, c) \mid f(r, c) = 1\}$. Thus the smallest rectangle can be found in the simplest way if it is upright. In that case, diagonally opposite corner points of the said rectangle are: (r_{min}, c_{min}) and (r_{max}, c_{max}), where

$$r_{min} = \min\{r \mid (r, c) \in S\} \quad \text{and} \quad r_{max} = \max\{r \mid (r, c) \in S\}$$

$$c_{min} = \min\{c \mid (r, c) \in S\} \quad \text{and} \quad c_{max} = \max\{c \mid (r, c) \in S\}$$

Figure 14.6(b) shows the minimum bounding upright rectangle of the shape shown in Fig. 14.6(a). The minimum bounding upright rectangles are not minimum bounding rectangles in true sense. Determining a true minimum bounding rectangle is computationally very expensive. However, we may obtain a close approximation of minimum bounding rectangle when sides of the bounding .

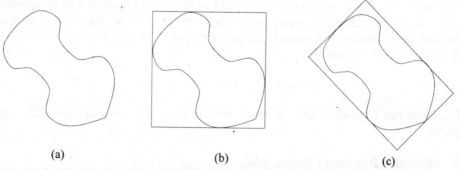

Fig. 14.6   (a) Original binary shape or region, (b) upright minimum bounding rectangle, (c) minimum bounding rectangle aligned along principal axes.

rectangle are aligned with the principal axes [see Section 13.5.1] of the region. Figure 14.6(c) shows such an approximation.

Suppose a shape S is bounded by a minimum rectangle B. Then $E = B - S$ is the set of points that are in B but not in S. Area of E (i.e. number of points in E) is zero if S itself is a rectangle. The shape of the bounding rectangle B is convex. Let us relax the constraint on the shape of B and consider it to be only convex. Then E is minimum when B is convex hull of S and is zero when S is also convex.

14.3.3 Concavity Tree

If the shape of any region S is not, in general, convex then the shape can be described recursively by concave regions resulting from it. These concave regions may be represented as nodes of a tree, called *concavity tree* [Sklansky (1972)]. Suppose the i-th node of the tree represents a region S_i, convex hull of which is denoted by B_i. Then all connected components of $E_i = B_i - S_i$ are children of the node S_i. An example of concavities of an object and corresponding tree are shown in Fig. 14.7.

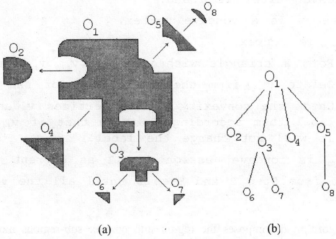

(a)   (b)

Fig. 14.7   Construction of concavity tree: (a) original binary shape or region and its hierarchical concave portions and (b) concavity tree corresponding to (a).

It may be noted that the concept of concavity tree bears similarity with describing three-dimensional object using *constructive solid geometry* (CSG) [Foley et al. (1992)]. Instead of describing the region recursively in terms of its concave regions, it can be described in terms of its convex sub-regions too. For that, region or shape should be decomposed into convex (or near-convex) regions.

14.3.4 Shape Decomposition

Often a region depicting an object is decomposed into sub-regions each of which corresponds to a meaningful part of the object. Sometimes the regions are decomposed with an objective that the sub-regions should be convex.

Decomposing single object

Triangles are always convex. So when an object or region is required to decompose into convex sub-regions, one may opt for decomposing it into triangles. Here we present a simple algorithm that decomposes a polygonal region into a set of triangular regions and a large convex region that may not be a triangle. Suppose the polygon is described by a set of vertices v_i ($i = 1, 2, 3, ..., n$). We call a vertex a *convex vertex* if the angle measured at that vertex is less than 180°, and a *concave vertex* otherwise. Therefore, each vertex carries a label either convex or concave. Algorithmic steps are as follows:

Algorithm 14.2

Step 1: Set the current position at $i + 1$.

Step 2: Check the labels of vertices sequentially starting from the current position. Note that $v_{i+n} = v_i$. Do the following if a concave vertex is found.

Step 3: Suppose v_i is a concave vertex.

   3a: If v_{i+1} is convex,

      (i) Form a triangle with vertices v_i, v_{i+1} and v_{i+2}.

      (ii) Delete v_{i+1} from the vertex list of the polygon.

      (iii) Check the convexity of the vertices v_i and v_{i+2}, and label them accordingly. (Note that if v_{i+2} is convex it will not change the label.)

   3b: If v_{i+1} is concave, assign $i + 1$ as current position.

Step 4: Repeat from Step 2 and Step 3 until all the vertices are convex.

Therefore, the algorithm decomposes the region into convex sub-regions most of which are triangles. However, the number and shape of the regions which the given region is decomposed into depend on the starting vertex, and thus, are not unique. Secondly, the given region can be decomposed into only triangles if the vertex v_i (in Step 2 and consequently in Step 3) is allowed to be convex too, and Step 4 is changed accordingly.

   Example Consider Fig. 14.8 that shows decomposition of a polygon using Algorithm 14.2. The polygon has nine vertices. Suppose convex vertices are labelled with '+' and concave vertices with '−'. Table 14.1 describes the results after each step.

   Residue polygon has all convex vertices: v_6, v_7 and v_8, and is a triangle (Triangle: 7) as shown in Fig. 14.8(f).

■

Table 14.1   Description of Fig. 14.8 that shows the decomposition of a polygon

Original

Vertices:	v_1	v_2	v_3	v_4	v_5	v_6	v_7	v_8	v_9			
Label:	+	+	+	−	+	+	+	−	−			

Fig. 14.8(a)

Vertices:	v_1	v_2	v_3	v_4	v_6	v_7	v_8	v_9		v_4	v_5	v_6
Label:	+	+	+	−	+	+	−	−				Triangle: 1

Fig. 14.8(b)

Vertices:	v_2	v_3	v_4	v_6	v_7	v_8	v_9		v_9	v_1	v_2
Label:	+	+	+	+	+	−	−				Triangle: 2

Fig. 14.8(c)

Vertices:	v_2	v_3	v_4	v_6	v_7	v_8		v_8	v_9	v_2
Label:	+	+	+	+	+	−				Triangle: 3

Fig. 14.8(d)

Vertices:	v_3	v_4	v_6	v_7	v_8		v_8	v_2	v_3
Label:	+	+	+	+	−				Triangle: 4

Fig. 14.8(e)

Vertices:	v_4	v_6	v_7	v_8		v_8	v_3	v_4
Label:	+	+	+	−				Triangle: 5

Fig. 14.8(f)

Vertices:	v_6	v_7	v_8		v_8	v_4	v_6
Label:	+	+	−				Triangle: 6

If the object or the region of interest is not a polygon then its decomposition is a non-trivial task. However, if different parts of the object have different shape (or, even simply size) characteristics then morphological algorithms can be developed to decompose the object. For example, consider Fig. 14.9. Figure 14.9(a) shows a binary image of a hammer. If we open the image with horizontal and vertical line structuring elements, Figs. 14.9(b) and 14.9(c) will result. Now subtracting (b) from (c) we get handle of the hammer as shown in Fig. 14.9(d). Finally, subtraction of (d) from (a) produces Fig. 14.9(e) that shows head of the hammer. In this approach, both algorithmic steps and structuring elements are completely problem dependent.

After decomposing the object, features (such as texture, moments, area, elongatedness) associated with each part is extracted/computed [see Chapter 13]. Then the object is described in terms of these parts and their inter-relationship using either graph or relational table or some other scheme. Finally, depending on the description scheme a suitable object recognition technique is chosen [see Chapter 15].

Separating images of overlapped objects

Recognizing objects and estimating their pose is one of the major objectives in image analysis research [Ballard and Brown (1982), Fu et al. (1987)]. When one such image understanding system is put to operate in real environment, recognition and pose estimation algorithms are usually developed using simple features. The simplest feature of an image is intensity or graylevel,

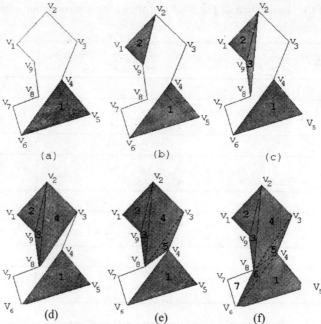

Fig. 14.8 Decomposition of a polygonal region (object) into convex sub-regions (parts). Convex sub-regions are triangles in this case.

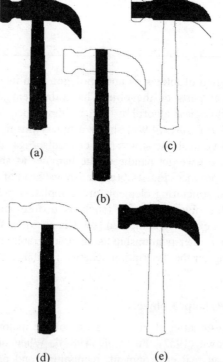

Fig. 14.9 Decomposition of an object (hammer) into semantically meaningful parts (handle and head).

and the corresponding representation is by a two-dimensional array. The objects may then be recognized by simple *image matching*[2] technique which performs the best when objects are well separated. This assumption may not be always true in real life, and an object may lie on another. A simple method for separating images of overlapped objects is described below [Chanda (1992)].

Suppose the input is a binary image which contains the silhouette of industrial objects. The objects are elongated, like screw-driver, spanner and hammer and each of their silhouette has at least one long straight strip. Let us call width of this long straight strip as *principal width*. In the image, an object may be overlapped by at most one other object and somewhere within this strip. An image frame contains only one connected component of 1-pixel. That means during processing of the image, we encounter only two types of situations:

1.   image contains a single object

2.   image contains two objects overlapping each other

Since we are working only with the silhouettes of the objects, which object is lying on which does not matter in subsequent processing.

Suppose, in binary image, *object* 1 is represented by set A of pixels of value 1 and *object* 2 is represented by set B of pixels of value 1. Each of these A, B, etc., has an elongated part (represented by a relatively thin and long straight strip), and some non-elongated parts. Now, after certain translation and rotation the sets A and B are transformed to A' and B', respectively. Hence, the silhouette of overlapped objects in binary image is represented by

$$I = A' \cup B'$$

The principal widths of the set of objects whose images are presented to the system is known (from the prototypes or models of the objects). Suppose these widths are w_1, w_2, w_3, and so on, and let w be the minimum among them. Secondly, the lengths of the straight strips are also known. Suppose these lengths are l_1, l_2, l_3, and so on, and let l be the minimum among them. Thirdly, the angle between the axes, i.e. lines parallel to the said long strips of the overlapped objects is not less than $t°$.

The goal is to generate images of isolated objects from the observed images of the overlapped objects, i.e. to generate images containing A' and B' individually starting from the binary image I. Algorithmic steps along with motivation, explanation and expected output of each step are as follows.

Algorithm 14.3

Step 1:   Determine the number of objects in the given image. If the number of objects is more than one, then determine their orientation.

Generate $S_i(I, K)$ by opening I [shown in Fig. 14.11(a) with structuring element K_i, i.e.

$$S_i(I, K) = \#(I \circ K_i)$$

where K_i ($i = 1, 2, ..., 180/d$) is straight line segme‍ shorter than l and much longer than w, and making an ang

---

$(i - 1)d°$ with r-axis. The interval $d°$ is chosen to be less than or equal to $\arcsin(w/l)$. This guarantees that for at least one value of i, K_i must lie within the thin straight strip of A' (say) for some amount of translation. As a result if I is opened with this K_i, the straight strip of A' will result and it may be said that the straight strip (as well as A') makes an angle approximately equal to $(i - 1)d°$ with r-axis. Non-elongated parts of A' are absent in the result of opening since the length of the structuring element is usually greater than the diameter of the non-elongated parts. Now, if the orientation of the structuring element is varied in either direction (or, in other words, value of i is increased or decreased), it is expected that the structuring element will not fit within A' (although at some places the structuring element may fit in practice). Therefore, $\#(I \circ K_i)$ falls sharply on both sides of the said value of i, and we see a sharp peak. If the width of A is such that for more than one value of i, K_i matches the straight strip we get a dome type peak. (However, even in this situation a particular i may show the best match.) The same is true for B' as well. Now if t is sufficiently greater than d then two well separated peaks are formed corresponding to the straight strips of A' and B'.

If $S_i(I, K)$ contains only one peak then the image contains one object only, and the image can be passed for subsequent processing such as image matching. If $S_i(I, K)$ [as shown in Fig. 14.10(a), in ideal case] contains two peaks for $i = j$ and k (say), then it can be said that there are two objects, one of which is overlapped by the other, and their orientations are roughly $(j - 1)d°$ and $(k - 1)d°$, respectively. Estimated angles are $0°$ and $40°$ for the image shown in Fig. 14.11(a).

Step 2: Once we know that the image contains multiple objects as well as their orientations, we extract thin straight strip of each object. Suppose orientation of A' is $(j - 1)d°$, then R, as defined below, represents the thin straight strip of A'.

$$R = I \circ K_j$$

Result is shown in Fig. 14.11(b).

Step 3: Now R is conditionally dilated by D, a small disk structuring element, with respect to the input image I until $(R_m - R_{m-1})$ contains two connected components only, where

$$R_0 = R$$

$$R_i = (R_{i-1} \oplus D) \cap I$$

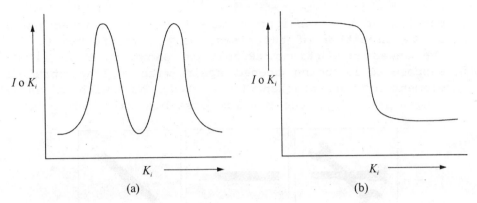

Fig. 14.10 Examples of ideal pattern spectrum: (a) $\#(I \circ K_i)$ versus angle when the length of the line structuring element K_i is fixed, (b) $\#(I \circ K_i)$ versus length when the angle of the line structuring element K_i is fixed.

Here the thin strip R of A' is grown by appending non-elongated parts of A' to itself. Dilation of R by a disk structuring element D makes it grow in all possible directions, but intersection with I retains only those points which belong to I. As a result, non-elongated parts of A' are grown and a part of straight strip of B' is also augmented to R at the place of overlap. If we count the number of connected components of $(R_m - R_{m-1})$ at this phase, the count will be more than two, because regions being appended are at two ends of the straight strip portion of B' as well as at some other non-elongated portions of A'. After some iterations non-elongated parts of A' are completely grown. If we continue the process, R will grow only along the straight strip of B', and the number of connected components of $(R_m - R_{m-1})$ will be two. We use this criterion to stop the iteration of conditional dilation. Finally, R_m becomes the object A' alongwith a part of thin strip of B'. The result is shown in Fig. 14.11(d). Steps 2 and 3 are repeated with K_k too, and S_n is obtained. In fact, R_m and S_n are the images of isolated objects with the exception that blister type regions are grown at the position where they overlapped. The results are shown in Figs. 14.11(c) and 14.11(e).

Step 4: Next, we obtain common part of R_m and S_n which is denoted by X, i.e.

$$X = R_m \cap S_n$$

X may be described in two different ways. In the first case, it may be said that X is union of a portion of the straight strip of A' and some unwanted portion that has come from B'. And in the second case, it is the union of a portion of the straight strip of B' and unwanted portions of A'. In either of the cases, we are interested to delete the unwanted portions. Result is shown in Fig. 14.11(f).

Step 5: Suppose X is being opened again with a line structuring element of orientation $(j - 1)d°$ and with a variable length from l_{min}, the minimum possible value of length, to

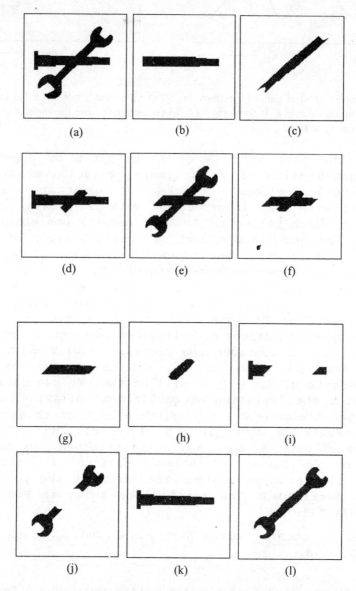

Fig. 14.11   Step-by-step results of separation of image of overlapped objects (see the text): (a) input binary image I of overlapped objects, (b) $I \circ K_j$, (c) $I \circ K_k$, (d) R_m, (e) S_n, (f) X, (g) X_1, (h) X_2, (i) $R_m - X$, (j) $S_n - X$, (k) goal image R', and (l) goal image S'.

l_{max}, the maximum possible value of length. As long as, the length of the structuring element is less than w_B sin $(k - 1) d°$, where w_B is the principal width of B, X opened by the structuring element gives back a set which is ideally same as X. However, in practice, the result of opening is not exactly the set X but is very very close to it. But as the length of the structuring element crosses this limit, unwanted portions are deleted and the result of opening retains portion of the straight strip of A' only since its length is much larger than the said limit. If we plot the #(X o K_i') versus length of K_i' then, in ideal case, we should get a pattern spectrum as shown in Fig. 14.10(b). Let K_j' be the structuring element of length greater than the value corresponding to which the curve in Fig. 14.10(b) shows the sharp fall. K_k' is another structuring element obtained in similar way.

Step 6: As described in Step 5, if X is opened by structuring elements K_j' and K_k', respectively unwanted portion of B' and A' would be deleted. Suppose

$$X_1 = X \text{ o } K_j' \text{ and } X_2 = X \text{ o } K_k'$$

Hence, X_1 is X without unwanted portions of B'; or in other words, X_1 is a portion of the straight strip of A' free from any significant noise due to presence of B'. Similarly, X_2 is X without unwanted portions of A'; or in other words, X_2 is a portion of straight strip of B' free from any significant noise due to presence of A'. Resulting X_1 and X_2 are shown in Figs. 14.11(g) and (h), respectively.

Step 7: From both R_m and S_n the common portion X, which contains the desired portion of the straight strips as well as some unwanted portions, is deleted, and then only the desired portion of straight strip is added to get the desired objects. For example, since both R_m and X contain same unwanted portions of B' and R_m is closer to the desired object A', X is deleted from R_m. As a result, R_m becomes free from unwanted portion of B'; but at the same time it loses a portion of straight strip because X also contains that portion of A'. Now, the union of the resultant image and X_1, which contains only the desired portion of straight strip of A', gives the desired image R' (say) corresponding to A'. Similarly, we obtain image S' corresponding to B'. That means, if R' and S' are defined as

$$R' = (R_m - X) \cup X_1 \text{ and } S' = (S_n - X) \cup X_2$$

respectively, then the images containing R' or S' are the goal images. The results of this step are shown in Figs. 14.11(i) and (k), and Figs. 14.11(j) and (l) for R' and S', respectively.

14.4 Relationship

The constraints of shape description requires description of relationship between regions obtained through segmentation process. Given the methodologies for decomposition of a shape as discussed in the last section, a complete description of any complex scene could be accomplished either through its global features or through features of each component and their inter-relationship. Formal representation techniques are discussed in this section.

14.4.1 Relational Description

Recognition by components is one of the fundamentals of human image understanding system. However, in most cases, the description becomes subjective or symbolic. Relationships are often described in terms of key words like above, inside, near, longer and brighter. Features which are evaluated through deterministic process are easy to express through formal definitions of conventional mathematics. Unfortunately, there are features and attributes whose description may not be completely deterministic, and in Chapter 15 a different set of treatments are presented to tackle them.

Let us start our definition of relationship considering primitives and features present in a scene. Since, an image consists of several distinct regions or parts or subparts which, in turn, could be described using discrete attributes, we can define their relationship by reviewing discrete mathematics.

Let A and B are two sets representing either parts or subparts or their features. Suppose further, if $a \in A$ and $b \in B$, then $A \times B$ denotes the set of all ordered pairs of elements of A and B, and a R b specifies relationship between the ordered pair (a, b). Therefore, a R b is a subset of $A \times B$. If relationship is described between two objects, the relationship is binary, and ternary in case of three objects, and quarternary for four objects, and so on. A ternary relationship could be an ordered pair and a subset of $(A \times B) \times C$ where the first component itself is a binary ordered pair. Reflexive, symmetric and transitive relations could be defined in any of the ordered pairs.

Example   Given here is an example of binary relationship presented in the form of a table. Consider four regions $\{a, b, c, d\}$ of the house shown in Fig. 14.12. Let us define a relation 'larger than' as follows. Suppose there are two regions X and Y, and their areas are denoted by A_X and A_Y, respectively. Now X is said to be 'larger than' Y if $A_X > A_Y$. Thus the relation 'larger than' is a binary relation defined on ordered pair. With respect to the regions of Fig. 14.12 the relation may be described by Table 14.2. The entry 1 denotes 'larger than' relation whereas 0 denotes 'not larger than'.

■

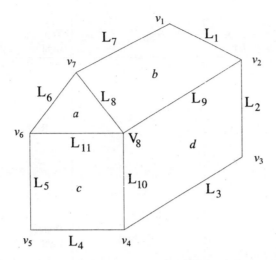

Fig. 14.12   An example figure (a house) to illustrate binary relations between its various kinds of features.

Table 14.2   Binary relation 'larger than' is described with respect to Fig. 14.12.

larger than	a	b	c	d
a		0	0	0
b	1		1	1
c	1	0		0
d	1	0	1	

The 'larger than' relation is a relation based on geometric attributes or features. Relations based on attributes colour, texture, etc., are also often used. However, relationships between different parts of an object or between diffferent objects of a scene are usually defined based on spatial or positional attributes. Some example of positional relations are 'top of', 'left of', etc. Consider Fig. 14.13 containing an object A, say, and its upright minimum bounding rectangle. Now we may simply say another object B is 'top of' A if the centroid of B lies above the top boundary of the said bounding box of A. Other positional relations such as 'left of', 'bottom-right of', etc., can be defined in a similar way.

Relational table is a convenient way of representing ternary or higher relations [Korth and Silberschatz (1988)]. If an ordered n-tuple $A_1, A_2, \ldots, A_i, \ldots A_n$ represents a set of attributes, a number of relations could be described between them and also between other n-tuples of the same scene. Tables 14.3–14.5 demonstrate such relationship between lines, surfaces and vertices of Fig. 14.12. If a particular attribute uniquely represents an ordered n-tuple, the attribute is called *primary key*. There may not be any primary key for a particular set and there could be a set of attributes which may form *primary composite key*. The attribute details are stored through the geometry of primitives. For example, line information could be stored through parametric form of line equation

$$x = x_1 + (x_2 - x_1)t \quad \text{and} \quad y = y_1 + (y_2 - y_1)t \quad \text{where} \quad t \in [0, 1] \quad (14.10)$$

for a line with endpoints (x_1, y_1) and (x_2, y_2). Similarly, for planar surface equation $Ax + By + Cz + D$

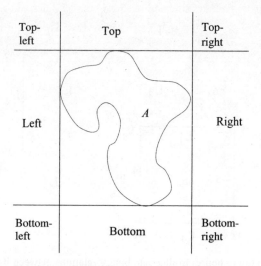

Fig. 14.13 Positions relative to an object A.

= 0, the coefficients (A, B, C, D) are stored. Table 14.3 gives the relational between the line segments and the vertices of the house in Fig. 14.12 whereas Tables 14.4 and 14.5 present the relationship between vertices and regions and the relationship between lines and regions, respectively. Obviously, several other forms of relational tables could be created depending on the derived attribute sets of the scene or its segmented regions.

Table 14.3 Relational table representing relations between line segments and vertices as shown in Fig. 14.12

	L_1	L_2	L_3	L_4	L_5	L_6	L_7	L_8	L_9	L_{10}	L_{11}
v_1	1						1				
v_2	1	1							1		
v_3		1	1								
v_4			1	1						1	
v_5				1	1						
v_6					1	1					1
v_7						1	1	1			
v_8								1	1	1	1

Table 14.4 Relational table representing relations between vertices and regions as shown in Fig. 14.12

	v_1	v_2	v_3	v_4	v_5	v_6	v_7	v_8
a						1	1	1
b	1	1					1	1
c				1	1	1		1
d		1	1	1				1

Table 14.5 Relational table representing relations between lines and regions as shown in Fig. 14.12

	L_1	L_2	L_3	L_4	L_5	L_6	L_7	L_8	L_9	L_{10}	L_{11}
a						1		1			1
b	1						1	1	1		
c				1	1					1	1
d		1	1						1	1	

The important aspect could be to investigate the invariance of such representation. Depending on the viewpoint transformation, a subset of the vertices, lines and surfaces would be visible and consequently, only the relational table for visible attributes are defined. The relational table for attributes which are most visible under projections is the important source of information for object identification or in a scene understanding system. Quite often a natural scene consists of multiple objects and as a result requires description of relations not only between parts of a single object but also between parts of different objects or their parts. Hierarchical relational description are often used to describe such combination of parts. Formally, relational description of an object is a pair (A, X) where A is a set of parts and X is a set of relations among the parts. Hierarchy is embedded in the part set A such that the element in A could be decomposed, depending on the level of hierarchy desired, into further 'atomic' subparts until no further decomposition is permissible. For example, in Fig. 14.12, let the surfaces (a, c) form the front face while the pair (b, d) form the side face. For the given scene, let us define the relations as *left-of* and *top-of*. Therefore, the house could be described as

```
H  =  ({FrontFace, SideFace}, {left-of, top-of})
left-of  (FrontFace, SideFace)
      FrontFace  =  ({a, c}, {top-of})
      SideFace  =  ({b, d}, {top-of})
```

This kind of description can also be implemented using a *graph* where elements of A (i.e. objects or its parts) are represented as *nodes*, and *edges* represent the elements of X (i.e. relation between nodes). Such a description of object is presented in the next section.

14.4.2 Region Adjacency Graph

The *region adjacency graph* (RAG) has already been described in Chapter 11 in the context of region segmentation. In this section we describe RAG for scene and object description [Pavlidis (1977)]. The term *adjacency* specifies spatial closeness between two parts. Naturally, it is part of binary relation. In scene description, adjacency measure between regions could be an effective descriptor. The region adjacency graph is a representation of this relation through a graph theoretic approach. Relevant terms of graph theory necessary for defining region adjacency graph are defined in Section 15.8.

Two regions are said to be adjacent if at least one boundary point of one region is adjacent to some boundary point of other region. A pixel is connected to each of its 8- (or 4-) neighbours. Two adjacent regions are closest if at least one boundary point of one region is connected to some boundary point of other region. Even if two regions are not connected, one could be adjacent to the other with some degree. There could always be a measure, for example, Euclidean distance measure, specifying the degree of adjacency between the regions. In case of an image and its derived regions, there is always a region, say background, to which some or all of the regions are connected or adjacent. Thus region adjacency graph may be constructed as follows [Pavlidis (1977)]. For a given scene or object, consider different regions (parts) obtained through the segmentation process form the nodes of a graph. A list of attributes or features corresponding to the region is attached with the node. For two adjacent regions, the corresponding nodes are connected by links. Links may be weighted with a numeric value representing degree of adjacency. Secondly, links may be directed signifying positional relations such as *top-of*, *left-of*, etc. A scene or an object described in such a way can then be analysed by structural pattern recognition techniques as described in Chapter 15. An example of RAG for Fig. 14.12 is shown in Fig. 14.14 where links are weighted with positional attributes.

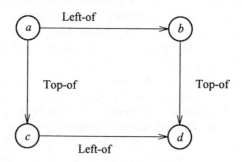

Fig. 14.14   An example of region adjacency graph (RAG) that describes the house in Fig. 14.12.

Summary

This chapter describes various schemes for object and scene description. The schemes can be grouped into two broad categories— boundary-based and region-based. Among boundary-based description schemes (i) list of connected points, (ii) polygonal approximation and (iii) Fourier descriptor are discussed in detail. Among region-based schemes (i) projection, (ii) minimum bounding rectangle and (iii) shape decomposition are described. Separation of images of overlapped objects is also presented. The description scheme for various relations among different parts of an object or that of a scene is given. Scheme for describing objects or scene using region adjacency graph is also discussed.

Problems

1. Justify with example that number of sides depends on the starting point(s) and error threshold in case of polygonal approximation.

2. Given a rectangle of any size. Represent its boundary in terms of straight line segments of unit length.

3. A 256 × 256 image contains an ellipse with its centre at (128, 128) and major and minor axes are 200 and 150 units, respectively. Select 64 points from its boundary maintaining equal (a) angular interval at its centre and (b) spatial interval along its perimeter.

Compute Fourier transform coefficients of these points' coordinates.

4. Take a document page having two or more column layout. Scan it with as good alignment as possible. Compute horizontal and vertical projections of the page image. Point out possible features that may be extracted from these projections.

5. Generate a 32×24 image of the character 'B' such that strokes are 7 pixels thick. Design a morphological algorithm to decompose the character into horizontal and vertical straight line segments and arcs.

6. Generate an isometric projection of a hexagonal prism. Construct a relational table representing 'adjacent to' relation between faces.

7. Generate an isometric projection of a hexagonal prism. Construct a relational table representing binary relations between lines and vertex. State the relations.

Bibliography

Ballard, D.H. and Brown, C.M., *Computer Vision*, Prentice Hall, Englewood Cliffs, New Jersey, 1982.

Chanda, B., 'Application of binary morphology to separate overlapped objects', *Pattern Recognition Letters*, **13**:639–645, 1992.

Cooley, J.W. and Tukey, J.W., 'An algorithm for the machine computation of complex Fourier series', *Math. Comput.*, **19**:297–301, 1965.

Foley, J., Van Daam, A., Feiner, S. and Hughes, J., *Computer Graphics: Principles and Practice*, Addison-Wesley, Reading, Massachusetts, 1992.

Freeman, H., 'Computer processing of line drawing images', *ACM Computing Survey*, **6**:57–97, 1974.

Fu, K.S., Gonzalez, R.C. and Lee, C.S.G., *Robotics*, McGraw-Hill, New York, 1987.

Korth, H.F. and Silberschatz, A., *Database System Concepts*, Tata McGraw-Hill, New Delhi, 1988.

Pavlidis, T., *Structural Pattern Recognition*, Springer-Verlag, New York, 1977.

Pavlidis, T., *Algorithms for Graphics and Image Processing*, Computer Science Press, Rockville, Maryland, 1982.

Persoon, E. and Fu, K.S., 'Shape discrimination using Fourier descriptors', *IEEE Trans. on Syst., Man and Cybern.* SMC-**7**:170–179, 1977.

Rosenfeld, A. and Kak, A.C., *Digital Picture Processing*, 2nd ed., Vols. 1 and 2, Academic Press, New York, 1982.

Sklansky, J., 'Measuring concavity on a rectangular mosaic', *IEEE Trans. on Computer*, C-**21**, 1972.

Chapter 15

Recognition

15.1 Introduction

Recognition or more specifically *pattern recognition* is a typical characteristic of human beings and other living organisms. The term *pattern* means something that is set up as an ideal to be imitated [Pavlidis (1977)]. For example, in our childhood a shape 'A' is shown to us and we are asked to imitate that. So the shape is the ideal one. On the other hand, if what we produce or draw obeying that instruction is close to that shape, our teacher identifies that as 'A'. This identification step is called *recognition* and the shapes we draw (i.e. objects we made) may be termed as *patterns*. Thus, the pattern recognition means identification of the ideal object. Recognition should, therefore, be preceded by development of the concept of the ideal or *model* or *prototype*. This process is called *learning*. In most real-life problems no ideal example is available. In that case, the concept of ideal is abstracted from many near-perfect examples. Under this notion learning is of two types: *supervised learning* if appropriate label is attached (by a teacher) to each of these examples; and *unsupervised learning* if no such labelling is available. It is obvious that for recognizing an object we must receive (or sense) some information or features from that object. Based on these features we assign the object being considered to one of the possible classes each of which represents a pattern. Hence, *classification* is the actual task to be done and we call it recognition if the classes are labelled with particular patterns. Sometimes, learning and recognition work together; outcome of recognition process modifies knowledge about the pattern classes. Unsupervised methods usually fall in this category.

Usually recognition process deals with physical items. Thus it depends on features from the items. Such process is called *sensory recognition*. There is another kind of recognition process which deals with abstract items such as an idea, a theory, a solution to a problem, a philosophical question, etc. This may be termed as *conceptual recognition* [Pavlidis (1977)] and is beyond the scope of this book. Here we will treat only sensory pattern recognition and more specifically *visual pattern recognition*.

Since objects are assigned to the classes based on the invariant features associated with them, it is obvious that objects of the same class must possess similar features and those which belong to different classes possess different features. Therefore, the set of features that distinguishes objects of different classes and is common to objects of the same classes is the key for classification and recognition. Identifying such a minimal feature set is an important step in the process of recognition. The process is called *feature selection*. Another major step is designing the *decision process*. The decision procedure should be optimum in a sense that the classification error must be minimum. This is developed usually through learning. That means given a set of training data, a set of decision rules is to be devised so that the training data are separated into the given set of classes in an optimum way. Note that each training data is a feature vector along with the class label which the object actually belongs to. This is an example of supervised learning. Unsupervised learning may be exemplified by clustering where feature vectors are supplied along with some indirect information about the classes. This may include number of classes, intra-class distance and inter-class distance among feature vectors. Decision methodologies adopt one of two major approaches: mathematical and heuristic. Mathematical approaches are based on the given set of models, and decision rules are devised satisfying optimal criteria of classification. On the other hand, when no such model is available decision rules are designed using human intuition and experience for a specific problem. The mathematical approach includes deterministic, statistical, fuzzy set theoretic and syntactic recognition; while heuristic methods include graph matching, tree searching, etc.

Surely the ultimate objective of any image processing task is to recognize the object(s) in an image. Having detected regions of interest, in the previous chapters, we have discussed several techniques to meaningfully describe these regions and their interrelationship. The descriptions are perceptually relevant in the sense that they have enough discriminating power to distinguish shapes with minor changes. In this chapter we concentrate on recognition aspects which are based on geometry and intensity-based features. If a complete set of discriminatory features for the pattern classes can be determined, the classification and recognition processes reduce to simple matching process. In most cases, recognition involves matching of object features in a scene with that of the models. Such matching, therefore, determines a measure of similarity between the object(s) in a scene with the object(s) in model data base.

15.2 Deterministic Methods

Suppose $\mathbf{f} = (f_0\ f_1\ f_2\ \cdots\ f_{n-1})$ is a vector representing n features of an object. Also suppose there are m classes: $C_0, C_1, \ldots, C_{m-1}$ where i-th class is represented by a prototype feature vector or model c_i of n elements. It is known that the object represented by the vector $\mathbf{f}$ belongs to one of these m classes. Then from the following notion of *minimum distance classifier* we can say that the object belongs to class C_k, if

$$d(\mathbf{f},\ \mathbf{c}_k) < d(\mathbf{f},\ \mathbf{c}_i) \qquad \text{for all } i \text{ and } i \neq k \tag{15.1}$$

where d is a metric. Any tie may be resolved arbitrarily. Defining or choosing an appropriate metric is an important requirement for classification.

15.2.1 Shape Distance Measure

Shape distance measure is a convenient similarity measure between shapes, because they are directly related to each other. In fact, lesser the distance greater is the similarity. It is very difficult to define the term 'shape' though it is widely understood. However, 'shapes' are often described in terms of features and the 'shape distance' measure is the distance between these feature vectors. Since, a shape can have both local and global features, the measure of distance could be global and local as well. For example, moments of a shape generate a set of global features, whereas measures like presence of corner, curvature and amount of convexity, etc., can be treated as local features specific to a subregion. A collection of local features may form a representative global feature and shape distance may be defined on such feature set.

If $\mathbf{c}_i$ and $\mathbf{f}$ are feature vectors of n elements representing i-th model and the object, respectively, the Euclidean shape distance between the model and the object is given by

$$d(\mathbf{f}, \mathbf{c}_i) = \sqrt{\sum_{j=0}^{n-1} (f_j - c_{ij})^2} = \| \mathbf{f} - \mathbf{c}_i \|$$ (15.2)

The Euclidean distance measure is invariant up to translation, rotation and isotropic scaling conditions. More general shape metrices or geometric invariant measures are often used to calculate shape distance. Though the Euclidean distance is most widely used to determine shape distance, weighted Euclidean and Mahalanobis distances are also used. For example, not all the features representing an object or a class are equally important and this observation leads to using *weighted Euclidean distance* defined as

$$d(\mathbf{f}, \mathbf{c}_i) = \sqrt{\sum_{j=0}^{n-1} w_j (f_j - c_{ij})^2}$$ (15.3)

where w_j are weighting factors forcing the importance of j-th feature in describing the shape. When statistical divergence properties of features are explicitly used as weights, we arrive at another useful measure, called *Mahalanobis distance*:

$$d(\mathbf{f}, \mathbf{c}_i) = (\mathbf{f} - \mathbf{c}_i)^T \Sigma_i^{-1} (\mathbf{f} - \mathbf{c}_i)$$ (15.4)

where Σ_i is the variance–covariance matrix of features of objects corresponding to the i-th class. Sometimes, the features are normalized before calculating the distance measure.

A *class* is often described as a collection of feature vectors. That means when no ideal model is available, a group of near-perfect examples defines the class. Suppose $\{\mathbf{c}_{kt}\}$ is a set of feature vectors representing the class C_k, then a couple of distance measures between shapes could be described.

- *Feature vector to feature vector distance* is the distance between a member of one class and a member of another class, and can be computed as Equation (15.2):

$$d(\mathbf{c}_{is}, \mathbf{c}_{kt}) = \sqrt{\sum_{j=0}^{n-1} (c_{isj} - c_{ktj})^2} = \| \mathbf{c}_{is} - \mathbf{c}_{kt} \|$$ (15.5)

- *Feature vector to class distance* is the distance between a member of one class and another class, and can be computed as

$$d(\mathbf{c}_{is}, C_k) = \min_t \{d(\mathbf{c}_{is}, \mathbf{c}_{kt})\}$$ (15.6)

Another form of this distance measure could be the distance between $\mathbf{c}_{is}$ and the mean vector of $\{\mathbf{c}_{kt}\}$.

- *Intra-class distance* is the maximum distance between any two feature vectors of the same class.

$$d(C_k) = \max_{s,t} \{d(\mathbf{c}_{ks}, \mathbf{c}_{kt})\}$$ (15.7)

- *Inter-class distance* is the minimum distance between a member of one class and a member of another class.

$$d(C_i, C_k) = \min_{s,t} \{d(\mathbf{c}_{is}, \mathbf{c}_{kt})\}$$ (15.8)

15.2.2 Discriminating Function

Once the distance measure is chosen, minimum distance classifier [Equation (15.1)] can be implemented straightaway. Let us consider a two-class problem. Then

Feature vector $\mathbf{f}$ is assigned to C_0 if $d(\mathbf{f}, C_0) < d(\mathbf{f}, C_1)$

Feature vector $\mathbf{f}$ is assigned to C_1 if $d(\mathbf{f}, C_0) > d(\mathbf{f}, C_1)$

In other words,

Feature vector $\mathbf{f}$ is assigned to C_0 if $d(\mathbf{f}, C_0) - d(\mathbf{f}, C_1) < 0$

Feature vector $\mathbf{f}$ is assigned to C_1 if $d(\mathbf{f}, C_0) - d(\mathbf{f}, C_1) > 0$

So, there exists a surface given by $d(\mathbf{f}, C_0) - d(\mathbf{f}, C_1) = 0$ that divides the feature space into two parts each of which contains exactly one class. This surface, in decision theoretic pattern recognition literature, is known as *discriminating surface* and its mathematical representation is called *discriminating function*. Suppose d gives the Euclidean distance, then the surface is a hyperplane. Let us define this plane, in general, as

$$a_0 f_0 + a_1 f_1 + \ldots + a_{n-1} f_{n-1} + a_n = 0$$

or

$$\mathbf{a}^T \mathbf{f}' = 0$$

where $\mathbf{f}'$ is $\mathbf{f}$ appended with a 1. Hence,

Feature vector $\mathbf{f}$ is assigned to C_0 if $\mathbf{a}^T \mathbf{f}' < 0$

Feature vector $\mathbf{f}$ is assigned to C_1 if $\mathbf{a}^T \mathbf{f}' > 0$

An example of discriminant surface (line in two-dimensional space) is shown in Fig. 15.1 for

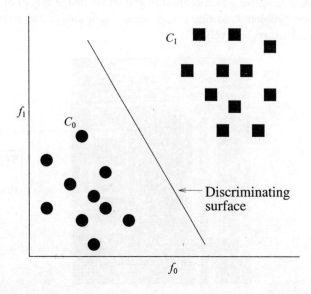

Fig. 15.1 Illustrating decision surface (line) for two-class problem in two-dimensional feature space.

$n = 2$. In general, for multi-class problem to each class C_i is associated a weight vector $\mathbf{a}_i$ such that

$$\mathbf{a}_j^T \mathbf{f}' = \begin{cases} > 0 & \text{for all } j \neq i \\ < 0 & \text{for } j = i \end{cases}$$

if the object corresponding to $\mathbf{f}$ belongs to C_i. Now the question is how to determine the weight vector? Consider, again, the two-class problem. Suppose the classes C_0 and C_1 are represented by set of prototypes: $\{\mathbf{c}_{0k}\}$ and $\{\mathbf{c}_{1k}\}$, respectively. Then the weight vector may be determined iteratively as follows. Let us initialize the weight vector arbitrarily and choose a weighting factor α $(0 < \alpha < 1)$. Then at p-th iteration

$$\text{if } \mathbf{a}^{(p)^T} \mathbf{c}_{1k}' < 0 \qquad \text{then } \mathbf{a}^{(p+1)} = \mathbf{a}^{(p)} + \alpha \mathbf{c}_{1k}'$$

and

$$\text{if } \mathbf{a}^{(p)^T} \mathbf{c}_{0k}' > 0 \qquad \text{then } \mathbf{a}^{(p+1)} = \mathbf{a}^{(p)} - \alpha \mathbf{c}_{0k}'$$

The iteration, is done by cycling through all the prototypes (preferably alternately) of both the classes until no significant change in weight vector occurs. The algorithm can be generalized to multi-class cases straightaway.

15.2.3 Template Matching

In many situations analysis of a scene requires identification of known patterns or models in it. *Template matching* is one of the earliest and simplest techniques which finds known pattern in a scene. The approach is, however, in most cases computationally expensive and recognition often suffers for a complex scene and with viewpoint variation. The method can be used for testing the existence as well as for localizing an object in the scene. Given a gray-scale image $f(r, c)$ of size $M \times N$ and a pattern or template which is another gray-scale image $g(r, c)$ of size $m \times n$ such that $m \leq M$ and $n \leq N$, the problem is to find g in f. An example image and a template are shown in Figs. 15.2(a) and 15.2(b), respectively.

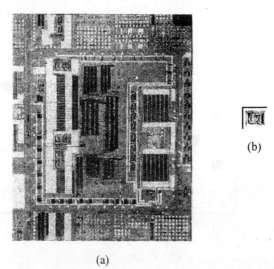

(b)

(a)

Fig. 15.2 Example images for template matching: (a) given image and (b) template image.

In case of localizing the object given as a template g in the image f the problem reduces to simple searching. The rectangular matrix (i.e. the domain of g) on which the pattern is defined is referred to as *mask* or window W. The idea of template matching, here, is to place the mask at all possible pixel locations of the image and compare the content of mask and the superimposed image region. That means the problem is to compute the degree of match between $\{f(r + s, c + t) \mid (r, c) \in W\}$ and $g(r, c)$ for all (s, t). Placing this number at the centre of sub-image where the mask is placed a *matching score matrix* is generated. The peak (s) at the matching score matrix indicates a good match. If the matching score is greater than a threshold, the pattern is said to be present at that location. On the other hand, in case of pattern recognition problem a set of templates $g_i(r, c)$ are given as models along with the image $f(r, c)$. Now suppose the image (of size equal to that of the template) contains an object. Then the problem is to find the best match between the image and one of the templates. Here again the image is said to contain the pattern if the best matching score exceeds a predefined threshold. In cases of binary images (with pixel values 1 and 0), the matching score is determined by counting the number of match of 1 for a particular mask location or mask type.

In the remaining part of the section, we do not distinguish between image and sub-image and consider the recognition problem only. Suppose we have a set of pattern templates given by $g_i(r, c)$ $(i = 0, 1, 2, \ldots)$ and $g_i(r, c)$ are normalized in such a way that

$$\sum_{(r,c)\in W} g_i(r, c) = 0 \quad \text{and} \quad \sum_{(r,c)\in W} g_i^2(r, c) = \text{constant}$$

for all i. Degree of matching may be measured through the distance between f and g_i, as we know, the better the match less is the distance between f and g_i. Then considering Euclidean distance, for the best match one should have

$$\min_i \{\Sigma_{(r, c)\in W} (f(r, c) - g_i(r, c))^2\} \Rightarrow \min_i \{\Sigma_{(r, c)\in W} f^2(r, c) + \Sigma_{(r, c)\in W} g_i^2(r, c)$$

$$- 2\Sigma_{(r, c)\in W} f(r, c) g_i(r, c)\}$$

$$\Rightarrow \max_i \{\Sigma_{(r, c)\in W} f(r, c) g_i(r, c)\}$$

Hence, $\Sigma_{(r, c)\in W} f(r, c) g_i(r, c)$ may be taken as a measure of similarity; when normalized with $\Sigma_{(r, c)\in W} f^2(r, c)$ and $\Sigma_{(r, c)\in W} g_i^2(r, c)$ it becomes correlation between f and g_i, i.e.

$$\rho(f, g_i) = \frac{\Sigma_{(r,c)\in W} f(r, c) g_i(r, c)}{\sqrt{\Sigma_{(r,c)\in W} f^2(r, c)} \sqrt{\Sigma_{(r,c)\in W} g_i^2(r, c)}} \tag{15.9}$$

We have assumed that $\Sigma_{(r, c)\in W} f(r, c) = 0$ too. Hence, f is assigned to C_k if $\rho(f, g_k) < \rho(f, g_i)$ for all $i \neq k$. It should be noted that $0 \leq \rho(f, g_i) \leq 1$. However, since the same f is being used for every g_i, we can simplify Equation (15.9) to obtain a measure of similarity with respect to g_i as

$$s(f, g_i) = \frac{\Sigma_{(r,c)\in W} f(r, c) g_i(r, c)}{\Sigma_{(r,c)\in W} g_i^2(r, c)} \tag{15.10}$$

Here also $0 \leq s(f, g_i) \leq 1$.

For binary image matching the amount of computation can be reduced in the following way. Let us construct three point-set as

$$\{S_f\} = \{(r, c) \mid f(r, c) = 1 \qquad \text{and} \qquad (r, c) \in W\}$$

$$\{S_{g_i}\} = \{(r, c) \mid g_i(r, c) = 1 \qquad \text{and} \qquad (r, c) \in W\}$$

$$\{S_h\} = \{(r, c) \mid \min\{f(r, c), g_i(r, c)\} = 1 \qquad \text{and} \qquad (r, c) \in W\}$$

Then

$$\sum_{(r,c) \in W} f^2(r, c) \qquad = \text{Card } \{S_f\}$$

$$\sum_{(r,c) \in W} g_i^2(r, c) \qquad = \text{Card } \{S_{g_i}\}$$

$$\sum_{(r,c) \in W} f(r, c) \, g_i(r, c) \quad = \text{Card } \{S_h\}$$

Thus, Equations (15.9) and (15.10) can be written for binary image as

$$\rho(f, g_i) = \frac{\text{Card } \{S_h\}}{\sqrt{\text{Card}\{S_f\}} \sqrt{\text{Card}\{S_{g_i}\}}} \tag{15.11}$$

$$s(f, g_i) = \frac{\text{Card}\{S_h\}}{\text{Card}\{S_{g_i}\}} \tag{15.12}$$

Now it is evident that $s(f, g_i) = 1$ if and only if for every $g_i(r, c) = 1$, $f(r, c) = 1$. In other words, $s(f, g_i) = 1$ if and only if $S_{g_i} \subset S_f$. That means (i) $S(f, g_i)$ is not a symmetric measure and (ii) $s(f, g_i)$ can be interpreted as a measure of similarity using erosion.

Let us define a function as

$$\lambda_i(k, l) = \sum_{(r,c) \in W} \delta_i(r, c; k, l) \tag{15.13}$$

where

$$\delta_i(r, c; k, l) = \begin{cases} 1 & \text{if } f(r, c) = k \text{ and } g_i(r, c) = l \\ 0 & \text{otherwise} \end{cases}$$

We also define $\lambda_i(k,.) = \lambda_i(k, 0) + \lambda_i(k, 1)$ and $\lambda_i(.,l) = \lambda_i(0, l) + \lambda_i(1, l)$. Then Equations (15.11) and (15.12) can be written in terms of these functions as

$$\rho(f, g_i) = \frac{\lambda_i(1, 1)}{\sqrt{\lambda_i(1, .)\lambda_i(., 1)}} \tag{15.14}$$

$$s(f, g_i) = \frac{\lambda_i(1, 1)}{\lambda_i(., 1)} \tag{15.15}$$

To make the measure symmetric we use morphological hit-and-miss transform instead of erosion. In that case the measure of similarity becomes

$$s(f, g_i) = \frac{\lambda_i(1, 1) + \lambda_i(0, 0)}{\lambda_i(1, .) + \lambda_i(., 0)}$$
(15.16)

Therefore, the number of operations for template matching should be of the order of $\theta(mn)$ for $m \times n$, i.e. the size of image template. However, this is true for a particular scale, orientation and position. Matching procedure should explore all possible values of these factors which leads to enormous computation. However, computational cost may be reduced by coinciding centroids and principal axes of object image and the template, and making area under them same as well.

15.3 Clustering

One of the ways to designing a classifier or, in other words, learning is deriving the deterministic functions as described in Section 15.2.2. This is a supervised method and needs a training set where features belonging to different classes are known a priori. When no such training set is available one should adopt unsupervised methods such as *clustering*. Clustering technique can be used for learning as well as for classification in an unsupervised manner. Basic objective of any clustering technique is to divide the data points of the feature space into a number of groups (or classes) so that a predefined set of criteria are satisfied. In some cases the number of classes are known. Criteria usually include inter-class distance and intra-class distance, density of points within a class, etc. A lucid and thorough discussion on clustering techniques may be found in [Tou and Gonzalez (1974), Andrews (1972), Duda and Hart (1973)] and other books on pattern recognition. Here we present only two widely used methods—*maximin algorithm* and *K-means algorithm*. The first one determines the number of possible classes that satisfy some clustering criteria; while the second one, given the number of classes, finds the best possible grouping of data by satisfying some criteria.

Maximin algorithm

Maximin (maximum-of-minimum) distance algorithm is a heuristic method that may be used to determine the number of classes that the data points belong to so that the inter-class distance is maximized.

Algorithm 15.1

Step 1: Select any arbitrarily chosen feature vector from the feature vector set $\{f_i\}$ as the first cluster centre c_0.

Step 2: Find the furthest feature vector with respect to c_0 and select it as the cluster centre c_1.

Step 3: For each of the remaining feature vector(s), find the minimum distance from it to the cluster centres $\{c_i (i = 0, 1, ...)\}$.

Step 4: Find the maximum of these minimum distances (computed in Step 3) and the corresponding feature vector.

Step 5: If this distance (i.e. maximum-of-minimum distances) is greater than a significant fraction (for example, a half) of, say, the average distance between cluster centres, select the feature vector as a new cluster centre and repeat from Step 3, else terminate the algorithm.

K-means algorithm

As said earlier, given the number of classes, *K-means algorithm* finds the clusters through an iterative procedure that minimizes intra-class distances. Suppose number of classes which the given data belong to is K (i.e. $m = K$). Then the algorithm may be described as follows:

Algorithm 15.2

Step 1: Choose first K different feature vectors as K different cluster centres $\mathbf{c}_0^{(0)}$, $\mathbf{c}_1^{(0)}$, ..., $\mathbf{c}_{K-1}^{(0)}$, where K is the number of classes and the superscript denotes the iteration number.

Step 2: At r-th iteration for each of the feature vectors, assign feature vector $\{\mathbf{f}_i\}$ to cluster C_k if

$$d(\mathbf{f}_i, \mathbf{c}_k^{(r-1)}) = \min_j \{d(\mathbf{f}_i, \mathbf{c}_j^{(r-1)})\} \qquad (15.17)$$

for $j = 0, 1, \ldots, K-1$ where d is a distance measure, or Euclidean distance.

Step 3: New cluster centres are computed by minimizing intra-class distances. If $c_k^{(r)}$ is the centre of C_k at r-th iteration, this is calculated by minimizing

$$D_k = \sum_{\mathbf{f}_i \in C_k} \| \mathbf{f}_i - \mathbf{c}_k^{(r)} \|^2 \qquad (15.18)$$

for $k = 0, 1, 2, \ldots, K - 1$. The cluster centre obtained by minimizing D_k in Equation (15.18) is the mean value of feature vectors belonging to C_k at r-th iteration, i.e.

$$\mathbf{c}_k^{(r)} = \frac{1}{n_k^{(r)}} \sum_{i \in C_k} \mathbf{f}_i \qquad (15.19)$$

where $n_k^{(r)}$ is the number of feature vectors assigned to C_k at r-th iteration.

Step 4: If $\mathbf{c}_k^{(r)} \approx \mathbf{c}_k^{(r-1)}$ for all k, that means there are insignificant or no changes in cluster centres, then the algorithm is terminated, else continue from Step 2.

Clusters thus obtained have minimum intra-class distance for a given set of feature vectors and number of classes.

15.4 Statistical Classification

Let us recall the method of determining optimum threshold for image segmentation through pixel classification. The process of image segmentation divides the image space into a number of regions of interest. This scheme can be extended to classification of feature vectors or patterns where similar type of patterns are grouped into one class or cluster. The term 'similar type', in this context, means closeness of feature vectors representing the objects. Again, the term 'closeness' reforms to the underlying sense of a distance measure and clearly the objective is to maximize the feature distance measure between any two classes (inter-class distance) while minimizing the same distances among patterns belonging to the same class (intra-class distance). However, we resolved the problem of optimum threshold by minimizing classification error. A thorough and comprehensive studies on statistical pattern recognition can be found in [Fukunaga (1990)].

15.4.1 Performance Evaluation

Performance of a classifier can be evaluated in many ways. Quantitative evaluation is the best done with the help of explicit training data set. One of the simple approaches of quantitative evaluation is by means of a *confusion matrix*. Suppose there are m classes $C_0, C_1, ..., C_{m-1}$ and a large set of test patterns (or feature vectors) $\mathbf{f}_i$, $i = 0, 1, ..., N - 1$. Test patterns are same as training pattern or training data; however, they are not used in designing the classifier. Now suppose $\mathbf{f}_i$ actually belongs to class C_j but classifier assigns it to class C_k. Then we increment the accumulator N_{jk} of a table as shown in Fig. 15.3. The rectangular array represented by $\{N_{jk}\}$ is

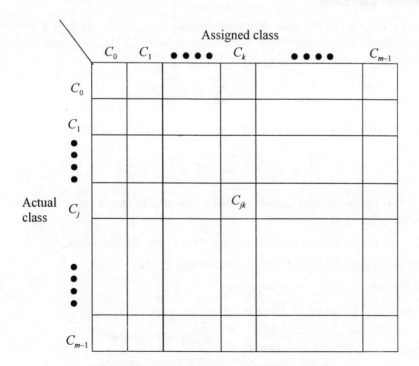

Fig. 15.3   Structure of a confusion matrix.

called the *confusion matrix*. Now if $j \neq k$ then any increment in N_{jk} means the *misclassification*. After testing all the N patterns we have

$$\sum_{k=0}^{m-1} \sum_{j=0}^{m-1} N_{jk} = N$$

Various measures of performance are suggested based on this matrix. The most common one is the percentage of correct classification, i.e.

$$C = \frac{\sum_{j=0}^{m-1} N_{jj}}{N} \times 100\% \tag{15.20}$$

If the classifier assigns the pattern $\mathbf{f}_i$ to class C_k when it actually belongs to class C_j, then a loss is incurred. Suppose this loss is denoted by L_{jk}. Then another measure of performance can be the total loss incurred, i.e.

$$T = \sum_{k=0}^{m-1} \sum_{j=0}^{m-1} L_{jk} N_{jk} \tag{15.21}$$

For obvious reason $L_{jj} = 0$. The major objective in classifier design is to maximize C or to minimize T.

15.4.2 Bayes' Classifier

We present in this section *Bayesian maximum likelihood classifier* which is a well-developed method from statistical decision theory. Consider Equation (15.21), total loss incurred due to assigning patterns to class C_k is

$$T_k = \sum_{j=0}^{m-1} L_{jk} N_{jk} \tag{15.22}$$

we may call it *conditional average loss* if

$$T_k = \sum_{j=0}^{m-1} L_{jk} p(C_j | \mathbf{f}) \tag{15.23}$$

where $p(C_j | \mathbf{f})$ is the conditional probability that a pattern is in class C_j if its feature vector is $\mathbf{f}$. We also denote by

$p(\mathbf{f} | C_j)$: the probability that a pattern from class C_j has feature vector $\mathbf{f}$,

$P(C_j)$: a priori probability that any pattern belongs to class C_j and

$p(\mathbf{f})$: is the sum of $p(\mathbf{f} | C_j)$ over all classes.

According to Bayes' formula [see Section 2.6]

$$p(C_j | \mathbf{f}) = \frac{p(C_j) p(\mathbf{f} | C_j)}{p(\mathbf{f})} \tag{15.24}$$

Substituting Equation (15.24) in Equation (15.23), we have

$$T_k = \sum_{j=0}^{m-1} L_{jk} \frac{p(C_j)p(\mathbf{f}|C_j)}{p(\mathbf{f})} = \frac{1}{p(\mathbf{f})} \sum_{j=0}^{m-1} L_{jk} p(C_j)p(\mathbf{f}|C_j)$$

Now $p(\mathbf{f})$ is constant in the evaluation of loss incurred due to any class, then for the purpose of comparison it is sufficient to take

$$T_k = \sum_{j=0}^{m-1} L_{jk} p(C_j)p(\mathbf{f}|C_j) \tag{15.25}$$

where $p(\mathbf{f}|C_j)$ is called the *likehood function* of class C_j. For two-class problem $\mathbf{f}$ is assigned to class C_0 if $T_0 < T_1$ and to class C_1 otherwise. Now

$$T_0 < T_1$$

implies

$$L_{00}\, p(C_0)\, p(\mathbf{f}|C_0) + L_{10}p(C_1)p(\mathbf{f}|C_1) < L_{01}\, p(C_0)p(\mathbf{f}|C_0) + L_{11}\, p(C_1)p(\mathbf{f}|C_1)$$

or

$$(L_{10} - L_{11})\, p(C_1)\, p(\mathbf{f}|C_1) < (L_{01} - L_{00})\, p(C_0)\, p(\mathbf{f}|C_0)$$

or

$$\frac{p(C_0)p(\mathbf{f}|C_0)}{p(C_1)p(\mathbf{f}|C_1)} > \frac{L_{10} - L_{11}}{L_{01} - L_{00}}$$

Suppose cost of misclassification due to any class be same, i.e., $L_{10} = L_{01}$ and $L_{11} = L_{00} = 0$, then

$\mathbf{f}$ is assigned to class C_0 if $p(C_0)p(\mathbf{f}|C_0) > p(C_1)p(\mathbf{f}|C_1)$

In general, for m classes,

$\mathbf{f}$ is assigned to class C_k if $p(C_k)p(\mathbf{f}|C_k) > p(C_j)p(\mathbf{f}|C_j)$

for all $j \neq k$. Simply speaking the pattern is assigned to the class for which the probability of feature vector within the class weighted by the class probability is greater than that for any other class.

15.5 Fuzzy Mathematical Recognition

In statistical methods of classification, basically probability of a pattern belongs to a class is determined. And then, the pattern is inferred to belong to a particular class for which this probability is maximum (in *maximum likelihood* approach). Determining probability means assigning some sort of uncertainty to the pattern with respect to classes. There is another method of assigning uncertainty to a pattern or object—fuzzy membership function [Pal and Dutta Majumder (1986)]. Consequently, the method is called *fuzzy mathematical pattern recognition*. One of the most widely used fuzzy recognition methods is clustering by *fuzzy c-means algorithm*, alternately called *soft clustering* as opposed to *hard clustering* by K-means algorithm [see Section 15.3] using decision theoretic approach.

Suppose there is a collection Φ of n feature vectors corresponding to n objects or patterns, i.e. $\Phi = \{\mathbf{f}_0, \mathbf{f}_1, ..., \mathbf{f}_{n-1}\}$ and c classes, $C_0, C_1, ..., C_{c-1}$ where $c \ll n$. Through hard clustering we generate a matrix $U = \{u_{ik}\}$ of size $c \times n$ where

1. $u_{ik} \in \{0, 1\}$

2. $\sum_{i=0}^{c-1} u_{ik} = 1$ for $k = 0, 1, ..., n - 1$

That means $u_{ik} = 1$ if feature vector $\mathbf{f}_k$ is assigned to the class C_i; otherwise $u_{ik} = 0$. If we relax the first condition to

1(a). $u_{ik} \in [0, 1]$

what we yield is called soft clustering. u_{ik} is probability or fuzzy membership function that $\mathbf{f}_k$ belongs to C_i. Here we consider fuzzy clustering as discussed below.

The most common criteria used in fuzzy clustering is intra-class weighted distance. Suppose V is the set of cluster centres, i.e. $V = \{\mathbf{v}_0, \mathbf{v}_1, \mathbf{v}_2, ..., \mathbf{v}_{c-1}\}$ then optimum clustering may be obtained by minimizing the objective functions:

$$J_m(U, V; \Phi) = \sum_{k=0}^{n-1} \sum_{c=0}^{c-1} u_{ik}^m \| \mathbf{f}_k - \mathbf{v}_i \|_A^2 \qquad (15.26)$$

where $\| x \|_A = \sqrt{x^T A x}$ is any inner-product norm. Optimal classification U^* of Φ is taken from the pair (U^*, V^*) that corresponds to local minimum of J_m. Approximate optimization of J_m by the fuzzy c-means algorithm is based on iteration through the following necessary condition [Bezdek (1981)] for its local extrema.

Theorem 1 If $D_{ikA} = \| \mathbf{f}_k - \mathbf{v}_i \|_A > 0$ for all i and k, then (U, V) may minimize J_m only if, when $m > 1$,

$$u_{ik} = \left[\sum_{j=0}^{c-1} \left(\frac{D_{ikA}}{D_{jkA}} \right)^{2/(m-1)} \right]^{-1} \qquad (15.27)$$

for $0 \le i \le c - 1$ and $0 \le k \le n - 1$, where

$$\mathbf{v}_i = \frac{\sum_{k=0}^{n-1}(u_{ik})^m \, \mathbf{f}_k}{\sum_{k=0}^{n-1}(u_{ik})^m} \qquad (15.28)$$

for $0 \le i \le c - 1$.

Singularity occurs when one or more intra-class distances become zero, i.e. $\| \mathbf{f}_k - \mathbf{v}_i \|_A = 0$ at any iteration. In that case (rare in practice) Equation (15.27) cannot be calculated. When this happens, assign zeros to each non-singular class and distribute non-zero memberships to the singular classes arbitrarily subject to the constraints 1(a) and (2). Corresponding algorithm may be described as follows [Pal and Bezdek (1995)].

Algorithm 15.3

Step 1: Choose initial cluster centres arbitrarily. Usually first c
feature vectors are taken as initial cluster centres, i.e.

$$\mathbf{v}_i^{(0)} = \mathbf{f}_i, \qquad i = 0, 1, ..., c - 1$$

Set $t = 1$ and choose the matrix A. For Euclidean distance
A is identity matrix. Choose also T, the maximum number of
iterations allowed.

Step 2: Calculate $u_{ik}^{(t)}$ from $V^{(t-1)}$ using Equation (15.27).

Step 3: Calculate $\mathbf{v}_i^{(t)}$ from $u_{ik}^{(t)}$ using Equation (15.28).

Step 4: Calculate error at t-th iteration as

$$E_t = \max_i \{ \| \mathbf{v}_i^{(t)} - \mathbf{v}_i^{(t-1)} \|_A \}$$

Step 5: If $E_t > \varepsilon$, a predefined error threshold, and $t < T$, then
increment t and go to Step 2;
else stop with $U* = U^{(t)}$ and $V* = V^{(t)}$.

Finally, degree of belongingness of a pattern to the classes may be ordered based on its membership values. Or, a pattern may be said to belong to a particular class if membership with respect to that class is maximum, which exceeds a decision threshold.

15.6 Syntactic Recognition

So far we have considered recognition methodologies based on non-structural features. Sometimes objects are represented in terms of structural features. For example, an object may be represented by chain-code of its boundary, or by its skeleton approximated with line and arc segments. One of the most prevalent methodology used for recognizing objects based on such features is syntactic technique [Fu (1982)]. The syntactic approach to pattern recognition problems provides a powerful method for describing a large set of complex patterns by using small sets simple pattern primitives and of grammatical rules that are recursive in nature. The technique has been adopted from *formal language theory*, and is sometimes called *linguistic approach*. Basic concept of syntactic pattern recognition is the specification of structural features, called *primitives* [see under lines and arcs in Section 14.2.3], and a set of rules, called *production rules*. These rules govern interconnection between the said primitives. Thus they form a *grammar*. For the sake of simplicity, we consider here only string grammar and its use in object recognition problem.

15.6.1 Grammar

Let us begin our discussion with the definition of grammar in context of syntactic recognition. A grammar may be defined as a 4-tuple [Noyes (1993)]

$$G = \{T, V, s, P\}$$

where

t—the finite set of *terminal symbols* or alphabets or constants (i.e. structural primitives) that represents the final substitution phase of the production of sentences (i.e. patterns or objects).

v—the finite set of *non-terminal symbols* or variables that represent the intermediate constructions; these variables are distinct from *T*.

s —a special distinguished variable in *V* that is the sentence (i.e. pattern or object) to be constructed. So, it is the *starting symbol*.

P—the finite set of *production rules* defining how symbols can be combined to form the sentences (i.e. patterns or objects).

A *language L(G)* is the set of all sentences that can be produced by the grammar *G*. In the present context, language corresponds to a class. Finally, the *parsing* of a sequence of symbols enables us to determine whether the sequence is a sentence in the language. Thus in syntactic pattern recognition gives a set of grammars each of which corresponds to a unique class and a sequence of primitives we parse the sequence using each grammar to determine whether the sequence is a valid pattern of the corresponding class.

It is required that *T* and *V* be disjoint sets. In the following discussion non-terminals will be denoted by capital letters *A, B, ..., S, ...*, etc. Lowercase letters of the begining of the alphabet i.e. *a, b, c, ...* etc., will be used for terminals. Strings of terminals will be denoted by lowercase letters toward the end of the alphabets *w, x, y, z*, etc. Strings of mixed terminals and non-terminals will be denoted by lowercase Greek letters *α, β, θ, ...* The empty sentence (the sentence with no symbols) will be denoted by $\emptyset$. Now, given a set *X* of symbols, we will use the notation *X** to denote the set of all sentences composed of elements from *X*.

Production rules are the most critical parts of the grammar or the system. String grammars are characterized primarily by the form of their productions. By putting certain restrictions on the form of the rules we can define different classes of grammars. Of particular interest in syntactic pattern recognition are the *regular grammars*, whose production rules have the following characteristics. The left-hand side of each rule contains only a single non-terminal symbol, and the right-hand side must contain either a terminal symbol by itself or a terminal symbol followed by a non-terminal symbol. However, two other grammars may be of our interest—*context-sensitive* and *context-free*. In case of context-sensitive grammar, length of left-hand side of rule is less than or equal to that of the right-hand side, and left-hand side may have more than one non-terminal symbol. On the other hand, in context-free grammar left-hand side of all the rules have only one non-terminal symbol. However, in both the cases, right-hand side of rule may have any sequence of symbols. Thus in the case of regular grammars productions are always of the form $A \rightarrow aB$ and $A \rightarrow a$ with $A, B \in V$, and $a \in T$, and in context-free grammar, productions are of the form $A \rightarrow \alpha$ with $A \in V$, and $\alpha \in (T \cup V)^* - \emptyset$; that is, α can be any string composed of terminals and non-terminals, except the empty string.

15.6.2 Recognition Strategy

Let us consider again two-class problem. Suppose objects of two classes, C_0 and C_1, are represented as strings of primitives. So we can interpret each primitive as a symbol permissible in some grammar. Suppose there are two grammars, G_0 and G_1, corresponding to these two classes. That means their production rules are such that G_0 allows the generation of sentences which correspond to objects of only class C_0; while G_1 allows generation of sentences corresponding to objects of only class C_1. Thus the language $L(G_0)$ generated by the grammar G_0 is the class C_0, and similarly $L(G_1)$ is same as C_1.

Once the two grammars G_0 and G_1 have been established, the syntactic pattern recognition process is, in principle, straightforward. Given a sequence of primitives representing an unknown pattern, the problem is to parse the sequence to determine in which language the pattern represents a valid sentence. If the sentence belongs to $L(G_0)$, the pattern is assigned to class C_0. Similarly, the object is said to belong to class C_1 if the sentence is valid with respect to the language $L(G_1)$. A unique decision cannot be made if the sentence belongs to both $L(G_0)$ and $L(G_1)$. If the sentence is found to be invalid over both the languages it is rejected.

In a step toward generalization, a class of objects may be defined by more than one grammar. Secondly, when there are more than two classes, the syntactic classification approach is the same as described above, except that more grammars (at least one per class) are involved in the process. Suppose, a class C_i is defined by n_i number of grammars $G_{i, 0}, G_{i, 1}, ..., G_{i,n_i}$. For m such classes total number of grammars is $\Sigma_{i=0}^{m-1} n_i$. In this case, the pattern is assigned to class C_i if it is represented by a sentence of only

$$L(G_{i,0}) \cup L(G_{i,1}) \cup ... \cup L(G_{i,n_i})$$

Ambiguity and rejection are declared in the similar way as before.

It should be noted that the rules of the grammar can be recursive (e.g. first rule of the regular grammar as given above). Thus parsing of a sequence of symbols is an application of *tree search* methods [see Section 15.7]. *Top-down parsing* starts with a starting symbol s and uses production rules of a grammar to verify that the given sequence of primitives corresponding to an unknown pattern can be constructed. A *depth-first* or a *best-first* search scheme can be used. *Bottom-up parsing* starts with a sequence and uses production rules of a grammar to produce s. If the parsing process fails to produce s, then the sequence is not a valid sentence with respect to that grammar.

15.7 Tree Search

Consider Fig. 15.4 that shows the discriminating functions (or decision boundaries) dividing two-

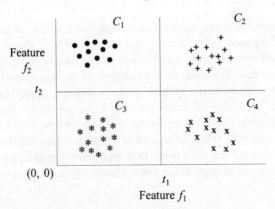

Fig. 15.4 Illustrates an example of discriminating functions for four classes in two-dimensional feature space.

dimensional feature space into four classes [see Section 15.2.2]. Similar classification can be achieved by a set of If-Then-Else rules as shown in Fig. 15.5(a). The concept may be represented by a *tree* as shown in Fig. 15.5(b) where terminal nodes represent the classes and non-terminal nodes are union of successor sets. In other words, the group of objects corresponding to a non-terminal node is decomposed into subgroups (i.e. successor nodes) based on the outcome of testing some criteria. This decomposition ends at terminal nodes corresponding to a unique object class. Finally, Object or pattern at any node except the root node inherits the properties or features of its parent node. Thus pattern classification and recognition can be achieved through tree search techniques. Root node is the entry point to the classifier.

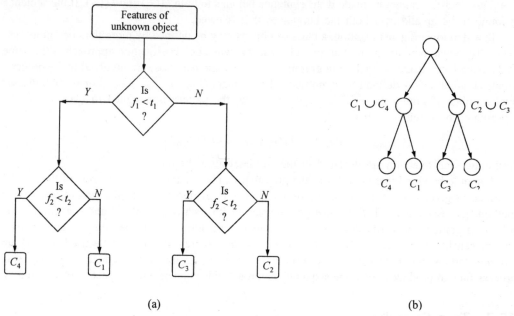

(a)   (b)

Fig. 15.5 Obtaining similar classification, as shown in Fig. 15.4, using simple If-Then-Else rules: (a) flow diagram and (b) corresponding tree representation.

The technique is the most suitable when rules are imprecise and heuristic in nature. In many cases, the mathematical form of decision boundaries is not easy to define. Given a set of features or attributes designating an unknown object, search starts at the root node of the tree. At any non-terminal node a rule is tested and depending on the outcome of the test, one of the successor nodes is chosen. Finally, a terminal node is reached if the unknown object belongs to the class corresponding to that node. This is called *top-down search*. As opposed to this, *bottom-up search* may also be adopted depending on the formulation of the problem. For example, in syntactic recognition procedure, parsing of a string of structural primitives (see Section 15.6) can be done in bottom-up fashion to arrive at the root node that represents the start symbol of a language defining certain class. Below we present some most commonly used search techniques.

Best-first search

This is a problem-solving technique used in *Artificial Intelligence* [Winston (1984)]. The search starts at a root node and the forward motion through the tree is guided by opening the best node among all children, i.e. successors of the current node. The algorithm is as follows:

Algorithm 15.4

Step 1: Form a one-element queue consisting of the root node.

Step 2: Until the queue is empty or the goal has been reached, determine if the first element in the queue is the goal node.

2(a): If the first element is the goal node, do nothing.

2(b): If the first element is not the goal node, remove the first element from the queue, add the first element's children, if any, to the queue, and sort the entire queue based on some measure of goodness (e.g. estimated distance from current state to the goal state).

Step 3: If the goal node has been found, announce success; otherwise announce failure.

Depth-first search

Depth-first search is the crudest of all the search techniques [Winston (1984)]. When no prior knowledge is available, it is possible to reach the goal node by picking every node and expanding it in all the possible successors. Other alternatives at the same node are not considered as long as there is an indication that the goal may be found. When the search cannot proceed, we go to the nearest parent node with unexplored alternatives and the above procedure is repeated, until all the alternatives for all the nodes in the tree are finished:

Algorithm 15.5

Step 1: Form a one-element queue consisting of the root node.

Step 2: Until the queue is empty or the goal has been reached, determine if the first element in the queue is the goal node.

2(a): If the first element is the goal node, do nothing.

2(b): If the first element is not the goal node, remove the first element from the queue and add the first element's children, if any, to the front of the queue.

Step 3: If the goal has been found, announce success; otherwise announce failure.

This is a costly procedure in terms of computing time, since most of the alternatives never lead to the goal. When the depth and the width of the tree are large, the depth-first search can be combinatorially explosive. Hence, the number of alternatives should somehow be constrained.

However, it is important to note that, when it is necessary to find all the possible paths, a depth-first search may be better, in particular, when combined with a suitable control mechanism to limit the number of alternatives.

A* algorithm

This algorithm is a useful method for traversing the graphs through optimal paths. A brief description is presented below, as given in [Winston (1984)]. In a search graph let c be the estimate of cost of going from a given node to the goal node. Then c can be expressed as the sum of two functions c_1 and c_2, where c_1 is the estimate of cost of getting from the initial state to the current node and c_2 is the estimate of cost of getting from the current node to the goal node. For computing the value of c_2, the heuristic information from the problem domain is used. So the evaluation function at the node $\mathbf{n}$ is given by

$$c(\mathbf{n}) = c_1(\mathbf{n}) + c_2(\mathbf{n}) \tag{15.29}$$

where $c_1(\mathbf{n})$ = cost of reaching node $\mathbf{n}$ from initial node, and $c_2(\mathbf{n})$ = cost of reaching goal node from node $\mathbf{n}$. The algorithm has the following steps.

Algorithm 15.6

Step 1: Create a search graph, **G**, consisting solely of the start node **s**. Put **s** on a list called OPEN.

Step 2: Create a list called CLOSED that is initially empty.

Step 3: LOOP: If OPEN is empty, exit with failure.

Step 4: Select the first node on OPEN, remove it from OPEN, and put it on CLOSED. Call this node **n**.

Step 5: If **n** is a goal node, exit successfully with the solution obtained by tracing a path along the pointers from **n** to **s** in **G**.

Step 6: Expand node **n**, generating the set **M**, of its successors and install them as successors of **n** in **G**.

Step 7: Establish a pointer to **n** from those members of **M** that were not already in **G** (i.e. not already on either OPEN or CLOSED). Add these members of **M** to OPEN. For each member of **M** that was already on OPEN or CLOSED, decide whether or not to redirect its pointer to **n**. For each member of **M** already on CLOSED, decide for each of its descendants in **G** whether or not to redirect its pointer.

Step 8: Reorder the list OPEN, either according to some arbitrary scheme or according to heuristic merit.

Step 9: Go to LOOP.

This algorithm when used along with the evaluation function c for ordering the nodes is called *algorithm A*. Let $c_1{}^*$ and $c_2{}^*$ be the optimal estimates of c_1 and c_2. Then $c^* = c_1{}^* + c_2{}^*$ gives the cost of optimal path from starting node to the goal node through the node $\mathbf{n}$. When both $c_1{}^*$ and $c_2{}^*$ are the lower bounds of c_1 and c_2, and if the c^* computed thus is used with graph search algorithm it is known as algorithm A*.

Now a tree can be viewed as an *acyclic graph*. Thus representing both model (or class representative or prototype) as well as the unknown object by graphs leads to a more general and robust approach called *graph matching*.

15.8 Graph Matching

In image analysis system the description of various objects of external world is maintained in a convenient form of abstract representation commonly termed as *knowledge base*. The tasks of *perception*, *recognition* and *interpretation* of the objects of the external world rely on the accuracy, search time and efficient implementation of this knowledge base. In a very simple sense, a knowledge base, thus contains *models* of generalized images, segmented images, geometric entities or analogical, or propositional entities corresponding to various objects of real world. The objects to be recognized or perceived are then tested for the best fit or *match* with the model(s) using various efficient search algorithms. Thus matching can be looked upon as finding correspondence between two representations. Graph theoretic approach is suitable for matching relational structures containing *n*-ary relations as *labelled graphs*. A brief discussion on graphs and graph theory is given in the following subsections.

15.8.1 Definitions

The analysis of various problems in real world involves the study of connectedness among a set of objects (or points in space) when the formulation of that problem is done accordingly. The problems of network analysis in electrical engineering, process scheduling in operating systems, analysis of molecular structures in chemistry, recognition of complex objects having various well-defined parts in scene analysis have a common feature of analyzing the topology of interconnections among the different elements. Thus all these problems can be looked upon as simple or complex graphs consisting of nodes representing parts of an object at different locations connected through links and edges. Hence the mathematical aspects of *graph theory* play very important role in the better understanding of the related real-world problems.

In graph theory a graph G is defined as an ordered triplet of $(V(G), E(G), \Psi_G)$ [Bondy and Murty (1976)] where

$V(G)$: a non-empty set of vertices,

$E(G)$: a set of edges that is disjoint from $V(G)$ and

Ψ_G: the incidence function, which associates with each edge from $E(G)$ an unordered pair of vertices from $V(G)$. If there exists an edge $e \in E(G)$ between two vertices u and v, where $u, v \in V(G)$, then $\Psi_G(e) = uv$.

Figure 15.6 shows a simple loopless graph for which we have

$$V(G): v_1, v_2, v_3, v_4, v_5; \qquad E(G): e_1, e_2, e_3, e_4, e_5, e_6, e_7$$

$$\Psi_G(e_1) = v_1v_2, \qquad \Psi_G(e_2) = v_2v_3, \ldots, \Psi_G(e_7) = v_3v_5$$

The graph is said to be *loopless* and *simple* if for all $\Psi_G(e) = v_1v_2$, $v_1 \neq v_2$ and there are no parallel edges between any two vertices.

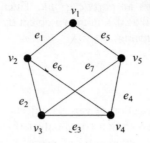

Fig. 15.6   A simple graph showing its vertices and edges.

15.8.2   Graph Isomorphism

Two graphs G_1 and G_2 are said to be *identical* when $V(G_1) = V(G_2)$, $E(G_1) = E(G_2)$ and $\Psi_{G_1} = \Psi_{G_2}$. Two identical graphs can be represented by identical diagrams. Two graphs are said to be *isomorphic* (or $G_1 \cong G_2$) if there are *bijective* functions Θ and Φ defined as

$$\Theta: V(G_1) \rightarrow V(G_2) \quad \text{and} \quad \Phi: E(G_1) \rightarrow E(G_2)$$

such that $\Psi_{G_1}(e) = uv$ if and only if $\Psi_{G_2}(\Phi(e)) = \Theta(u)\Theta(v)$.
   The isomorphism between two graphs can be detected using standard algorithms. However, the algorithm discussed below works on directed graphs or *digraphs*. Any undirected graph may

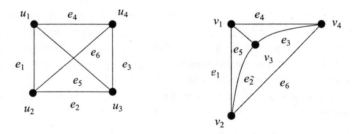

Fig. 15.7   Two isomorphic graphs.

be viewd as a digraph by replacing each edge with two oppositely directed edges. Two digraphs generated in this way are isomorphic if and only if the originals are isomorphic.
   We define *indegree* and *outdegree* of a vertex in a graph as the number of edges entering or leaving the vertex, respectively. While testing for isomorphism between two digraphs, we compare the vertices of the graphs which have equal indegree as well as outdegree. Also the two graphs must have equal number of vertices. We label them as $(1, 2, ..., n)$, where n is the total number of vertices.
   The algorithm discussed below employs a backtrack technique. We define $G_1(k)$ as a *subgraph* of G_1 induced by a set $S_1(k)$ of k vertices such that $S_1(k) \subseteq V_1$. The subgraph $G_1(0)$ is trivially isomorphic to empty subgraph of G_2. Suppose at k-th step, we have found a subgraph of G_2 consisting of the vertices from the set $S_2(k)$ where $S_2(k) \subset V_2$ and $G_2(k)$ is isomorphic to $G_1(k)$. Then we try to extend this isomorphism to $G_1(k + 1)$ by choosing a vertex v from $V_2 - S_2(k)$ so

that v corresponds to one of the remaining vertices of S_1. If it does so, we set $S_2(k + 1) \leftarrow S_2(k)$ $\cup \{v\}$ and try to extend it for $(k + 2)$. Otherwise, we back up to $G_1(k - 1)$, and try to choose a different vertex to form $S_1(k)$. Ultimately, if we can reach $G_1(n)$, the graphs are isomorphic. Alternatively, if we reach $G_1(0)$, the graphs are not isomorphic. Steps of graph isomorphism algorithm is described below.

Algorithm 15.7

```
flag ← false
k ← 0
ISOMORPH( )
if (flag) then  G₁ ≅ G₂,  the correspondence is  i ↔ f_i¹

else  G₁ ≇ G₂
```

Procedure ISOMORPH(S)
```
k ← k + 1
if  S₂ = V₂ then flag ← true
for v ∈ V₂ - S₂ while not flag do
if (MATCH)
then  f_k ← v²
          ISOMORPH(S₂ ∪ {v})
else  k ← k - 1³
return
```

Procedure MATCH
```
return true if vertex v ∈ V₂ - S₂ can be matched to vertex k ∈ V₁
return
```

Summary

A good number of books and edited volumes are available on pattern classification and recognition techniques. The recognition problems, usually, are well formulated and the solutions incorporate both mathematical and heuristic approaches. In this chapter, we provide only a brief and introductory treatment of the topic. More specifically basic concepts and tools for visual pattern recognition are presented here. We first provide a measure of similarity between shapes that leads to image matching. This measure is commonly expressed as distance between identical features of scene and the model. Both mathematical (such as deterministic approach, statistical approach, fuzzy mathematical approach) as well as heuristic (such as tree searching and graph matching methods) techniques are discussed. Mathematical methods are based on deterministic approach (exemplified by decision theoretic approach) or uncertainty measurements (exemplified by statistical and fuzzy

---

[1] i-th vertex of G_1 corresponds to f_i vertex of G_2.
[2] Label vertex v as k-th vertex of G_2.
[3] Go back to $(k - 1)$-th level of isomorphism.

mathematical) approach. Both supervised (for example, determining discriminating function) as well as unsupervised (for example, clustering) learning mechanisms are presented. Recognition of visual pattern based on structural features is also discussed.

Problems

1. In a pattern recognition problem, feature vectors have two elements. Three class centres are given by $(20 \ 20)^T$, $(20 \ 100)^T$ and $(100 \ 20)^T$, respectively. Plot class centres in the feature space. Find discriminating functions and draw corresponding boundaries between the classes considering Euclidean distance.

2. Suppose in a two-class pattern recognition, problem classes are represented by mean vector and covariance matrix as given below.

$$\text{For class-I:} \quad \mu_1 = \begin{bmatrix} 20 \\ 30 \end{bmatrix}, \quad \Sigma_1 = \begin{bmatrix} 5 & 0 \\ 0 & 10 \end{bmatrix}$$

and

$$\text{For class-II:} \quad \mu_2 = \begin{bmatrix} 50 \\ 80 \end{bmatrix}, \quad \Sigma_2 = \begin{bmatrix} 8 & 0 \\ 0 & 20 \end{bmatrix}$$

Find discriminating functions between the classes considering Mahalanobis distance.

3. Suppose in a two-class pattern recognition problem, classes are distributed as Gaussian where mean vectors and covariance matrices are as follows:

$$\text{For class-I:} \quad \mu_1 = \begin{bmatrix} 2 \\ 3 \end{bmatrix}, \quad \Sigma_1 = \begin{bmatrix} 1 & 0 \\ 0 & 3 \end{bmatrix}$$

and

$$\text{For class-II:} \quad \mu_2 = \begin{bmatrix} 5 \\ 7 \end{bmatrix}, \quad \Sigma_2 = \begin{bmatrix} 2 & 0 \\ 0 & 1 \end{bmatrix}$$

Determine the class boundary considering Bayesian classification scheme. Assume a priori probabilities of class-I and class-II are 0.4 and 0.6, respectively.

4. Given a set of features vectors that are believed to come from more than two classes. Suggest a deterministic scheme that can group these data into least number of classes as optimally as possible.

5. Suppose two classes are represented by two grammars G_1 and G_2, where

$G_1 = \{T_1, V_1, S, P_1\}$
$T_1 = \{a, b, c, d\}$
$V_1 = \{A, B, C, D, s\}$
P_1:
$S \rightarrow aA$

$G_2 = \{T_2, V_2, S, P_2\}$
$T_2 = \{a, b, c, d\}$
$V_2 = \{A, B, C, D, s\}$
P_2:
$S \rightarrow aA$

$$A \to aA$$
$$A \to aB$$
$$B \to bB$$
$$B \to bC$$
$$C \to cC$$
$$C \to cD$$
$$D \to dD$$
$$D \to dC$$
$$D \to d$$

$$A \to aA$$
$$A \to dA$$
$$A \to aB$$
$$B \to bB$$
$$B \to bC$$
$$C \to cC$$
$$C \to cD$$
$$D \to dD$$
$$D \to d$$

Determine class belongingness or ambiguity or rejection of the following sequences of primitives:

(i) $a^m \, b^n \, c^m \, d^n$

(ii) $a^m \, d^n \, a^p \, b^q \, c^{m+p} \, d^{q-n}$

(iii) $a^m \, b^n \, c^p \, d^q \, c^{m-p} \, d^{n-q}$

(iv) $a^m \, b^n \, c^p \, d^q \, c^{m-p} \, d^{n+q}$

Assume indices are all positive integers and $m > 1$.

Bibliography

Andrews, H.C., *Introduction to Mathematical Techniques in Pattern Recognition*, Wiley-Interscience, London, 1972.

Bezdek, J.C., *Pattern Recognition with Fuzzy Objective Function Algorithms*, Plenum, New York, 1981.

Bondy, J.A. and Murty, U.S.R., *Graph Theory with Applications*, Macmillan Press, London, 1976.

Duda, R.O. and Hart, P.E., *Pattern Classification and Scene Analysis,* Wiley-Interscience, New York, 1973.

Fu, K.S., *Syntactic Pattern Recognition and Applications*, Prentice-Hall, Englewood Cliffs, New Jersey, 1982.

Fukunaga, K., *Introduction to Statistical Pattern Recognition*, 2nd ed., Academic Press, San Diegi, California, 1990.

Noyes, J.L., *Artificial Intelligence with Common LISP*, Galgotia, New Delhi, 1993.

Pal, N.R. and Bezdek, J.C., 'On cluster validity for fuzzy c-means model', *IEEE Trans. on Fuzzy Systems*, 3:370–379, 1995.

Pal, S.K. and Dutta Majumder, D., *Fuzzy Mathematical Approach to Pattern Recognition,* Wiley-Eastern, Calcutta, 1986.

Pavlidis, T., *Structural Pattern Recognition,* Springer-Verlag, New York, 1977.

Tou, J.T. and Gonzalez, R.C., *Pattern Recognition Principles*, Addison-Wesley, London, 1974.

Winston, P.H., *Artificial Intelligence*, Addison-Wesley, Reading, Massachusetts, 1984.

Index